Tourism Promotion and Power
CREATING IMAGES, CREATING IDENTITIES

NIGEL MORGAN AND ANNETTE PRITCHARD
University of Wales Institute, Cardiff

JOHN WILEY & SONS
Chichester • New York • Weinheim • Brisbane • Singapore • Toronto

Copyright © 1998 by John Wiley & Sons Ltd,
Baffins Lane, Chichester,
West Sussex PO19 1UD, England

National   01243 779777
International (+44) 1243 779777
e-mail (for orders and customer service enquiries): cs-books@wiley.co.uk
Visit our Home Page on http://www.wiley.co.uk
or http://www.wiley.com

Other Wiley Editorial Offices

John Wiley & Sons, Inc., 605 Third Avenue,
New York, NY 10158-0012, USA

WILEY-VCH Verlag GmbH, Pappelallee 3,
D-69469 Weinheim, Germany

Jacaranda Wiley Ltd, 33 Park Road, Milton,
Queensland 4064, Australia

John Wiley & Sons (Asia) Pte Ltd, 2 Clementi Loop #02-01,
Jin Xing Distripark, Singapore 129809

John Wiley & Sons (Canada) Ltd, 22 Worcester Road,
Rexdale, Ontario M9W 1L1, Canada

Library of Congress Cataloging-in-Publication Data

Morgan, Nigel.
  Tourism promotion and power : creating images, creating identities
/ Nigel Morgan and Annette Pritchard.
      p.   cm.
  Includes bibliographical references and index.
  ISBN 0-471-98341-1
  1. Tourist trade. I. Pritchard, Annette. II. Title.
G155.A1N633   1998
338.4'791—dc21   98–5757
                                                              CIP

British Library Cataloguing in Publication Data

A catalogue record for this book is available from the British Library

ISBN 0-471-98341-1

Typeset in 10/12pt Times from authors' disks by Mayhew Typesetting, Rhayader, Powys.
Printed and bound in Great Britain by Bookcraft (Bath) Ltd, Midsomer Norton, Somerset.
This book is printed on acid-free paper responsibly manufactured from sustainable forestry, in which at least two trees are planted for each one used for paper production.

Contents

Acknowledgements

There are a number of people to whom we are extremely grateful for their help and support in producing this book. We would especially like to thank Dr Eleri Jones, Dean of Resources at the University of Wales Institute, Cardiff, Faculty of Business, Leisure and Food for her constructive comments and patience in reading the entire draft – *diolch yn fawr*. We would also like to thank a number of our postgraduate students (particularly Cheryl Cockburn-Wootten, Nicola Foster, Martin Selby and Sheena Westwood) for their support and suggestions and for sharing research experiences. The responsibility for any flaws in the few product, of course, rests with the authors. We are also grateful to all those people and organisations who kindly gave their permission to reproduce their advertisements and brochures.

Above all, it is important for us to express our gratitude to our respective families for all their help and encouragement throughout our lives. Nigel Morgan wishes especially to thank Carol, Derek, Elsie and Iorworth. Annette Pritchard wishes to thank her mother, father and grandmother and her dearly missed nain, daid and grandad. Without the support of all of them we would never have been in a position to write this book and it is dedicated to them. '*Hanner y daith, cychwyn.*'

Nigel Morgan and Annette Pritchard
Cardiff, May 1998

Part One:
Into the Tourism Image

1 Introduction

This book, like many others, focuses on the represented image, but, unlike the majority of other such works, it investigates the tourism image. Images serve many functions at many different levels and in tourism, images are used in a number of practical ways to convey ideas and messages. Firstly, images can be used to communicate messages about particular places and products. Secondly, they can be used to redefine and reposition such places and products (often, though not always, after changes have been made to the product). Thirdly, images can be used to counter negative, and enhance positive, perceptions of products, places and peoples. Finally, images and representations of products, places and peoples can be used to specifically target key market areas, especially in an age of highly targeted and sophisticated market segmentation.

These are all practical areas where promotion, through tourism imagery and representation, plays a vital role in a highly competitive and constantly changing marketplace. Such images and representations are also, however, at work on a much deeper, and arguably a much more significant, level. Tourism processes have broader cultural meanings which extend far beyond the actual consumption of tourism products and places. Tourism identities are packaged according to particular dominant value systems and meanings. Just as tourism sites are associated with 'particular values, historical events and feelings', so values, feelings and events are used to promote such sites, reinforcing the dominant ideologies.[1]

At the dawn of the third millennium, images are the currency of cultures, reflecting and thereby reinforcing particular shared meanings and beliefs and particular value systems. Tourism marketers through their marketing images create identities which represent certain ways of seeing reality, images which both reflect and reinforce particular relationships in societies. These are relations which are grounded in relations of power, dominance and subordination which characterise the global system. As this book will explore, when we look at tourism imagery, we can see identities crafted by marketers which reflect and distort historical and colonial relations, which reinforce current economic realities and which affirm gendered relations.

In these and other ways, the images and representations which are used in tourism marketing reveal as much about the dynamics of societies as do the more explored images of film, photography and art. The problem with tourism images and representations, perhaps unlike other images, is that too often they are read at face value. Many of us, as students, practitioners and consumers of tourism, are in fact content to do this – maybe to do more would be to pose questions which we would be reluctant to answer. We are quite happy to examine how a tourism resort may use imagery to reposition itself or how a country may depict its inhabitants to communicate a welcoming image to a target audience. We are less comfortable with investigating what lies behind these images and perceptions. Questions concerning where these constructed identities 'locate' particular peoples in our view of the world, what they reveal about how races and genders are perceived and how historical, economic, social and political relationships structure our world are too infrequently posed. This is the aim of this book – to invite the reader to look into the tourism image and consider how they see global identities reflected there.

Tourism, image and power

Some authors, including Lanfant,[2] Dann[3] and Selwyn,[4] have begun to address the cultural significance of tourism. Within the slowly evolving tourism arena particular power interests are seen to compete and significant examples can be found of work which looks at the language of tourism and how meanings can be read from that language.[5] Similarly, others, such as Silver,[6] Mellinger[7] and Cohen,[8] have examined how races, nationalities and genders are portrayed in tourism and what those representations reveal about the representers' view of the world. However, despite this growing body of work, tourism's relationship to power still merits further attention, particularly as, when it is recognised, it is too often discussed as being specific to destinations of the developing world.

Whilst it is true that the power context of tourism is beginning to be researched, much of the work which examines power and the tourism image still remains on the periphery of tourism studies. The greatest volume of image work is vocational or business-oriented and many authors, including Crompton,[9] Gunn,[10] and Kotler,[11] have discussed practical image-related issues in place, destination and tourism product marketing. There are now numerous texts which discuss the mechanics of promotion, citing examples of good and bad practice and outlining what image promotion can and cannot achieve.[12] What there are very few examples of, however, are attempts to bridge the division between the two ways of discussing tourism image creation – the gap between the more established economic perspective and an emerging sociological perspective. At the beginning of the 1990s John Urry wrote that the 'sociology of tourism is currently not keeping up with tourism's economic and social development'.[13] Almost a decade later, that scenario has not radically changed. Cara Aitchison recently commented that it is a sign of tourism's immaturity that tourism sociology texts still feel compelled to justify themselves by arguing that greater social understanding of tourism will lead to greater economic development. She summarises this situation, saying 'one can't help but notice the uphill struggle that sociology has within a subject which is still dominated by economics.'[14]

Thirty years after the emergence of tourism as a field of study there remains little crossover between those taking a business perspective and those pursuing a more sociological or historical perspective. Whilst it certainly does not purport to be a sociology of tourism, this book does attempt to go some way towards bridging this knowledge divide. In doing so we believe that such shared knowledge will encourage a more rounded analysis of the role of image creation and representation in tourism. In the following chapters we will highlight particular issues facing marketers and examine instances of success or failure in positioning places and products for particular audiences through imagery. Where we depart from other such examinations, however, is that we will argue that a knowledge of the origin of such images, an understanding of the interplay of the power relationships upon which they are based, and an appreciation of the roles which such representations create for the represented can lead to a much more insightful analysis of tourism processes.

As the tourism industry and its study mature, they will need to recognise their wider responsibilities and the significance of such issues. Image creators should be aware that what they create springs from an assemblage of interconnected forces which can by no means be described as ideologically neutral or without cultural value or meaning. Image creators are themselves products of particular societies, which have particular relationships with other societies. Some are dominant, others less so. The images and representations which they create thus not only construct, but also reinforce ideas, values and meaning systems at the expense of alternative ways of seeing the world.

In saying this, we are not suggesting that a conspiratorial perspective should be adopted when examining such images and representations. Instead we may do well to regard such phenomena as products of a consensual, as opposed to a conspiratorial, world view – indeed, we shall argue later in this chapter that tourism images are created by what can best be described as consensual marketing. It is consensual since, although the dominant world view is created within the centres of power by the enfranchised rather than by the disenfranchised on the margins of power, it is often a collaborative relationship, largely for economic reasons. Clearly, however, it is the powerful and the enfranchised who shape the ideological arena and it is important to examine how touristic images of particular places and peoples contribute to how such places and peoples are portrayed and perceived globally. Those images can be considered on racial, ethnic, geographical and gendered bases. We need to acknowledge that such constructions reveal much about the dynamics of relationships between peoples, cultures, genders and states – constructions which dominate the currency of culture and ideology.

Raymond Williams once commented that if 'all cultural processes were initiated by humans themselves' then it follows that 'none of them could be clearly understood unless they were seen in the context of human activities as a whole'.[15] Thus, '. . . since tourism-related activity has become an important process of development, the social, economic and political relations which result are part of overall issues of power and control.'[16] Kinnaird and Hall continue, arguing that those power relations can be articulated through race, class and gender, to which we would add sexuality, age and abilism. Despite its presentation as free time, framed by choice, flexibility, spontaneity and self-determination, the study of tourism leads the researcher not to the periphery but to the core of global power structures. As sociologists and increasingly, historians, begin to explore the subject, tourism is beginning to be seen as an arena which articulates these power structures, just as leisure and leisure history have been regarded for some time.[17] Gender and race, for example, are attracting the attention of more and more tourism researchers and one such writer, Linda Richter, suggests that there 'are striking opportunities to apply gender and race to a panoply of tourism issues focused on the distribution of power, privilege and political socialisation'.[18] Certainly, as the subject becomes less dominated by economics, it is beginning to be recognised that tourism simultaneously reflects and reinforces social, cultural and economic divisions ultimately rooted outside the tourism experience itself.

Why focus on the touristic image?

It has been said that 'All tourism is about illusion, or perhaps more kindly, about the creation of "atmosphere".'[19] In fact, Crick has argued that in tourism 'the emphasis has shifted away from production itself to image, advertising and consumption.'[20] It is surprising then that, until recently, the study of tourism promotional imagery has been superficial. In the words of Dann:

> Considering the sheer size of the international tourism industry today, there is a remarkable lack of analysis of the many ways it is promoted.[21]

Extant work has concentrated on the images used to market destinations, their accuracy, reliability and ability to satisfy or attract tourist demand.[22] Too few authors have gone beyond this to investigate what tourism marketing images reveal about societies' prevailing views and beliefs and much of the mainstream tourism literature, particularly that interested in image and marketing, fails to recognise the existence of issues of power. Whilst economic power is addressed in some tourism texts, the cultural power of tourism imagery and discussions of the discourse of tourism imagery rarely figure. This is particularly surprising, since tourism is a subject fundamentally concerned with perceptions of image and identity.[23]

As we will explore in Chapter 2, tourism images neither mirror nor reflect destinations and peoples since, like all images, they 'are not objective nor transparent but are produced within sites of struggle'.[24] In view of this, it can be argued that a tourism image reveals as much about the power relations underpinning its construction, as it does about the specific tourism product or country it promotes. The images projected on brochures, billboards and television reveal the relationships between countries, between the genders and between races and cultures. They are powerful images which reinforce particular ways of seeing the world and can restrict and channel people, countries, genders and sexes into certain mind-sets. Moreover, such is the covert and pervasive influence of these images that so far few have sought to question their impact or relevance. Indeed, the tendency to regard tourism imagery as somehow value-neutral is related to the fact that too often the tourism industry itself is treated uncritically. Yet the significance of how places and experiences are portrayed should not be understated, since, as Richter points out:

> The image process socialise[s] visitors and residents alike to a political impression of themselves *vis-à-vis* what they are seeing or remembering. Such impressions are not neutral. They imply gradations of power and influence, of value and dispensability, of what can be bought and what is not for sale.[25]

Theoretical ways of seeing tourism

We are arguing here that tourism processes *manifest power* as they mirror and reinforce the distribution of power in society, operating as mechanisms whereby inequalities are articulated and validated. Such views are slowly gaining acceptance, but tourism itself is only beginning to develop a putative theoretical base and, as this chapter will now explore, a number of competing theories are only slowly evolving. This book cannot tackle all the questions of power which need addressing, but it does seek to discuss how many of them are articulated and reflected in a particular part of tourism marketing – the tourism image. However, before we can begin to discuss the role of image or the power structures which animate tourism, we need to look briefly at these theoretical viewpoints which are emerging in order to explain and locate the phenomenon of tourism. In his *The Language of Tourism*[26] Dann identifies four major theoretical strands in the body of tourism literature: the established perspectives of strangerhood, authenticity and play, and the emergent perspective of conflict. To these we would add the embryonic interactionist and poststructural feminist perspective and would advocate that the conflict perspective be extended to incorporate notions of consensual marketing. An appreciation of such perspectives is pertinent to developing an understanding of touristic images and their subtexts. What is interesting, as we shall return to, is that each of the three more established perspectives see tourism from the tourist's perspective, not from that of the visited peoples or destinations.

Tourism as strangeness or authenticity

The longest established tourism perspectives are those of strangerhood and authenticity. The first was largely constructed by Eric Cohen who argued that tourism is a manifestation of people's desire to visit other places and other peoples in order to experience the differences which exist in the world.[27] This view suggests that the desire to experience difference and to search for both novel and strange experiences are prime motivators of the tourism phenomenon. Cohen argued that not every tourist exhibits the same desire to experience 'difference' and that different types of tourist exhibit different kinds of strangerhood or foreign tolerance rating. He envisaged a range of tourist types, from the organised mass tourist with little interest or inclination to experience differences at one end and, at the opposite end of the spectrum, the drifter, a person almost exclusively orientated to the element of difference.[28] This classification of tourists is, however, somewhat problematic as tourists' identities are by no means fixed and drifters may well become pillars of the establishment in later phases of their life cycles. Similarly, Selwyn has pointed out that:

> one is left wondering about the ethnographic justification for the various claims that are made. It is by no means clear. . . that 'drifters' and intellectuals are necessarily 'more alienated' from their society than 'organised mass tourists.'[29]

Cohen has developed his earlier classification of tourists to include five varieties, each of which exhibit different world views which are themselves predicated on their relationship to both their own and other societies (recreational, diversionary, experiential, experimental, and existential). Central to this definition is the concept of alienation and only the recreational tourist escapes the alienation exhibited by all the other tourist types. Feelings of alienation in turn prompt other tourists to search for fulfilment elsewhere – away from their own societies and within others. As a result, such tourists are progressively less inclined to be dependent on the comforts and structures provided by the tourist industry because they are more open to and, in some cases, are actively engaged in the search for strange and authentic experiences. One of the greatest difficulties with this view is that this concept of alienation (which is utilised by both Cohen and MacCannell) is increasingly regarded as untenable in our postmodern, consumer-oriented world.[30]

The concept of alienation also informs the next major perspective in tourism theory, although in this case, it is described more as the search for the authentic or sacred. The 'authenticity' of any tourist experience is an issue which has caused much controversy amongst tourism academics. The debate has centred around whether tourists consume 'authentic' representations of other peoples' societies and lives or whether they are duped by 'inauthentic', 'pseudo' events and products manufactured for the undiscriminating tourist masses. Boorstin, in an analysis which focused on contemporary American tourism, argued that tourism is in fact an arena in which the tourist 'finds pleasure in inauthentic contrived attractions, gullibly enjoying the "pseudo-events" and disregarding the "real" world outside'.[31] He considers that, far from offering authenticity and truth, tourism is, in fact, a self-sustaining system of illusion generated by the industry and the media, illusions which subsequently structure the ill-informed tourist choices. This view was extended by Turner and Ash who went so far as to say that the tourists' search for new places to visit culminates in 'a small monotonous world that everywhere shows us our own image . . . the pursuit of the exotic and diverse ends in uniformity'.[32]

Such approaches have been much criticised for adopting a value-laden approach to tourism, implicitly criticising the mass tourist whilst favouring the self-reliant traveller who is seen to be of independent means.[33] Highlighting the definitional problem of distinguishing between the tourist and the traveller, Thurot and Thurot have pointed out that: 'The leisure of the masses, which is very recent, has received from the intellectuals more criticism in 10 years than aristocratic leisure received in 2,000 years.'[34] In addition to this criticism, the inauthentic nature of the tourist's as opposed to the traveller's experience has been questioned. Arguably both could be regarded as equally inauthentic, although in one of the seminal texts on tourism theory, MacCannell argued that, far from being a quest for the inauthentic, tourism is in many ways, an authentic journey.[35] He sees it as a journey upon which tourists embark in order to escape modern day alienation, a journey taking them to a more authentic and complete reality. The tourist of today is thus searching for meaning in premodern 'times' and places in pristine, natural landscapes and primitive cultures. In many ways they are therefore seen to be searching for a more real and thus a more 'authentic' experience in order to overcome the alienating features of everyday modern life. In this view, tourism is regarded as being concerned with the production of an authentic experience, but one which is convenient for both visitor and visited. Tourism, because it enables people to visit other places and thus other 'times', also provides people with the opportunity to seek authentic experiences. However, the practical problems involved in questing for the truly authentic mean that tourists cannot gaze on other people's everyday lives. To circumvent this problem the industry constructs tourist spaces providing a staged authenticity.[36]

Various authors have extended MacCannell's notion of tourism as a sacred journey or as some kind of modern day pilgrimage in which the tourist goes through a surrogate spiritual cycle of death and 'rebirth'.[37] In undertaking the pilgrimage, the tourist temporarily visits an unfamiliar location. At that location he or she worships at the feet of various tourist 'shrines' and as a result of this recreational process the tourist is emotionally uplifted and spiritually refreshed. Alienation has been mediated – at least for another year! A number of authors have, however, criticised these authentic and sacred perspectives – some have questioned the universality of the notions, arguing that not all tourists can be regarded as pilgrims,[38] whilst others, such as Schudson, have argued that tourism can be viewed equally as escape rather than a pilgrimage.[39] There are therefore clearly many kinds of tourists rather than one generic category of 'the tourist', and one person can exhibit different types of travel behaviour at different times and in different places.

The views of MacCannell have also been criticised for their reliance on works of literature to inform their theoretical consideration of tourism – primarily because he restricts his analysis to works published before 1960. As such, he cannot account for the new forms of tourism which have emerged since the Sixties and as a result: 'He told his readers about a society which had virtually disappeared. Because he lacked an actual picture of tourism, he never discovered the present social reality.'[40] Similarly, it can be argued that such concepts of reality and authenticity have become increasingly problematic given the commercial and institutional nature of tourism. As Relph argues:

> An inauthentic attitude to place is nowhere more clearly expressed than in tourism . . . [where] individuals and authentic judgement about places is nearly always subsumed to expert or socially accepted opinion, or the act and means of tourism becoming more important than the places visited.[41]

Others have concurred with this view – Urry, for instance, has argued that the tourist gaze 'cannot be left to chance' and that 'People have to learn how, when and where to "gaze".'[42] In addition, Crick has suggested that the very nature of the inauthentic or authentic debate is spurious and inappropriate since we live in a world whose cultures are by no means static. Cultures are instead being continually re-invented and are subject to changes stimulated by both internal and external forces,[43] and, since cultures constantly develop, evolve and change, whose version of reality or authenticity is being offered and consumed during this spiritual journey?

Tourism as play

It is clear then that the view that tourism is authentic or somehow sacred is by no means universal. For one, Urry, whilst agreeing that 'There is a clear distinction between the familiar and the faraway and . . . such differences produce distinct kinds of liminal zones', disagrees with the premise that tourists are engaged in a search for the authentic.[44] His argument is based on the premise that tourism is all about leisure, the antithesis of regulated and organised work. As such, it is about pleasure and the consumption of 'unnecessary' goods and services which provide such pleasure. Tourism is also in some sense an experience of difference, of extra-ordinary, rather than ordinary encounters, offering the tourist pleasures which are very different from those experienced in normal life. Pleasure may be experienced in many ways, in many different contexts, but it is pleasure and difference which separate the touristic experience from everyday life.

It is important to note, however, that despite the emphasis on enjoyment, Urry does not see tourism as an unstructured experience. Rather, he sees it as 'socially organised and systematized', an experience in which the role of the 'many professional experts who help to construct and develop our gaze as tourists' is vital.[45] In the course of this book, we will seek to endorse this view of these tourism professionals, agreeing with Urry's view that:

> By considering the typical objects of the tourist gaze one can use these to make sense of elements of the wider society with which they are contrasted . . . tourism is significant in its ability to reveal aspects of normal practices which might otherwise remain opaque.[46]

By looking into the tourist image, therefore, we can investigate and explore what is obscured. The visual is central to the tourism experience: images entice people to visit places and once there, people 'gaze' at that which initially drew them, photographs are then taken and postcards are sent to those unfortunately left out of the gaze. In such a process particular images are carefully selected and 'endlessly reproduced and recaptured'.[47] Thus, while tourism is all about daydreaming, 'such daydreams are not autonomous, they involve working over advertising and other media generated sets of signs.'[48]

At the heart of Urry's discussion is his conception of 'the strolling flaneur' as 'a forerunner of the twentieth-century tourist'. A *flaneur* was one of the strolling boulevard paraders in mid-nineteenth century Paris, observing and being observed themselves, but never interacting with those they encountered. For Urry he (for the *flaneur* was 'invariably male'), was 'the modern hero, able to travel, to arrive, to gaze, to move, to be anonymous. . .'.[49] It is interesting that this prototype tourism consumer is commonly thought of in terms of freedom and pleasure, a view which is central to Urry's understanding of tourism. However, as Elizabeth Wilson points out, rather than being framed by freedom, we should also recognise that the *flaneur* was also driven by profound insecurity and anxiety.[50] In this, Urry's *flaneur* emerges as little different from MacCannell's alienated tourist, despite the initial, seemingly obvious, differences between the two views.

Similarly essential to Urry's analysis is its reliance on concepts of pleasure, the antithesis of work, and on difference. In doing so, although his analysis essentially revolves around the notion of a postmodern experience, it is interesting that the concepts which he uses are drawn from an earlier 'modern' era where the dichotomy between work and play was more distinct and complete. This leads us to the centre of the debate regarding the role and status of postmodernism in theory and in society, a concept which underpins Urry's *The Tourist Gaze*. Postmodernists regard consumption as the defining experience of people's lives; they see postmodernism as a 'condition' which is experienced differently throughout the western world – some countries are more postmodern than others, whilst within countries some places, usually cities, are more postmodern than others.[51] Despite this, they argue that in varying degrees the West as a whole is becoming postmodern as labour markets become more flexible, families less stable and gender less distinct. These processes are seen to parallel or perhaps, more accurately, develop as a result of the globalisation of the economy and the internationalisation of culture.[52]

It is therefore argued that postmodern societies are those in which formerly defining structures and divisions such as class and work are blurring and there is a sense that society and its social divisions are less solid and rather more fluid. As such, people no longer have the 'comforts' of social foundation or of common and distinct interests and shared interests which characterised the 'modern' era. The result of these changes is a society in which an individual's identity and interests are determined by what he or she consumes and goods are valued for their symbolic as well as their use-value. Such an individual, bereft of familiar foundations, is thus 'perpetually anxious, insecure, restless and unable to settle, a voyeur adrift in a sea of symbols'.[53] This is a situation which might surely stimulate an increase in the feelings of alienation and the desire for authenticity previously suggested by commentators such as MacCannell. Leading this social revolution, according to Urry, are the 'baby boom' and 'professional-managerial class' whilst the remainder of society will presumably follow the trends.[54]

If postmodernism is really a key shaper of societies, it should be recognisable among young people, the very group which is most likely to be attuned to the phenomenon. That does not, however, appear to be the case and Ken Roberts, in a recent exploration of British youth cultures, convincingly reiterates the importance of the labour market and argues that work and the forces of production are not yet ready to be consigned to the some postmodern periphery.[55] Roberts argues that despite the claims of a shift to a postmodern society, the changes which have occurred have not led to consumption or leisure becoming the major definers of identity and experience. Instead he sees a society in which:

> . . . the main systematic differences in leisure practices are still linked to the old predictors. Lifestyle formation is still normally within social, ethnic and gender groups.[56]

In such a vision of the late Nineties, young people 'are still able to build identities from the customary materials – sex, sexuality, social class, and also, in some cases, nationality, religion and ethnicity'.[57] In this sense, the forces which mould identities and which express power still prevail at the end of the twentieth century. Leisure emerges not as a defining *shaper* of identity, but as a *sphere* in which identities are articulated, identities which reflect inequalities constructed elsewhere.

Just as the 'defining' nature of postmodernism can be questioned, so too can the significance of forms of tourism which are frequently pointed to as evidence of an increasingly postmodern world. Canada's much-discussed West Edmonton shopping mall[58] and the virtual tourist may herald less a brave new world, where people no longer need to leave their home towns or computer armchairs to travel, and more presage the next stage in the development of long-established trends. As Enloe has pointed out in her discussion of the relationship between women and international politics, the turn-of-the-century visitor to the World Fairs could: 'without leaving her own country . . . experience remote corners of the world, choosing "to visit" the Philippines, Alaska, Japan or Hawaii'.[59] These Fairs and their successors were much more than mere entertainment, they also fulfilled a political and ideological role, helping the 'public imagine an industrializing, colonizing global enterprise'.[60] Given this, we must question both the truly postmodern nature of today's touristic phenomena and the failure to fully incorporate analyses of the rationales behind such phenomena into postmodern analyses of tourism.

Tourism as interaction

The three theoretical perspectives discussed so far have become part of the accepted and established body of knowledge within tourism, although all three can be criticised as theories which are not grounded in experience.[61] As such, they fail to explain the tourist's reality since a given individual may or may not be seeking personal development, play, or even succour from alienation. Despite this, however, there is an undeniable tendency to undervalue the actual experience of the tourist in the pursuit of some all-encompassing theoretical framework. A different strand of sociological thought is now developing which tries to move away from the dominant characteristics of tourism, arguing that we need to look anew at the subject and at the relationships between those who visit and those who are visited. In this perspective, Wearing and Wearing argue that, until now, sociological analyses of the tourist experience have been almost exclusively male-orientated and male-directed. Although there has been a fracturing of this universality with the introduction of the notion of 'difference', whether this be in terms of race, ethnicity, class, abilism, age or gender, the dominant perspective through which difference has been viewed and explained has remained a male perspective bound up with viewing the tourist as a *flaneur* and the destination as the image the gazing tourist consumes.[62]

This emergent approach argues that it is now time to supplement this rather static, bi-polar perspective with alternative perspectives which see tourism as an arena of interaction which also impacts on the tourist.[63] As well as offering the tantalising and ideologically desirable premise that within this space tourists (and presumably those visited) can learn and grow, the Wearings also suggest that more of a focus on interaction would escape the masculine 'subject–object' relationship which has to date dominated analyses of tourism. This view is also helpful in moving the debate on from the increasingly stale polarisation of tourism as an authentic or inauthentic experience, a debate which is increasingly irrelevant as the experience itself becomes the reality.[64]

Wearing and Wearing argue that the subjective meanings and realities which are constructed by tourists in the tourist space should be incorporated into analyses of tourism. These meanings help to construct not only the tourist self but also the tourist space, a space which is more than just a place or an image. In this way, tourism itself becomes more than just an industry or a passive experience but an interactive process which offers opportunities for self development and growth.[65] The tourist destination is therefore no longer a mere image or object to be consumed by the watching tourist, instead it is a chora, 'a space whose meaning can be constantly redefined by its inhabitants',[66] an arena in which 'Tourists can . . . grow by interacting with other tourists and hosts. Tourists should thus be seen as "chorasters" rather than "flaneurs"'.[67]

Incorporating this perspective into image-based research would mean that researchers could no longer assume that 'each individual's experience of the tourist destination will be similar'.[68] We would indeed agree that this is the case, however, we would also argue that the touristic image is one arena or chora where experiences, identities and interactions are informed by the predominant ideological constructions which shape those meanings and experiences. The tourist chora is therefore an arena where the visitor and the visited are joined by the image creator. As we shall suggest in Chapter 3, the touristic relationship is not just two-way but at least a triangular, and in reality, probably a multi-dimensional relationship since it must take account of the many players, drawn from creators, consumers and hosts, which shape the interaction.

The tourist chora could be seen as one which may open up new opportunities and horizons or, alternatively, it may reinforce particular meanings and divisions in society – as Wearing and Wearing themselves point out:

> The power differentials between Western tourists and the dominant discourses of their culture and those of the host culture can mean that the tourist may merely impose his/her ideas onto the host culture.[69]

In this way the tourists will be confirmed in their own beliefs or ideological systems. Certainly, it is the case that in many situations the tourist chora itself may limit opportunities for interaction and therefore the ability to challenge or accept the dominant ideological meanings. In some chora, for instance in all-inclusive resorts, the opportunities for interaction will be extremely limited and controlled. In others, the tourist is essentially purchasing a transferable product, as, for example, the sun and sand product. In yet other destinations the power relationship characterising those who visit and those who are visited are so opposed that interactions will be severely constrained.

Although the perspective is a valuable contribution to the development of tourism theory and a significant attempt to advance the debate, it emerges that there are some major criticisms of the view. Firstly, there are extremely limited opportunities for interaction and meetings of cultures are brief and highly structured, and, importantly, informed by stereotypical representations. Indeed, rather than being challenged by these interactions, the stereotypes appear to be confirmed on both sides, as suggested by Evans-Pritchard's and Laxson's studies of interactions between tourists and native Americans, analyses which we explore in Chapter 8.[70]

Secondly, one must question the practicality of such an approach, particularly given that the participants in the interaction are polarised in terms of economic, political and social power. Clearly, this situation gives further weight to the argument for bringing image into wider debates about politics and power since the tourism image significantly contributes to the defining and maintaining of stereotypes at both a macro and micro level.

Tourism as conflict

Power, and the issues which surround its influence, has been relatively peripheral to the discussion on tourism theory to date. However, there is a developing body of theory which argues that power is central to analyses of tourism and it is the one which will structure our analysis of tourism imagery. In doing this we will be drawing on Foucault's ideas of discourse, power and the body, but first we begin with Said's highly perceptive text, *Orientalism*, first published in 1978. Said's analysis of Orientalism or more precisely, how the West 'deals' with the Orient is grounded in Foucault's conception of discourse. It sees the relationship between East and West as one of power and domination and subordination as opposed to one which is mutually supporting and sustaining. One of the key themes of Said's argument is that:

> without examining Orientalism as a discourse one cannot possibly understand the enormously systematic discipline by which European culture was able to manage – and even produce – the Orient.[71]

Underpinning this perspective is the belief that 'ideas, cultures, and histories cannot seriously be understood or studied without . . . their configurations of power, also being studied.'[72] In society, we need to ask why certain cultural forms have more prominence than others, just as some ideas are more influential than others. The hegemony of certain forms and ideas over others can only be properly understood if the power relations which underpin them are similarly examined. It is only then that, in the case of the East, we can see how 'European ideas about the Orient . . . [reiterated] European superiority over Oriental backwardness'.[73] Said goes on to argue that the Orient in fact was 'almost a European invention . . . a place of romance, exotic beings, haunting memories and landscapes [and] remarkable experiences'.[74] As its primary and oldest colony, the Orient has been engaged in a relationship with Europe where the latter has dominated the former. One cannot understand one without the other and a failure to examine their relationship misses the critical point that 'the Orient has helped to define Europe (or the West) as its contrasting image, idea, personality and experience.'[75]

We would argue that such concepts can be applied very usefully to the study of tourism imagery and the representations which it advances. Within tourism imagery we can see the management and production of cultures and even historical relationships. Just as the West and the Orient were culturally juxtaposed, so too were Europe and Africa[76] and similar processes can still be observed in tourism. Tourism, depending on one's perspective, can be variously seen as play, the opposite to work, as the sacred as opposed to the profane, or as the strange as opposed to the familiar. These are concepts which support and reflect varying interpretations of society but which to date have yet to be grounded in power, ignoring that 'Tourism is as much ideology as physical movement'.[77] Concepts of alienation and authenticity are grounded in modern, industrial societies and social structures, yet, despite this, there appears to be a reluctance to address the factors which shape those ideologies. This failure to properly observe the power configurations which inform and structure tourism has led to, at best a partial study of the phenomenon, and, at worst, an obfuscation of the forces which underpin this global industry.

Tourism is a cultural arena in which such hegemonic ideas of superiority and inferiority are continuously played out. Developing Said's analysis, it could be argued that tourism is yet another chapter in the series of relationships between the West and the Orient in which the West has always retained 'the relative upper hand'.[78] The Orient is no longer just studied, displayed and theorised about, it is now represented and visited touristically. As a tourist site, the Orient is now constructed around notions of Western superiority and dominance over Oriental inferiority and subservience. These are concepts which are explored in more detail in Part III of this book, where we shall see that tourism writing and imagery frequently portray Asia's peoples as childlike and primitive and its landscapes as feminine and vulnerable. At this stage, however, it is essential to point out that western society has in fact managed and produced the Orient and, as such, it is a clear example of those who represent having power and authority over those who are represented.[79]

The conflict perspective has been criticised for overly constricting the ability of those who are dominated to negotiate with or to subvert those who dominate. Whilst there is certainly a danger here of denying the autonomy of the represented, most of the criticism stems perhaps from a view of power which is rather more crude and unilinear than that provided by discourse analysis. In discursive approaches power, rather than merely radiating from the centre or the top of society, is seen as circulating throughout societies. A more appropriate metaphor for understanding the way that power operates within society is that of a spider's web – power permeates all aspects of the web and it is not merely negative, it is also productive.[80] Perhaps the clearest way to understand this idea is to discuss how knowledge operates. Knowledge is closely intertwined with power and is therefore highly political despite the tradition in the West to confer upon it a non-political or impartial status. This is because knowledge is produced by individuals and those individuals cannot be divorced or separated from their human or social circumstances. People are members of societies and cultures, they are products of particular historical and social relationships and as such, they share certain perspectives and ways of seeing. This process has implications for the knowledge which is produced in society and the power which is linked to it.

We have focused in detail on Said's vision of the relationship between the West and the Orient – its 'Other' – to introduce the theme of the conflict perspective. It clearly highlights how a dominant West defined the Orient in relation to itself, measured against its norms and values; it is however, but an example of a wider discourse. Race is just one dimension of what is the Other, what is different – a difference which is measured against western, white, bourgeois, heterosexual men.

Those who do not conform to this pattern are defined in relation to it and how they differ, how they are Other, determines how they are seen in the tourism image – this is the central theme of our thesis in this book. Western, white, bourgeois, heterosexual man is Haraway's 'master subject'[81] who describes and represents people who are not like himself. As Rose comments, 'He understands femininity, for example, only in terms of its difference from masculinity. He sees other identities only in terms of his own self-perception; he sees them as . . . his Other.'[82]

At this stage, it is appropriate to introduce the notion of consensus into this debate, specifically in relation to the dominance of the master subject in constructing tourism image. The notion of consensus has been explored in cultural and media studies[83] but has to date received little recognition in discussions of tourism marketing. As we hinted above, people utilise frames of reference to make sense of and to explain the world in which they live. These frames of reference mediate our interpretations of reality and, not surprisingly, the realm of tourism marketing is similarly influenced by these mediating frameworks. What is promoted and how it is promoted is a product of the particular political, social and cultural system in which it operates – and that is one dominated by the norms and values of the master subject. As a major, possibly *the* major, contemporary institution for the circulation of ideological values, the marketing media are totally unlike previous similar institutions, such as the state, religion or education, in that their *raison d'être* is to sell rather than to socialise or propagandise. There is, therefore, no question of there being a directing intelligence or conspiracy behind the ideological bias of promotional images which is seeking to secure loyalty to the 'system'. To suggest this is, in fact, to miss the point.

The media's 'world view' or frame of reference is based on particular values and assumptions which are drawn upon when the image creators represent places and people. The result is a certain way of seeing the world[84] – a way of seeing which confirms or creates particular images and which contributes to how potential tourists view the world and its inhabitants. The consensual paradigm provides a useful framework for analysis which can be used to examine the roles and impact of the media in society as it is by no means a deterministic view. It contends that historical relationships do not determine how peoples and places are represented in tourism but that history, colonialism, and the social, economic and cultural are forces which dynamically influence these representations. Tourism, like the other realms discussed by Said, is a realm where 'cultural work, political tendencies, the state and the specific realities of domination' exert influence.[85] The master subject scripts tourism representation and Others are measured, portrayed and described – imaged – according to 'his' norms. As we shall see in more detail in Chapter 8, so pervasive is 'his' way of seeing the world that even when 'he' does not directly create the image, Others read from 'his' script.

The result is a process or system of representation which at times threatens individual cultural identities, indigenous cultural values and lifestyles and which mediates the incorporation of societies into a particular world system. The language of tourism is thus a language of power as central to Said's argument is the concept that language and representations are underpinned by political, intellectual, cultural, and moral power.[86] Tourism has a language of its own, a 'language of modernity, promotion and consumerism',[87] it is a language which tries to encourage or entice people into another world for a particular period of time, such as a vacation. It does this by 'addressing them in terms of their own culturally predicated needs and motivations'[88] and, as with any language, conversations are not unidirectional. The language of the image creator and marketer is joined by the language of the tourist, who draws on many sources of image, both touristic and non-touristic, when engaging in a conversation. Here, perhaps we should reiterate that the image creators and potential tourists both share and are products of particular social systems. As we have already suggested, image creators are drawing on shared meaning systems to create images which will appeal to tourists from similar societies. Therefore at the same time, particular ways of seeing the world and its inhabitants are reinforced at the expense of alternatives. The language of tourism can therefore be seen as the master subject's language of social control – 'As a bearer of cultural messages, it contains norms and values, prescriptions and proscriptions.'[89]

As we will explore in the following chapters, tourism imagery as a means of tourism communication provides an ideal vehicle for the study of such overt cultural messages.[90] These cultural messages are communicated through markers or signposts which can use either verbal or non-verbal media and which appeal on a multi-sensory level.[91] As we will see in Chapter 2, representations are grounded in the dominant ideology – an ideology which is itself grounded in political, social, economic and institutional practices and realities. It is important to note, however, that whilst we have focused on them in detail here, representations of the 'Other' which are based on ethnocentric stereotypes, symbols and texts are by no means the sole arena for such constructed realities.[92] Similar processes are at work elsewhere, for instance, in heritage tourism. In an analysis of Texan tourism authorities, Hollinshead argues that certain perspectives on the past are selected through social and ideological engineering, arguing:

> Nowhere is the empowerment of discourse more evident than in articulating the past, in deciding which truths become ennobled and whose past, present and future dominates.[93]

These are similar issues and questions to those raised by Edensor and Kothari in their analysis of the masculinisation of the heritage of Stirling in Scotland.[94] It emerges then that tourism is 'both a constructed and constructing phenomenon, it is a communicator and shaper of society's ideology'.[95] Reality is constructed and history is edited. This is not to say that alternative perspectives or views cannot be developed or cannot exist in conflict with dominant views as any arena in which power is manifested will also be an arena of conflict.[96] As such, tourism is recognised to be no different from any other sphere where the issue of perspective and constructed views of reality dominate. This is, however, a view which has been seriously neglected by most tourism marketing texts.

Ways of seeing the tourism image

So far this chapter has discussed the concepts of meaning, language, and representation in tourism. It has also attempted to provide some indication of how these

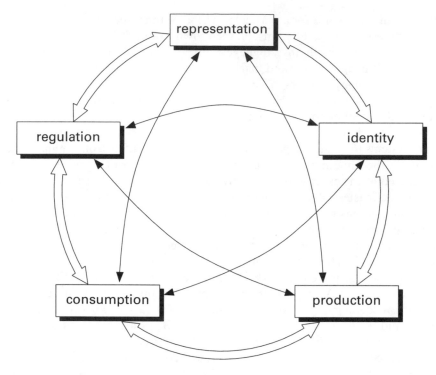

Figure 1.1   The Circuit of Culture.

Source: Hall S. (ed.) (1997) *Representation: Cultural Representations and Signifying Practices*, Sage, London: 1. Reprinted by permission of Sage Publications.

concepts interact and intersect to create different 'realities'. To fully understand how they construct tourism imagery, however, we need to turn our attention to what has been described as 'the circuit of culture'. This recognises that language, representation and meaning do not exist as isolated concepts but are inexorably intertwined in a continuous circle whereby language utilises representations to construct meanings (Figure 1.1). As Boorstin commented:

> overtime, via advertising and the media, the images generated of different gazes come to constitute a closed self perpetuating system of illusion.[97]

In this way, tourism imagery is one element in the circuit of culture, reflecting and reinforcing the circuit of knowledge and power. To paraphrase Stuart Hall, who was more concerned with a holistic analysis of culture, tourism representation is a 'key moment' in the circuit of tourism discourse. The tourism image therefore emerges as one sphere into which we can look in order to understand the dialogues between, and amongst, the creators, the consumers and the consumed. Those dialogues enable all three groups to create shared meanings and to interpret and see the world in similar ways.

This circuit of culture is the basic, underlying idea which underpins all the chapters in this book, as all consider how the circuit is operationalised in the tourism image. Chapter 2 develops this theme, investigating how we can interpret and understand the multi-layered meanings of the tourism image by explaining, evaluating and contrasting semiotic and discursive approaches to image analysis. In Chapters 3 and 4 we discuss how the image is created and consumed, a relationship which is extremely close. In the first of these chapters we explore the roles of the creator and the consumer in the circuit of culture, arguing that by consuming the image the tourist is also creating and recreating it. The chapter also suggests that there are many audiences for the touristic image beyond the obvious one of the potential tourist consumer. Chapter 4 investigates the role of the tourism image media and the image creators within the circuit, touching on the debate over the influence of advertising on society. It suggests that the relationship between 'projected' and 'official' tourism images and the 'organic' images derived from other non-tourist sources is circular, since the circuit of culture reveals that the tourism image is grounded in a wider cultural discourse. Thus, tourism and culture have a symbiotic relationship whereby tourism makes use of cultural meanings to frame its imagery, meanings which are drawn from many areas in society. In Part II of the book Chapters 5, 6, and 7 examine shifting global power structures and consider how they are mediated in the touristic image. These chapters question whether these new power structures, including the rise of Asia, the changing roles of women and the emergence of new markets, are leading to a reconfiguration of the cultural meanings currently informing tourism imagery. In Part III we focus in more detail on two key aspects of power and discourse and evaluate how the master subject currently scripts the portrayal of genders, races and different ethnic groups in the tourism image.

Throughout the book we are seeking to suggest some alternative perspectives and agendas for tourism. In particular, we will explore the role tourism imagery plays in contemporary image-dominated cultures and its relationship with popular culture. In considering these issues, we try to open up the meaning and significance of tourism images in our culture via the experience of seeing and consuming tourism images. We want to connect the discussion of the role of image in tourism to the wider debates surrounding the role of imagery in society – debates which have been topical in media studies and cultural geography for some time.[98] Thus, in a sense, this book examines the tourism image sociologically, since it is a phenomenon which is shaped by and which itself shapes wider social and cultural forces. It demonstrates that what many tourism marketing texts have hitherto neglected is the importance of the relation of tourism imagery to the ways in which we interact with the wider world. There has been remarkably little concern over the manner in which destinations and their peoples have been portrayed, packaged and presented by 'the cultural brokers of tourism'.[99] Such issues are crucial, however, since:

> Without an understanding of the predispositions and motives of tourists, and how these in turn are moulded, manipulated and sometimes even created, knowledge of tourists and tourism will always be lamentably deficient. . . .[100]

Despite the existence of the five key strands in tourism theory which we have outlined, tourism as a subject area is still maturing. As we enter an increasingly media-dominated world it is time for tourism to develop and expand its frame of reference to embrace debates elsewhere which are crucial to its functioning. We are dealing with a complex reality which by necessity requires a complex analysis encompassing the totality of peoples' existence if we are to truly understand the power relations which imbue and underpin tourism.[101] It is essential, therefore, that we move towards an analysis of tourism imagery which embraces issues of class, race, ethnicity, abilism, age, sexuality and gender, for these are the realities which shape peoples' lives and thus tourism processes.

References

1   Shields, R. (1990) *Places on the Margin*, Routledge, London: 11 and 29.
2   Lanfant, M.F. (1995) 'International Tourism, Internationalization and the Challenge to Identity', 24–43 in Lanfant, M.F., Allcock, J.B. and Bruner, E.M. (eds) *International Tourism: Identity and Change*, Sage, London.
3   Dann, G. (1996) *The Language of Tourism: A Sociolinguistic Perspective*, CAB International, Oxford.
4   Selwyn, T. (1996) 'Introduction', 1–32 in Selwyn, T. (ed.) *The Tourist Image: Myths and Myth Making in Tourism*, John Wiley and Sons, Chichester.
5   reference 3 above.
6   Silver, I. (1993) 'Marketing Authenticity in Third World Countries', *Annals of Tourism Research*, 20: 302–318.
7   Mellinger, W.M. (1994) 'Towards A Critical Analysis of Tourism Representations', *Annals of Tourism Research*, 21 (4).
8   Cohen, C.B. (1995) 'Marketing Paradise, Making Nation', *Annals of Tourism Research*, 22 (2): 404–421.
9   Crompton, J.L. (1979) 'An Assessment of the Image of Mexico as a Vacation Destination and the Influence of Geographical Location upon that Image', *Journal of Travel Research*: 18–23.
10 Gunn, C. (1988) *Vacationscapes: Designing Tourist Regions*, Van Nostrand, New York.
11 Kotler, P. *et al.* (1994) *Marketing Places. Attracting Investment, Industry and Tourism to Cities, States, and Nations*, The Free Press, New York.
12 reference 11.
13 Urry, J. (1991) 'The sociology of tourism', 48–57 in Cooper, C., *Progress in Tourism, Recreation and Hospitality Management,* vol. III, Belhaven Press, London.
14 Aitchison, C. (1997) book review of Apostolopoulos, Y. *et al.* (1996)(eds) The Sociology of Tourism: Theoretical and Empirical Investigations, Routledge, London, *Leisure Studies* (16) 53–54: 53.
15 Williams, R. (1985) 'Culture', 15–22 in MacLellan, D. (ed.) *Marx: The First Hundred Years*, OUP, Oxford: 23.
16 Kinnaird, V. and Hall, D. (1994) 'Introduction' in Kinnaird, V. and Hall, D. (eds) *Tourism: a Gender Analysis*, John Wiley and Sons, Chichester: 5.
17 Rojek, C. (1985) *Leisure and Capitalist Theory*, Tavistock Publications, New York; Clarke, J. and Critcher, C. (1985) *The Devil Makes Work*, MacMillan, London; Wilson, J. (1988) *Politics and Leisure*, Unwin Hyman, London; and Hargreaves, J. (1986) *Sport, Power and Culture*, Polity Press, Cambridge.
18 Richter, L.K. (1995) 'Gender and Race: Neglected Variables in Tourism Research', 71–91 in Butler, R. and Pearce, D. (eds) *Change in Tourism. People, Places, Processes*, Routledge, London: 72.
19 Dubinsky, K. (1994) '"The Pleasure is Exquisite but Violent": The Imaginary Geography of Niagara Falls in the Nineteenth Century', *Journal of Canadian Studies*, 29 (2): 64–88 quoting Mary Ainsly. 65.

20 Crick, M. (1989) 'Representations of international tourism in the social sciences: sun, sex, sights, savings and servility', *Annual Review of Anthropology*, 18: 307–344.

21 Dann, G. (1996) 'The People of Tourist Brochures', 61–82 in Selwyn, T. (ed.) *The Tourist Image: Myths and Myth Making in Tourism*, John Wiley and Sons, Chichester: 61.

22 Chon, K.S. (1990) 'The Role of Destination Image in Tourism: A Review and Discussion', *Tourist Review*, 45 (2): 2–9.

23 reference 18: 71.

24 Mellinger, W.M. (1994) 'Towards A Critical Analysis of Tourism Representations', *Annals of Tourism Research*, 21 (4): 756–779: 776.

25 reference 18: 81.

26 reference 3.

27 Cohen, E. (1972) 'Towards a Sociology of International Tourism', *Social Research*, 39: 164–82.

28 reference 3: 12–17.

29 reference 4: 6.

30 reference 4: 3.

31 Boorstin, D. in Urry, J. (1990) *The Tourist Gaze. Leisure and Travel in Contemporary Societies*, Sage, London: 7.

32 Turner, L. and Ash, J. (1975) *The Golden Hordes. International Tourism and the Pleasure Periphery*, Constable, London: 292.

33 See Urry, J. (1990) *The Tourist Gaze. Leisure and Travel in Contemporary Societies*, Sage, London; Dann, G. (1996) *The Language of Tourism: A Sociololinguistic Perspective*, CAB International, Oxford; and MacCannell, D. (1973) 'Staged Authenticity', *American Journal of Sociology*, 79 (3): 589–603.

34 Thurot, J. and Thurot, G. (1983) 'The ideology of class and tourism. Confronting the discourse of advertising', *Annals of Tourism Research*, 10, 173–89: 184.

35 MacCannell, D. (1973) 'Staged Authenticity', *American Journal of Sociology*, 79 (3): 589–603.

36 reference 35.

37 Lett, J. (1983) 'Ludic and liminoid aspects of charter yacht tourism in the Caribbean', *Annals of Tourism Research*, 10: 35–56; Shields, R. (1990) *Places on the Margin*, Routledge, London; Urry, J. (1990) *The Tourist Gaze. Leisure and Travel in Contemporary Societies*, Sage, London: 9; and Graburn, N. (1977, 1989) 'Tourism, the sacred journey', 21–36 in Smith, V. (ed.) *Hosts and Guests: The Anthropology of Tourism*, 2nd ed., University of Pennsylvania Press, Philadelphia.

38 Cohen, E. (1979) 'Rethinking the sociology of tourism', *Annals of Tourism Research*, 6: 18–35 and Cohen, E. (1979) 'A phenomenology of tourist experiences', *Sociology*, 13: 179–201.

39 Schudson (1979): 1252–3, quoted in reference 3: 9.

40 Thurot, J. and Thurot, G. (1983) 'The ideology of class and tourism. Confronting the discourse of advertising', *Annals of Tourism Research*, 10: 173–89: 188.

41 Relph, E. (1983) *Place and Placelessness*, Pion, London: 83.

42 reference 31: 9.

43 Crick, M. (1988) 'Sun, sex, sights, savings and servility: representations of international tourism in the social sciences', *Criticism, Heresy and Interpretation*, 1 (1): 37–76: 65–66.

44 reference 31: 11.

45 reference 31: 1.

46 reference 31: 2.

47 reference 31: 13.

48 reference 31: 13.

49 reference 31: 137–8.

50 Wilson, E. (1992) 'The invisible *flaneur*', *New Left Review*, 191.

51 reference 31: 86.

52 Featherstone, M. (1991) *Consumer Culture and Postmodernism*, Sage, London, and

Featherstone, M. (ed.) (1988) *Postmodernism: Theory, Culture and Society*, Sage, London.

53   Roberts, K. (1997) 'Same activities, different meanings: British youth cultures in the 1990s', in *Leisure Studies*, (1) 1–16: 12, paraphrasing Denzin, N.K. (1992) *Images of Postmodernism*, Sage, London.

54   reference 31: 89. See also Lash (1990) *The Sociology of Postmodernism*, Routledge, London.

55   Roberts, K. (1997) 'Same activities, different meanings: British youth cultures in the 1990s', in *Leisure Studies*, (1) 1–16: 16.

56   reference 55: 1.

57   reference 55: 13.

58   reference 31: 147–8.

59   Enloe, C. (1989) *Bananas, Beaches and Bases. Making Feminist Sense of International Politics*, Pandora, London: 26.

60   reference 59: 26.

61   see Botterill, T.D. and Crompton, J.L. (1996) 'Two Case Studies Exploring the Nature of the Tourist's Experience', *Journal of Leisure Research*, 28 (1): 57–82.

62   Urry, J. (1991) 'Tourism, Travel and the Modern Subject', *Vrijetijden Samenleving*, 9 (3/4): 87–98.

63   See Kelly, J. (1994) 'The symbolic interaction metaphor and leisure: critical challenges', *Leisure Studies*, 13: 81–96.

64   MacCannell, D. (1976 and 1989) *The Tourist. A New Theory of the Leisure Class*, 2nd ed., Schocken Books, New York; and Urry, J. (1990) *The Tourist Gaze. Leisure and Travel in Contemporary Societies*, Sage, London.

65   reference 61.

66   Wearing, B. and Wearing, S. (1996) 'Refocussing the tourist experience: the "flaneur" and the "choraster"', *Leisure Studies*, 15 (4): 229–244: 235.

67   reference 66: 235.

68   reference 66: 230.

69   reference 66: 239.

70   Evans-Pritchard, D. (1989) 'How "They" See "Us"', *Annals of Tourism Research*, (16): 89–105; and Laxson, J. (1991) 'How "We" See "Them": Tourism and Native Americans', *Annals of Tourism Research*, (18): 365–91.

71   Said, E. (1991) *Orientalism. Western Concepts of the Orient*, Penguin, London: 3.

72   reference 71: 5.

73   reference 71: 7.

74   reference 71: 1.

75   reference 71: 1–2.

76   Achebe, C. quoted in Segal, L. (1990) *Slow Motion. Changing Masculinities, Changing Men*, Virago, London: 173.

77   reference 59: 28.

78   reference 71: 7.

79   reference 71: 3.

80   Foucault, M. (1980) *Power/Knowledge*, Harvester, Brighton: 119.

81   Donna Haraway quoted in Rose, G. (1993) *Feminism and Geography. The Limits of Geographical Knowledge*, Polity Press, Cambridge: 7.

82   Rose, G. (1993) *Feminism and Geography. The Limits of Geographical Knowledge*, Polity Press, Cambridge: 7.

83   Seymour-Ure, C. (1974) *The Political Impact of the Mass Media*, Constable, London; and McQuail, D. (1987) *Mass Communication Theory*, Sage, London.

84   Berger, J. (1983) *Ways of Seeing*, British Broadcasting Corporation and Penguin, London and Harmondsworth.

85   reference 71: 15.

86   reference 71: 12.

87   reference 3: 4.

88   reference 3: 2.

 89   reference 3: 3.
 90   see Uzzell, D. (1984) 'An alternative structuralist approach to the psychology of
      tourism marketing', *Annals of Tourism Research*, 11: 79–99; Urry, J. (1990) *The
      Tourist Gaze. Leisure and Travel in Contemporary Societies*, Sage, London;
      MacCannell, D. (1976 and 1989) *The Tourist. A New Theory of the Leisure Class*,
      2nd ed., Schocken Books, New York; Dann, G. (1988) 'Images of Cyprus projected by
      tour operators', *Problems of Tourism*, XI (3): 43–70; Gartner, W. (1993) 'Image
      Formation Process', *Journal of Travel and Tourism Marketing*, 2 (2/3): 191–215.
 91   see MacCannell, D. (1989) 'Introduction to special issue on the semiotics of tourism',
      Annals of Tourism Research, 18; and Graburn, N. (1995) 'The past in the present
      Japan: nostalgia and neo-traditionalism in contemporary Japanese domestic tourism',
      47–70 in Butler, R. and Pearce, D. (eds) *Change in Tourism. People, Places, Processes*,
      Routledge, London.
 92   see Hollinshead, K. (1993) 'Ethnocentrism in tourism', 652–62 in Khan, M. *et al.* (eds)
      VNCR's Encyclopaedia of Hospitality and Tourism, Van Nostrand Reinhold, New
      York, discussed by Dann, G. (1996) *The Language of Tourism: A Sociolinguistic
      Perspective*, CAB International, Oxford: 25; also Evans-Pritchard, D. (1989) 'How
      "They" See "Us"', *Annals of Tourism Research*, (16): 89–105; Laxson, J. (1991) 'How
      "We" See "Them": Tourism and Native Americans', *Annals of Tourism Research*, (18):
      365–91; and Cohen, C.B. (1995) 'Marketing Paradise, Making Nation', *Annals of
      Tourism Research*, 22 (2): 404–421.
 93   Hollinshead, K. (1993) 'Ethnocentrism in tourism', 652–62 in Khan, M. *et al.* (eds)
      VNCR's Encyclopaedia of Hospitality and Tourism, Van Nostrand Reinhold, New
      York, discussed by Dann, G. (1996) *The Language of Tourism: A Sociolinguistic
      Perspective*, CAB International, Oxford: 25.
 94   Edensor, T. and Kothari, V. (1994) 'The Masculinisation of Stirling's Heritage', in
      Kinnaird, V. and Hall, D. (eds) *Tourism: a Gender Analysis*, John Wiley and Sons,
      Chichester.
 95   reference 93.
 96   Hollinshead, K. (1992) 'White gaze, "red" people – shadow visions: the
      disidentification of "Indians" in cultural tourism', *Leisure Studies*, 11: 43–64; and
      Brunner, E. (1994) 'Abraham Lincoln as authentic reproduction: a critique of
      postmodernism', *American Anthropologist*, 96 (2): 397–415.
 97   reference 31: 7 on Boorstin, D. (1964) *The Image: A Guide to Pseudo-Events in
      America*, Harper, New York.
 98   Hall, S. (1997)(ed.) *Representation: Cultural Representations and Signifying Practices*,
      Sage and the Open University, London; and Williamson, J. (1978) *Decoding
      Advertisements*, Marion-Boyars, London.
 99   reference 3: 61.
100   reference 3: 61.
101   Swain, M. (1995) 'Gender in Tourism', *Annals of Tourism Research*, 22: 247–266: 225.

2 Reading the image

In Chapter 1, we discussed the idea that tourism and particularly tourism imagery should be seen within a broader cultural context since it reflects and reinforces the underpinning cultural infrastructure. In this chapter we review how to *read* such images and focus on aspects of analysing tourism advertisements: in particular, the chapter analyses semiotic and discursive approaches to understanding images. This discussion builds on the previous chapter's assertion that all imagistic promotion is value-laden and that the values expressed are highly selective and in many senses socially conservative, restrictive and constricting – what we will now explore in detail is how and why that is the case in tourism.

It would be naive to underestimate the significance of promotional imagery, the 'distinctive visual backcloth' of the world in which we live today.[1] The world is being imaged and it is simplistic to think that we are immune to the ideological messages which are being transmitted. Promotional images not only reflect the prevailing cultural values of a society, drawing upon current images and stereotypes, but also play a vital role in shaping these values through their contribution to the process of socialisation. In promoting products, marketers illustrate certain aspects of society and this selection process reflects and reinforces preferred interpretations from the collective cultural knowledge and information. Thus, certain norms and values are promoted at the expense of others, and as we will argue in this book, certain scripts are privileged above others, particularly those which favour the white, male, heterosexual gaze.

The imagistic culture

There is undoubtedly tremendous current interest in image. Image is exhorted as the defining experience of the decade, as the new reality. Politicians debate nuances of style instead of substance; teenagers seek out brands to reinforce their self-image; and destinations spend millions of dollars to create or recreate their identities. It is said that we are undergoing an 'image revolution' on an unprecedented scale and that the 'old' images of cinema, television, photography and print (whilst still highly significant and visually engaging) are being replaced with 'new' images. Through new technology 'a whole range of available image forms – and consequently of ways of seeing, looking, watching' are increasingly 'being mobilised and made use of'.[2] There is a proliferation of screen culture and a rush to embrace the pleasures of virtual life and cyberculture, a call to live our lives in a cyberspace populated with virtual tourists, virtual scholars and virtual lovers. We:

increasingly live in a three-minute . . . culture . . . [where we] keep switching from
channel to channel unable to concentrate on any topic or theme for longer than a few
minutes.[3]

Many of us live in what have been described as postmodern service-based, media-
dominated societies in which lives are represented as well as lived.[4] Whilst we
suggested in Chapter 1 that there is some doubt about the defining nature of
postmodernism, it is evident that developed societies are fascinated by immediate
consumption and it is the representations rather than the realities of consumption
which actually structure and influence our purchasing behaviours. Urry problem-
atises the distinction between representations and reality, arguing that much of
what we view as reality today in fact consists of representations which we consume
– 'social identities [which] are constructed through the exchange of sign values'.[5] In
this sense, we live in a world where the concept of reality is increasingly irrelevant,
as everything is a copy, or a text upon a text, and what is fake seems more real
than the real. To many, Main Street, Disneyland is as authentic as any other
American street.

This is a scenario which is growing in significance because of the 'visualisation'
of society. As we increasingly depend on the visual to signify reality, we must
attach an even wider significance to representations and images and their importance, for these are in fact constructing our reality – or the reality we consume. We
are encouraged to participate in particular versions of reality and it is important
that we understand the nature of these 'realities' and the sources from which they
spring. This is to view our cultural realities in terms of their wider context, as the
end products of the social realities which underpin them, social realities which are
grounded in struggle. This is because societies are characterised by the struggle for
power as social groups, classes, races and genders are in competition at many levels
and the struggles are not just within societies, but between them. Middle-class
women in the Philippines or in India may have a real stake in maintaining the
status quo, unlike working class women living in the same town. The cultural
sphere, like the economic and political spheres, is one of the spheres where these
struggles are engaged. It is an arena in which the more powerful groups – often
western, white and male – establish and maintain dominance through image
creation. The study of image in tourism can therefore illuminate not only how our
realities are being shaped and, in many cases, reconstructed, but can also reveal the
complex power relationships which inform this process.

Image promotion

Image promotion is concerned with transferring meaning onto a product from the
outside, through repeated imagistic association.[6] Perhaps the best way to illustrate
this process is to take an advertisement for St Maarten in the Caribbean which
appeared in KLM's June 1996 in-flight brochure (Figure 2.1). A young, conven-
tionally attractive white couple lounge under a sun umbrella at the entrance to a
large cave, gazing out onto an empty beach and blue sea on which floats just one
boat in the distance (possibly theirs). The cave walls which frame the scene give it

Figure 2.1   Advertising as communication. Reproduced by permission.

a window-like quality – their (and our) window onto the Caribbean. The main advertisement copy says: 'Sint Maarten. Governed by the Dutch and the French, ruled by the sun and the sea.' The unmistakable assumptions (to the western audience) on which the advertisement is based – that the Caribbean means blue seas, empty golden beaches, romance and relaxation and that it is expensive and colonially familiar – illustrates the way in which the brand-imaging of destinations links them symbolically to a wider world of social values. Like all advertisements, this is a two-way communication process – to accept the selling message is to accept the values it presupposes. Similarly, by representing these values as part of the visual backdrop, the advertisement naturalises them and cements their hold on society.

The destination which is projected as an object of desire (Sint Maarten) is presented as a cultural symbol charged with social significance: 'On this tiny island, even the crowned heads of Europe bow to the gods of sun and sea.' Simultaneously, the consumer who is the target of the advertiser is induced to adopt the socio-cultural identity attributed to the young couple who already consume the product. It is noteworthy that there is no mention of the local Sint Maarten population. Governance is colonial and the island is 'ruled' by the forces of nature. Within this there appear to be echoes of European superiority over non-European peoples and cultures, peoples and cultures which are somehow more backward, more 'natural' and therefore more primitive. Clearly, such image promotion is ideological. Relationships outside the image *per se* structure the exchange and their significance is increased by the tendency to treat the tourism image as an item of play removed from the real world.

Arguably, all such marketing-inspired imagery, whether in advertisements (both printed and electronic), on packaging or in brochures, is ideological. Perhaps at this stage it is useful to define ideology. Wernick in his book *Promotional Culture* provides a good working definition of this ambiguous and contested concept, suggesting that it 'refers simply to that level of reality, at once individual and collective, subjective and objective, at which people orient meaningfully to their world. . . . Such a definition is both universal – ideology as an irreducible element of all collective and individual life – and neutral.'[7] Ideology is not exclusively identified here with dominant or dominated consciousness, since both oppositional and critical perspectives are also themselves forms of ideology. All image promotion, even the most rational, is ideological since it places its audience in the role of consumer and seeks to create a positive attitude amongst that audience towards the advertised product. However, images like the Spanish advertisement in case study 2.1, which imbue their products with cultural and psychological appeal, also impinge on their audience's sense of identity, orientation and appeal.[8]

Case Study 2.1   Reading Spain, Reading Passion For Life

This advertisement appeared in the April 1996 *Sky* magazine. It portrays an attractive young dark-haired woman, clearly a flamenco dancer caught by the camera in mid-movement. The advertisement is vibrant in both movement and colour: the woman wears a rich red dress and a golden shawl swirls around her as she pivots, her arms raised in a classic flamenco move; the backdrop is a vivid red, dominated by what we take to be a setting sun. We are told in the small copy of the advertisement that 'Flamenco dancing is at the heart of Spanish culture'. Moreover, we are told that the dance, and by inference, the woman and Spain, is 'a struggle of contradictions. The expressive gesture, form and posture and the frenzied movements blending into one another in an eternal play of seduction'. All of which suggests a loss of self-control, a suggestion which is in direct contrast to the reality of the dance, since flamenco is highly structured and controlled.

The advertisement omits any tangible product information, any references to price or any aspect of the purchase. Moreover, the advertisement portrays Spain primarily as an idea or concept. References to the product's tangible qualities are subordinated to a display of its psycho-cultural significance. The tone of the advertisement is very personal – it is 'A Personal View' by the photographer Javier Vallhonrat and it is also a personal appeal to the individual consumer. Since everybody and anybody might want the product, as destinations are so substitutable and all are seeking differentiation, the advertiser is moved to make a personalised appeal on behalf of a product infused with the distinctiveness of symbolic mysticism. It would be impossible to imbue products with such symbolism if that symbolism itself was unintelligible or without ideological appeal. Highly symbolic advertisements such as this, must therefore find not only effective pictorial and verbal devices to imbue the product with significance, but also they must build that significance from elements of a clearly understood cultural code. In other words, the success of the image is dependent on the creator and the consumer sharing cultural meanings. Yet, representing Spain and Spanish women in this way endorses and continues a particular view of Spanishness – the circuit of culture in operation.

The self invited to indulge in the product (Spain) is the same as the one whose fantasy ideal is projected onto the product – a fantasy ideal of female Spanish beauty and culture. In order to attract the relevant audience and persuade them to

Figure 2.2 'Reading Spain'. Reproduced by permission.

try the product, the advertisement sets out to construct a personal and social identity of what is the 'real' Spain for its potential users. That this Spain may be only a cameo of Spanish life is not addressed. It simultaneously offers the flamenco dancer as a glimpse of Spain and grafts her identity onto that of the destination. Spain thus is female, seductive, contradictory and expressive. Through this advertisement, imagistic promotion has successfully (re)coded a product (Spain) as a desirable psycho-ideological sign (the flamenco dancer).

As we will explore in more detail in Chapter 3, a variety of approaches have been used to explain the relationship between society and promotional activities such as advertising.[9] Whichever approach is favoured, it is always the case that imagistic promotion makes use of emotive words and images, often to associate products with a lifestyle to which the audience aspires. Families featured in advertisements are always happy, healthy and usually affluent, individuals never appear tired, ill or bored after purchasing a product. Advertisements are always upbeat and associate products with good feelings and things. They also presuppose a consumerist orientation – a feeling that the world is there for the consumer's delight and gratification – at a price.

In these ways, imagistic promotion does build on the values, desires and symbols which exist in society but it goes beyond mere reflection in neutral fashion. Imagistic promotion 'typifies what is diverse, filters out what is antagonistic or depressing, and naturalizes the role and standpoint of consumption as such'.[10] The world it presents to us is therefore, 'flat, one-dimensional, incorporative and normalized'.[11] In tourism (as in other imagistic promotion) symbols are used to suggest desires and goals: fast cars, luxurious houses and designer clothes convey success; whilst stereotypes such as the ideal mother, the exotic temptress, the honeymooning couple, the group of fun-loving young people, or the high-powered male executive convey familiar scenarios and lifestyles with which the audience identifies. What is important is to understand the bases from which these stereotypes spring, to see the ways in which they are reflected in the tourism image and to consider their impacts on how we construe the world.

Understanding the power of the image

Promotional imagery in all its forms is one of the most important and pervasive cultural factors influencing and intruding into everyday life. Such imagery in television commercials, in printed advertisements, on billboards and in brochures operates by establishing a relationship between a type of consumer and a type of product and by seeking to promote differentiation between products. The term 'image' is commonly held to refer to the organised representation of an object, a person or a place in an individual's cognitive system and embraces both a definition of that object, person or place and a recognition of their attributes. Images therefore represent mental constructs and objects, peoples and places are all open to different images.

How we evaluate these images appears to be considerably influenced by socially shared values which are defined by cultural, economic and social factors.[12] People from particular social groups or societies make sense of the world in similar ways and representations help us to make sense of the world by communicating or signifying meaning. Image could thus be described as a form of shorthand, symbolising the meaning and value which we and others associate not only with objects but also with peoples and places. To be white or black, poor or rich, male or female, Irish, Welsh, African or American brings with it particular associations which help us make sense of the world and to define others in it. As Stuart Hall has said: 'the question of meaning arises . . . in the construction of identity and the marking of difference.'[13]

We can witness the process of definition and meaning in the existence of commonly held perceptions amongst groups of people which result in common ways of seeing other peoples and places and thus, ultimately in the creation of stereotypes.[14] Stereotypes are of course by no means static or unchanging or universal but are socially and temporally specific and open to variation between groups and across time. The temporal and spatial specificity of knowledge means that meanings and interpretations can change over time from one historical context to another. As such the meanings discussed in this book can themselves be contested as there is not one correct but alternative and equally plausible, interpretations. However, as we argued in Chapter 1, not all interpretations are equally accepted as powerful groups, often western, male and Caucasian, attempt to regulate, structure or shape the ideological arena. Thus the power of social groups is critical to the rise and fall of stereotypes and some groups are more powerful and more successful in getting their interpretations heard than others since 'some people . . . [have] more power to speak about some subjects than others',[15] including tourism imagery.

Tourism is one such arena where we can observe this process. It is 'a world discovered by entrepreneurs, packaged and then marketed'.[16] As such, the tourist gaze is moulded by professional image creators and brochure writers – marketers who are themselves products of certain societies and social groups (very often the same as the tourist). The images they create echo the referent systems, the cultures and ideologies, together with the dreams and fantasies of their particular groups. The end result is a system of meanings communicated by signs, which are at once the product of, and the reinforcement and recreation of particular ways of seeing and interpreting the world. We need to focus on these signs, images and meanings to come to terms with the wider role of tourism in the world, in other words to understand how tourism reinforces and encourages particular ways of seeing and thinking.

Tourism is grounded in real world relationships – historical, economic, political, social and cultural. Culture is about meanings which are communicated via representational systems and within these systems we make use of signs or symbols to interpret those meanings. Language is 'one of the "media" through which thoughts, ideas and feelings are represented in a culture',[17] language which is not merely verbal, but also visual. Language is a signifying practice and Hall *et al.* provides an excellent introduction to the process of cultural representation and signifying practices.[18] For our purposes, it is essential that the reader understands what is meant by a signifying practice. Language signifies meaning and as such the components of language function symbolically in that they 'operate as *symbols*, which stand for or represent the meanings we wish to communicate'.[19] These symbols or signs enable meaning to be exchanged, interpreted and decoded. This process is only possible, however, when the exchange or communication takes place between people who share 'concepts, images and ideas' which enable them to make sense of the world in broadly similar ways.[20] Thus, the advertisements for Sint Maarten and for Spain only work because the signs and symbols are mutually understood (figures 2.1 and 2.2). Various approaches have attempted to explain how these representation processes work and the following pages will focus on two approaches – semiotic and discursive – which share many common features, but, crucially, differ on others.

Semiotic approaches to understanding images

The semiotic approach is concerned to understand the mechanics or 'poetics' of how language produces meaning[21] and, as such, is the study of the language of signs and thus meaning in culture. Semioticians 'read' culture and central to their approach is the belief that cultural objects and practices convey and depend on meaning which is communicated via cultural signs and which, like any other language, can be analysed and read. Words, images and objects function as signs which construct meanings and thus carry messages which can be interpreted by those who share the same cultural codes. In this way, the qualities of any product are understood to *signify* more than their intrinsic value or use to the consumer just as diamonds, flowers, gold and perfume have all acquired a 'because she's worth it' image and identity through advertising. Based on evoking emotion through the illusive promise of pleasure, products offer happiness or other states of existence by their mere acquisition.[22] In pursuit of suggesting this promise, products are provided with images since advertisements can offer little product information and in fact, in tourism advertisements often serve as substitute products. Existing images from other spheres of life are utilised and adapted to create distinctions between products and consumers and images and ideas are thus connected with certain products rather than originating from them. In this way, advertisements select particular elements from the world and rearrange them to present the mythical world of the product and the advertisement.

A variety of techniques are used in this process, techniques which can be analysed and thus decoded. Sign, signifier and signified are all terms used in the process of decoding the ideological meaning of advertisements.[23] A sign is something which holds meaning for people, it may be an object, word or picture. We can disentangle the idea of the sign in order to understand how the process works since the sign is made up of two elements which are inextricably linked – the signifier and the signified – both of which are needed to produce meaning. The signifier is the object which features in the advertisement – the pictures, words and symbols and, in the case of electronic media, the sounds used in advertisements – whilst the signified refers to the concept or meaning suggested by the signifier.

Signifiers in advertisements are sophisticated since they are more than mere vehicles for one dimensional meanings and can be manipulated to produce other, more subtle meanings. Moreover, advertisements are not just about encoding meanings but about transferring those meanings to create others and advertisers have adopted a number of major referent systems to lubricate this process. These systems, based on history, science and nature, are idealised, evocative and above all reusable because they are transferable, adaptable and constantly evolving. By positioning a product adjacent to other objects or items pre-existing meanings can be transferred from the latter (the referents) to the former. Thus, in the St Maarten advertisement (Figure 2.1), the attractive young couple lying together on the beach transfer romance to the destination. This transference of meaning is only possible, however, if the reader and advertiser share a common set of values and knowledge – without these the process is bound to fail.[24]

This transference of meaning is a somewhat complicated exercise which requires further explanation since it is underpinned by the concepts of denotation and connotation.[25] Denotation and connotation are two levels of meaning within the study of signs. Denotation refers to the basic recognition of an object and is concerned with the simple description of signs. In the advertisement for Spain, for example (Figure 2.2), the denotation phase would at one level simply recognise a woman dancing against what might be a sunset, and read the text which hints at passion. At a higher level, connotation links the sign itself to society, to the social ideology, the beliefs, concepts and values which inform society and the descriptive is transformed by the reader into something which has meaning beyond its 'objectivity'. So, in our example, the Spanish advertisement works at a much broader cultural level by inviting the reader to realise that this is not just a woman dancing, but that she 'is' in fact Spain and is evoking a particular view of the country – female, hot, passionate, seductive, expressive and contradictory – a blend of 'spiritual and physical'. The mode of representation is that of a photograph and as such, this 'naturalises the symbolic message' by making it appear uncontrived.[26] Unlike some other advertisements, however, in case the reader misinterprets the sign, the text specifically directs their understanding. This ideological transference of meaning takes the object into the realm of myth.[27]

From this example, we can see that representations work at a broader socio-cultural level and as such, can be read to establish their meaning. Proper semiotic analyses require that the reader goes through a series of steps in order to fully understand how meaning is produced. Within the denotation phase, the reader needs to decode all the elements of an image to provide a composite picture of the image. Once this has been established the reader needs to proceed to the next phase, the connotative or mythic phase, in order to establish the image's wider cultural meaning. It is crucial to note that it is the reader who enables this exchange to take place. In fact, as Urry points out, we are all amateur semioticians:

> One learns that a thatched cottage with roses round the door represents 'ye olde England', or the waves crashing on to rocks signifies 'wild, untamed nature'; or especially, that a person with a camera draped around his/her neck is clearly a tourist.[28]

Similarly, Culler comments that:

> All over the world the unsung armies of semioticians, the tourists, are fanning out in search of the signs of Frenchness, typical Italian behaviour, exemplary Oriental scenes. . . .[29]

In this way, Dann and Potter can write about a Caribbean yacht (a denoted sign) representing a James Bond lifestyle (a connoted meaning). The transference here is through brochure photographs, but it can be made by colour, language or other methods such as replacing the product with one possessing qualities with which its marketers would like it associated, as the flamenco dancer represents Spain. In this way the process is ideological and the reader or viewer is the recipient but also the recreater of the advertisement's message, whilst the process occurs in an environment where assumptions are accepted as being 'true'. For instance, the process assumes that consumers who are free to purchase any commodities, buy what they choose. The basis of that choice and the factors which influence the consumer are not considered.

Such semiotic analyses have been applied to various arenas of representation, including advertising, photography, popular culture, travel and fashion.[30] Other studies have utilised semiotic techniques but grounded their work in an examination of the power relationships which characterise society.[31] Examples of both of these ways of using semiotics can be found in tourism, for instance in the work of Selwyn[32] and Sinclair.[33] MacCannell, in his introduction to 'The Semiotics of Tourism', a special issue of the *Annals of Tourism Research*, goes so far as to say that 'there is a privileged relationship between tourism and semiotics'[34] and Dann has argued that:

> nowhere . . . is a semiotic perspective considered more appropriate than in the analysis of tourism advertising with its culture coded covert connotions, in the study of tourism imagery and in the treatment of tourism communication as a discourse of myth.[35]

To date Urry's is the most well-known work concerned with the 'signs' which construct the tourists' gaze, although others, notably Thurot and Thurot, have utilised semiotic analyses to underpin a neo-Marxist interpretation of tourism.[36] Despite the interest of these commentators, semiotics is a relatively new analysis in tourism and Dann has argued that there is a need for 'further "semiotic ethnography" of tourist brochures'.[37] Whilst recognising the scope for more analyses of this kind, we would suggest that those approaches which are concerned purely with the poetics of meanings suffer from a number of flaws, primarily the tendency to treat language as 'a closed, static system'.[38] Systems of representation do not merely convey meaning, but also contribute to the production of knowledge – which is closely related to social practices enabling some to have more power to speak than others. Semiotics' limitation therefore is related to its inability to fully incorporate issues of knowledge, power and historical specificity into its analysis of meaning. As Foucault argued:

> The history which bears and determines us has the form of a war rather than that of a language: relations of power not relations of meaning . . . 'semiology' is a way of avoiding its violent, bloody and lethal character by reducing it to the calm Platonic form of language and dialogue.[39]

Discursive approaches to understanding images

Semiotic approaches have been criticised for isolating representations and meanings from the arena of power and knowledge, yet as we have seen, culturally powerful groups have more power to speak about some subjects than other groups.[40] As such, some peoples or groups within society have the authority to represent whilst others are represented and certain ways of talking about a subject are accepted whilst others are rejected.[41] It is impossible to understand the process of representation without reference to this relationship, a relationship which is the essence of discourse. As Foucault argued, discourse is about the production of knowledge in a particular time and place. Knowledge is never neutral or objective but is closely related to power since it is part of the social distribution of power – it regulates, channels and constructs identities and meaning and provides us with common sense realities in our social and cultural lives. Social control is thus exercised and representations defined through the control of knowledge since our shared mental and conceptual maps depend '. . . on the relationship between things in the world – people, objects and events . . . and the conceptual system, which can operate as mental representations of them'.[42] Unlike semiotics, the discursive approach is more concerned to study the production of knowledge through language, since it 'defines and produces the objects of our knowledge'.[43] This production is a process which:

> 'rules in' certain ways of talking about a topic, defining an acceptable and intelligible way to talk, write or conduct oneself, so also by definition, it 'rules out', limits and restricts other ways of talking, of conducting ourselves in relation to the topic or constructing knowledge about it.[44]

Discursive approaches are concerned less with the poetics and more with the politics of representation, in other words, with its impact and consequences. In contrast to semiotics, discourse therefore not only examines how meaning is produced but also how such meanings are linked with knowledge and power in society, recognising that knowledge 'defines the way certain things are represented, thought about, practised and studied'.[45]

Regardless of actual veracity, knowledge which is 'linked to power not only assumes the authority of "the truth" but has the power to make itself true'[46] and impacts on people's beliefs, behaviours, and actions. As Foucault argued:

> Truth isn't outside power . . . It is produced . . . by . . . multiple forms of constraint . . . . Each society has its . . . 'general politics of truth', that is the type of discourse it accepts and makes function as true.[47]

Foucault's conception of power is very radical since, instead of viewing power as something which is exercised by a small minority at the top over a large majority at the bottom, it argues that power is rather more web-like. It sees power not as a monopoly commodity, but one which is 'exercised through a net like organisation'.[48] It is a more sophisticated analysis of power relations than a Marxist one which would explain power purely in the context of class relations as it recognises that power bestrides social categories. It permeates all levels of existence and operates in every social site, both public and private, and we are all involved in its circulation – power goes '. . . to the depths of society'.[49] It is important to recognise, however, that Foucault does not deny the dominance of powerful groups in societies but argues that there are many mechanisms which mediate and contribute to the exercise of power which influence and regulate appropriate behaviours.

For Foucault, the body was the ultimate site of struggle between different forms of power and knowledge. He examined how Western societies have exerted power over the body – the vessel of social and sexual normality and thus the key site where power has disciplined and punished any deviation from the norm.[50] Foucault was concerned with how the body was conceived, with how it was controlled, and with how its possibilities and limitations were circumscribed by the discourses which defined it. He regarded the human body not as merely a natural, physical form, but one inscribed by power and knowledge which varies over time. This is:

> a radically historicized conception of the body – a sort of surface on which different regimes of power/knowledge write their meanings and effects.[51]

Foucault's focus on the body provides a valuable analytical tool for those interested in the operation of power and knowledge in tourism and, more specifically, in the tourism image. For, as Fiske comments, power is at work everywhere, in all activities:

> Clothing, cosmetics, slimming, jogging are all means of incarnating rules and intextuating the body. The relationship[s] between the body beautiful and the body ugly . . . are social relationships of norms and deviations, and therefore political relationships aimed at naturalising in the body the norms of those with most power in the social formation.[52]

The body is, in fact, central to the pleasure arena. How it is positioned and conceived and how power and pleasure are manifested and exercised within it must therefore be critical areas for investigation within tourism. There is a hierarchy of 'preferred images of the body'[53] and Dann comments that:

> images define what is beautiful, what should be experienced and with whom one should interact. Understanding the people of tourism is thus, above all else, an analysis of images.[54]

Meanings in tourism are grounded in relations of power, who represents what, whom and how are critical and often contested issues since how other places and peoples are represented has consequences for the meanings which are produced in society. Whilst some groups are more influential in this process of definition than others, we are all caught up in the same web of power which Foucault described. We can thus examine the flow of representations about tourism, places and peoples and how society and its social order is depicted within these.

In much the same way as meaning is not imposed but mediated through local rituals influencing people, behaviours, and bodies, we can all be seen as products of particular formations of power and knowledge – living in a particular historical context and a particular institutional regime. The web of power, knowledge and meaning binds us to a particular regime of truth in which the body is central. Thus, travel writings and tourism promotional images which portray people in particular places such as Africa, South America and Eastern Europe as primitive, static and unchanging may or may not be accurate. However, if most believe that they are, then this has important consequences for how we perceive and treat such people and their significance in society. These beliefs operate as 'truth' and this regime of truth inscribes particular meanings on bodies which in turn feed back into the web of power and circuit of culture (Figure 1.1). Similar issues apply to how black bodies are perceived and constructed as 'Other' in white-dominated societies – Dyer, for example, examined how black bodies are bound up with labour, with meanings grounded in slavery, meanings which persist today, although this particular form of production has largely vanished.[55]

We can see particular examples of this operating in tourism, as well as in other representational forms, such as photography and film. The process can be clearly seen in the construction of museum exhibitions, which have been described as 'systems of representation that produce meaning through the display of objects'.[56] Indeed, there are significant parallels between the spheres of tourism and ethnographic museums – just as the latter's collections originated in the search to preserve the '"exotic", "preliterate", "primitive", "simple", "savage", or "vanishing races"',[57] so we can see such terms similarly employed to describe particular peoples in the tourism promotional literature. The representation of peoples and places are by no means natural or innate, instead they are historically power-specific and make use of geographical, social, and cultural distinctions which are constructed and 'located historically in the struggle for power between what has been called "the West and the Rest"'.[58]

All cultural producers, from advertisers, designers, to museum curators and authors, are involved in the creation of 'myths' and therefore inevitably wield symbolic power. Museum exhibitions are artefacts shaped by the interplays between curators, designers and the museum institution – the result of a series of deliberate actions: collections are purchased; exhibitions are planned, written and constructed. Such exhibitions are thus 'necessarily selective . . . authored and partial.'[59] In interpreting such exhibitions, semiotic approaches would be interested in the articulation of meaning, whilst discursive approaches would be more orientated towards the political implications of the representations – described by Lidchi as the politics rather than the poetics of representation.[60] A discursive analysis would argue that the practices of collecting and displaying are powerful activities and that an analysis of the relationship between power and knowledge should be incorporated into any investigation of exhibitions. Museums appropriate and display objects for certain ends and the objects are incorporated and constructed by the articulation of pre-existing discourses. In this way, the museum becomes an arbiter of meaning since its institutionalised power allows it to articulate and reinforce the scientific credibility of frameworks of knowledge or discourse formations through its method of display.

We have to read and decode such representations if we are to translate the meanings which they convey. Tourism representations can be discussed in exactly the same terms and, just as Lidchi's focus was on how museum exhibitions represent 'other cultures', so our focus in the following chapters will be on how tourism represents peoples and places. Such discussions, we would argue, are vital and, it is particularly important that tourism representations are brought into the debate surrounding how 'the West classifies, categorises and represents other cultures'.[61] This is a debate which is concerned not just with how representations are created and what they signify but also how those representations are grounded in a political relationship between the core and the periphery, that is, between the powerful western nations and their less powerful counterparts. The representations of peoples and places in tourism can no longer be seen as an innocent or somehow value-neutral activity, removed from the political mainstream of society. In tourism, as in other spheres, the representation of others is all about possessing and knowing other cultures – such actions are purposeful and motivated.

The tourism marketer aims to present the unfamiliar to the tourist and to achieve this the unfamiliar is encoded, with certain meanings promoted and others discarded. Potential tourists are directed towards particular interpretations at the expense of others and thus 'reality' is interpreted through a process which is grounded in unequal relationships of power – tourism promotion does not simply 'happen' – text is written, photographs are taken, people and places are represented. Tourism representations are thus themselves products of the culmination of particular historical, social and political events and relationships. The discourse of tourism promotion does not merely reflect 'reality', instead relations of power contextualise and structure the representation of particular peoples and places at particular times so that 'what we are presented with is a representation of . . . life, authored and partial'.[62] It is a representation which reflects the 'power relationships between those subjected to such classification and those promoting it'.[63] Representations are thus removed from the reality of lives and alternative interpretations of that reality.

Marketing and promotion provide but one discourse on the relationship between those who promote and those who are promoted. Foucault suggested that representations are the culmination of several discourses or bodies of knowledge, known collectively as discursive formations, which work:

> to construct a specific object/topic of analysis in a particular way, and to limit other ways in which that object/topic may be constructed.[64]

Discursive approaches have been criticised in the past for failing to properly indicate the 'influence of the material, economic and structural factors in the operation of power/knowledge' precisely because of their concerns with discourse *per se*.[65] They have also been criticised for viewing power and the struggle against it as unrelated.[66] Despite their flaws, however, they do provide a much more comprehensive analysis of representations than semiotics in the sense that they are more concerned with the politics of representation, a politics which can no longer be divorced from the underpinning economic and structural realities. Discourse is thus about the production of knowledge but has absolute geographies and temporal contexts.

Urry argues that:

> The (tourist) gaze is constructed through signs and tourism involves the collection of signs. When tourists see two people kissing in Paris what they capture in the gaze is the 'timeless romantic Paris'.[67]

We would argue that these signs are not just restricted to signs of the destination – for example to signs of Paris, the Caribbean, Ireland or Egypt. To a discursive analyst these signs also signify other beliefs and meanings about society, the social world, the place of men and women and the place of other countries, races and nationalities within the world. At one and the same time they replicate and reinforce particular ways of viewing the world and go some way towards defining acceptable roles and responsibilities. It is important, therefore, to look not just at those elements which signify or sum up, for example, Egypt but it is also vital to look at what such signs say about Egypt in the world order, or more correctly first world perceptions of Egypt and accepted and acceptable Egyptian activities and roles.

If we return to our example of the Spanish advertisement (Figure 2.2), whereas a semiotic analysis would be concerned to understand the meaning of the sign, one based on a discursive perspective would see the body as significant. The body is that of a young woman, photographed and thus objectified by a man; hers is a body which is also heavily inscribed with sexual meaning. Although the text describes the flamenco dance, it also describes her and also, by deliberate implication, Spain. Such an analysis would also be concerned to highlight the political implications of the imagery – in that it is not only the female who is seen as seductive and full of contradictions, but also Spain, a view which has implications for how Spain views itself and how it is viewed by the world. In using such imagery those with the power to do so are seeking to reposition Spain as Spanish, an idea to which we will return in Chapter 7.

Tourism marketing is but one strand of contemporary society, a society dominated by historical, social, economic and cultural relationships which favour particular groups and particular perspectives. At the same time, it is a product of those very relationships – the essence of consensual marketing. People and places are constructed in particular ways, to appeal to particular groups and in doing so, the options for representations are limited and circumscribed. The process of representation thus constructs and presents one culture for the consumption of another yet such systems of representation are contested entities – some interpretations are more valid than others at a particular time, depending on the particular power relationships in existence. In tourism promotion, whilst we can read representation in much the same way as Lidchi read ethnographic museum collections, at first appearance, the impact and implications of such representations may not be regarded as so serious. They have no educational remit and obviously tourism promotion is all about selling vacations. Yet, this should by no means undervalue the importance of the tourism image as it should be seen as one more element in the holistic discursive formation, one more strand in the process of representation which disadvantages some 'truths' at the expense of others. More importantly, however, pleasure (a large element of tourism) should not be consigned to the periphery, somehow outside power and politics since, as Foucault argued, pleasure and power are closely intertwined.

References

1   Urry, J. (1990) *The Tourist Gaze. Leisure and Travel in Contemporary Societies*, Sage, London: 12.
2   Robins, K. (1996) *Into the Image*, Routledge, London: 5.
3   reference 1: 92; see also Lash, S. (1990) *The Sociology of Postmodernism*, Routledge, London.
4   reference 1.
5   reference 1: 85.
6   Wernick, A. (1991) *Promotional Culture*, Sage, London: 15.
7   reference 6: 23.
8   reference 6: 31.
9   Argyle, H. (1975) *Bodily Communication*, Methuen, London.
10 reference 6: 42.
11 reference 6: 42.
12 Ajzen, I. and Fishbein, M. (1980) *Understanding Attitudes and Predicting Social Behaviour*, Prentice Hall, Englewood Cliffs, NJ.
13 Hall, S. (1997) 'Introduction' 1–12 in Hall, S. (ed.) *Representation: cultural representations and signifying practices*, Sage and the Open University, London: 4.
14 Taft, R. (1959) 'Ethnic stereotypes, attitudes and familiarity: Australia', *Journal of Social Psychology*, 49: 177–86.
15 Hall, S. (1997) 'The work of representation' 13–74 in Hall, S. (ed.) *Representation: cultural representations and signifying practices*, Sage and the Open University, London: 42.
16 Crick, M. (1989) 'Representations of international tourism in the social sciences: sun, sex, sights, savings and servility', *Annual Review of Anthropology*, 18: 307–44: 308.
17 reference 13: 1.
18 Hall, S. (ed.) (1997) *Representation: cultural representations and signifying practices*, Sage and the Open University, London.
19 reference 13: 1.
20 reference 13: 4.
21 reference 13: 6.
22 Williamson, J. (1978) *Decoding Advertisements*, Marion Boyers, London.
23 Culler, J. (1976) *Saussure*, Fontana, London.
24 see references 22 and 1.
25 see references 18 and 22 for further discussion.
26 Barthes, R. (1977) 'The Rhetoric of the Image' 32–51 in Barthes, R. (1977) *Image, Music, Text*, Hill & Wang, New York: 45.
27 Barthes, R. (1972) *Mythologies*, Cape, London.
28 reference 1: 139.
29 Culler, J. (1981) 'Semiotics of Tourism', *American Journal of Semiotics*, 1: 127–40.
30 Barthes, R. (1967) *The Elements of Semiology*, Cape, London; and reference 27.
31 reference 22 and Fiske, J. (1994) *Understanding Popular Culture*, Routledge, London.
32 Selwyn, T. (1993) 'Peter Pan in South East Asia. Views from the brochures' 117–37 in Hitchcock, M., King, V. and Parnwell, M. (eds) *Tourism in South East Asia*, Routledge, London.
33 Sinclair, D. (1995) Tourism in Guyana: a Semiotic Analysis, unpublished MPhil thesis, University of West Indies, Barbados, quoted in Dann, G. (1996) *The Language of Tourism. A Sociolinguistic Perspective*, CAB International, Oxford.
34 MacCannell, D. (1989) 'Introduction', 1–6 *Annals of Tourism Research*, 16 (1): 3.

35 Dann, G. (1996) *The Language of Tourism. A Sociolinguistic Perspective*, CAB International, Oxford: 6.

36 Thurot, J. and Thurot, G. (1983) 'The ideology of class and tourism: confronting the discourse of advertising', *Annals of Tourism Research*, 10: 173–89.

37 Dann, G. (1996) 'The People of Tourist Brochures', 61–82 in Selwyn, T. (ed.) *The Tourism Image. Myths and Myth Making in Tourism*, John Wiley and Sons, Chichester: 61.

38 reference 15: 42.

39 Foucault, M. (1980) *Power/Knowledge*, Harvester, Brighton: 114–5.

40 reference 15: 42.

41 Foucault, M. (1980) *Power/Knowledge*, Harvester, Brighton.

42 reference 15: 18.

43 reference 15: 44.

44 reference 15: 44.

45 reference 15: 6.

46 reference 15: 49.

47 reference 41: 131.

48 reference 41: 98.

49 Foucault, M. (1977) *Discipline and Punishment*, Tavistock, London: 27.

50 Foucault, M. (1978) *The History of Sexuality*, Harmondsworth, Penguin.

51 reference 15: 51.

52 Fiske, J. (1994) *Understanding Popular Culture*, Routledge, London: 92.

53 Mercer, C. (1986) 'Complicit Pleasure', 50–68 in Bennett, T., Mercer, C. and Woollacott, J. (eds) *Popular Culture and Social Relations*, Open University, Milton Keynes: 67.

54 reference 37: 79.

55 Dyer, R. (1986) *Heavenly Bodies: Film Stars and Society*. St Martens, New York.

56 Lidchi, H. (1997) 'The Poetics and the Politics of Exhibiting Other Cultures', 151–222 in Hall, S. (ed.) *Representation: cultural representations and signifying practices*, Sage and the Open University, London: 153

57 reference 56: 161.

58 Hall, S. (1992) 'The West and the Rest: discourse and power', in Hall, S. and Gieben, B. (eds) *Formations of Modernity*, Open University Press/Polity Press, Cambridge, discussed in reference 56: 161.

59 reference 56.

60 reference 56.

61 reference 56: 153.

62 reference 56: 179.

63 reference 56: 191.

64 reference 56: 191.

65 reference 15: 51.

66 Bennett, T. (1986) Introduction: Popular Culture and 'the turn to Gramsci', vii–xi in Bennett, T., Mercer, C. and Woollacott, J. (eds) *Popular Culture and Social Relations*, Open University, Milton Keynes.

67 reference 1: 3.

3 Creating and consuming the image

As we outlined in the introduction, the circular nature of culture suggests that it is not only the media, but also consumers who are active participants in the production of touristic identities and representations. In this chapter we begin our investigation of this relationship with a brief consideration of the role of advertising in tourism marketing since, as we have seen, tourism activities are 'literally constructed in our imagination through advertising and the media. . .'.[1] Whilst a number of models have been generated from within the industry to explain the nature and impact of advertising,[2] it is essential that we consider the role of tourism advertising within a wider framework. The role of advertising in society and the relationships which characterise the advertiser and the consumer have been the subject of much debate in media studies and sociology and various critiques have been offered to explain these relationships, many of which are pertinent to our discussion.[3] In contrast, just as discussions of tourism marketing have failed to consider the wider implications of the relationship between advertising and society, there has been a similar reluctance to fundamentally examine the stresses within the advertising process.

Readers of some tourism texts may well be forgiven for assuming that the image creation process is largely seamless since they often neglect the very real tensions which underpin the relationships between the advertiser (the client), the advertising agency, the market research company and the consumer. In this chapter we highlight the fact that the relationship between the advertiser and the advertising agency is a complex one, which might also be further complicated not merely by a geographical but also by a *cultural* distance between the two. We also point out that the relationship between the image creator and the image consumer is by no means straightforward as there are many creators and consumers of the imagery. Some of the former may well be engaged in promoting the same destination for diverse and even contradictory objectives, whilst others may be concerned to target a diverse range of audiences. It is not only the potential tourist, but also the local tourism industry, local residents and perhaps, above all, politicians who are also potential consumers of tourist promotional activity.

It is, however, the involvement of the tourism consumer which has caused the greatest amount of controversy and tension in the advertising process. It is unrealistic not to involve consumers in campaigns – they influence the market research process which itself informs the image creation process. Those consumers are as much the products of their own societies as are the marketers and their attitudes have been shaped and formed not only by their experiences, education, cultures, social values and histories, but also by the marketing images to which they have been exposed. In this way, they are vital players in our notion of consensual image creation and an investigation of the image/consumer relationship reveals the underlying structures which link image-consumers and image-creators and shape their views of the tourism world. The relationships and tensions which underpin how the image is created and consumed are, for ease of discussion, considered separately, but they are in reality facets of a holistic process and we invite the reader to consider how creation and consumption are intertwined, as they are in the case study of the symbiotic relationship between tourist advertisements and tourists' own photographs (case study 3.1).

The impact of tourism advertising

Modern tourism marketing is a continuous communication with existing and potential customers and an organisation's total communications programme consists of a mix of promotional activity including advertising, sales promotion, public relations and personal selling to achieve marketing targets. Promotion can be a short-term activity (such as a sales offer), but when seen at a strategic level, it is a mid- and long-term investment aimed at building up a consistent and credible corporate or destination identity. Brochures, media advertisements, the behaviour of staff, in-store merchandising and sales promotions can all create the image of the organisation and all aspects of the promotional effort should project the same image to the tourist.

The ultimate purpose of image creation is to influence buyer behaviour and manipulate demand. The impact of image, however, is much more wide-reaching in societal and cultural terms, an issue which we shall turn to later in this chapter. Before doing so, however, we need briefly to consider the marketing impact of the image. In a summary of the latest research into advertising techniques from a practitioner perspective, Davies et al. identify four models employed in planning advertising.[4] These are: sales response, persuasion, involvement and saliency. All four of these techniques are popular in tourism marketing, although some products and organisations rely more heavily on some than others. Tour operators and travel agencies, for example, may use sales-response linked to sales promotions more frequently, whilst destinations are more likely to use involvement and saliency in their campaigns.

The sales response technique is a very simple price-based strategy encouraging the purchase of a product purely on the basis of its price. Persuasion, the second technique, is widely used and demonstrably successful. This takes the advertisement as its starting point and employs its impact and message to persuade the audience that the product presented is the most desirable available. Whilst it sounds straightforward, persuasion is not a simple technique, for it is capable of sophisticated variation, particularly where the 'brand advantage' is made emotionally rather than rationally persuasive.[5] The third advertising technique is involvement, a technique which aims to arouse the audience's interest, thus creating a self-referent relationship whereby the audience imagine themselves within the advertisement's framework and (hopefully) feel good about the brand. The next stage is a commitment to the brand, with a concomitant increase in sales. Involvement is a more sophisticated technique, characteristic of style-market products such as alcohol and clothing, although it is also highly relevant for some tourism products. At the leading edge of developments in advertising is the fourth and final technique – saliency. This relies on innovative, radical, even controversial brand images and attempts to achieve much more simple than 'brand' awareness as it tries to 'move' the target audience emotionally closer to the brand product. Saliency is therefore concerned with the product's presence in the audience's consciousness, generating a feeling of 'that product is for me'.

In the last three of these advertising techniques direct sales is not the main objective. In the 1980s advertising was regarded as contributing significantly to sales figures yet recent commentators dispute this assumption, arguing that this impact of advertising is usually applicable to new products or variations in products with an obvious competitive advantage.[6] Instead the impact of advertising is not to increase sales directly, particularly in relation to established brands, and where it does have this effect, the increase is generally insufficient to recoup the cost of the campaign. The value of advertising lies in improving people's attitude towards brands, thus leading to long-term sales. Interest is created by the culmination of long-term advertising memories; whilst consumers discard those which are uninteresting, they retain memories of those advertisements which are unusually appealing or provocative. The latter form the basis of successful brand image building and maintenance, a process accomplished over a considerable period of time with high returns since the impacts are also long term.

As a discretionary product, tourism competes for customers' time and money against essential items of expenditure; in addition, as a service industry, promotion in tourism is even more vital than in other industries. Despite arguments over the essential differences between the marketing of goods and services, it is well established that the tourism product is intangible, inseparable, variable and perishable. There is little that is tangible for the customer to examine beforehand or to take away afterwards; the service is inseparable from its production; the experience is variable and often subject to factors beyond the marketers' control; and finally, the product is perishable and cannot be stored for future sale. Clearly, you cannot test drive a vacation beforehand, and thus promotion becomes critical, having a greater role in establishing the nature of the product than in most other markets. This means that the skill in tourism marketing lies in creating the perceived value of the product, in packaging it and in promoting the experience in a way which gives a product a competitive edge. In this respect, creating the image becomes paramount – 'Promotion *is* the product as far as the tourist-prospect is concerned. The customer buys a trip or a holiday purely on the basis of symbolic expectations established promotionally through words, pictures, sounds, images, etc.'[7]

As a result, modern tourism advertising's task is to create a memorable image for the product which will be recalled at the time when the consumer has to choose between products. This long-term role of image promotion is becoming more and more significant in tourism as the way in which consumers choose tourism products is changing. Business tourism is increasing rapidly and for those who can afford vacations, they are becoming leisure experiences to be enjoyed at varying times of the year. Many tourists in Europe now enjoy as many as four or five trips a year.[8] Similarly, in the US an increasing percentage of 'two career couples' has accelerated the trend towards shorter, more frequent vacations. Longer vacations of over ten nights are declining, whilst trips of three nights rose by almost one-third during the late Eighties.[9] Historically the western tourism industry considered that there were certain key 'windows' when tourists chose their annual vacation destination and thus, the advertising was targeted in bursts.[10] This is increasingly untenable and tourism marketers have adjusted their ideas to the need to keep their products and brands on the potential tourists' agenda throughout the year. As a result, we are all consuming tourism advertising throughout the year.

As we have made clear, we are not concerned here with revisiting the practicalities of tourism marketing or with discussing the wider tourism marketing or even the promotional mix. Those are topics which are extensively addressed in an increasing number of specialist texts aimed at the tourism student and practitioner.[11] Instead, we assume some familiarity with tourism and marketing and are aiming at those who want a deeper insight into one particular aspect of tourism promotion and, more especially, with its relationship with society. As the previous chapter indicated, we are concerned, above all, with the discourse of tourism imagery and in the following pages we explore the role of the tourism image media and the image creators and consumers within the circuit of culture (Figure 1.1). The major tenet of the argument suggests that there are many creators and many audiences for the touristic image, all of whom influence the kinds of images portrayed and the image process itself. In many ways these less recognised audiences are as, if not more, influential than the widely discussed opinions of the consumer.

Advertising and society

Advertising has been the subject of much debate and, in many cases, commentators have portrayed it in a negative light regardless of their own individual ideological perspectives. Fowles has pointed out that both non-Marxists and Marxists have heavily criticised advertising and proponents of both ideological perspectives regard it as a manipulative force designed to seduce. Advertisers and consumers are seen to be engaged in a relationship characterised by the former's power at the latter's vulnerability:

> The offender, conceived of as big business or capitalism, is looming, omnipotent, able to exert its will under any and all circumstances. The offended, the misled public is pliant, supplicating, malleable.[12]

Advertising is thus the mechanism, or lubricating fluid which oils the wheels of capitalism since it stimulates the twin forces which drive that system – materialism and consumption. In the rush to own and consume, people are encouraged to purchase items which they neither really want or need. Lasch, in fact, describes advertising as much more than a promoter of consumption[13] – as does Fowles, who sees it as a consumption which 'promises to fill the aching void' and attempts 'to surround commodities with an aura of romance; with allusions to exotic places and vivid experiences, and with images of females' breasts from which all blessings flow'.[14]

Critics of both Marxist and non-Marxist analysts of advertisements argue that such writers attach too much significance to the power of advertising, pointing out that many individuals recognise that advertisements are misleading and dishonest and deny being unduly influenced by them. In addition, they argue that the symbolisation of products through promotional imagery merely reflects to society its own cultural norms and values. They see the 'intervention of advertising into the formation of consciousness' as 'neutral – a kind of inert gas. At most a reinforcement of whatever ideological codes and conditions have, for other reasons come to prevail.'[15] This is a rather simplistic view of how imagistic promotion works; because such images are intended to sell there are clearly certain orientations and values which the advertising images will mirror and some which they will not – both in the values appealed to and in the symbols employed, there is an inherent bias towards the conventional, the dominant perspective.

It is not the *overt* advertising messages but the *underlying* connections between products, images,[16] (and people) which encourage and reproduce particular ways of seeing the world, its inhabitants and the ways in which they interact. These covert messages are insidious and remain long after the image of the product and its claims have been forgotten. In this way advertisements operate through ideology and are instrumental in the reproduction of society's structures, continually using and reusing particular myths and values. By these mechanisms advertisements are linked to the wider social structure through referent systems; as advertisements work through ideology, so ideology works through advertisements. Advertisements thus:

> obscure and avoid the real issues of society, those relating to work: to jobs and wages and who works for whom. They create systems of social differentiation which are a veneer on the basic class structure of our society.[17]

Far from suggesting that discussion of advertising has gone too far, Fowles argues that the concepts which underpin both Marxist and non-Marxist critiques of advertising remain underinvestigated. He suggests that advertising should be viewed from a rather different perspective, one which recognises that advertising as a medium draws from and contributes to popular culture. Within this perspective, Fowles suggests that the relationship between advertising and the consumer is also in need of reformulation. Instead of seeing this relationship as one of seducer and seduced, or in terms of the powerful as opposed to the powerless, he suggests that consumers and advertisers should be regarded as engaged in a mutual exchange of meaning. Advertising can thus be seen as 'the richest and most faithful daily reflections that any society ever made of its entire range of activities'.[18]

The perspective suggested by Fowles in many ways parallels Hall's circuit of culture discussed in Chapter 1. Image creators are engaged in the business of advertising and advertisements link the tourism industry with its consumers (the potential tourists) via the advertising agency and the tourism media. Since the aim of tourism advertising is to effectively communicate messages to potential consumers, it must speak to them in the most attractive way, 'articulating their impulses and satisfying their needs'.[19] If those engaged in constructing and delivering such messages are to effectively communicate with the consumer they need to root them in shared cultural symbols. As McCracken has argued, meanings originate from within the cultural sphere and are subsequently made use of or appropriated by advertising to facilitate the consumption of products. In purchasing these products the consumer thus participates in this process which could be described as a cultural exchange – meanings are used, represented, accepted and thus reinforced and the cycle is ready to begin again.[20]

Advertising and consumers

The notion that the image creator and the consumer are engaged in a mutual exchange affirms the need to review the relationships between advertising and consumers. Just as there are many arguments regarding the relationship between advertising and society, there are similar controversies surrounding the relationship between advertising and consumers and the dilemma over whether advertising mirrors social values or actively creates them is central to much of the existing work on advertising.[21] Fowles suggests that the relationship between advertising and the consumer cannot be described in a simplistic cause and effect way regardless of whichever perspective one takes. Advertisements are highly selective in the images which they portray and sustain:

> Advertising cannot create social actualities . . . To believe it can impose stereotypes of its own making upon the public is to hold demeaning and . . . unsupportable views about the nature of the public. Consumers do not all accept the idealizations in advertising and then pattern themselves determinedly on them.[22]

Consumers live very different lives from those found in advertisements which tend to mimic idealized states of existence and portray flawless individuals in enviable situations. Advertising does, however, suggest stereotypes or clichés of attractiveness, desirability and desirable situations and the relationship between advertising and the consumers is circular:

> Advertising does not, and cannot, create these stereotypes from sources that exclude the public, nor does advertising passively mirror stereotypes; it is actively involved in the dialectical process of making and remaking them. . . .[23]

This produces an increasingly tightly defined relationship between the consumer and the advertiser in which need and image are ever more closely aligned and in which 'refined preferences' lead to even more 'refined images'.[24] For the consumer, the advertisement takes vague notions of important states and lends those a form or an image. The consumer understands that advertisements do not replicate real life situations and indeed, 'The consumer does not want advertising to deal in realities . . . the consumer appreciates advertising that offers gossamer.'[25] Advertisers and agencies in turn respond to consumer preferences by offering 'desired depictions' drawn from popular culture. The consumer is 'a spectator in meanings . . . on the prowl not for any and all meanings but for those that are, or will be, of personal value . . . . The spectator is also looking for those products whose symbolic overtones suit the meanings the spectator wishes to elicit in oneself or in others.'[26]

The consumer thus *selectively* decodes the messages encoded in the advertising and as such has a powerful and interpretative role to play in this exchange of meaning. Advertising of all descriptions does encounter some resistance from the consumers, indeed its sheer volume engenders a tendency for rejection – consumers have many sources of information on which to draw and they are selective in their attention to advertising and in its interpretation. They may decode advertising in a number of ways[27] – and may respond positively, negatively or compromise in some way. A preferred meaning exchange would be one in which the advertisers' meaning is accepted; an oppositional exchange would lead to the advertisers' meaning being rejected; and a compromise exchange is one negotiated between the consumer and the industry.

For some writers, the significance of advertising is even greater than that recognised by this mutual exchange – for them, whilst the consumer is accorded a voice, the emphasis is more on the advertiser. Marchand's work in *Advertising the American Way* contradicts Fowles' argument that advertising cannot create social actualities. Instead, he argues that the information provided by advertisements played a key role in 'teaching' immigrants how to be American (and consumers) in the 1920s and 1930s.[28] His suggestion is that advertisements feature visual images of society which then provide people with guidelines of cultural standards and appropriate behaviours in much the same way as did theatrical nineteenth-century tableaux. In contrast, whilst Williamson regards consumers as naive, she does not see them as the receivers of packaged messages courtesy of the advertisers. Instead, the consumers, like the advertisers, are themselves part of the process which produces meaning and people provide 'the connecting link . . . for the ideological students of ideas. This only exists inside our heads.'[29] As O'Barr argues in his book, *Culture and the Ad*:

> Meaning resides only in those who do the work of interpreting, whether they be the makers of advertisements, critical interpreters, or naive readers.[30]

Both Williamson and Marchand argue that advertisements provide an edited and selective view of society and fulfil a role in helping the consumer to understand the accepted social 'realities' and both agree that analysis of such advertisements leads to a greater understanding of society. O'Barr goes further, pointing out that the views of the consumers or audience of advertisements are largely inaccessible and very rarely sought – Marchand, like Williamson, fails to investigate what members of the audiences for advertisements actually thought. In order to begin to go some way towards rectifying this tendency, instead of taking a purely theoretical stance, O'Barr is more concerned with the notion of audience response and the consumers' interaction with advertising. He suggests that:

The interpretative triangle of author, audience and critical interpreter – is the base on which meaning is generated. Understanding how advertisements mean what they do requires attention to all three.[31]

He contends that whilst there are numerous texts that examine the relationship between advertising and the critical interpreter there are few which examine the consumer of advertising, despite the fact that meanings are neither universally shared nor uniform. In a relationship which involves the product and consumer in the creation of meaning, we need to understand what advertisements mean to consumers and to give insufficient weight to the consumer is to obscure a reality in which:

> advertisements work in the sense of convincing us to adopt attitudes and act on them – only when the meaning is our own, whether we supplied a portion or all of it.[32]

Too much focus on what advertisements mean to their creators detracts from what they mean to their consumers, disguising the fact that 'The process of interpretation is a collaborative effort of audience and creator',[33] which takes place within a much broader cultural context. In order to redress this imbalance O'Barr investigates the relationship between the consumer and advertising via the tourists' own photographs (case study 3.1). Tourism advertising, more than any other type of advertising, facilitates such an examination since tourists take vacation photographs which are themselves representations and can be compared with the representations of advertising. In this way we can ascertain 'the degree of congruence between the representations shown within the advertisements and those created outside . . . as a result of advertisements'.[34]

Case Study 3.1   Tourist Photographs – the Creator/Consumer Interface

O'Barr suggests that advertisements are much more than mere mirrors or responders to consumers and their needs. Instead he argues that advertisements 'lay down templates from which Americans [and others] construct images of others and judge relations with them'.[35] He does not merely claim this, however, but actively seeks to discover whether it can be sustained. In doing so he asks whether there is evidence to show that consumers, in this case, tourists, receive, understand and act upon advertising messages. The medium he examines are tourist photographs which, he argues, 'constitute a visual record that may confirm a correspondence between the templates suggested in advertisements and the images preserved on film'.[36]

In an investigation of tourist photos, he found that they suggest a link between advertisements and travel photographs. Tourists sought out iconographic representations of other peoples, races and cultures – 'the Other' – to photograph 'not the Japanese but the Japanesy, Geisha girls and pagodas [and] . . . peasants picking coffee'.[37] They pursued 'photographic trophies' which themselves became the essence of the touristic experience, trophies which provided visible proof that the tourist visited, saw and took a picture to reflect the experience.

The photographs did not merely record these touristic icons, however, they also showed both the visited and visitor in social situations. Pictures showed 'native peoples doing whatever it is they do in the part of the world the tourist visited'[38] and when the visited and visitor were photographed together the relationships between the two were hierarchical. 'The tourists are photographed with their favourite guides, bargaining for souvenirs in native markets, or supping drinks they did not mix.'[39] Tourists shop, pose by monuments and see the sights in clothes which they may well have specially bought for the trip, such as a new safari jacket or swimsuit. Those who are visited, however, do 'quaint native things. Gondoliers manoeuvre boats through Venetian canals [and] . . . Maasai warriors walk beside rural roads in Kenya'.[40] Such photographs reveal the differences between those who visit and those who are visited in terms of power and inequality.

Can such photographs be interpreted as evidence of the influence of advertising on consumers or do they merely demonstrate that advertising mirrors society? O'Barr argues that whilst there will always be an element of the latter, 'the representational process also provides in each reflection a new model for future behaviour'.[41] What is occurring here is a complex interaction between advertising, tourism and popular culture. Such touristic sites and representations were not merely created by advertising or even by the tourists, instead much of what is considered worthy and appropriate in tourism is the result of many discourses, an extended interaction between not only popular culture, advertising and consumers, but also other spheres such as history, art and literature. It is difficult to disentangle one from the other and to claim that one came first and stimulated the others is spurious. Thus 'whichever comes first, the culture or the ad, a cycle is quickly established: Advertisements depict differences because consumers expect them and consumers expect differences because travel advertisements play them up.'[42]

In fact, photographs provide a way to understand 'very different aspects of twentieth century tourism' since 'the development of photography has been intrinsically linked with the tourist'.[43] We will return to the role of the camera in tourism representation in Chapter 8 – as Cohen has pointed out: 'the role of photography in tourism and even more, the study of tourism through photography, are relatively neglected topics in tourism studies', an astonishing fact given that 'we could learn a great deal from the analysis of [tourist] photographs'.[44] We have already seen that perceptions are formed by cultural processes, and O'Barr suggests a similar function of photography both in terms of the tourists' photographs and how the tourists are encouraged to frame and take photographs by advertisements and professional 'help' texts. In a similar vein, Nir, in analysing photographs of the Bible Lands, found that they can also be shaped by religious and professional interests. Previewing the ideas of O'Barr, Nir's earlier exploration of the relationship between those who photograph and those who are photographed emphasised the 'clash between European photographers and their colonial subjects'. Photographers exploited the locals, for whom 'photography was an experience to which one was asked to submit . . . to be subjected to a stranger's gaze'.[45] In exploring the relationship between the creation and the consumption of the image, what tourists consider worthy of a photograph – how they select their subjects, what they deem worthy of inclusion in photographic albums – could not be more revealing. As case study 3.1 demonstrates, these selections are largely constructed by the promoted image – in their 'private' photographs tourists seek out, recreate and thus reinforce, the 'public'[46] photographs of the tourism advertisements and travel literature.

Tensions within the imaging process

The way in which tourist photographs echo tourism advertising images may suggest that there is little tension between the created image and its consumption. For many the analysis of the relationship between advertising, the consumer and society, may well be complete once the reader has interpreted the image. If we were to leave the discussion here, however, we would be failing to investigate properly the relationships which inform the exchange of meaning. It is by no means a smooth process as the transference, or exchange of meaning, is a dynamic process which links the client (the advertiser), the advertising agency and the consumer within the cultural sphere.

Advertisements are usually highly polished creations, although the end product belies the tensions which inform its creation since 'any advertisement is the product of contesting forces'.[47] As such, the final execution is usually a compromise between the wishes of the client and the advertising agency. Creative agencies frequently clash with cautious clients who may be nervous about the creative concepts and executions put forward, although as the people who ultimately fund campaigns, clients' opinions cannot be ignored. However, just as clients may alter the scope or direction of executions, for advertisers their agency provides a repository of knowledge and experience. This situation may be particularly critical when sometimes far-flung national tourism organisations wish to appeal to physically and culturally remote consumers.

Advertising agencies are obviously highly skilled in creating memorable and salient executions. It is important to remember that, as we outlined in Chapter 1, agency employees are members of particular cultural systems which of necessity inform their view of the world. Consider, for instance, that advertising agencies tend to be located in the metropolitan centres of the West, with New York and London dominating (something to which we return in Chapter 8). It would be naive to assume that this has no impact on the cultural foundations of advertising as these western agencies – reading from scripts composed by the master subject – create advertisements which are primarily designed to appeal to western consumers. Western advertisers and consumers both draw on shared cultural meanings, selecting and reinforcing cultural messages and symbols which are themselves products of their societies and histories. Tourism advertising (like other forms of advertising) sells and dramatises dreams and aspirations rather than realities[48] – but it is important to question whose dreams and 'realities' are represented. Essentially, they are Western dreams sold for western consumption – dreams which are not universal but which are socially constructed and which privilege white, male, heterosexual fantasies.

Tensions between the consumers and the creators

Perhaps the greatest potential source of tension in the advertising relationship exists between the consumer and the advertisement since 'It is only within the mind of the individual spectator that symbols are turned into meanings, that the welcomed content finds its purpose.'[49] The consumer is, of course, much more than merely an interpreter of meaning, he or she can be an active contributor to the image generation process itself and this is particularly true in the late Nineties, when companies are increasingly concerned to consult the consumer over the suitability of advertising campaigns. Part of the rationale for this is that significant sums of money are expended annually on image promotion. In 1997 total global advertising spend approached $300 billion, with the United States accounting for $110.1 billion, Europe $83.5 billion and Asia Pacific $84 billion.[50]

Given the huge sums of money involved, it is not surprising that many companies look to research to minimise the risks involved in the promotion process. Research is used to improve the efficiency and effectiveness of the images used in promotion but it can also demonstrate accountability and cost effectiveness. It is a highly specialised area of marketing research, 'concerned with the objective evaluation of advertising as a method of mass communication and persuasion'[51] and an increasing reliance on consumer research brings its own tensions to an already controversial process in which:

> even advertising practitioners themselves are often unable to agree if the creation of a successful campaign is pure inspiration or calculated science.[52]

The increasing trend to ask the consumer has by no means been welcomed by all of those involved in the business of image creation. Indeed, some practitioners in the advertising industry argue that instead of debating which techniques should be used to evaluate the latest image campaign, they should instead be addressing whether advertising campaigns should be researched at all.[53] Of particular concern to them is the very real threat which such populist research poses to the creative process of image design. The danger is that the public, through their involvement in research, could replace the creative judgements of the skilled practitioner (case study 3.2). This is certainly alarming given that there is, in fact, relatively little evidence to suggest that the public can be relied upon to create effective image campaigns, reposition products or attract target markets – as Jones has argued, research can be a 'disastrous substitute for judgement'.[54] Advertising practitioners have a much longer history than their marketing research counterparts and in the rush to consult, and for some, to rely on, the public's judgement, innovative and potentially powerful campaigns may be rejected on the basis of 'research fact'.

Case Study 3.2   To Innovate Don't Ask the Consumer

Most tourism professionals spend most of their mature working lives acting on information and beliefs which are outdated and most of the senior managers running companies were last on the front line with customers at least ten years ago. In today's dynamic marketplace, this 'out-of-touchness' encourages irrelevant products, redundant organisations and obsolete managers.[55] Marketing research is also based on the historical beliefs of the customers and their perceptions of the products and services they buy. By its very nature market research investigates *existing* markets and refines *existing* propositions – it rarely talks to customers about their views on new concepts. Similarly, benchmarking helps organisations to compare themselves with the competition – it cannot help them to leapfrog the competition. In fact, what most companies are doing is watching their rivals, not watching the customer.

Over the last 30 years the marketplace has seen three waves of marketing philosophy. In the 1970s, business was supply-driven and in the 1980s research-driven when companies spent a great deal of time asking the customers what they wanted. The third and prevailing wave is described by Peters as concept-driven.[56] He argues that 'We need to establish what the customer might want if it were available or what the customers might want but were too ill-informed to ask for.'[57]

The crux of this problem is that consumers are being asked to give their opinion on what are often complex or controversial messages and images in very short spaces of time and perhaps in very artificial environments. It is not surprising then that such research may well provide 'an authoritative way of dismissing the quirky, distinctive ideas which make advertising live'.[58] What if, in a focus group, half the respondents loved a campaign and half hated it? The majority of researchers would recommend that the advertisement be changed and therein lies the danger of an over-reliance on research to guide the development of powerful promotional campaigns. Arguably, however, such a position challenges an underlying theme in the tourism literature as Middleton suggests that 'Print must convey the messages that target customers are known to want and respond to, on the basis of market research.'[59] This is to ignore the reality of marketing in many organisations and overplays the closeness of marketing research and marketing promotional activities. Research and marketing are often separate departments with separate agendas, whilst research is often used to prop up certain campaigns and claims and in many cases, such is the pressure of timescales and the lack of planning that the campaign is already running whilst research is conducted. In addition, for emerging or new destinations with no positive or negative images to reinforce or change, market research is of little help in creating the image. In these situations the images used are those created by the agencies and marketers – images which they think will succeed and which they anticipate will project the 'right' image for the destination.

There are, of course, many organisations involved in tourism image creation – from the smallest accommodation operators to the largest airlines and inter-national hotel chains and national tourism agencies. It is vitally important to consider who is creating and producing the image since the images portrayed will vary substantially depending on the initiating agency and the purpose of the advertisement. It may seem an obvious point, but such competitive identities can potentially confuse and undermine the message. For example, a *CNN* adver-tisement by investment group Euromed portrays a Tunisia hugely removed from the tourist advertisements for the same country. Suited, western-style businessmen predominate in a highly urban, high-tec environment whilst for tourism purposes a rather different souq, Arabic, Bedouin desert-style image is portrayed by the Tunisian Tourist Board.[60] These are two different advertisements of the same country produced for different audiences with quite different marketing objectives. This approach is by no means unique to Tunisia, but is common to all destinations since most places are seeking to attract inward investment, employment oppor-tunities and residents in addition to tourists (see case study 3.3). The messages communicated to each audience are quite different, revealing that there is no objective 'reality' of a place but different facets emphasised to different groups, a process which necessarily brings tensions.

Case Study 3.3   Curacao: 'Caribbean Treasure' or 'An Island of Business'?

Two advertisements appeared in the June 1996 issue of KLM's in-flight magazine as part of a larger feature on Curacao in the Dutch Caribbean – one was placed by the Curacao Tourist Bureau Europe, the other by Curacao Investment Promotion. The two different advertisements reveal the way in which the differing 'realities' of a place are promoted within the image, both visually and through the text. In the tourist advertisement the photographs and the text focused on the island's natural environment, the comfort of the resort and its natural environment – 'whether you're a diver, a shopper or an adventurer' it has an attraction for you. There is no sense that the island is a business centre. In contrast, whilst the advertisement designed to attract inward investment refers to the 'sun, sand and . . . beautiful clear sea' it highlights its 'strategic location', its infrastructure and its democratic tradition. In its visual imagery the green of the seas is replaced by a rather grey shot of the island's international airport.

The same concepts are presented here with a different emphasis, but to the same reader – remember these were placed within two pages of each other. Thus 'a truly unique and exceptional vacation destination' becomes 'a major international financial center'; the 'charm of its people' becomes a talented 'workforce'; 'international cuisine' contrasts with multi-lingualism; a 'historic marketplace' with a place which has continued 'moving with the times'. Finally, its Dutch heritage is transformed from 'attractive architecture' to the ability to access 'European markets.'[61]

Just as images reflect the motives of the creators, the audiences at which they are aimed are similarly diverse. There are at least four important image audiences in the case of public sector tourism organisations – potential tourists, the local tourism industry, politicians, and local residents. Whereas it is an obvious point that consumers can influence images through marketing research, politicians, the tourist trade and residents also play a role in influencing the projected image (case study 3.4). Public sector agencies are frequently inhibited by the need to include equal representation for industry operators and geographical areas in their publications. The tensions this can cause were vividly exposed in the way in which a 1997 Welsh local authority brochure was renamed *Mid Wales Lakes and Mountains: From the Brecon Beacons Through the Heart of Wales to the Berwyn Mountains.* Whilst this may well have adequately reflected the conflicting demands of the local tourism operators it is clearly a less than snappy marketing title.[62]

Thus, whilst brochure covers are often designed by professional tourism officers together with graphic designers, the local politicians, residents or tourism operators often also play a part in choosing the desired image, whether directly or indirectly.[63] Recognising the web-like nature of knowledge and power outlined in Chapters 1 and 2, it is important to note that within each of these groups some are more powerful than others and more adept at communicating their viewpoint – residents in Torquay are more likely to be able to influence the promotion of their destination than residents in the black South African homelands, for example.

Case Study 3.4   Residents Force Image Change on Resort of Torquay

There was considerable controversy surrounding the 1960 brochure cover for the seaside resort of Torquay in South West England. The cover, a slightly risqué photograph of a young couple on a beach, was met with opposition from residents and some tourism traders who considered it an unsuitable image for 'the Queen of the English Riviera'. The brochure was quickly labelled the 'Bikini-Girl Guide' by the local press. Although not everyone criticised the photograph since the local Hoteliers Association described its detractors as 'a few old Grundies', the controversy was such that in the following year the resort returned to its more typical cover illustration of palm trees and yachts. These latter images dominated the Torquay brochure cover throughout the 1950s and 1960s and re-emerged in the mid-1980s as the heart of the current image campaign.

The tensions between the creators and the represented

Although many image creators are actively pursuing both stakeholder and consumer consultation, the concept of discussing image creation with the actual inhabitants of a destination is rather more radical. This highlights another source of tension within the advertising process as it could result in image campaigns which are unacceptable to the host community. Arguably, one such instance is the way in which Prince Vlad, a historical figure regarded as a national hero in Romania, is distorted into 'Prince Vlad the Impaler-Dracula' and used as a brand image in brochures marketing the destination:

> You should share in the romantic stories of unearthly love . . . in . . . the Count's castle. As for the Count's sinister reputation, remember that he is harmless, unless you 'enter free and of your own will', under his cloak. . . Lunch in the very house in which Prince Vlad Dracula was born, in 1431, then witness a witch trial. . . [and] follow in Harker's footsteps. . . .[64]

This misrepresentation of a national figure for tourism consumption is not welcomed by many in Transylvania. Similarly, in Whitby in North-East England there is disquiet over the use of the same Bram Stoker Victorian Gothic novel *Dracula* to promote the seaside resort. Stoker visited the small port to gather material for his classic horror and featured it in three chapters of the novel. Yet, although this association brings significant tourist trade to the town, some residents are concerned that the link attracts American and European visitors who are obsessed with drugs and the occult and would prefer the tourism authorities to highlight the port's links with the seafaring explorer Captain Cook.[65]

In contrast, in a current campaign, the Wales Tourist Board (WTB), the national tourism agency for Wales, is pursuing a much more 'inclusive' approach to their branding activities which may well have the affect of negating such criticism and even of reducing some external political pressures. Here, the brand proposition has not been constructed by, for instance, a London-based advertising agency and implemented with no reference to the Welsh people. Rather, in a groundbreaking move, the key brand attributes and values are being researched amongst the people

of Wales to ensure that they are acceptable and representative but not stereotypical. This approach reflects the WTB's unique remit amongst UK tourist boards
to safeguard the country's culture as well as to promote tourism. As Robin Gwyn
of the WTB's public relations section recently said of the campaign:

> There would be nothing worse than a lot of highly paid professional organisations
> coming together to work out an idea that is not something the people of Wales could
> relate to.[66]

This approach also has the effect of assisting destination brand managers to exert
some control over the product. The 'inclusive' approach of 'Wales The Brand'
provides an imaginative way forward, since, by researching the core brand values
amongst its indigenous population, the tourist board is not only ensuring that the
brand's associations are acceptable, but also that they are more likely to reflect the
product.

It is also perhaps an example of power being exercised by people who are not
normally involved in the image creation process – but it is possible that this is a
power which directly stemmed from a hostile reaction to one of the WTB's
previous marketing campaigns. The campaign in question was centred around the
slogan 'Now there's Wales for you.' Developed by a London agency, it was felt to
convey 'Welshness' in the phrasing but produced an outcry in the Welsh press and
broadcast media over its stereotypical and patronising tone. As such it is an
example of how a group of people 'consumed' a representation of an identity, a
representation which was subsequently rejected and regulated by those who were
not in fact the intended audience for the campaign. This example is as representative of the rather circular nature of cultural values and meanings as is the
relationship between popular culture and tourism imagery, it is merely another
aspect of this process.

Such examples reveal the multi-dimensional reality of image creation and consumption in that, in addition to recognising the multiplicity of creators, it is also
important to recognise that the potential tourist is not the sole consumer of the
imagery. There is also a need to influence groups including retail agents and
suppliers, as well as opinion formers such as journalists and travel writers. In
addition, local, national and international politicians and professional groups may
be targets of image projection.[67] Paymasters, other departments, other agencies
and countries are also important consumers of images – not just potential tourists.
It is important to recognise that image creation activities are one of the obvious
manifestations that an agency is engaged in promoting. Producing brochures,
posters and media advertisements demonstrates – to their managers, their political
paymasters and to other destinations – that marketers are doing their job.

In such ways, image is not just important to the audiences but to the producers,
belying the simplicity of statements which suggest that 'all print is designed to
serve the customers' needs, not those of the producer'.[68] There are many audiences
and customers for print material – and not always the most obvious ones.
Brochures and other image vehicles are also highly visible and prestigious symbols
for stakeholders and opportunities for politicians' photocalls. For many places
their tourism promotional activities, such brochures and posters, symbolise their

separate political and social identities as well being vehicles to attract tourists (case study 3.5). Moreover, in their promotion, places are thus *seen* to be on various agendas – for tourism, inward investment, and regeneration opportunities.

Case Study 3.5   Problems of Multi-tiered Destination Image Promotion in Wales

Place promotion has been defined by Ward and Gold as: 'the conscious use of publicity and marketing to communicate selective images of specific geographical localities or areas to a target audience'.[69] It is important to realise, however, as they go on to point out, that there is a critical paradox inherent within place marketing. On one level, place promotion in Western Europe has traditionally been regarded as an aspect of public or quasi-public policy. Thus it should be undertaken to benefit the public good and local authorities should not, when marketing them-selves, stress their advantages at the expense of neighbouring authorities. At another level, however, place promotion is now strongly influenced by the spread of the market principle and places must therefore compete with each other.

This paradox of public policy and market forces is further complicated in local states. Often, political considerations within local government dictate the range of photographs which are included on a brochure cover. Frequently, a local authority's literature has to be seen to include photographs which illustrate all the key areas, towns, or resorts within its boundaries. Whilst this has its political advantages in that it appeases local pressure groups and local residents, it can compromise the effectiveness of the images. The reality of local state promotion therefore provides a very specific example of Ward and Gold's 'uneasy co-existence between the public policy and the marketing approaches to place promotion'.[70]

In terms of how places are portrayed by official tourism marketers, the fact that places are 'multi-sold' complicates their projected images.[71] For instance, in the case of Wales, there are thirteen different national bodies promoting the country overseas for different purposes and to different audiences, whilst the local state also has a promotional role and often conveys conflicting messages.[72] It is there-fore, important to realise that places exist in the minds of many audiences at different times and in different ways. Places sometimes project different messages for different audiences – sometimes on the same stand at shows and events, depending on whether tourists or investors are sought.

A secondary problem is that destination brochures produced on the political boundaries of a local state raise a number of potentially problematic policy issues for the strategic planning of tourism marketing, including possible duplication of effort and resources. It is also possible that potential tourists might fail to recognise and even be confused by marketing areas based purely on administrative boundaries. These issues are by no means unique to Wales since they are found wherever place marketing is undertaken by several agencies operating at, or collaborating with, different tiers of government. There is a question over the efficacy of marketing practices that are liable to over-arching political influences which undermines the extent of integration of destination image promotion across comparable tiers of a geo-political system and between levels of local and national government.

Wales, together with England, Northern Ireland, and Scotland, is one of the four home countries of the United Kingdom. The WTB, an independent statutory body, is the primary agency responsible for marketing Wales to potential visitors and for developing and improving the country's tourism product and infrastructure. Wales as a destination has an impressive range of tourism products as well as a rich and varied natural environment and a strong cultural and linguistic identity. Until 1996 prospective visitors to Wales could choose from a vast array of tourist brochures. In addition to the main WTB vacation brochure, three regional companies charged with marketing Wales – North Wales Tourism, Mid Wales Tourism and Tourism South & West Wales – produced a range of brochures, whilst two-thirds of Wales' 45 local authorities produced brochures of one type or another.

In 1994 the WTB's strategy highlighted the volume of brochures being produced and emphasised the need for a more structured approach to the production of tourism literature.[73] Certainly such was the, then, range of promotional literature that there were dangers of, at best, duplication of effort, and, at worst, a confusion of projected message emanating from Welsh destinations. The WTB is trying to create a unique 'brand' Wales through the projection of core themes – conveyed through Celtic imagery and typeface, the Welsh language and the slogan 'Wales-Cymru. Land of Inspiration'. In particular, it urges the use in all promotional literature of the Welsh flag and the Welsh dragon as brand signatures.

Very few of the pre-1996 local authority brochures attempted to contribute towards developing this cohesive brand. The majority of local authorities paid minimal reference to this potentially unique dimension, and in some cases ignored it completely. Most were more concerned with promoting their own areas and authority names – most of which had little meaning to the potential tourist. Of 27 brochures only six used the Welsh language on the cover and of the images in all 27 brochures only 2% were uniquely 'Welsh' images. As many as eight authorities did not include anything distinctively Welsh or Celtic in their brochure.

If the strategy to differentiate Wales is to be effective, it is vital that the same messages are communicated and reinforced in all promotional literature, however by pursuing their own agendas, the local authorities were actually undermining the WTB's attempt to establish a unique brand 'Wales'. This reflects the political realities of place marketing where destination promotion is often the responsibility of a variety of agencies and organisations operating at different government levels. Whilst competition extends consumer choice, the volume of brochures produced and the confusion of marketing messages is clearly counter-productive. However, such are the political imperatives which impel local authorities towards their place promotional activities, that the notion of cross-boundary cooperation instead of each promoting their own authority name has been difficult to achieve. Since 1996 there are now 14 marketing areas which form the basis for coordinated marketing schemes, operating under the auspices of 22 new unitary authorities.[74] There have, however, been 'teething' problems with the new scheme and some authorities have tried to opt out of the new areas. The future success of Wales' multi-tiered promotional activities remains to be proved.

It emerges that many places have to be seen to be operating in the promotional arena for political reasons and place promotion has become increasingly important in the last two decades. As many western countries have suffered decline in their traditional industries, so have many areas turned to tourism as an agent of economic revival. Yet, as more and more countries, states, regions and cities invest in tourism and in place marketing, the competition for potential tourists becomes fierce:

> No longer are places merely the settings for business activity. Instead, every community has to transform itself into a seller of goods and services, a proactive marketer of its products and its place value. Places are, indeed, products, whose identities and values must be designed and marketed.[75]

As every place becomes increasingly competitive, not to be seen is not to be considered. In this sense, arguments of effectiveness and cost-efficiency often become spurious and are ignored, despite the increasingly results-driven marketing agendas. In our highly competitive world, the image of places, as well as products and organisations, are crucial. As we have seen, however, there are many factors which influence image creation, it is a process which is by no means seamless and without tension. In this chapter we have explored the relationships between advertising, society, the image creators and the image consumers, investigating some of the strains which are articulated within the image creation process. In the next chapter we turn our attention to the relationship between popular culture and the tourism image since it is popular culture which provides the stock of knowledge upon which the tourism advertisers and consumers draw in constructing their views of the world.

References

1 Urry, J. (1990) *The Tourist Gaze. Leisure and Travel in Contemporary Societies*, Sage, London: 13.
2 Scott-Malden, D. (1991) *Recent Developments in Advertising Theory: A Review of the Work of Davies, Riley-Smith, MacClay and Millward Brown* (unpublished).
3 Williamson, J. (1978) *Decoding Advertisements*, Marion Boyers, London; Wernick, A. (1992) *Promotional Culture. Advertising, ideology and symbolic expression*, Sage, London; and Fowles, J. (1996) *Advertising and Popular Culture*, Sage, London.
4 reference 2.
5 Shimp, T. (1993) *Promotion Management and Marketing Communications*, 3rd ed., Dryden Press, Fort Worth.
6 reference 2.
7 Season, T.V. (1989) 'Promotional Strategies in Tourism', 335–339 in Witt, S.F. and Moutinho, L. (eds) *Tourism Marketing and Management Handbook*, Prentice Hall, Hemel Hempstead: 336.
8 Wales Tourist Board (1997) *The 1996 All Wales Visitor Survey*, Wales Tourist Board, Cardiff.
9 Kotler, P., Haider, D.H. and Rein, I. (1993) *Marketing Places: Attracting Investment, Industry, and Tourism to Cities, States and Nations*, The Free Press, New York: 207.
10 Morgan, M. (1996) *Marketing for Leisure and Tourism*, Prentice Hall, Hemel Hempstead: 230.
11 Middleton, V.T.C. (1994) *Marketing in Travel and Tourism*, 2nd ed., Butterworth Heinemann, Oxford; Holloway, J.C. and Robinson, C. (1995) *Marketing for Tourism*, 3rd ed., Longman, Harlow; Wearne, N. and Morrison, A. (1996) *Hospitality Marketing*, Butterworth Heinemann, Oxford; Kotler, P. *et al.* (1996) *Marketing for Hospitality & Tourism*, Prentice Hall, New Jersey; and Horner, S. and Swarbrooke, J. (1996) *Marketing Tourism, Hospitality and Leisure in Europe*, Thomson Business Press, London.
12 Fowles, J. (1996) *Advertising and Popular Culture*, Sage, London: 65.
13 Lasch, C. (1978) *The Culture of Narcism: American Life in an Age of diminishing expectations*, WW Norton, New York.
14 reference 12: 72–3.
15 Wernick, A. (1991) *Promotional Culture. Advertising, ideology and symbolic expression*, Sage, London: 42.
16 Williamson, J. (1978) *Decoding Advertisements*, Marion Boyers, London.
17 reference 16: 47; see also Ewen, S. (1976) *Captains of Consciousness. Advertising and the Social Roots of the Consumer Culture*. McGraw Hill, New York, for a historical Marxist critique of advertising.

18 McLuhan, M. (1964) *Understanding Media: the extensions of man*, McGraw Hill, New York: 232.

19 reference 12: 48.

20 McCracken, G. (1986) 'Culture and Consumption: A theoretical account of the structure and movement of the cultural meaning of consumer goods', *Journal of Consumer Research*, 13: 71–81.

21 reference 16.

22 reference 12: 159.

23 reference 12: 160.

24 reference 12: 160.

25 reference 12: 163.

26 reference 12: 195.

27 Hall, S. (1980) 'Encoding/decoding', 128–38 in Hall, S. (ed.) *Culture, Media, Language*, Hutchinson, London. See also Fowles, J. (1996) *Advertising and Popular Culture*, Sage, London.

28 Marchand, R. (1985) *Advertising the American Way: Making Way for Modernity 1920–1940*, University of California Press, Berkeley.

29 reference 16: 101–102.

30 O'Barr, W. (1994) *Culture and the Ad. Exploring Otherness in Advertising*, Westview Press, Boulder, Colorado: 7.

31 reference 30.

32 reference 30: 8.

33 reference 30: 10.

34 reference 30: 12

35 reference 30: 103.

36 ibid.

37 ibid.

38 ibid.

39 ibid.

40 reference 30: 105.

41 reference 30: 106.

42 reference 30: 13.

43 Botterill, T.D. and Crompton, J.L. (1987) 'Personal Constructions of Holiday Snapshots', *Annals of Tourism Research*, 14 (1): 152–56: 152.

44 Cohen, E. (1987) review of Yeshayahu, N. (1985) The Bible of the Image: The History of Photography in the Holy Land, 1839–1899, University of Pennsylvania Press, Philadelphia, *Annals of Tourism Research*, 14 (1): 157–162: 157.

45 Yeshayahu, N. (1985) The Bible of the Image: The History of Photography in the Holy Land, 1839-1899, University of Pennsylvania Press, Philadelphia: 5.

46 Berger, J. (1980) *About Looking*, Pantheon Books, New York.

47 reference 12: 77.

48 Marchand, R. (1985) *Advertising the American Way: Making Way for Modernity 1920–1940*, University of California Press, Berkeley.

49 reference 12: 104.

50 *The World in 1997* (1996), The Economist Publications, London: 106.

51 Chisnall, P.M. (1994) *Consumer Behaviour*, 3rd ed., McGraw-Hill, Maidenhead, Berkshire: 55.

52 Research International 1, Background Papers, Market Research Society, Advertising Research Seminar, 'The Research International Approach to Advertising Evaluation Research': 1.

53 Silvester, S. (1994) 'Is Research Killing Advertising?' Research International Background Papers, Market Research Society, Advertising Research Seminar.

54 Jones, quoted in Bovee, C.L. *et al.* (1995) *Advertising Excellence*, international edition, McGraw-Hill, New York: 7.

55 Peters, G. (1996) *The Next Wave: imagining the next generation of customers*, Pitmans, London: 9.

56   ibid.

57   ibid.

58   reference 53: 9–10.

59   Middleton, V.T.C. (1992) *Marketing in Travel and Tourism*, 2nd ed., Butterworth Heinemann: 195.

60   Euromed/Tunisian Tourist Board television advertisement run on CNN during summer 1996.

61   advertisements in *Holland Herald*, KLM June 1996: 17–19.

62   'Move to avert fresh row over name of visitor brochure', *Western Mail* 5 June 1997: 5.

63   For example, a Welsh flag was included on the 1993 Vale of Glamorgan brochure cover following comments made by a councillor representing Plaid Cymru, the Welsh Nationalist Party, that more specific Welsh images should be incorporated.

64   Romantic Romania. Fascinating Tours operated by Romantic Travel, Romania.

65   'Whitby takes fright at the spectre of a Dracula invasion', *The Times* 14 June 1997: 12.

66   quoted in Shipton, M. (1997) 'A new era – a brand new Wales', *Wales on Sunday* 4 May: 20–21.

67   Cooper, C. *et al.* (1993) *Tourism Principles & Practice*, Pitman Publishing, London: 258.

68   reference 59: 195.

69   Ward, S.V. and Gold, J.R. (1994) 'Introduction', 1–17 in Ward, S.V. and Gold, J.R. (eds) *Place Promotion. The Use of Publicity and Marketing to Sell Towns and Regions*, John Wiley and Sons, Chichester: 2.

70   reference 69: 11.

71   Ashworth, G.J. and Voogd, H. (1990) *Selling the City*, Belhaven Press, London.

72   Pritchard, A. and Morgan, N.J. (1995) Evaluating vacation destination brochure images: the case of local authorities in Wales', *Journal of Vacation Marketing*, 2 (1): 23–38.

73   Wales Tourist Board (1994), *Tourism 2000. A Strategy for Wales*, Wales Tourist Board, Cardiff.

74   Wales Tourist Board, (1994) Marketing Areas Study, Wales Tourist Board, Cardiff; and Wales Tourist Board, (1994) 'Promotional Literature – Towards a More Rational Approach. A Wales Tourist Board Consultation Paper', Wales Tourist Board, Cardiff.

75   reference 9: 10.

4 Culture and the image

In this chapter we explore the distinction between so-called 'projected' or 'official' tourism images and the 'organic' images derived from other non-tourist sources. Building on Gartner's conceptualisation of the image formation process as a continuum of sources,[1] we suggest that the circuit of culture reveals this to be more of a loop which constantly revolves, looping back on itself. Within this loop, particular ideas and associations, through continued use and reuse, have come to dominate the stock of knowledge from which official agencies (such as tourist boards) and those engaged in the production of popular culture (such as film-makers and writers) draw their representations of people and places. Tourism and culture can thus be said to have a symbiotic relationship whereby tourism makes use of cultural meanings to frame its imagery, meanings which are drawn from many areas in society. We investigate the developing link between tourism agencies and producers of popular culture (particularly film and television industries) and examine the synergistic relationship which exists between these two agents of image creation. As a prelude to this, however, we briefly consider the existing body of work on imagery in tourism.

The image and tourism promotion

Image emerges as a key marketing tool in an industry where potential consumers must base buying decisions upon mental images of product offerings rather than being able to physically sample alternatives.[2] As a result of this important role, image has been discussed as a critical variable in the tourism marketing mix since the 1970s and studies have highlighted its many roles. There is an extensive literature which examines the relationship of image to destination choice and in terms of tourist decision-making.[3] Related to these issues, and equally well-researched are those of travel satisfaction,[4] the image formation process,[5] image modification and change[6] and image measurement.[7] Finally, the relationship between image and tourism development has also been studied.[8]

Image in tourism covers a wide range of activities and agencies. Its role reflects that of promotion in general, which is aimed at influencing attitudes and behaviour of audiences in three main ways: to confirm and reinforce; to create new patterns of behaviour and attitude; or to change attitudes and behaviour.[9] Thus, tourism operators use images to portray their products in brochures, posters and media advertising; airlines, hotels and resorts do the same; as do destinations, attempting to construct an image of a destination that will force it into the potential tourist's evoked set, or destination short list, leading to a purchase decision. Whatever the tourism product, its image is the public face of how it is marketed and the importance of image promotion in tourism marketing should not be under-estimated.

A key theme within tourism image research is that of destination image and the field has been studied by researchers in psychology, geography, marketing and tourism, recreation and leisure. All these studies indicate that destination images are subjective, and temporally and culturally-specific, although few studies have successfully tackled a definition of destination image – indeed, Pearce has commented that 'image is one of those terms that will not go away, a term with vague and shifting meanings'.[10] Where some definition has been attempted a number of common themes have emerged.[11] Collectively, destination image has been described as 'an amalgam of impressions, beliefs, ideas, expectations and feelings towards an area . . . suggesting the involvement of both cognitive and evaluative components'.[12] Perhaps the most useful definition of the concept of 'image', which can be applied to a product, a person or a country is Echtner and Ritchie's adaptation of Dichter's definition: 'an image is not only the individual traits or qualities but also the total impression an entity makes on the minds of others.'[13] One thing is clear – destination image is multi-faceted and multi-dimensional and it is not only tourists who hold images of tourism places, although studies focusing on the tourists' perceptions have dominated. Tourists; intermediaries such as travel and advertising agencies (often based in the tourism generating region); the industry (suppliers in the destination); the destination state (governments, states and authorities); and the indigenous population (often neglected, but key stake-holders in terms of tourism development) all have differing images of the same destination. The tourist image is therefore highly inter-subjective.[14]

This multi-faceted role of image makes its analysis extremely complex – for instance, it has to consider the role of the image creator and the meaning systems which inform their creations – which in turn reinforce particular ways of imaging or seeing the world. How a Madison Avenue advertising executive sees tourism in Fiji or the Seychelles is probably far removed from how the indigenous population would see their own 'reality'. But the implications of this are felt far beyond a difference of view since, as we shall return to in Part III, the former has the authority to represent the latter and thus contribute to the reinforcement of a particular ideology. Whilst there is clearly an element of subjectivity in place definition, authors such as Urry, Hughes and Said[15] have drawn attention to the evolution of predomi-nant ways of seeing the world over time and in this sense there are commonly held views which underpin the construction of images, myths and clichés of places and peoples. Critics may argue that all of us have differing expectations and perceived realities of destinations, however, this is to deny the pervasive influence of social, historical and cultural processes. Similarly, the social group within which an indi-vidual moves greatly influences perceptions.[16] In such ways 'common' stereotypes of destinations and their peoples emerge, but as we will explore later in this book, those stereotypes are the everyday reflections of dominant ideologies.

Destination image is certainly an important determinant of tourist buying behaviour. Research by Pearce,[17] Woodside and Lyonski,[18] and Goodrich,[19] demonstrates a clear relationship between positive perceptions of destinations and positive purchase decisions. Although these perceptions may not be based on 'fact' or first-hand experience, they nevertheless exert a vital influence on a potential tourist's decision to visit a destination. Similarly, negative images, even if unjustified, will deter potential tourists and result in a decision not to purchase. As Hunt recognised in the late Seventies:

> It is possible that images, as perceived by individuals in the travel market, may have as much to do with an area's tourism development success as the more tangible recreation and tourism resources.[20]

There is a considerable debate surrounding the influence of tourism promotion activities. For instance, it is argued that potential consumers compare vacation brochures and, on the basis of that comparison, make a decision on their preferred destination.[21] Despite this contention 'little empirical evidence exists to explain the process in any detail',[22] now, however, recent research suggests that destination selection is a rather more complex and haphazard process than that suggested in the comparative destination evaluation models.[23] Destination choice appears to be something which is not carefully planned but is almost random and open to outside events or influences such as advertisements or special offers. The only internal influences which could be identified as being important in terms of destination selection include the tourists' past experiences, recommendations from friends and relatives and the needs of their children, where applicable. Certainly, there appears to be little detailed evaluation of what particular destinations or resorts have to offer the potential vacationer.[24] These research findings pose some interesting questions regarding the role of promotional tools in the tourist decision-making process. This is particularly so, as it suggests that much tourist literature does not serve to persuade uncommitted potential vacationers but rather to confirm the intentions of those already planning to visit.

If it emerges that destination images are formed according to both personal and social influences, it is also the case that these images are dynamic. Gunn has suggested that tourist images are in a state of transition throughout the travel experience. As a result, an important development in place image theory has been the comparison of a destination's image at different stages in the tourist's decision-making process.[25] At each stage the potential tourist may hold different images of a destination, images which are constructed by the amount, source and objectivity of the available information. This range of imagery has been described as a hierarchy of place images, ranging from initial perceptions based on organic sources, to a modified or re-evaluated image upon visiting the destination.[26] This modification results in what has been described as a much more 'realistic, objective, differentiated, and complex image'.[27] The influences upon this changing image are many and varied and include both external influences (maybe encountered at the destination itself) and internal influences (such as personal motives).

This takes us to the heart of our review of the tourism image literature. In 1972 Gunn categorised the sources of consumer images into two typologies. The first are 'organic' images which stem from a lifetime of socialisation and which include popular culture, the media, literature and education. The second source was classified as 'projected' images, direct attempts to influence consumer images of destinations. Official tourist organisations and agents are responsible for the projected image and include commercial sources such as brochures and advertise-ments.[28] Many authors have built on Gunn's work to create further classifications of image sources, such as Phelps' primary and secondary images and Fakeye and Crompton's complex image, both of which deal with the difference between images after experience.[29] By far the most sophisticated adaptation of Gunn's work is Gartner's identification of eight 'image agents'. Gartner suggests that the image formation process can be seen as a continuum of separate agents acting both independently and in combination with each other. The continuum is constructed on the differing levels of credibility, market penetration and control applicable to each agent.[30]

There is a wide recognition amongst tourism academics, therefore, that desti-nation images are influenced by a much wider spectrum of information sources beyond those produced by tourism agents. This has resulted in the contention that the influence of commercial image creation is relatively weak in comparison to other marketed products.[31] Whilst official influences like brochures, posters and adver-tisements may not play as critical a role in influencing purchase decisions as in other products, Nolan found that the material of official tourist information services was highly rated in terms of usage and perceived credibility.[32] Furthermore, Schmoll has argued that the influence of official messages is perhaps stronger than is consciously acknowledged and Dilley concludes that the power of officially projected images should not be underestimated.[33] Despite the refinement of the image typologies, however, the differentiation between 'organic' and 'projected' images remains, albeit in a continuum rather than in a two-dimensional relationship. This is because many studies have been concerned to examine the functional remits of organisations which are involved in image formation. Looking at the functions of organisations and images, however, obscures the mutually dependent and symbiotic nature of culture on the one hand and advertising, in our case tourism advertising, on the other, a relationship we will now examine in more detail.

Reconstruing the image media

There are many components to the promotional mix (Table 4.1) and how an organisation blends the mix depends on a number of factors, particularly the nature of the product to be marketed and the target audience.[34] Tour operators rely heavily on television advertising, whilst niche market operators tend to focus on printed media advertising in specialist publications.[35] Whilst image creation affects all aspects of the promotional mix, the key vehicles for its projection in tourism are electronic and print media advertisements and brochures, although, of course, these operate in conjunction with other activities, particularly sales pro-motions. There are therefore a range of media in which advertisements are placed promoting the merits of destinations, airlines, attractions and hotels – these are the traditional promotional media for the tourism image and they would be classified as projected or official image sources.

However, as we suggested above, such classification into projected or official sources ignores the reality of the circular cultural exchanges outlined in Chapter 1. In practice, all these media borrow from other cultural spheres and the tourism

Table 4.1   The Principal Tourism Promotional Tools.

Activity	Notes
paid for media advertising	includes TV, press, radio and outdoor. Also includes tourist board and other travel-related guides, books and brochures that accept advertising
direct mail/door to door distribution	includes general sales literature or print items specially designed for the purpose
exhibitions/shows/workshops	important alternative forms of distribution and display for reaching retail, wholesale and consumer target groups
personal selling	via meetings, telephone contact, workshops. Primarily aimed at distributors and intermediaries purchasing for groups of consumers
sales literature	especially promotional brochures and other print used in a servicing role
sales promotion	short-term incentives offered as inducements to purchase, including temporary product augmentation. Covers sales force and distribution networks as well as consumers
price discounting	a common form of sales promotion; includes extra commissions and bonuses for retailers
point of sale displays merchandising	posters, window dressing, displays or brochures and other materials both of a regular and temporary incentive kind
familiarisation and educational trips	ways to motivate and facilitate distributor networks through product sampling. Also used to reach and influence journalists
distribution networks and commission	organised systems or channels through which prospective customers achieve access to products, includes computerised links between principles and distributors

Source: After Middleton, V.T.C. (1994) *Marketing in Travel and Tourism*: 150, Butterworth-Heinemann.

image is all around us in the sense that our views of peoples, places and products are heavily influenced by cultural processes. As Fowles notes in *Advertising and Popular Culture*:

> The symbol domain of popular culture . . . offers lavish pickings to advertisers trying to construct attractive messages for reticent consumers. Advertisers will appropriate such popular culture material as celebrities, music, [and] comedic styles.[36]

This suggests that a division between organic and projected imagery is increasingly artificial – images which are drawn from popular culture influence tourism marketers, tourism writers and tourism consumers. These images include those in

literature, art, music, films, television programmes and other product advertisements. Images swamp us every day – from news broadcasts on *CNN* to billboards
and radio messages – as we live in a media-driven world. In this global media, it is
that of the US which dominates, especially in the celluloid market. It is this
cultural power of the US and the West – empowering them to define and represent
peoples and places – which must be recognised in discussions of the role of image
within the tourism promotional mix.

The division between 'official' and 'organic' imagery seems increasingly tenuous
given that we live in a world where cultural icons inform tourism imagery. The
supermodel Claudia Schiffer promotes Montenegro in the former Yugoslavia; films
and songs provide emotive symbols for tourist destinations, as *O Georgia*, sung by
Elton John, does for Georgia, USA; and powerful cultural symbols such as the
Coca-Cola logo sell Atlanta. As popular culture informs tourism advertising, so
advertising – through using and reinforcing particular symbols, icons and images –
lubricates the circulation of culture throughout and between societies. Thus,
tourism brochures selling timeless, romantic Paris, using images of lovers kissing
by the Seine, shape, reinforce and enhance what we understand to be Parisian or
French images. Such images, however, are themselves products of French post-war
humanist photography which produced a distinctive body of images which shaped
a particular view of Frenchness and French culture.[37]

Similarly, in other tourism destinations we can see how culture and tourism fuses
and exchanges images – as when history, film, sports events and tourism imagery
intersected at Atlanta in 1996. Burnt to the ground in the American Civil War by
General Sherman's army (an event vividly represented in the movie classic *Gone
with the Wind*), the city in its promotion for the 1996 summer Olympics recon-
strued history, historical film representation and a new vision of regeneration. The
world's premier sports event was billed as the city's second rebirth, after that of
1864.[38] This is by no means an isolated example as tourism writers and marketers
frequently rely on these wider cultural markers in their portrayal of destinations.
The UK tour operator Airwaves' *America Latina* brochure informs the would-be
traveller that 'Visiting Cuba is like dipping into five centuries of history'[39] and that
its political isolation has created a timewarp on the island, forever locked in the
Forties and Fifties:

> . . . the island is redolent with this imagery, whether it is Hemingway's old haunts, . . .
> the Tropicana Night Club which still somehow echoes to the sound of Nat King Cole,
> the hotels run by "Long Legs Diamond" and the events of the Bay of Pigs – it is
> almost as if Alec Guinness was still our man out there.[40]

The meshing of popular culture in film, song, literature, art and photography is an
extremely complex process as audio and visual images interweave to create an
overall impression. Whilst film and television are visual, their soundtracks are
vitally important to the creation of atmosphere. This interweaving of media is
further blurred by the cross-referencing of images and the synthesis of film,
television, video and computer images, often disseminated by an increasingly small
number of vertically and horizontally integrated global companies, a situation
which should be borne in mind when reading the following pages.

Perhaps one of the oldest sources of travel images is literature, which itself has provided the germ for many films, songs and plays, as well as tourism promotion. The Irish Tourist Board (*Borde Failte*) now markets not only the country's built heritage and natural environment, but its literary giants, including, amongst others, Oscar Wilde, George Bernard Shaw, Samuel Beckett, W.B. Yeats and James Joyce. As well as promoting places, literature can also prompt tourism development and shape tourism identities, as when references appear in brochures and on road signs. In the UK Dorset is 'Hardy Country' after Thomas Hardy; Yorkshire is 'Brontë Country' after the Brontë Sisters; Stratford is associated with William Shakespeare and Swansea in South Wales with the poet Dylan Thomas. In the USA New Orleans actively associates itself with the *Vampire Chronicles* novels of Anne Rice[41] and Salem with Arthur Miller's play *The Crucible* (case study 4.1). Interestingly, the same piece of literature can be associated with very different places. As we have already discussed, Bram Stoker's *Dracula* and its movie progeny provide Transylvania in Romania with a powerful tourism and cultural icon, and Whitby on the Northeast coast of England, also featured heavily in the novel, hosts an annual Dracula festival and has a Dracula experience attraction.

Case Study 4.1   Salem – The Witch City of *The Crucible*

In the search for differentiation, some destinations turn to rather unusual associations to create a distinctiveness – for example Salem, Massachusetts has branded itself 'The Witch City'. When Arthur Miller visited Salem in 1952 to research his *The Crucible* he described the town as '"morose and secret", bypassed by industry, "dripping . . . in the cold black drizzle like some abandoned dog."'[42] Centuries after the trials, the town was still embarrassed about what had happened. Yet after the triumph of Miller's play a Witch Trail was set up and today signs show where various citizens had been arrested, interrogated, or hanged whilst even the local police carry the slogan 'Salem, The Witch City, Massachusetts, 1626' on their patrol cars and uniforms.

Using literary markers is a device which is by no means restricted to professional destination marketers. Travel writers frequently use such figures to introduce destinations to their readers. In an introduction to a 1997 article in the US travel magazine, *Condé Nast Traveler*, on the Malay Archipelago, readers are told that Joseph Conrad wrote of the destination 'in the opening pages of his novel *The Rescue* [as] a "region of shallow waters and forest-clad islands . . . still mysterious between the deep waters of two oceans. . ."', and that 'From a far distance, Malaysia evokes the brooding romance that haunts Conrad's tales.'[43]

The moving image

Whilst literature continues to play a vital role in popular culture, the defining media of the second half of this century are television and film. Television is a sensory medium and the dominant vista for the image in the post-industrial world:

> More than any other form of mediated communication, television is intimate, multi-modal and multisensory, transmitting voice, music, sound effects, graphics and imagery to eye and ear. . . Before viewers' eyes dance phantasmic scenes, an ever novel kaleidoscope of symbolic activity.[44]

Television can directly influence the tourism image through the broadcast of tourism commercials but it is the popular entertainment featured on television which exerts the most powerful influence on the images of places and peoples. It is the most effective medium for promoting the look and the sound of a place, whether in the form of a fifteen second network commercial or a half hour narrow-cast cable or satellite 'infommercial' on a travel channel. A different version of such ideas is the video travelogue and the vacation programme, such as *Wish You Were Here* in the UK or the *CNN Travel Show*. These are key tourism image vehicles, often developed in close cooperation with the area tourism authorities, yet there is very little research measuring the impact of such programmes on image formulation or the vacation decision-making process. The essence of these programmes is to blend travel and entertainment and each week the regular presenters are joined by guest celebrities who present a short personal view of three or four destinations. Despite these 'personal' views, the shows very clearly portray 'soundbite', 'snapshot' representations of destinations which often rely on stereotypes heavily grounded in socio-historical and cultural process, as case 4.2. illustrates.

Case Study 4.2 A Personal View of Adelaide, Australia

Featured on the UK holiday programme, *Wish You Were Here*, the piece starts with a voice-over introduction announcing that its presenter will be 'Living it up down-under and getting to grips with the locals', phrases which refer to popular UK conceptions of Australia and to the sexy image of the presenter, Lesley Joseph, a vampish UK sit-com star.

Good beaches, interesting cities, a wine valley and a plethora of wild animals is a lot to ask of any destination, but Lesley Joseph found them all in Australia. After flying for 24 hours and thousands of miles, the first thing she found in Adelaide was a cricket match – 'wasn't it sweet of them to put it on so I wouldn't feel homesick?' In fact, there was much more in Adelaide to make Lesley feel at home – statues of Queen Victoria; city buildings which were described as not looking out of place in British cities; and Victorian-style mansions on the outskirts of Adelaide.

Having been treated to these iconic symbols of home, the UK viewer is introduced to his or her first symbol of Australia – a koala bear: 'I knew I was in Australia when I met this baby – a hairy grey baby' (shot of Lesley cuddling a koala). The viewers' next encounter with Australia is with the beach but, just in case they feel out of place, they need not worry because Glen Elle reminds Lesley of 'Brighton back home' and she tells us that it was also the first landing point for European settlers in 1836. Moving on to some modern day icons, the viewer is next confronted with a shot of some *Baywatch*-style lifeguards whose attentions Lesley is trying to attract, echoing her on-screen sexy image. She is unsuccessful, however, and asks 'what's Pamela Anderson got that I haven't got?'. The Barossa Valley, Australia's greatest wine producing area, is the next point of call. We are told that the first settlers in the Valley were Lutherans who have given the villages a German feel. The piece concludes on Kangaroo Island, a place where people can see what everyone expects to see in Australia – kangaroos and other wild animals. The whole item is accompanied throughout by didgeridoo music, hinting at Australia's unseen aboriginal heritage.

As one can see, the representations of Australia aimed at a UK audience draw on many spheres: colonial history, Queen Victoria, cricket (the archetypal English sport exported as a result of Empire), and popular entertainment in the shape of *Baywatch* and Lesley's own UK television series *Birds of a Feather*. Key Australian icons include the beach, koala bears, kangaroos, sunshine, wine and Aboriginal music. These representations help to construct an identity of a white Australia in which the indigenous population is in the background, heard but not seen. This identity is grounded in a set of meanings which the UK consumer is understood to recognise and share in, beginning the cycle of culture once more.

Source: 'Wish You Were Here', HTV television programme screened in the UK on 22 May 1997.

Television holds tremendous opportunity for tourism marketers, and not just as a vehicle for advertisements or to showcase on travel shows – indeed, this is perhaps the least significant role of television in promoting touristic images. Who can estimate the impact of the numerous 'nature' and 'wildlife' programmes featuring the countries of Africa on potential tourists' images of that continent? Similarly, the Hawaiian location of the television detective series *Hawaii Five O* and *Magnum P.I.* were very effective showcases for the island, as was the setting of the UK detective series *Bergerac* on Jersey. This relationship between depiction on television and the tourism image is complex and not restricted to some simple form of product placement since it can significantly alter the image of a place, as in Dallas, Texas which was able to redefine its 'stodgy image' as a result of the long-running television show, *Dallas*.[45]

In some cases, depiction on television may even alter the 'reality' of a place and television shows have been catalysts for the recreation of places as living environments and tourism sites. Parts of the city of Miami, Florida were actually recreated in the image of the American television show *Miami Vice*. Here we witness the circulation of meaning, with popular culture representing a particular view of a place and the place itself recreating its own identity in this image. What we see is a process which Chambers described in relation to the individual but can be extended in this case to the place. Here, we see a place:

> Caught up in the communication membrane of the metropolis . . . in front of a cinema, TV, video or computer screen . . . the realisation of 'self' slips into the construction of an image, a style, a series of theatrical gestures.[46]

In the early 1980s when *Miami Vice* first appeared the city was wary of a negative impact as the show was heavily associated with crime and drugs. Yet the programme, as well as providing a platform for Miami as a destination, (associating it with designer fashion, designer stubble, vibrant music and beautiful people) actually became the catalyst for environmental and economic regeneration. The show's producers needed brightly coloured visuals and energetic Latin music to crystallise a certain image of Miami, so, for shooting purposes, many of Miami Beach's faded art deco buildings were repainted in pinks and oranges.[47] However, amongst the millions of television viewers who consumed that image were Miami's residents and marketers who embraced the fictionalised representation of their city and began to take renewed pride in its buildings and internationally renowned art-deco architecture, repainting and renovating their own buildings as seen in the show. Here a television show created an identity which was made more 'real' and which served to underpin further celluloid representations of the city as case study 4.3. demonstrates.

Case Study 4.3 The Miami of *The Specialist*

Just as *Miami Vice* has helped to create a particular Miami 'reality', the same process is extended and reinforced in movie representations of the city. In many ways the 1994 movie *The Specialist* typifies Miami as a symbol within popular culture. This movie, starring Sylvester Stallone, Sharon Stone and Eric Roberts, is an 'explosive and steamy thriller' set in the 'sultry heat of Miami'. In presenting its story, however, the movie represents a very particular image of Miami – a city of yacht parties, dinner dances, stretch limousines and beautiful people. The movie creates a very clear image of a *chic* place, a city which blends the elegance of art deco architecture with stylish, blue and pink-lit skyscrapers. We see a place in which one can flirt with a danger which is glamorous and exoticised.

Our first view of Miami opens with an art deco neon sign of a woman smoking. The camera, constantly moving back to reveal more of the scene, next focuses on a glamorous nightclub singer who stands next to a white piano, in front of a swaying palm tree framed by a light which seems to symbolise a tropical full moon. Sexy, late-night female vocals fill the air. This, like the other party scenes, is set along the city's revitalised waterfront and a sense of Miami's changing face is evoked in the opening scenes. Sharon Stone comments 'I used to live here when I was a little girl', to which Roberts replies: 'A lot has happened here since you've been gone – one of them is me.'

Roberts is a powerful Cuban-American crime boss who invites Stone, with 'I'll show you my Miami'. He is a sophisticated designer gangster in a dinner jacket. Like his city, he is portrayed as Hispanic, sexy and now having acquired the trappings of an affluent lifestyle. Yet the dangerous side of his/its nature is never far away – as he says 'Whatever I want I take'. Here the global audience sees and hears evocative, powerful images of Miami, a city which is glamorous yet dangerous, *chic* but exotic, it is American but it is Hispanic, like the Latino music which throbs throughout the movie, it pulsates with life.

Recognising the power that film, television and travel programmes can have in raising the profile of places, tourism agencies are working increasingly with film-makers to promote their destinations as possible locations. In this increasingly close relationship between the media and tourism marketers, we can see the further erosion or blurring of a clear distinction between 'projected' and 'organic' images. This is the ultimate in tourism product placement – to place your destination in a film or television series. Locations are important choices for film-makers and the power of film is beginning to be recognised by the tourism industry, as seen in the huge tourism agency presence at festivals such as the annual Cannes Film Festival and the Los Angeles' Locations Fair. The product placement sub-industry has grown vigorously over the past two decades.

as Hollywood producers have sought additional sources of income to offset rising production costs, and as advertisers have searched the media horizons for underused and less resisted venues for their promotion.[48]

As a result, in *Home Alone II: Lost in New York* the Plaza Hotel is heavily featured and the family spend an inordinate amount of time considering Avis car rental. Product placement is a phenomenon which is not confined to the film or television industries. Public relations agencies often attempt to place favourable stories about tourism products and places in magazines and newspapers. Publicity generated through public relations and journalist familiarisation visits are frequently sought and their marketing potential well established.

Films are another aspect of this kind of publicity, yet their impact is not so commonly discussed. In the wake of the box office success, *Gandhi*, India experienced a 50% increase in tourism;[49] *Deliverance*, an early 1970s action movie set in Raeburn County, Georgia, was the catalyst for the establishment of its raft and adventure tourism industry; whilst visitor figures to Fort Hayes in Kansas, featured in Kevin Costner's *Dances with Wolves*, increased by 25% during 1990–91 following the film's release (Table 4.2).[50] Similarly the recent *Braveheart* and to a lesser extent, *Rob Roy* generated incredible interest in Scotland (Figure 4.1). Ironically the latter was largely filmed in Ireland, highlighting that the power of 'constructed reality' dominates over any sense of objective reality. Celluloid exposure is of course uncontrollable and can have negative results. In this way in the late 1980s the film *Mississippi Burning* attracted negative publicity for Philadelphia, Mississippi, a small town which had gained notoriety in the Sixties when three civil rights workers were murdered by the Ku Klux Klan. The film was shot on location there but in the resultant publicity, the town gave the impression that it had changed little in twenty years.[51]

Table 4.2 The Interplay Between Tourism and Film.

Some Like It Hot	Hotel del Coronado, San Diego, California, USA
To Catch a Thief	Carlton Hotel, Cannes, France
The Prisoner	Portmeirion, Wales
Crocodile Dundee	Australia
Deliverance	Raeburn County, Georgia, USA
Dances With Wolves	Fort Hayes, Kansas, USA
Braveheart and Rob Roy	Scotland
Room With a View	Florence, Italy
Close Encounters of the Third Kind	Devil's Tower Monument, Wyoming, USA
Forget Paris	Paris, France

Often, film images persist decades later, for example, Austria still relies on *The Sound of Music* as a communicator of its natural beauty whilst some places seem to have an eternal fascination for movie-makers and writers. The Empire State Building is a film icon and a place icon for New York, its fame in the one realm reinforcing and recreating its fame in the other (*King Kong*, *An Affair to Remember* and *Sleepless in Seattle*). A handful of world cities have acquired iconic status which are reinforced via film – we have the constant image of Rome as *La Dolce*

Liam Neeson playing the lead role in Rob Roy, filmed on location in Scotland in 1994.

"Michael (Caton-Jones), the Director, always told us when we were prepping the film that it was going to be tough, and he had picked some magical locations in the Highlands of Scotland. I had heard and read a lot about them. Even though I have been to Scotland, I have never been this far North. The scenery is extraordinary. It's wonderful to stand here dressed like this and know that these hills and mountains haven't changed in millenia. Indeed Rob Roy and his clans would have trudged these hills and would have seen these views and seen these sunsets."

Jessica Lange on location in Scotland for Rob Roy in 1994 playing Mary MacGregor.

"I love it here in Scotland. At one point, after I first got here I thought that this would be a place to live, to raise children. There is a purity here. There's something so wonderfully - not innocent, but somehow not tainted like the society we live in. It's somehow remained pure in a way.

"I think feeling so strongly about the place, about the land here, really made a huge difference in playing the character. I mean the spirit of the place seemed to somehow enter into the portrayal of Mary MacGregor.

"There wasn't a day went by that I didn't walk outdoors, or take one of my five-mile walks and that I wasn't awe struck by everything I saw. I love the sky, the changes in the weather and the islands. We went to the islands, the sacred island of Iona. It is a mystical place, I think, this part of the world."

Figure 4.1 The Stars of *Rob Roy* Promote Scotland. Reproduced by permission of the Scottish Tourist Board.

Vita, of romantic Paris, of swinging London, of groovy and hippie San Francisco, and gritty but sophisticated New York. Since the 1950s Las Vegas, like New York and Los Angeles, has acquired an unique place in film-making and many movies have been set wholly or partly in the city, including *Diamonds are Forever*, *Viva Las Vegas*, *The Godfather*, *Bugsy*, *Leaving Las Vegas* and *Casino*. Although it is difficult to prove a direct link, the case study 4.4 illustrates that film has a cumulative impact on image formation.

Case Study 4.4 The Impact of Film on Las Vegas' Image

Various research techniques have been developed in order to establish the images, attitudes and perceptions which people hold of particular brands or products. However, given their very nature, the measurement of such factors is frequently problematic. The problem is that images, attitudes and perceptions are subjective and in many cases even subconscious. As a result they are not easily qualifiable and certainly not quantifiable. In the following study to explore Las Vegas' 'brand personality' amongst UK residents, some of whom had visited the city and some who had not, a variety of projective techniques were used to construct a comprehensive analysis of the destination's overall image. Taken as a whole, these techniques enable a powerful picture of respondents' impressions of Vegas to be developed. The most interesting finding to emerge was the strength and consistency of the imagery, most of which seemed to derive from film and television and the similarity of image amongst those who had experience of the destination and those who had not. None of the participants could recall being exposed to what could be termed 'projected imagery' in the form of advertisements for Las Vegas. In the case of those who had not visited the destination, their perceptions of Las Vegas were almost exclusively drawn from popular culture, and in the case of those who had been, such imagery was still evocative, even overpowering their actual experiences.

In a focus group setting the respondents' top-of-the-mind associations of Las Vegas centred around the 'traditional', adult Las Vegas product and reveal the possible power of cinematic portrayals of the city. Features such as gambling, sex, Mafia-connections and entertainment were the key descriptors. Personalities associated with Vegas included Howard Hughes, Bugsy Seagal, the Fifties 'brat-pack', Elvis Presley and Tom Jones. Participants specifically mentioned the movies *The Godfather*, *Honeymoon in Vegas* and *Casino* and there were glamorous overtones of limousines, champagne and glittering night-life.

Las Vegas' user and product imagery were explored by two techniques, sentence completion and visual collage boards. User imagery refers to respondents' perceptions of the typical vacation visitor to Las Vegas and product imagery reflects what respondents would expect to find there in terms of accommodation, attractions, entertainment and environment. Using visual collage boards, respondents were asked to select and explain which particular individuals most typified their perceptions of visitors to Vegas. Such techniques can reveal images, feelings and associations which respondents hold of particular destinations and tourism products. In the case of Las Vegas, these tended to confirm a view of a traditional, adult product. The people who would visit were seen to be relatively affluent, empty-nesters, largely American, 'brash', 'loud' and 'self-confident', 'somebody from Roseanne'. International visitors were thought to be first-time visitors and were overwhelming described as in search of 'fun', a 'good time' and entertainment. One respondent completed the sentence, '*people who go to Las Vegas are . . .* pseudo-riche unhappy Americans, glamorous but bored and looking for happiness.'

The same techniques were also used to explore respondents' perceptions of what Las Vegas had to offer as a destination in terms of accommodation, entertainment and environment. When asked what Las Vegas offers there was unanimity in that it offers 'everything and anything you want', '24-hour entertainment of your choice' and above all 'escape'. This last was a common theme and one respondent commented that: 'Las Vegas offers dreams, glitz, glamour and a chance to forget reality.' It was 'not pretentious – it doesn't pretend to be something it's not – but what it is, fun and spectacle. It's for all sorts of people out for fun and entertainment'. Hotels in Las Vegas were seen to be 'like theme parks with rooms', 'big', 'bright', 'brash' and 'entertainment-centred'. Entertainment in Las Vegas was seen as varied, comprehensive and offering a wide range of choice, with something for everyone. For some it was 'over the top, with showgirls . . . everywhere', it was 'in your face, you can see a volcano explode, watch a sea battle, then go and see showgirls all in the space of a five minute walk'. One respondent with experience of the destination commented that entertainment is 'non-stop . . . and often free', whilst another who had not visited saw it as 'like Butlins, only bigger, a lot bigger'. Above all it was 'fun, fun, fun'.

Other techniques were used to explore Las Vegas' brand fingerprint or the respondents' relationships with a brand, examining the thoughts and feelings held about a destination through the senses (sights, sounds, smells, tastes, touch and feelings). The respondents' images and impressions of Las Vegas can be seen in Table 4.3. When asked to describe Las Vegas if it was to come to life, the results were interesting. Although some saw it as a large, middle-aged man and others as 'a sexy, young showgirl, all feathers and lipstick', the overwhelming personification was of Las Vegas as a middle-aged, American lady '. . . acting and trying to look younger'. She seems glamorous but in a faded way, with 'gaudy, expensive clothes, driving a big car and wearing lots of jewellery, make-up and perfume'. She

Table 4.3 Las Vegas' Brand Fingerprint Amongst UK Residents.

Sights	*Sounds*
bright neon lights and dark skies	loud, up-beat music and 'buzz'
limousines	traffic
'showy' clothes and make-up	gaming machines and roulette wheels
sparkling diamonds	last bet calls
amusement parks	people and many languages
smog	clinking glasses and champagne corks
wide, straight streets and huge buildings	popping
lots of people 'hanging out'	
Smells	*Taste*
perfume	American fast food, steak and ribs
sweat	alcohol and cigarettes
alcohol, smoke and food	cosmopolitan, expensive food
cars and pollution	bitter tastes
	Coca-Cola
Touch	*Feelings*
money	overwhelmed and frantic
metal	surprised, amused and happy
heat	exhilarated, adrenaline
	guilt, fear and loneliness
	excitement, expectation and anticipation
	distaste and turned off

would also be 'chattering away in a loud voice about anything and everything but on a superficial level'. Underneath this exterior, however, there is a sense of insecurity – she is 'gregarious, outgoing and extrovert but maybe underneath desperate and lonely', even being seen as 'the original whore with a heart of gold' and 'big, brash, crude but refined in some ways'. Perhaps the most interesting finding in this study was the consistency of image amongst those who had been to the destination and those who had not experienced it. Las Vegas has the ability to evoke extremely powerful images, probably largely related to its frequent portrayal in films, songs and books, as one participant commented: 'We all know what Las Vegas is about – money, Mafia and sex – you see it in the films all the time.'

It is important to recognise in tourism marketing terms, however, that the power of film can also be a somewhat transitory media and 'a one-time impression is the beginning, not the end of place promotion'.[52] Devil's Tower, Wyoming, thanks to the 1977 film *Close Encounters of the Third Kind*, became a household name in US in the 1970s. The Tower plays a key role in the film and during its cinema run and television re-runs the area enjoyed a tremendous increase in visitors.[53] The year after its release visitor numbers increased by 75% and over a decade later, 20% of visitors credited viewing the film as their prime source of destination knowledge.[54] Whilst today it is no longer such a tourist attraction due to its isolated location and lack of local support its visitor numbers are still well above the pre-*Close Encounters* figure.[55]

The painted and printed image

Despite the undeniable power of film and television, visual tourism images are also found elsewhere. Together with literature, perhaps art is the oldest source of tourism imagery and today provides a marker for travel writers and marketers. In an article on Belle-Ile, an island off the Northwest coast of France, *Condé Nast Traveler* readers are told that 'The cliffside panorama that seduced Henri Matisse and Claude Monet a century ago remain unmarred by modern development. . . .'[56] Moreover, we have the further recommendation that Matisse described Belle-Ile as 'the most beautiful corner of France', his endorsement ensuring that the island became 'A beacon to French artists and writers'.[57] One of the destinations which most prominently makes active use of its association with the arts is Italy. The Italian State Tourist Office's brochure, *Italia. Travels in Wonderland*, is laden with images of paintings, sculpture and architecture, and with references to literature and music from classical antiquity to the Renaissance and the Romantic Movement. The brochure's cover sets the pattern, depicting Bernini's sculpture, Apollo and Daphne, whilst its first page of text reminds the potential traveller that 'the history of art as we understand it today could never have been written without Italy and its masterpieces.'[58] In addition, 'Goethe, Stendhal, Dickens, Montesquieu, Montaigne, Byron, Shelley and Dumas' all journeyed through Italy on The Grand Tour, 'as did all the cultivated youth of Europe, for whom a journey to Italy was a sort of conclusion to their education, a great University in the open air'.[59] The implication is clear – that for the modern traveller to complete his or her education, a visit to Italy is essential.

As well as in art, film and literature, above all, of course, the images used to promote and describe tourism destinations and products appear on billboards, in brochures and in print media advertisements. In all of these media, the images often draw on or make use of popular culture, including films, television series and songs associated with places. As we shall return to in greater detail in Part III, they often draw heavily on historical, social and cultural relationships. One such medium is the billboard which represents a spatially fixed medium for image promotion. They can advertise nearby attractions to road travellers, airlines use them to advertise at airports and destinations use them to promote their key identities. Tour operators also use them to advertise, as in the recent controversial Club 18–30 poster campaigns in the UK (case study 6.2). These posters were deliberately provocative and were eventually banned by the Advertising Standards Authority, but not before the company had secured considerable media coverage for the campaign.[60]

Advertisements placed in magazines and newspapers are also a very popular and successful promotional vehicle. The virtue of this is its selectivity, since so many publications are available that advertisers can reach any target group by knowing their reading habits – for instance, there are over 11 000 different magazines in the US alone.[61] Countries, states, cities and tourism organisations often buy full-page advertisements in widely-read business magazines such as *Fortune*, *Forbes* and *The Economist* and newspapers offer an easy way to communicate messages about a place, including news about festivals or events. Interestingly, advertisements for non-tourism products on billboards and in newspapers and magazines are also participants in the image process, particularly for tourist destinations. In this way, the current wave of advertisements for Irish beers in Europe contributes to the construction of images of Ireland (case study 4.5). These advertisements are populated by key stereotypes, notably smiling, red-headed girls, running through rolling green fields and phlegmatic, genial old farmers drinking stout. The same process is in operation for Scotland by whisky, for France by *Cointreau* and for the American south by *Southern Comfort*.

Case Study 4.5   Ireland Exploits Liquid Assets

There is a huge enthusiasm for Irish-style drinking establishments and as a result, O'Hagen's, McGinty's and O'Neill's bars have opened from Abu Dhabi to Australia; from Moscow to Mongolia. In order to create these bars, with *craic*, the warmth of the atmosphere, the food and the Irish music, the brewers Guinness have brought together a number of specialists under the banner of the Guinness Irish Pub Concept. This is a complete off-the-shelf package. There are five designs – including the Irish country pub, the traditional Irish pub shop and the Victorian Dublin pub costing an average of between £150 000 and £200 000. Guinness is also working with a music agent to organise tours for Irish musicians to Irish pubs and has commissioned a top chef to produce a range of Irish recipes which can be reproduced anywhere in the world.[62] To ensure that the traditional Irish welcome is also part of the franchise deal, the brewers are also employing a Dublin recruitment agency to supply genuine Irish bar staff with big personalities. More than 100 pubs have been created in this way around the world.[63]

Advertising is only one key image tool, another prime example of the printed image is the travel brochure. It has been said that 'The travel world is awash with brochures. . .'[64] and for many organisations the design, production and distribution of their annual tourism brochure is the single most important and most expensive item in the marketing budget. The advantages of brochures are their relatively low cost, flexibility and portability. Indeed, the brochure is arguably the key image tool in tourism and Holloway and Plant described it as 'probably the most important single item in the planning of tourism marketing'.[65]

Brochures are produced for both promotional and information purposes and tend to involve the use of colour photographs and prose laden with adjectives to sell attractive images of destinations and hotels to potential customers. In these brochures, both text and photographs are heavily grounded in popular culture. Whilst hotels and attractions do use brochures, it is tour operators and destinations who rely most heavily on the brochure, which has been described as 'a thick, glossy, full-colour catalogue, designed to persuade people to purchase the product'.[66] It is a vital tool in image management and has long been regarded as one of the most influential and widely utilised means of destination promotion,[67] not least because of the product substitute role of printed material and the extent to which it 'establishes expectations of quality, value for money, product image and status'.[68]

Case Study 4.6   A View of Wales – 'It Really is a Magazine, Not a Holiday Brochure.'

The brochure produced by the Wales Tourist Board is an excellent illustration of the way in which the traditional vacation brochure is changing (see Figure 4.2 for 1996). Presented as the *Wales Tourist Board Holiday Magazine*, it contains personal, individual views of Wales and its attractions written by well-known Welsh celebrities and people with connections with Wales. The managing editor, Roger Thomas's editorial comments that 'The magazine is intended as a good read. I hope you'll be entertained – and surprised – by its contents.'

The cast of characters includes Oscar-wining actor Sir Anthony Hopkins, UK prime-time news presenter John Humphrys, internationally renowned botanist and broadcaster David Bellamy, world record-breaking athlete Colin Jackson, historian Sir Roy Strong, and Carlo Rizzi, Musical Director of the Welsh National Opera. Here we have the complete embodiment of the interplay between the many forms of culture, sport, history, the media and the tourism image.

Not only do brochures draw on popular culture, but the brochure itself is changing – some destinations are presenting their brochures as magazines, and including guest articles and short stories. There is evidence to suggest that these brochures are likely to be retained for longer, almost as 'coffee-table magazines' (case study 4.6). Some brochures for the new generation of 'fashion hotels' are objects of beauty in themselves and where once they would be illustrated by the inevitable shot of a couple in soft focus on the balcony, now they contain images which would not look out of place in *Elle Deco* and *The World of Interiors*.

Figure 4.2 A View of Wales. Reproduced by permission of the Wales Tourist Board.

The image in song

The audio plays an important part in creating the tourism image, often as sound-tracks to accompany visual images. In fact, it would be a mistake to separate the two as this denies the close relationship between the two senses. An emotive song can conjure up accompanying visual images, whilst some images evoke certain sounds and songs. Music, of course, is an important asset in demarking time and space and in transporting viewers and listeners to different places. Songs are highly significant vehicles for tourism images since 'Music has the ability to stimulate extraordinary emotional feelings'.[69] Songs such as *'I Left My Heart in San Francisco'*, *'I Love Paris'* and *'Viva Las Vegas'* carry tremendous images. *'If You're Going to San Francisco'* became an anthem and a cultural icon in the 1960s for the 'flower-power' generation and, for them, still evokes strong images. Despite the fickle nature of popular music the song retains those associations for successive generations and has helped to position the city as an easy-going, relaxed destination (Table 4.4).

In the same way the music group the Beach Boys symbolised the California surfbeat culture and The Beatles the Mersey beat of Liverpool. One fact of interest is that visitors to Liverpool associate the city with The Beatles and expect a high level of entertainment provision in the destination, an expectation which is not completely met by 'reality'.[70] The power of music is also deliberately exploited by marketers, including those in tourism. For instance, haunting strains of Irish music are the background sounds when Ireland is the destination; rock and roll and Elvis Presley music are used to sell the US in general; blues music markets the southern US states and country music the US corn belt states in particular. As Fowles comments: 'Popular music, beyond delivering emotional gratification to a listener, also serves as a ticket to membership in a group with similar tastes.'[71] In this sense, music is also orchestrated to appeal to particular social groups and to make connections with these groups, perhaps a recent case in point being Spain's use of flamenco music in its 'Passion For Life' campaign aimed at the cultural, upscale tourist.

Table 4.4   The Tourism Image in Song

San Francisco	I Left My Heart in San Francisco
New York	New York, New York
Las Vegas	Viva Las Vegas
California	California Girls
Spain	Carmen
Barcelona	Barcelona
London	A Nightingale Sang in Berkeley Square
Paris	I Love Paris
Ireland	Danny Boy
Dublin	Molly Malone
Rio de Janeiro	The Girl From Ipanema
Japan	Madame Butterfly

The celebrity image

So far we have focused on the relationship between the tourism image and popular culture, especially in film and song. Taking such ideas a stage further, it is interesting to look at the symbiotic relationship between the tourism image and celebrities such as film or sports stars and fashion models (case study 4.7). They are able to penetrate the commercial clutter of advertising and thus hold viewer attention for a few milliseconds longer. Due to their celebrity status they 'represent another quality of popular culture that is of great interest to advertisers',[72] including tourism marketers. In such ways, 'the star exerts an imaginary but actual presence in the conduct of the individual – sometimes strongly but more often only referentially'.[73] Stars emerge as presenters of tourism and sports programmes and as endorsers of tourism products:

> The solemn, heartfelt stature that stars enjoy with spectators . . . wants to be exploited
> . . . waits to be exploited. Because, luckily for advertisers, most stars are for hire, it is
> only a matter of time before the star takes on a secondary, commercial role as
> spokesperson.[74]

Stars do not just act as endorsers, but become icons of tourism themselves. Winterset, Iowa, now attracts over 30 000 tourists a year just because it is actor John Wayne's birthplace.[75] Thus the locations of movie star homes and birthplaces now provide the reason to visit some places. Similarly, locations associated with the movies and their stars, such as the Hollywood 'Street of Stars' in Los Angeles, become the very tourist attraction. Recognising this, the British Tourist Authority recently produced a Film Map of Britain which highlights for visitors the sites of famous films, not all of which are directly portrayed in the movies. In the final culmination of this symbiotic relationship, Universal Studios in Los Angeles, which began as a film studio, has been developed into a tourist attraction encompassing entertainment motion-rides based on the studios' films, night-clubs and retail outlets. Similar processes, meshing tourism, television and film, are echoed at the Disneyworld sites, at the MGM attraction in Florida and, on a smaller scale, at Coronation Street World in Manchester, UK. Similarly, the MTV network is considering moving into the theme park business and is examining the feasibility of a $500 million investment in a music-oriented resort.[76] In this way, the circuit of culture moves around again, as not only are places represented in film and music, but they become famous through films and are visited as such.

Case Study 4.7   Wales' Star-studded Campaign

Wales' recent campaigns make effective use of celebrities, including US Masters winning golfer Ian Woosnam, Oscar-winning actor Sir Anthony Hopkins and world renowned singer Tom Jones. The involvement of these celebrities attracted tremendous media attention in an eyecatching poster campaign. The campaign, launched in 1994, was the first time that the Wales Tourist Board used endorsements from the world of showbusiness, fashion and sport.

The first phase of the campaign featured giant posters of Sir Anthony Hopkins, Ian Woosnam and Tom Jones against beautiful Welsh landscapes. A surreal approach was used on the poster featuring Tom Jones, whose face was superimposed on a photograph of a rocky outcrop on Tenby beach in Southwest Wales. The posters were part of the overall 1994 marketing drive, being featured on 746 strategic billboard sites in London, the East and West Midlands, the Northwest of England, Wales and the West and in 4000 advertisements on London underground trains. Subsequent phases of the campaign added Alice of Lewis Carroll's *Alice in Wonderland*, who regularly holidayed in Wales, designs of the (then) Welsh-based fashion house, Laura Ashley, and Dylan Thomas, the Swansea-born poet. Interestingly, however, there were two key celebrities who could not be used in the marketing initiative. The two most well-known celebrities associated with Wales – HRH Charles, Prince of Wales and the late Diana, Princess of Wales – could not be featured in an advertising campaign due to issues of royal protocol, and, ironically, the former is more probably associated with Scotland, one of Wales' competitor destinations.

Not only do celebrities endorse and become tourist products, but they are often actively involved in their creation as in the Hard Rock Hotel, Las Vegas, and the restaurant chains of the Fashion Cafes and Planet Hollywood (case study 4.8.). Since sports, film and music icons are able to transcend national barriers and cultural boundaries, such ventures hold tremendous commercial appeal. Tiger Woods, Andre Agassi, Shaquille O'Neal and Monica Seles are among the stars promoting the All Star Cafe chain which has five outlets worldwide whilst Planet Hollywood (of Bruce Willis, Sylvester Stallone and Arnold Schwarzenegger) is considering a $30 million joint venture with the ITT Sheraton group to build a Planet Hollywood casino-hotel. These are all examples where celebrities and the world of entertainment have become enmeshed in tourism and hospitality. This process is not restricted to the high-profile, high-earning film and sports stars and supermodels – frequently when fashion models are seen on calendar shoots, in style magazines and fashion catalogues, they are invariably in exotic, often tropical locations and, within this, not only is the destination often credited within the advertisement, but also the hotel in which they stayed and the airline which flew them there.

Case Study 4.8 Celebrity Hotels and Restaurants

In a cultural crossover between film, fashion, pop music and tourism, the hotel that you stay in is fast becoming a high-fashion lifestyle statement. More and more hotels and restaurants are owned by celebrities – the actors Bruce Willis, Sylvester Stallone and Arnold Schwarzenegger are perhaps the most well known but by no means the only celebrities to do this. Rock stars Bono and The Edge of U2 own The Clarence in Dublin, record producer Chris Blackwell owns the fast-growing Island Outpost group which includes the Art Deco Hotels in Miami, whilst pop icon Madonna co-owns The Blue Door restaurant at the Delano in Miami.
   These new style hotels are attempting to make design statements and persuade guests that whether they check in or just drink in their bars, choosing them says as much about them as the clothes they wear. As soon as it opened the Royalton in New York became a trendy meeting place for stylists, fashion models and editors

and movie stars and, if the hotels are like film sets, the guests are actors. The guest register, once the subject of discretion, is now a matter of open pride and some PR companies will fax journalists a list of celebrity guests. Thus, you can learn that Tina Turner was one of the first guests at the Clarence – a happy symbiosis for both star and hotel, a mutually beneficial cycle of fame.

Not only can you stay in these hotels, you can purchase lifestyle accruements to reflect their fashionability. The hotels are being merchandised, so that The Marlin in Miami's South Beach sells its own branded T-shirts and the Island Outpost its own compact disc of world music. In a crossover between tourism, stardom and literature, the Chateau Marmont in Los Angeles has produced a literary anthology by famous hotel guests past and present which is available in the UK. The circuit of culture spins around again.

The virtual image

There are, of course, new image vistas opening up which blend visual and audio imagery as technological change creates ever expanding media horizons. Now you can watch a *Star Trek* movie, buy a *Star Trek* video game in which the film actors provide the voices and then stay at the Hilton Las Vegas and enjoy the *Star Trek* experience. Likewise, you can watch *Jurassic Park*, experience the ride at Universal Studios and play the interactive computer game. Newer image vehicles for tourism include audio tapes, videotapes and faxes and thousands of travel companies – from hotels to airlines and destinations – already have a presence on the Internet. Moreover, with traffic along America's electronic superhighways tripling each year,[77] the significance of this medium is likely to grow, especially amongst younger people – future consumers who, brought up with such technology, may well use it to make independent travel bookings.

In addition to the Internet, there are other new vistas for the image. New multimedia self-booking kiosks, already having completed trial runs in the UK, could become commonplace, as could video links to travel agents allowing customers to see live footage of resorts.[78] The use of virtual reality images will allow the potential consumer to view the location and 'experience' certain aspects of the product. Visitors planning a Hawaiian vacation can, for $8.95, buy the Visit Hawaii CD, the Hawaii Visitors Bureau's official travel planner on CD-ROM. The disc contains:

> valuable visitor information, hundreds of images of the most beautiful islands in the world, traditional and modern Hawaiian music, a wealth of Hawaii's history and cultures, maps, a photo guide to beaches, parks, and sights of interest, a calendar of events, a talking Hawaiian dictionary, and much more![79]

Such comprehensive, interactive media may threaten traditional promotional methods in the very near future, as Horner and Swarbrooke comment: 'Brochures are increasingly being accompanied by video cassettes. These help the organization to show real images of the holiday, destination or hotel.'[80] Whilst such developments are of obvious marketing importance, we would raise the question, whose *real* images? In virtual reality and interactive tools, the customers are still consuming constructed images, created in just the same way as the older media images. Of more interest to us in this book are the kind of images which these new media are carrying. They are not fundamentally altering the ways in which the world is seen – for the new interactive electronic media are, just like the more traditional print and electronic media such as television and radio, dealing in the same limited stereotypical views of peoples and places.

As this chapter has illustrated, the relationship between tourism advertising and popular culture is a blurred one. This blurred relationship is also one which characterises the consumers' reception of these two spheres. Typically 'the viewer permits the two symbol fields to mix together and specific instances of the two fields to blend'.[81] This mixing or blurring is facilitated and increased by the ways in which advertising and popular culture are composed. Again, as we witnessed in Chapter 3, there is a continuing 'promotional reflexivity' in the media.[82] Here, in the media 'the mutual entanglement of promotional signs in one domain with those in another has become a pervasive feature of our whole produced symbolic world'.[83]

It is interesting to consider whether we can regard travel programmes as an example of this phenomena in much the same way as music videos have been discussed. Music videos are at one and the same time elements of popular culture but also advertisements for songs, albums and pop groups. As such they fuse the advertising and popular culture domains even more directly than what has previously been discussed. The MTV CEO Tom Freston recently described such channels as 'environments that are uniquely conducive to the marketing of music'. Yet Gow points out that viewers of music video channels such as MTV and VH-1 'would most likely scoff at the notion that the music video is nothing more than a new type of advertising'.[84]

It may well be commercially driven but consumers do not view either the videos or the channel itself as advertising or as a means by which to increase sales of a specific product. In many ways, MTV and the music video parallel the development of the vacation or holiday programme. These programmes are part of popular culture in the sense that they are construed as popular entertainment but once again this is popular entertainment which can also be construed as a form of advertising. In the UK some eight million people each week watch programmes such as *Holiday*,[85] programmes which could be said to be a series of advertisements for destinations, resorts, even hotels and airline carriers and tour operators. As such, *Wish You Were Here* and the *Holiday* programme blend the domain of the popular with that of advertising and are further examples of a media relationship in which everything seems to be promoting everything else.

It seems reasonable to argue that just as consumers of MTV see the product more as about entertainment than advertising, so too do consumers of these travel programmes. The importance of these programmes to tourism organisations has not yet been properly researched. There is, however, some evidence that consumer interest in destinations is markedly stimulated by being featured on such programmes.[86] The relationship between the consumer and this particular mix of advertising and popular culture is itself a further development in the consumer–advertising relationship which has yet to be properly examined. Similarly, the importance of these programmes as vehicles for disseminating knowledge to their loyal viewers, who at a later stage in the process may well be aspiring tourists, is something which has received surprisingly little attention in the tourism literature and is a topic to which we shall return in Part III.

This chapter has demonstrated how tourism borrows from the world of 'popular' and 'high' culture. It borrows to promote itself but, in some cases, the tourism site is recreated in the image portrayed in other representations, as in the case of Miami. In other cases (such as parts of Los Angeles) the site of popular culture becomes the tourist attraction – the two are closely intertwined and mutually dependent, exchanging symbols between spheres. In doing so, they reinforce particular symbols, views and identities and, even as marketers find new ways to project their images, the same stereotypical identities are being per-petuated. Nowhere can this be more clearly seen than in the hotels of Las Vegas which enmesh film, literature and history with entertainment and tourism, with the characters from *The Wizard of Oz* welcoming guests to the 'MGM Grand Hotel and Theme Park', whilst the 'Excalibur' hotel mixes Arthurian legend with that of Robin Hood, 'Treasure Island' stages sea-battles and 'The Luxor' recreates the land of the Pharaohs, mixing millennia of Egyptian history. At the hotels of 'Paris at Ballys', 'Monte Carlo', and at 'New York New York' (complete with Statue of Liberty) the resort has brought global tourist icons to the desert, creating new tourist sites in the image of 'reality'.

We need to ask what images are being created, endorsed and circulated in this relationship, in this cycle of cultural representation. There has, as we have outlined, been a considerable amount of work on the tourism image but there has been no attempt to locate it within popular culture and the circuit of culture. This has led to the distinction between projected and organic imagery, a distinction which is only tenable in terms of the function of image origins. Given the link between popular culture and tourism and the fact that they reflect each other, we need to reconsider how we regard the tourism image. We have seen here and in the previous chapter, that such is the process of image creation and consumption, that this distinction is rather artificial. In the circuit of culture, by consuming the image, the tourist is perpetuating and in a way, recreating the image. In Part II we move on to consider how shifting global power structures between countries, cultures, peoples and genders may or may not be influencing these dominant ways of seeing.

References

1   Gartner, W. (1993) 'Image Formation Process', *Journal of Travel and Tourism Marketing*, 2 (2/3): 191–215.
2   Kent, P.J. (1990) 'People, Places and Priorities: Opportunity Sets and Consumers' Holiday Choice', in Ashworth, G. and Goodall, B. (eds) *Marketing Tourism Places*, Routledge, London: 42–62.
3   Goodrich, J.N. (1978) 'The relationship between preferences for and perceptions of vacation destinations: application of a choice model', *Journal of Travel Research*, Fall 8–13; and Mayo, E.J. and Jarvis, L.P. (1981) *The Psychology of Leisure Travel: Effective Marketing and Selling of Travel Services*, CBI, Boston.

4   Chon, K.S. (1990) 'The Role of Destination Image in Tourism: A Review and Discussion', *Tourist Review*, 45 (2): 2–9.

5   Gunn, C. (1989) Vacationscape: Designing Tourist Regions, Bureau of Business Research, University of Texas, Austin; and reference 1.

6   Pearce, P.L. (1982) 'Perceived changes in holiday destinations', *Annals of Tourism Research*, 9: 145–64; Gunn, C. (1989) Vacationscape: Designing Tourist Regions, Bureau of Business Research, University of Texas, Austin.

7   Gyte, D.M. (1987) 'Tourist cognition of destination: an exploration of techniques of measurement and representation of images of Tunisia', Trent Working Papers in Geography, Trent Polytechnic, Nottingham.

8   Hunt, J.D. (1975) 'Image as a factor in Tourism Development', *Journal of Travel Research*, 13 (3): 1–7; and Gunn, C., (1989) Vacationscape: Designing Tourist Regions, Bureau of Business Research, University of Texas, Austin.

9   Seaton, T.V. (1989) 'Promotional Strategies in tourism', 335–339, in Witt, S.F. and Moutinho, L. (eds) *Tourism Marketing and Management Handbook*, Prentice Hall, Hemel Hempstead: 337.

10 Pearce, P.L. (1988) *The Ulysses Factor*, Springer-Verlag, New York: 162.

11 Crompton, J.L. (1979) 'An Assessment of the Image of Mexico as a Vacation Destination and the Influence of Geographical Location upon that Image', *Journal of Travel Research*, 18, Fall 18–23; Embacher, J. and Buttle, F. (1989) 'A Repertory Grid Analysis of Austria's Image as a Summer Vacation Destination', *Journal of Travel Research*, 28 (1): 3–7; and Um, S. and Crompton, J.L. (1990) 'Attitude determinants in tourism destination choice', *Annals of Tourism Research*, 17 (3): 432–48.

12 Foster, N.J. *et al.* 'Tourism Destination Image: A Literature Review and Evaluation', unpublished paper. The authors are indebted to N.J. Foster of University Wales Institute, Cardiff for allowing us to see drafts of her PhD in progress.

13 Echtner, C.M. and Ritchie, J.R.B. (1991) 'The Meaning and Measurement of Destination Image', 2–12 *Journal of Tourism Studies*, 2 (2): 4, adapting Dichter, E. (1985) 'What's in an image?', 75–81 *Journal of Consumer Marketing*, 2 (1): 75.

14 Selby, M. Urban Tourism in Cardiff, University of Wales Institute Cardiff, PhD in progress.

15 Urry, J. (1990) *The Tourist Gaze. Leisure and Travel in Contemporary Societies*, Sage, London; Hughes, G. (1992) 'Tourism and the geographical imagination', *Leisure Studies*, 11: 31–42; and Said, E. (1991) *Orientalism, Western concepts of the Orient*, Penguin, London.

16 Kent, P.J. (1989) 'The Desire to Conform? Another Role of Image in the Destination Choice of Potential Tourists', 18–35 in *Leisure Participation and Experience: Models and Case Studies*.

17 Pearce, P.L. (1982) 'Perceived changes in holiday destinations', *Annals of Tourism Research*, 9: 145–164.

18 Woodside, A.G. and Lysonski, S. (1990) 'A general model of traveller destination choice', *Annals of Tourism Research*, 17: 432–448.

19 Goodrich, J.N. (1978) 'The relationship between preferences for and perceptions of vacation destinations: application of a choice model', *Journal of Travel Research*, Fall: 8–13.

20 Hunt, J. (1979) in Rosenow, J. and Pulsipher, G. (eds) *Tourism – the Good, the Bad and the Ugly*, Media Production Marketing, Lincoln, Nebraska: 179.

21 Coltman, M.M. (1989) *Tourism Marketing*, Van Nostrand Reinhold, New York.

22 Gilbert, D.C. (1991) 'An examination of the consumer behaviours process related to tourism', 78–105 in Cooper, C.P. (ed.) *Progress in Tourism, Recreation and Hospitality*, vol. III, Belhaven Press, London: 78.

23 Wales Tourist Board, (1993) Marketing Areas Study, Wales Tourist Board, Cardiff.

24 reference 23.

25 Selby, M. and Morgan, N.J. (1996) 'Reconstruing place image: A case study of its role in destination market research', *Tourism Management*, 17 (4): 287–94.

26 Gunn, C. (1989) *Vacationscapes: Designing Tourist Regions*, Van Nostrand, New York.

27 Echtner, C.M. and Brent Ritchie, J.R. (1991) 'The Meaning and Measurement of Tourism Destination Image', *Journal of Tourism Studies*, 2 (2), December: 2.
28 reference 26.
29 See Selby, M. and Morgan, N.J. (1996) 'Reconstruing place image: A case study of its role in destination market research', *Tourism Management*, 17 (4): 287–94.
30 reference 1.
31 Nolan, D.S. (1976) 'Tourists' use and evaluation of travel information sources', *Journal of Travel Research*, 14, Winter, 6–8; Gitelson, R.J. and Crompton, J.L. (1983) 'The Planning Horizons and Sources of Information used by Pleasure Vacationers', 2–7 *Journal of Travel Research*, 21 (3); Gray, C. and Herbert, M. (1983) Choosing a Country for a Holiday, Seminar on The Importance of Research in the Tourism Industry, Helsinki, ESOMAR; Hodgson, P. (1983) 'Research into the Complex Nature of the Holiday Choice Process, Seminar on The Importance of Research in the Tourism Industry, Helsinki, ESOMAR; and McLellan, R.W. and Dodd Foushee, K. (1983), 'Negative Images of the United States as Expressed by Tour Operators from other Countries', *Journal of Travel Research*, 22 (1): 2–5.
32 Nolan, D.S. (1976) 'Tourists' use and evaluation of travel information sources', *Journal of Travel Research*, 14, Winter, 6–8.
33 Schmoll, G.A. (1977) *Tourism Promotion*, Tourism International Press, London; and Dilley, R.S. (1986) 'Tourist Brochures and Tourist Images', *Canadian Geographer*, 30: 59–65.
34 Kotler, P. *et al.* (1997) *Marketing for Hospitality & Tourism*, Prentice Hall, NJ ch. 16.
35 Horner, S. and Swarbrooke, J. (1996) *Marketing Tourism Hospitality and Leisure in Europe*, Thomson Business Press, London: 310.
36 Fowles, J. (1996) *Advertising and Popular Culture*, Sage, London: 103.
37 Hamilton, P. (1997) 'Representing the Social: France and Frenchness in Post-War Humanist Photography', 75–150 in Hall, S. (ed.) *Representation: Cultural Representations and Signifying Practices*, Sage and the Open University, London. These photographers included Henri Cartier-Bresson, Andre Kertesz and Robert Doisneau.
38 Dyer, B. (1991) 'Booming Atlanta', *Chicago Tribune*, 5 May 1991: 17, quoted in Kotler, P., Donald H. Haider and Irving Rein, (1993) *Marketing Places: Attracting Investment, Industry, and Tourism to Cities, States and Nations*, The Free Press, New York: 216–7.
39 Airwaves America Latina 1996/97: 9.
40 reference 39: 8.
41 *The Observer* (1996) 11 August.
42 ibid.
43 Torregrosa, L.L. (1997) 'Malaysia to the Max', *Condé Nast Traveler*, July 70-81: 72.
44 reference 36: 114.
45 Kotler P. *et al.* (1993) *Marketing Places. Attracting Investment, Industry and Tourism to Cities, States and Nations*, The Free Press, New York: 173.
46 Chambers, I. (1986) *Popular Culture: the Metropolitan Experience*, Methuen, London, quoted in Fiske, J. (1992) *Reading the Popular*, Routledge, London: 106.
47 reference 45: 172–3.
48 reference 36: 144.
49 reference 45: 215.
50 Riley, R.W. and Van Doren, S. (1992) 'Movies as tourism promotion', *Tourism Management*, September, 257–274: 270–1.
51 reference 45: 192–3.
52 reference 45: 185.
53 reference 50: 270–1.
54 ibid.
55 reference 45: 185.
56 Hack, S. (1997) 'Rock a La Mode', *Condé Nast Traveler*, July, 94–103: 95.
57 ibid.
58 The Italian State Tourist Office's brochure, *Italia. Travels in Wonderland*.
59 ibid.

60 Pritchard, A. and Morgan, N.J. (1996) 'Sex Still Sells to Generation X', *Journal of Vacation Marketing*, December 3 (4): 69–80.

61 reference 45: 174.

62 'Irish exploit liquid assets', *Independent on Sunday* Business Supplement, 1 December 1996: 7.

63 ibid.

64 Middleton, V.T.C. (1994) *Marketing in Travel and Tourism*, 2nd ed., Butterworth-Heinemann: 189.

65 Holloway, J.C. and Plant, R.V. (1992) *Marketing for Tourism*, 2nd ed., Pitman Publishing, London: 148.

66 Horner, S. and Swarbrooke, J. (1996) *Marketing Tourism Hospitality and Leisure in Europe*, Thomson Business Press, London: 310.

67 Wicks, B.E. and Schutt, M.A. (1991) 'Examining the role of tourism promotion through the use of brochures', *Tourism Management*, December: 301–12.

68 reference 64: 193.

69 Lull, J. (1992) 'Popular music and communication: An Introduction', 1–32 in Lull, J. (ed.) *Popular Music and Communication*, Sage, Newbury Park, California: 12.

70 Selby, M. (1995) Tourism and Urban Regeneration: The Role of Place Image, MSc thesis, Department of Management Studies, University of Surrey.

71 reference 36: 121.

72 reference 36: 116.

73 reference 36: 119.

74 ibid.

75 reference 45: 209.

76 *Sunday Business* 26 January 1997.

77 Wales Information Society Project (1997) Wales Information Society, Cardiff: 10.

78 'Agents will be bypassed by BT's self-booking kiosks', *Travel Trade Gazette*, 5 June 1996: 4.

79 advertisement in *The Islands of Aloha. The Official Travel Guide of the Hawaii Visitors Bureau*, 1997: 82.

80 reference 66: 206.

81 reference 36: 184.

82 reference 36: 101.

83 reference 36: 12.

84 Gow (1992) 'Making Sense of Music Videos: Research during the inaugural decade', *Journal of American Culture*, 15 (3): 35–43: 35.

85 British Audience Research Bureau 1996.

86 Personal Communication with Wales Tourist Board Senior Travel Trade Officer.

Part Two:
The Image and Changing Markets

5 Fragmenting identities, fragmenting power

Part I indicated that tourism representations are significantly shaped by social, economic and cultural forces, particularly history and colonialism. To date, and probably for the foreseeable future, the most important tourism-generating countries will tend to be concentrated in those societies and amongst those particular groups which currently dominate the global system. Equally, the tourism image creators will continue to be drawn from and will rely on existing power structures and their output will reflect the ways of seeing which inform and underpin these power structures. Such structures are by no means static, however, and a rudimentary knowledge of history alerts us to the transient nature of power and empire, transience which we can discern today. Our world is constantly changing, power centres are shifting, old orders are giving way to new, and there are emergent economic, social, political and cultural powers – all of which has important consequences for tourism.

Later in this book we shall examine the influence of various powerful scripts on the process of image promotion, particularly those of the master subject – the male, Western and white scripts. We will discuss how these scripts are grounded in historical relationships and how they dictate the construction of particular identities and relationships. At this stage, however, it would be useful to discuss the dynamic nature of power in the international global system. Initially, power is primarily economic, but with economic power comes political, social, cultural and ideological influence, all of which impact on tourism representation. The world is rapidly shrinking as businesses become internationalised, and societies increasingly diverse and multi-cultural. Demographic changes reveal that the West is 'growing old and will never be young again',[1] creating new challenges for tourism. Many societies have seen a liberalisation of sexuality and the opportunities for women are rising both in the ageing West and in a youthful East, where many of the most significant changes are occurring. Above all, the world is witnessing the Asian renaissance – already the new economic powerhouse – the countries of this region are becoming increasingly important politically, socially and culturally.

The emergence of these new structures will have significant implications for the tourism industry and therefore for those involved in creating its images and dreams. This rapidly changing global environment means that marketers are constantly having to revise their marketing strategies to reflect the changing complexion of societies. This chapter will examine the increasingly fragmented reality of lifestyles, especially in the post-industrial tourist-generating societies. In particular, it focuses on the demographic and economic trends and their impact on tourism marketing. In recent decades consumers and markets have changed radically, resulting in a 'de-massification' of markets. Sampson has described this process as '. . . not so much that of market segmentation but rather market fragmentation'.[2] Clearly, marketers can no longer describe and target consumers in simple terms, but have to develop sophisticated marketing strategies and in doing so, they are experiencing varying degrees of success. Sometimes they have recognised changing trends, other times they have ignored them and occasionally they have alienated emergent groups. Whilst such changes will have important implications, it remains to be seen to what extent they will fundamentally challenge the prevailing power structures of the tourism industry. A discussion of such marketing strategies and their outcomes forms the basis of Chapters 6 and 7. First, however, this chapter identifies and discusses some of the ways the current structures are at some times being challenged, and at others reaffirmed.

The shrinking world

Communications, increasing travel opportunities, falling trade barriers, multi-cultural societies and a convergence of tastes and preferences are all contributing to the creation of a 'smaller' world, although there are also counter forces to globalisation, in particular a rise in nationalism and anti-immigration policies. This move towards globalisation is perhaps the most influential contemporary trend, one which will create both threats and opportunities for tourism operations, and which will both cement and challenge existing power bases. This new world economy is increasingly dominated by inter-company trade and person-to-person communications, and multi-national companies and not states are the dominant power players. Indeed, there are a number of significant threats to the power of nation states, both from within and without. One such trend is the pressure for internal devolution, decentralisation and thus the devolvement and fragmentation of power in many states as communities, countries and regions seek more self-determination. As we shall see in Chapter 7, this trend has provided the impetus for destinations in Eastern Europe, Spain and Wales to carve out new, more self-confident tourism identities.

The internationalisation of business

Of all the challenges facing today's managers, 75% identify globalisation as their greatest concern.[3] Indeed, such is the acceleration of internationalisation that some commentators have written about the end of nations and the rise of markets. Many companies now have sub-regional marketing programmes with, for instance, a South East Asian, a European and a North American policy, whilst many international non-commercial organisations (such as Greenpeace) are also gaining unprecedented prominence. Investment flows between countries have risen dramatically over the last decade as trade barriers have come down and more and more businesses have developed global portfolios to reduce vulnerability to regional downturns, for instance, whilst Europe suffered a major recession for most of the 1990s, many of the Asian economies have been booming.

Those western companies (particularly those providing consumer goods and services) who have focused globally have enjoyed greater profitability than those who have concentrated on domestic markets.[4] Although many western companies have been multi-national since the 1960s, few have been truly *global* companies. This involves companies 'taking advantage of global markets and their economies of scale, *and* being culturally representative of the markets in which the companies operate'.[5] British Airways, one of our case studies in Chapter 7, is responding to this rise of a global economy and the much-heralded world traveller by seeking to become the first truly global airline. However, just as there appears to be a recognition of the need for companies to be culturally representative and thus more diverse, this itself is challenged by the emergence of a parallel trend which suggests that what we are witnessing is a convergence as opposed to a divergence of global tastes.

The convergence of tastes

For years marketers have sought to create homogeneous global brands so companies can achieve economies of scale in management and marketing and promotional costs. Now, despite the continuance of local, national and regional differences, there is growing evidence of the rise of cross-cultural tastes and the entertainment and software industries are already truly global industries. The US has been the most successful society in packaging its culture and its brands for global consumption. It has been largely responsible for promoting a 'world snacking-culture' and Coca-Cola, McDonald's, Disney, Levi's and Hollywood all promote individualism, free-market philosophies and a youth culture.

Entertainment and sport are the leading agents of this global culture, as satellite television channels and corporate sponsorship promote soccer to the US and Asia, American football and baseball to Europe and golf to the world. As tastes converge, arguably we can see the emergence of cross-national consumers as in the case of the first Euro-consumers – the well educated, the young and the frequent business travellers. These consumers can be reached via advertising in English, the language which has the highest comprehension level in Europe, especially in northern Europe, averaging over 55% comprehension in Scandinavia.[6] This will be accelerated by the growing availability of pan-European media, such as the increasing penetration of cable and satellite channels across Europe, projected to reach almost 60% of European households by 2003.[7] As Glen Peters (amongst others) has suggested, what we are witnessing is a globalisation of tastes and cultures, but one which, in the medium term, will still cater for more local preferences with a micro overlay of attention to local tastes and preferences.[8]

The trend towards globalisation and a convergence of global culture is not yet irreversible, however, and indeed, the iconic representations of this phenomenon (largely drawn from American culture) have been attacked in countries as diverse as India and France. In India demonstrators have smashed Pepsi bottles and set fire to Kentucky Fried Chicken restaurants[9] whilst in France politicians believe that the French culture is under threat from Americanised, English-speaking cultural and ideological saturation. Steps have been taken to combat this with legislation requiring French radio stations to broadcast at least one quarter of their daily output in the French language. At the end of the twentieth century we are clearly witnessing a collision of tastes, but at this point it is difficult to predict whether it will result in the emergence of some composite and shared identity or whether we are seeing the ideological triumph of one powerful (Americanised) culture at the expense of other, weaker ones. Despite the convergence of cultures, there remains a strong desire to retain difference in the face of homogeneity so that, even in the most multi-cultural, multi-ethnic societies, cultures and customs appear as a mosaic, with each contributing group retaining their individuality whilst contributing to a new, richer whole.

The rise of multi-cultural societies

Just as we are seeing trends running towards and against globalisation, we are also seeing significant changes within nation states which undermine simplistic, one-dimensional ways of describing peoples and places. As we shall see in Part III, peoples, countries and regions have caricatured identities – stereotypes which are used by marketers to sell tourism products and places to consumers. These carica-tures are extremely pervasive and enduring yet they are grounded in historical relationships and are representative of mono-cultural myths, not the contemporary multi-cultural realities. The stereotype of the bowler-hatted, pin-striped, cricket-loving 'Brit' hardly reflects the diversity of England, Scotland, Northern Ireland and Wales, never mind the various identities of immigrants who have increasingly settled in Britain over the past century. Multi-culturalism has arrived and one-dimensional representations of national identities are increasingly unrepresentative of most contemporary societies, particularly as previously powerless ethnic minori-ties grow in economic, cultural and political influence. Yet, despite the advent of multi-cultural societies, the tendency for marketers to rely on these clichéd identi-ties seems to be increasing in our media- and image-saturated world. It is not the purpose of this book to provide a comprehensive analysis of the implications of multi-culturalism, however we are interested in its impacts on tourism and the most useful way to assess some of these impacts, is to focus on the world's most significant multi-cultural nation – the USA.

The USA is one of the world's key tourism generating countries. Although most Americans do not travel beyond the borders of the US, many take vacations within the States and their domestic tourism market is huge. A country with a population of over 250 million, it is an extremely ethnically diverse market. The major racial subcultures in the States are Caucasian (itself divided along ethnic and cultural lines), African-American, Hispanic-American, Asian-American and American-Indian. The USA is in the midst of one of its largest immigration waves in decades. In 1990 8% of the population (or twenty million people) were foreign born, about 25% of them having arrived in the country since 1985.[10] Of these foreign-born persons, over four million were Mexican, by far the largest group, with the

Philippines accounting for over 900 000. The foreign-born immigrants are making the greatest impact in California, where over one-fifth of them live.[11]

Differences in lifestyles, economic wealth, political influence and consumer spending patterns exist between all these groups, yet the dominance of the white consumer remains barely challenged. As we shall see in Chapter 6, it is only since the 1990s that tourism marketers have begun to look beyond the needs of white tourists and to date, the overwhelming majority of consumer research has focused on Caucasians. The scant research which has focused on other racial groups has concentrated on the consumer *differences* between whites and African-Americans[12] – once again reinforcing the notion that the white experience is the norm against which all other groups are measured and evaluated.

By far the largest and most politically powerful racial minority in the USA are African-Americans, currently accounting for 30 million people or 12% of the population and spending an estimated $250–270 billion annually.[13] Recognising the power of this market, over $750 million is spent annually on advertising to African-Americans. The decision facing marketers is how best to reach this segment: whether to advertise in the general mass media on the assumption that African-Americans have the same consumption habits as Caucasians, or whether to advertise in media directed exclusively at African-Americans.[14] While it remains true that a significant portion of the African-American population is not as well off economically as the white majority, there is an important and growing African-American middle class and it is these consumers who are beginning to attract the interest of the tourism marketers. Most research indicates that the value orientations of middle class African-Americans are quite similar to those of middle-class whites. Indeed, they are often more 'middle class' and, are, for example, more committed to a need for achievement than the white middle class. This has important implications for notions of cultural and ideological power and change for if groups embrace established 'norms and values' then such norms and values are reinforced – white American ways of seeing migrate across racial boundaries and become 'American' ways of seeing.

The fastest growing minority in the States are the Asian-Americans yet despite its importance, there is little evidence of any tourism-related market research focusing on this group. In 1990 it accounted for seven million people or 3% of the population. Of these approximately 23% were Chinese, 19% Filipino and 12% Japanese. In fact, about 40% of all new immigrants to the US are currently from Asia and they are concentrated in a small number of large cities – about 58% of them living in Los Angeles, San Francisco and on Hawaii. By the early Nineties about 10% of California's population was Asian and by the year 2000 approximately five million Asians will live in the State.

Asian-Americans are largely family-oriented, highly industrious, and strongly driven to achieve a middle-class lifestyle. They are also high academic achievers, more computer-literate than the average and many of them run their own businesses or are in managerial or professional occupations. In particular, the ethnic Chinese are extremely influential, both in the US – where a million ethnic Chinese live in California alone, the largest Chinese community outside Asia[15] – and globally. The ethnic Chinese, from Taiwan to Los Angeles and London, are the most successful entrepreneurs in the world and Chinese around the globe hold between $2 and $3 trillion in assets.[16] These attributes make them an attractive market for an increasing number of marketers,[17] yet, as we shall see in Chapter 10, Asians almost exclusively feature as part of the tourism product rather than as tourist consumers in western travel literature.

Although Asians are the fastest growing minority group, it is the Hispanic-Americans who will outnumber African-Americans as the largest minority group in the US within 20 years. Representing about 9% of the US population or 22 million people, they are younger than other segments, have larger families and have a 26.8% growth rate anticipated for the decade 1990–2000. They are already the dominant minority in New York, Los Angeles, San Diego, Phoenix, San Francisco and Denver and are the majority in San Antonio, Texas. The three largest Hispanic subcultural groups are Mexican-Americans (60% of Hispanic-Americans), Puerto Ricans (12%), and Cubans (5%). They are heavily concentrated in certain geographical locations, with over 70% living in California, Texas, New York and Florida.[18] Their impact is perhaps most obviously witnessed in the extent of bilingual signage and announcements which are common to these locations. Again, however, just like the Asians, they never feature as potential tourists in travel literature.

Whilst the USA is the most influential multi-cultural and multi-racial society, similar societies also exist in Europe. In the UK there are over 270 000 black households in London alone, forming a significant market for products and services.[19] In fact, the UK has a large ethnic minority population, numbering three million, that is 6% of the population. As in the USA, different ethnic communities vary in economic power and it is extremely misleading to speak of such minorities as a single, homogeneous category. One of the most striking facts is the growing success of the Indian community which out-performs all other ethnic minorities except the Chinese, on most counts, and often the white ethnic majority as well. A profile is emerging of the UK's Indian community which is 'increasingly self-employed, home-owning, privately educated and white-collar professional'. For instance, 61% of Indians between the ages of 21 and 23 have two A levels or their equivalent, compared to 43% of whites and 40% of blacks. Conversely, the Afro-Caribbean UK communities have been rather less successful and only 40% of black families are owner-occupiers compared to 83% of Indian households.[20]

Multi-culturalism holds many implications for tourism marketing. As we can see from the USA, there are elements within ethnic minorities who have secured substantial economic power and will provide attractive opportunities for marketers – as in the development of black heritage trails (Chapter 6) – and such economic power is frequently a precursor to political and ideological power. Miami, for instance, recently elected its first Hispanic mayor. However, although ethnic minorities are growing in power, the majority ethnic groups retain power in most societies – ethnic minorities are disproportionately poorer, have lower educational attainment and are more likely to become criminalised. In the US blacks and Hispanics constitute two-thirds of the prison population; in England and Wales almost a quarter of female prisoners are from ethnic minority groups and the same pattern applies elsewhere: North Africans in France; Moluccans and Surinamese in the Netherlands; gypsies in Hungary; native peoples in Canada; and Aborigines in Australia.[21] There still remains a real reluctance to see beyond the needs of the white majority and the example of the African and Asian-American middle classes suggests that the achievement of economic power need not necessarily stimulate change or an increasing diversity of societal norms and values. In Part III we will examine how such norms and values impact on tourism imagery and suggest that the dominance of the prevailing white script remains fundamentally unchallenged.

The transformation of work

Just as globalisation, facilitated and accelerated by technological change, is a key force in shaping the world, a second key shift is occurring in work practices. Indeed, particularly in the post-industrial world, work is being transformed and 'the job' as we understand it may disappear as outsourcing and consultancy increase part-time and short-term arrangements between employee and employer – certainly the dominance of the 'nine to five' work pattern has already vanished. Technology is the prime agent of this transformation, as telecommuting and self-employment increase. The Internet and its associated technologies represents the most significant opportunity for companies and individuals to shape the future and there are currently over 60 million people on the Net.[22] Moreover, whilst the growth in the number of Internet hosts is slowing, it still grew at a rate of 70% during 1997.[23] The implications of these changes will be far-reaching, creating greater job insecurity, heightening the importance of self-marketing and speeding up the drift to a low-wage future for many people in many countries. By necessity, as work itself is transformed – its nature and very definition being reshaped – so the construction and role of leisure and tourism in people's lives will change. The transformation of work will impact on global power structures. It has the potential to strengthen the power of existing groups, to create new power bases and, at the same time, could reinforce the disenfranchisement of those on the peripheries.

Blurring the boundaries of work and leisure

As the computer becomes part of everyday life and as it becomes more flexible – with the advent of laptops and palmtops, often with miniature high-speed fax/modems – the traditional boundaries between where we live, where we work and where we play are becoming blurred. Working from home is not a new phenomenon as freelancers and the self-employed have long existed: what makes this a revolution is not its novelty but the *scale* on which it is occurring. The growth of information technology and the restructuring of large corporate and governmental bodies around the world is making work flexible on an unprecedented scale. Up to two million people in the UK currently work at home full time. While half of these are self-employed, one-third are 'telecommuters', the numbers of which are growing rapidly. In a recent UK survey 62% of companies reported some form of telecommuting and in the USA almost twelve million people are already telecommuting – working digitally from the home or on the move. The latest figures suggest that this could soon be an option for as many as one in three workers in some countries.[24]

The shift to a service-based, low-wage world

Whilst technological change offers new opportunities for some workers, for others
it poses more of a threat, creating a heavier workload for some and taking work
away from others. The digital revolution has not eased the workload of many busy
executives, it just means they can take their work with them wherever they go.
Technological advance has also reduced the requirement for many skills, resulting
in downsizing and an increase in early retirement in many developed economies.
Moreover, many of those in work are working longer hours. A recent UK survey
found that two-thirds of fathers work in the evenings and 60% work at week-
ends,[25] whilst a new word has found its way into organisational vocabularies –
'presentism' – coined to describe the way in which many employees, worried about
job insecurity, have to be seen to be indispensable, the first into work and the
last out.

The shift from a manufacturing to a service-based economy in the post-
industrial world has also been key in encouraging the trend towards flexible
employment. Over the last two decades the contribution of manufacturing to gross
domestic product (GDP) has declined in the developed world, whilst that of
services has increased. In some countries, such as Japan and Germany, the manufacturing sector remains important at about 40% of GDP, but in others, such as
the US, the UK and France it is down to less than a third. Manufacturing jobs in
the developed economies have also been hit by automation and high labour costs –
for example, in Germany factory labour costs are $25 an hour, whereas in China
the figure is between 50 cents and a dollar.[26] If the countries of the developed
world are to maintain employment they must look to providing value-added
activities and concentrate on what they do best. Japan and Taiwan have a niche in
electronics; Germany in designing and building reliable machines; the US in
communications; whilst London is the world's top financial centre.[27] There is a
trend towards shifting the traditional labour-intensive manufacturing jobs into the
lower-wage economies of the developing world and the developed world will seek
to compete in the higher value-added service industries: 'Marketing, distribution,
media and communications . . . and leisure are the established areas where the
developed world will continue to grow jobs.'[28] Certainly with information-related
services, including tourism, cross-border competition is increasing and cheap
networking and communications will make it possible to run most information-
oriented services from almost anywhere in the world.

The global haves and the have-nots

The last decade has witnessed a widening gap between the rich and poor countries
and between the 'haves' and 'have nots' within those countries, and in many ways
technological advance and the transformation of work, rather than empowering
the disenfranchised, has often cemented their marginalisation. In this age of
information and knowledge, the speed with which countries, companies and
individuals rise to the challenge of technology will depend on the time and money
they are able and are willing to invest in the training and infrastructure needed to

compete in a reshaped marketplace. Those who do make effective use of the new channels of information will be able to access global markets, but those who do not are likely to become increasingly peripheralised. These new media channels are likely to be shaped in certain ways – thus the prevalence of the English language in media and communications is likely to reinforce existing power structures and affirm the powerful position of English-speaking countries and peoples. Sixty per cent of radio broadcasts, 70% of addressed mail, 85% of international telephone calls and 80% of *all* data transfers are currently in English.[29] Moreover, with it firmly established as the language of business, the power of English and its speakers is likely to remain in the medium term.

Following this theme, perhaps one of the key future divisions between individuals, businesses and places may well be between those who are 'local' and those who are 'cosmopolitan' or 'global' rather than the traditional division between capital and labour. The élite of the future will have virtual offices, be linked into the global communications systems and enjoy a cosmopolitan lifestyle in a 'virtual' global village. They will be world travellers for business and pleasure and will demand high levels of service and amenities. Similarly, some places will have a global role whilst others will remain local or regional. Cities like London, New York, Los Angeles and Tokyo have already become world cities where the global élites – politicians, business people and entertainers/celebrities – congregate. They are likely to be joined by Asian world cities in the next decade, including Singapore; Kuala Lumpur (the Malaysian capital which has just completed the Patronas Towers, the world's tallest structures); and Putrajaya, a megacity which will be Malaysia's commercial capital by 2008.[30]

Rich and poor countries

If three main segments of world markets are identified – industrialised countries, developing countries and less developed countries – the second segment accounts for 19% of the world's population and 32% of the world's income.[31] Since these countries are outpacing the industrialised countries, they offer very attractive business prospects, both in terms of generating tourists and offering a higher quality destination product. Yet, despite this, there is no doubt that the rich are becoming richer and poor relatively poorer. The decline in the credibility of the United Nations and the dominance of the US is widening the gap between rich and the poor countries and Professor Paul Roger has argued that too much power and influence residing with the US and its Northern European allies runs the risk of further deepening this gulf.[32] For example, the gap between Africa's rich and relatively stable countries and its poor and sometimes collapsing countries is growing every year and most of its 700 million people became poorer in 1997.[33] Figures from the World Bank indicate that the globe's poorest countries have an average annual income of only $308, whereas in the richest countries the equivalent figure is almost $22 000.[34] Colonialism has been replaced by neo-colonialism in which the rich core countries are able to exploit the poorer peripheral ones through the activities of multi-national corporations – huge organisations which are head-quartered in the core countries.[35] These corporations are immensely powerful and are far richer than many countries. As Bradshaw and Wallace point out in their *Global Inequalities*, General Motors was worth $133 billion in 1992, the same as the combined wealth of Malaysia ($57 billion), Pakistan ($42 billion) and Egypt ($34 billion).[36]

Technological change has the potential to empower the world's disadvantaged countries and, as the new global infrastructure, the information superhighway could certainly erase the differences between centre and peripheries. People living in hitherto isolated rural communities will be able to compete with urban workers via the information superhighway.[37] However, whether this shift will ever facilitate a fundamental challenge to existing power bases remains to be seen. The information society is a reality for a very small portion of the globe. North America accounts for over 70% of the world's Internet connections, Europe for just under 25%, and Australia and Japan for 4% – the rest of the world accounts for only 1% of connections, a stark indication of the global power balance.[38] It will take some time to 'wire' those currently excluded whilst the power of the existing users becomes ever more entrenched – traffic along America's electronic superhighways triples each year.[39]

The widening gap between rich and poor consumers

The world is not simply being divided into rich and poor countries: within rich nations the gulf between the 'haves' and the 'have-nots' is widening. In the 1990s many of the world's developed countries have seen recession, falling property and real estate values, and high unemployment rates with associated insecurity about jobs and the future. Clearly the free-spending leisure future predicted in the early Eighties has not materialised and many countries have seen the gap between their rich and poor widen. Of all the G8 economies, only Germany has seen this gap narrow (as a result of more prosperity in the former East Germany), whilst in the USA and the UK the gap has widened considerably. The distribution of income has become increasingly unequal in recent years in the UK – the bottom 40% of households accounted for only 12% of expenditure in 1995, half that of 1979.[40] Moreover, basic essentials account for over a half of their spending, whilst the richest households devote almost 60% of their spending to luxuries, especially travel and leisure activities.[41] According to the 1993 US Census, in the USA almost a quarter of children under the age of six live below the poverty line and the figures for ethnic minority groups are startling. Fifty per cent of all African-American children and 40% of all Latino children under six live in poverty.[42]

Case Study 5.1   Technology is the New Divide

It will be the elites of the information age – driven by the application of the microchip to virtually everything   who will profit in the future. A new industrial revolution is in progress and the disenfranchised who will be excluded are today's new underclass: the 'digitariat'. In the UK, one of Europe's most 'wired' countries, 40% of people do not regularly use any of the weapons of the new revolution –

computers and mobile phones – 80% do not know how to get connected to the Internet and of those on-line, only 9% use it regularly. It is not just the numbers of people who do not use the new technology which is significant, however, it is their socio-economic profile. Only 9% of the UK's lowest socio-economic groups – the so-called C2DEs – have ever used the Internet compared to a quarter of the highest socio-economic group – the middle and upper classes – the ABC1s.[43]

This paints a picture of a two-nation UK, even more widely polarised in terms of access to the advantages of the information age than the monetary gulf between rich and poor. The information age – the convergence of immensely powerful but ever cheaper computers with optic fibre telephone lines of almost unlimited capacity – was supposed to herald a new age of equal opportunity in which information was to be accessible to all at an affordable price, but that does not seem to have materialised.

As *between* countries, one of the main divisions *within* such societies in the future may well be related to access to technology. Some adults are technophobic[44] but many more are denied access to empowering technologies by their economic and cultural powerlessness. As case study 5.1 illustrates, those with access to the information society are likely to be drawn from the higher socio-economic groups in the developed world. Relatively more people in the Third World are likely to be excluded from the Internet (at present over 80% of the world's population has no access to a telephone, let alone a computer[45]) – a medium which has huge potential for tourism marketing. Indeed, the on-line travel segment is estimated to grow by 1000% by the year 2000,[46] yet its access will be limited and the existing ways of seeing are therefore likely to continue to prevail.

The Asian renaissance

One of the regions which is likely to emerge as one of the global 'haves' is Asia and as the year 2000 moves closer, it is fast becoming a dominant region of the world – economically, politically and culturally, despite recent economic turbulence.[47] The Asian continent from India to Japan, from the old USSR to Indonesia, now accounts for three billion people, more than half of the world's population, half of whom are under 25. By the early years of the next millennium, more than half a billion of these Asian households will be 'middle class' – a market the size of the US and Europe combined. Asia is thus dominated by countries which are demographically and politically young. For most of these states the Cold War was a period of post-colonisation and they only attained independence in the 1940s and Fifties. Hong Kong has already returned to China but when Macau also returns at the end of the 1990s, every inch of territory in Asia will be controlled by Asians for the first time in 400 years.

Whilst the old Asia was divided by culture, language, politics, religion and geography, the new Asia, 'forged by economic integration, technology, especially telecommunications, travel and mobility of people, will look like one coherent region'.[48] Asians, especially the Chinese, are characterised by hard work, thrift and education-orientation and the new economies of Asia have created millions of entrepreneurs. In addition an enormous resource of talent is returning in 'a reverse brain drain' as young Asians return East, many of whom are joined increasingly by young Westerners seeking opportunities. Clearly, Asia is reaching high levels of sophistication, as exemplified by Hong Kong which will soon again boast the world's tallest building when Nina Tower opens in 1998.[49] Naisbitt comments about perceptions of the East: 'Many in the West who have never been to Asia, or who have not been there for a long time, have the mindset that Asia is a fairly primitive place, when, for example, Asia's best hotels and best airlines are better than those in the West.'[50]

Case Study 5.2   Focus on Japan

Although Japan's growth may have peaked, the country is emerging from the recession of the late Eighties and early Nineties, as one commentator has said: 'Aggressive innovation throughout the lean years of the early Nineties is now bearing fruit.'[51] This economic success is combined with new legislation to encourage the Japanese to take holidays and it is rapidly becoming one of the world's key tourism-generating countries – with an annual outbound tourism market of approximately 12 million[52] – both its economic and social structure indicate a boom in leisure. In Japan, the significant post-war educational reforms have resulted in major changes to the social class structure and it has been described as a 'new middle class' society where 'the vast majority of Japanese people today consider themselves to be members of the middle class'. Moreover, the country has a 'very equality-oriented education system that provides virtually everyone with a common, homogeneous education through to the age of eighteen'.[53]

In 1995 Japanese exports totalled $443.1 billion, up 62% on 1989, the last year of the global boom. The same year Japan's gross domestic product totalled $5110 billion, not far behind America's $7246 billion and more than four times the UK's $1057 billion. Moreover, measured at market exchange rates, its per capita income in 1996 was $40 897 – 47% higher than the USA's $27 799 and 126% higher than the UK's $18 097. In addition, its unemployment rate of 3.4% was one of the lowest in the world. Yet, even Japan will be left behind as the countries of Southeast Asia, led by China, increasingly hold economic sway – 'If the explosion of wealth in East Asia continues, the number of people aspiring to Western-style consumerism is likely to treble by 2030.'[54]

Despite this increasing economic power of Asia, it does not necessarily follow that the prevailing ways of seeing and describing the East will change. As case study 5.3 illustrates, the way in which American advertising has viewed Japan has to some extent evolved over the twentieth century to reflect changing political and social relations. However, it also demonstrates the dominance of existing ways of seeing in its discussion of the continued construction of Japanese women as exotic, as Other. Indeed, the old stereotypes are actually gaining ground, 'as much by Oriental consent as by direct crude economic pressure'[55] from the developed world, especially its cultural leader – the United States. As Said points out: all the universities in the Arab world are run according to some pattern inherited from or imposed by the old colonial powers; and whilst there are dozens of institutions in the West studying the East, there are none in the East devoted to studying the US (the greatest influence in the region) and few of any stature devoted to studying the Arab or Islamic Orient. Above all, the greatest contribution to the continued shaping of the Orient as 'Oriental' is the triumph of Western consumerism, not merely in the prevalence of Levi's and Coca-Cola:

> . . . but also by cultural images of the Orient supplied by American mass media and consumed unthinkingly by the mass television audience . . . there is . . . a very powerful reinforcement [of Orientalism] in economic, political, and social exchange: the modern Orient, in short, participates in its own Orientalizing.[56]

Case Study 5.3   How the Japanese are Seen by Themselves and by the USA

In the twentieth century representations of the Japanese have shifted from depictions of them as an 'exotic' 'Other' to portrayals of them as equal economic partners – crucially, however, Japanese women continue to be represented in ways which are exotic and erotic. In his *Culture and the Ad* O'Barr analyses images of Japan drawn from the *National Geographic* magazine in the twentieth century. His discussion covers many issues but in this case study we examine what his study reveals of the changing touristic representations of Japanese men and women in Japanese and American advertisements, in particular we focus what he rather surprisingly does not highlight – the exoticism of the women.

The prewar early years – Japan the 'Exotic Other'

In this period Japan was portrayed in the pages of *National Geographic* as an extremely exotic destination, its portrayal heavily utilising stereotypical images such as Geisha girls, rickshaws and pagodas. Official literature produced by the Japanese Tourist Bureau invited tourists to visit 'Old Japan' to experience traditional ceremonies, ancient rites and scared shrines, all in modern American-style comfort, of course. Japan is 'Ageless . . . immortal . . . rare loveliness . . . exquisite beauty . . . with the ultra-modern convenience and Western World comforts and diversions'.[57]

The postwar years – Japanese men become 'westernised'

The advent of World War II saw Japan disappear from the world tourist map and it did not reappear until the 1960s, in contrast to travel advertisements for other Asian countries which appeared soon after the War.[58] It is during the 1960s that we see a divergence in the images used to represent Japan – whilst the images of women remain 'exotic and submissive',[59] for instance in airline ads, we see a shift in how Japanese men are represented. They, 'never powerful in the prewar advertising', now cease to be exotic. Instead they are depicted wearing Western clothes and working in 'serious business contexts'.[60] Interestingly, however, the women are represented in ways very similar to the exotic period, a gender difference which O'Barr neglects to mention. Two Japanese Airlines advertisements encapsulate these diverging gendered identities. In one, provocatively entitled 'We're all you expect Japan to be', a beautiful, kimono-attired woman invites the reader to sit. She is wide-eyed and smiling at the camera, indeed, the advertisement tells us that she:

is much more than an airline stewardess. She's an artful conjuror. She . . . [epitomises] serenity, and peace, welcome . . . and personal attention, that is Japan at its most charming.[61]

In contrast, in 'How to fly, Japanese style', we see two middle-aged businessmen. One is American, attired in a Japanese robe and eating sushi with chopsticks. The other is Japanese, dressed in a western suit, he eats steak with a knife and fork. This advertisement encapsulates the new relationship between America and Japan, at least in terms of businessmen. It is one of mutual respect and equality – a relationship which does not apply to women, however. In the same advertisement we are told that service is:

> reflected in the smile of your JAL hostess. . . Her delicate grace as she pours your sake. The very special way she makes you feel like an honoured guest at a family banquet.[62]

The 1980s and beyond – degrees of 'equality'

In the 1980s we see yet another dimension in Japan's changing relationship with America. In an advertisement entitled 'How we traded with the Navajos – Seiko Watch Executives', an advertisement for Citicorp Travelers Checks, we see the Japanese as tourists in the USA. The visited have become the visitors. But, who is visiting and who is being visited is of great importance, bearing in mind our previous discussions of gender and racial roles. The visitors are all camera-toting businessmen trying on Indian hats. Women do not feature at all in this scene, reinforcing the notion that only Japanese businessmen have achieved parity with the USA. Similarly, who is the visited? Considering that the visiting relationship carries echoes of who is powerful and who is powerless, who is rational and who is spectacle, it comes as little surprise that the tourists' gaze focuses not on white America, but on the most powerless and disenfranchised group in the USA – the North American Indian. Whilst representations of Japan have changed over the century in response to shifting political and economic power, the change has not been a fundamental one – representations still reinforce very sexist and ethno-centric views of Asian women and, Japanese men are portrayed in positions of power – but only in relation to one of the West's most disenfranchised groups. In the first instance the Orient is very clearly participating in the Orientalisation of its women, and, in the second, American advertisements have mediated the economic power of the Japanese by juxtaposing them with the Navajos, an even more peripheralised Other.

The global rise of women

This economic rise of Asia has been paralleled and, to some extent, led by a rise in the position of women. Where educational opportunities are available to them, women around the world are increasingly gaining higher standards of education than are men and where they have political representation they are voting more for welfare and environmental protection in contrast to men. In parts of Asia, we are witnessing what Naisbett has described as a 'quiet, yet powerful revolution'.[63] For example, Japan and Sweden now share the oldest average age for first-time marriage – 27 for women and 30 for men.[64]

Within Asia, we can discern the beginning of two Asias. Whilst most women continue to live traditional lives, there is the emergence of 'millions of affluent

Asian women . . . as a force the entire world must reckon with'.[65] In China, women are participating in all aspects of Asian life in unprecedented ways, as workers, voters and consumers, constituting 25% of all entrepreneurs.[66] Asian women are increasingly achieving educational parity with their male counterparts and their participation in the workforce compares favourably with US and European figures. In this sense, in this part of the world, where women's lives have been 'role bound' for centuries, new opportunities are emerging.[67] These options are the culmination of many processes, including labour shortages, full employment, education and 'gender-blind' technology.[68] As one Singapore newspaper has commented:

> in only one generation some Asian countries have created a corps of career women who are upwardly mobile, globally minded, affluent and ambitious. That is no mean feat.[68]

Despite this success story, women in Asia are paid less than men and are subject to a glass ceiling, as they are in the West, whilst their emerging economic success has yet to be echoed in social and political change. Women in Asia are, however, being politicised and there a number of examples of women organising to demand such change.[70] The achievements of women in Asia should not be denied and indeed, it should be recognised that change has occurred against a social and cultural tradition in which women have been homemakers and in which 'males are strong and aggressive (*yang*), women passive and nurturing (*yin*)'.[71] Women are clearly challenging the old male power bases and, as Naisbett concludes in his analysis: 'Asia in the twenty-first century will find leadership in its own women and they, in turn, will find partnership with women in the West, moving towards global critical mass.'[72]

In the West, the position of women has also changed dramatically in recent decades and their importance as consumers, as influences on buying behaviour and political change is greater than ever before. As Beeghley comments, whereas women used to be asked what their husbands did for a living, now men are frequently asked what do their wives do?[73] Women's consumer needs have long been neglected by marketers, but their rise in power and influence should be ignored at their peril in the future. By the year 2000 white females will account for almost 40% of the US workforce, having risen by 11% since 1960.[74] Carol Nelson comments:

> Thirty-five years ago . . . the typical American woman graduated from high school, married, had children, and stayed at home with her family. . . . 'Career' woman as a peer of the career man was practically unheard of.[75]

Yet, although the gap has narrowed, women in the US continue to earn less than their male counterparts – 72% of male earnings in 1993, compared to 61% in 1960 – and given the slow narrowing will not achieve parity for some time.[76] It is also perhaps a misnomer to talk about 'the rise of women', precisely because 'women are an ever-more fragmented market'.[77] Throughout the West women are divided in terms of their responsibilities, their level of financial security, and their amount of free time, as well as a range of socio-economic factors. There is also a significant difference between the experience of women in industrialised and developing countries and in parts of the less developed world. In many of these countries patriarchal states and religions severely circumscribe female roles. As an article in *Asiaweek* has commented:

> Many women don't know they have a right to divorce their husbands and think Islam permits their spouses to beat them. And a great number regard a role beyond wife and mother as unthinkable.[76]

The divisions are, however, much too complex to be discussed in terms of a West–East divide. Women are becoming increasingly important in some Asian economies, whilst in the West, misogynist philosophies find echoes in the religious right in parts of the US, in spirit if not in practice, in their often-voiced concerns of the demise of the family and moral values. Women constitute a disadvantaged group in many societies and their situation is improving only slowly. Worldwide they still only make up 10% of all national-level legislators and 6% of cabinet-level posts – even in the US where discussions of equality are frequently heard, only 11% of Senate and House members in Washington DC are women.[79]

Whilst change is occurring it is a gradual process and, as our discussions in Chapters 6 and 9 illustrate, even where there is an extremely economically powerful female segment – such as women business travellers – the tourism industry often fails to recognise its needs. In developing services and promotional campaigns aimed at business people, most of the world's airlines subsume women into a male norm and facilities and advertising images are designed to appeal to an exclusively male clientele. Despite the rise of women, particularly in the tourism-generating countries, they are still not being recognised by the tourism industry and are often heavily sexualised, appearing in the tourism image only as decorative adornments to tourism products and destinations. Stereotypical ways of representing them still dominate and they are overwhelmingly associated with family and passivity, rather than individuality and activity.

The changing household

The lessening of women's dependency on men is accelerating as a result of a number of forces, including: industrialisation; urbanisation; widening marital choices; premarital sex; abortion; divorce; and women's employment.[80] These are trends which are by no means confined to the West as Asia is beginning to experience the same changes in response to the incorporation of women into the workforce. As a result, 'traditional' family life has been affected and perhaps one of the most fundamental challenges facing the West is the rise of the household and the parallel decline of the family. This poses a significant challenge to the tourism industry given that portrayals of the typical tourist represent white, heterosexual couples and families. The lifestyles of those who are Other – such as ethnic minority groups and gays – rarely feature.

The family is changing out of all recognition in the western industrialised world. The term 'family' refers to two or more persons related by blood, marriage or adoption, who reside together – a pattern which is declining in the West as there has been a rise in 'households'. A household may include unmarried couples, family friends, roommates or boarders. There has been a sharp decline in the nuclear family, an increase in blended families and in single-parent families. In the US 30% of all households are non-family households, outnumbering the once traditional family – those married couples with children – and one-third of children are born outside marriage. In addition, divorce is rising throughout the western world and changing working patterns have also changed the concepts of what is a traditional family. Today fewer than 4% of American families consist of what was once considered the 'traditional' arrangement of a bread-winning husband and a home-making wife.[81]

Social and demographic change is also enhancing the importance of the singles markets and single males are expected to become an especially important target market in the future.[82] In the UK the number of people marrying each year has been declining for the last 20 years, from seventeen per 1000 to eleven per 1000 in 1995. In 1990 in the USA 23 million or 22% of homemakers were adult males and that number is rising as household size shrinks and the number of one-person households increases. Male homemakers are typically found in non-family type situations, as single persons – over 80% have no children, compared to 58% of women. They are also concentrated in the under-35 and over-65 age groups. Thus, with many people postponing marriage and children, there has been a decline in the nuclear family and a concomitant growth in travel products aimed at childless couples – in the UK two-thirds of current holiday trips do not involve children.[83]

If the next century may be the era of the household, in an age of increasing sexual liberalisation, it may also see the wider recognition of 'alternative' lifestyles. In particular, homosexuality has been openly recognised, although it has not necessarily been accompanied by general acceptance. Marketers have begun to see the economic power of the so-called 'pink pound', as we explore in case study 5.4, but heterosexuality remains the norm against which others are measured – a fact which has profound implications for the tourism experiences of gay people, as we will see in Chapter 6.

Case Study 5.4   Focus on the Gay Market

The true size and value of the gay market is impossible to ascertain, since few reliable statistics exist on sexual orientation. There are also practical problems in obtaining data about marginalised activities and gay studies often rely on 'anecdotal evidence, informal "interviews" and participation observation'.[84] It does seem, however, that the market is growing as a result of greater social permissiveness, growing out of the gay pride movement. The market is also increasing as more and more homosexuals (especially lesbian women) openly develop families, conceive or adopt children and build 'quasi-traditional families'.[85]

A number of writers, including Ritchie and Holcomb and Luongo, have recognised that the gay tourism market includes a potentially large market of upscale, well-educated professionals.[86] In the US almost 40% of unmarried partners of homosexuals hold a college degree, compared to 18% of unmarried heterosexual partners and 13% of married spouses. While 86% of the partners of gay men and

81% of the partners of gay women have an above high school education, only 74% of heterosexual unmarried partners have a high school diploma.[87] Readers of US gay magazines also have an upscale profile – 7% have doctoral degrees, compared to less than 1% of the general US population and their median household income in 1992 was $51 300 compared to a national average of $30 050.[88] It is widely reported that gay male couples have higher average incomes and more free time than heterosexuals, since fewer than 5% of gay male couples have children.[89] Whilst this obviously has some substance, it is important to remember that this is rather a simplistic view; as in other market segments, there are upscale and down-scale gays. Moreover, in many countries female employees earn less than their male counterparts so lesbian couples' average incomes will be less than average gay male couples' incomes.

It does seems, however, that gays are more likely than average to buy dis-cretionary items, such as consumer goods, health club membership and especially travel products.[90] As a result, in the late 1990s, this high income, free-spending gay and lesbian community, the so-called 'pink pound', has become the latest target of mainstream marketers as a viable consumer group. In the USA, with 10% or 18.5 million of the population estimated to be homosexual, companies have been targeting the gay community for some time. Absolut Vodka has been targeting gay consumers since 1979 and sponsors of the IV Gay Games in New York included AT&T, Continental Airlines and Miller Beer.[91] Although gay tourists who attend events like the Gay Games are a minority of consumers, they 'tend to be "hyper-consumers" who not only consume more, but also influence the purchases of their gay and straight friends and colleagues', thus providing vital word of mouth endorsements for products, brands and companies.[92] Gays are also extremely brand loyal to gay-friendly companies and once gay consumers see that a company is reaching out to them they are much more loyal to those efforts than straight consumers – sponsorship of gay events makes them 'much more likely to buy the sponsor's products or services'.[93] Absolut Vodka, for instance, 'has built so strong a franchise among gays and lesbians that the brand is automatically acknowledged as a sponsor or presence at major events', even when it is not there.[94] Such marketing can have a lasting impact, provided the effort made is sustained.

The future is age, the future is youth

Of all the demographic changes shaping the world, perhaps the greatest single demographic event is the age spilt between the developed world, which will continue to age, and the developing world which will be younger than ever. An ageing population is not an exclusively developed-country phenomenon, since in China, with its one child per couple policy, over a fifth of the population will be over 60 by 2030, and Thailand, Taiwan, and South Korea also face a similar situation.[95] Nevertheless, it is the case that more than half the world's population today is under 20 years of age and 90% of them live in the poorer developing world. In contrast, an 'Age Wave'[96] is sweeping the developed world's population, a process which has been well documented elsewhere.[97] Increased life expectancy as a result of improving medi-care and rising standards of living are shifting the age profile ever upwards. In the developed world people live, on average, 25 years longer than they did at the beginning of the century and by the turn of the century about one in seven people in North America and Japan will be over 64.[98] In the US the number of elderly consumers is growing twice as fast as the overall population – over 30 million Americans or 12% of the population are over 65 and that number will double in the next 50 years. At the same time, falling birth rates mean that in most Western European countries the birthrate is too low to sustain even the current population.[99]

Case Study 5.5   Focus on Seniors' Lifestyles

Targeting elderly consumers is a profitable activity, but it is not easy, since they are not an homogeneous group. In fact, it has been suggested that elderly consumers are more diverse in interests, opinions, and actions than any other segment of the adult population.[100] Moreover, age is not necessarily a major determinant of how older consumers respond to marketing activities. Recognising that the elderly are not a uniform group, marketers have tried to segment this group. One basis is simply on age, splitting them into the young-old (65–74), the old (75–84) and the old-old (85 and over). Another is on the basis of motivations and quality of life orientation, splitting them between the new-age old and the traditional older consumer.

Although the population is ageing, recent research suggests that older consumers are enjoying increasingly active lifestyles. Firstly, the Henley Centre which provide UK leisure research information, argue that older people are increasingly taking part in active leisure pursuits, particularly swimming. Secondly, the Centre suggests that they are also increasingly participating in more upmarket activities such as concert and theatre visits and short breaks and leading the shift towards eating out at restaurants. Finally, although one might expect this market segment to be among the more conservative in terms of participation in traditional activities, they are turning to more varied leisure activities,[101] becoming less homogeneous and less easy for marketers to access.

This evidence complements other recent research which indicates that in many areas the behaviour and attitudes of older and younger people are becoming similar as older people are becoming younger in outlook. Leisure activity patterns, including going to the cinema, participating in do-it-yourself activities, eating out and watching videos, are blurring across age groups. Described as a process of 'attitudinal convergence', it seems reasonable to suggest that this will also be translated into a convergence in vacation behaviour patterns.[102] This will be accentuated as today's cohort of third age consumers, aged 45 to 59, move into the older age groups, giving a further boost to the leisure profiles of tomorrow's older consumers. Clearly, marketers are going to have to become adept at providing a range of active and varied leisure services to people in their 50s, 60s and 70s, previously marketed only to those under 50 years of age, particularly as this market will enjoy 20 to 30 years of post-working life.[103]

This 'greying' trend is well established in the tourism marketing literature[104] but, as we shall see in Chapter 6, the image creators do not seem to know how to craft messages which appeal to this segment. In particular, many of the brochure images are very stereotypical and often alienating. The main target of the marketers are the Baby Boomers rather than the over-fifties generation, who, together with younger consumers – Generation X – are often overlooked. Recently the definition of Generation X was convincingly shifted by Ritchie to the birth years 1961–1981, in other words, those aged between 17 and 37 in 1998. Interestingly, thus defined, they have actually outnumbered Boomers in the United States since 1980, accounting for 78.4 million, or 30% of the population in 1995, whilst Boomers accounted for a smaller, if noisier, 26%.[105]

These demographic statistics should be of interest to all tourism marketers, particularly with the arrival of 'new' tourism generating regions with younger age profiles, notably in Asia. A new, younger travel consumer group may emerge, defined by globalisation, itself accelerated by technological innovation and the emergence of a global youth culture. These 'Xers', 'marketing savvy, cost-conscious and skeptical of "hype"',[106] are the first generation to have grown up in a media, information-saturated environment – an environment of sophisticated advertising, video games and personal computers, in which television has been a mature medium throughout. They have been described as having a healthy scepticism of advertising and marketing[107] and it will be interesting to see how marketers frame their appeals to these consumers in the future.

This chapter has provided a selective overview of the global trends which the tourism marketers (and others) will have to address. We have tried to identify those key trends which impact on power relationships, although recognising that there are equally significant ones which space has not allowed us to consider – notably the rise of movements dedicated to promoting disabled rights and environmental concerns. The economic, social and political changes outlined in this chapter may in time lead to shifts in the cultural and ideological spheres. Yet in spite of this change, the overriding impression of our brief review is the strength and continuity of the dominant discourses in the face of change. The current tourism structures are highly dependent on the old ideologies and the world is 'hooked into the Western market system'.[108] Tastes are standardising, not only in consumer goods and services, but in cultural images which are 'supplied by American mass media and consumed . . . by the mass television audience'[109] – forces which may decrease the challenge of alternative cultural and ideological systems and lifestyles by channelling them into existing frameworks and thus diluting their impact.

Global changes are occurring and perhaps new referent systems will begin to emerge to frame the touristic process. A key theme in this discussion has been the increasing fragmentation of lifestyles, which means marketers will have to become more niche-oriented and more targeted in their media selections. Those marketers who recognise and cater for these new markets may well outperform their less innovative rivals and in one scenario, maybe the future will hold more acceptance for currently marginalised groups like the gay community and better provision for previously neglected groups like tourists with special needs. At the same time, however, this shrinking world, created by information technology, the convergence of tastes and the transformation of work may also create a polarised world, divided between the 'high-tec', 'cosmopolitan alrights' and the 'low-ed' 'digitariat', a division between those living in the global village and those marginalised in a local ghetto. This increasingly two-tier world may accentuate two-tier tourism – privileged tourism for the haves and a less fulfilling tourism for the have-nots. As we will see in Chapter 6, the tourism image currently focuses on heterosexual couples, families and the youth market, but groups such as seniors, women, gays and non-whites are relegated to the margins. The next chapter looks at these themes in more detail, highlighting the relationship between the image creators and the roles they assign to certain groups in the world of the tourism image via a number of case studies. These are inevitably highly specific in that they are snapshots in time but they provoke and pose interesting questions about the ways we use frames of reference to make sense of the world.

References

1 Peter Laslett, quoted in Henley Centre, (1994) 'Today's older consumers: an emerging third age of personal fulfilment or a wasted era of frustrated possibilities?', Henley Centre Leisure Futures.

2 Sampson, P. (1982) 'Consumer classification – the state of the art', *European Research*, 10 (4), October.

3 Peters, G. (1996) *Beyond the Next Wave. Imagining the next generation of customers*, Pitmans, London, quoting a 1995 American Management Association survey of its members: 25.

4 reference 3.

5 Yip, G.S. (1992) *Total Global Strategy*, Prentice Hall, quoted in Peters, G. (1996) *The New Wave. Imagining the next generation of customers*, Pitman, London: 25–6 (our emphasis).

6 Reader's Digest Eurodata, 1990, quoted in Horner, S. and Swarbrooke, J. (1996) *Marketing Tourism, Hospitality and Leisure in Europe*, International Thomson Business Press, London: 220.

7 Mooij, M. de (1994) *Advertising Worldwide*, Prentice Hall, London, quoted in Horner, S. and Swarbrooke, J. (1996) *Marketing Tourism, Hospitality and Leisure in Europe*, International Thomson Business Press, London: 224.

8 reference 4: 28.

9 reference 4: 31.

10 Schiffman, L.G. and Kanuk, L.L. (1994) *Consumer Behaviour*, 5th ed., Prentice Hall, Englewood Cliffs NJ: 447.

11 'The United States' New Immigrants Tide', *Brandweek*, 1 March 1993, 17, quoted in Schiffman, L.G. and Kanuk, L.L. (1994) *Consumer Behaviour*, 5th ed., Prentice Hall, Englewood Cliffs NJ: 448.

12 Real, T. (1996) 'Looking Good: How Cultural Tourism has Changed the face of North American Travel Destinations', 171–84 in Robinson, M. *et al.* (eds) *Tourism and Culture. Image, Identity and Marketing*, The Centre for Travel and Tourism, Sunderland.

13 Grossman, L.M. (1992) 'After Demographic Shift, Atlanta Mall Restyles Itself as Black Shopping Center', *The Wall Street Journal*, 26 February.

14 reference 10: 455.

15 Naisbitt, J. (1997) *Megatrends Asia. The Eight Asian Megatrends That Are Changing The World*, Nicholas Brealey Publishing, London: 18.

16 reference 15: 8 and 13.

17 reference 10: 455.

18 Hoffman, M.S. (1993)(ed.) *The World Almanac and Book of Facts: 1993*, Pharos Books, New York and Johnson, O. (1992)(ed.) *1993 Information Please Almanac*, Houghton Mifflin, Boston; quoted in Schiffman, L.G. and Kanuk, L.L. (1994) *Consumer Behaviour*, 5th ed., Prentice Hall, Englewood Cliffs NJ: 445.

19 BBC1 Breakfast News Broadcast, 18 November 1996.

20 *The Observer* (1996) 11 August, quoting HMSO, (1996) Social Focus on Ethnic Minorities.

21 Shaw, S. (1996) 'A bull market for prisons', The World in 1997, *The Economist*: 92.

22 reference 15: 16.

23   CyberAtlas (1997) Demographics. Http://www.cyberatlas.com/demographics.html. The authors are indebted to Mike Snelgrove's MPhil in progress for this reference.
24   'A word about the home office', *The Independent on Sunday*, 1 December 1996: 80–81.
25   'Myth of "new man" hides blight on families', *The Guardian*, Saturday 9 November 1996: 18.
26   reference 4: 51.
27   reference 4: 52–3.
28   reference 4: 54.
29   'Brain Storms', *The Guardian*, 5 November 1996: 2–3.
30   reference 4: 30.
31   Weber, J.G. (1974) 'Worldwide strategies for market segmentation', *Columbia Journal of World Business*, 9 (4) winter, quoted in Chisnall, P.M. (1995) *Consumer Behaviour*, 3rd ed., McGraw Hill, Maidenhead, Berks: 327.
32   reference 4: 37–8.
33   Smith, P. (1996) 'Africa turns Asian', The World in 1997, *The Economist*, 89–90: 89.
34   Bradshaw, Y.W. and Wallace, M. (1996) *Global Inequalities*, Pine Forge Press, Thousand Oaks, California: 20.
35   reference 34: 49.
36   ibid.
37   Wales Information Society Project (1997) Wales Information Society, Cardiff: 29.
38   The British Council (1996) The Internet and ELT: An Overview. http://www.britcon.org/english/internet/engoverl.htlm#History. The authors are indebted to Mike Snelgrove's MPhil in progress for this reference.
39   reference 37: 10.
40   'Targeting the Rich and Poor', Executive Summary 17 July 1995, Mintel International Group Ltd.
41   ibid.
42   reference 34: 34.
43   reference 29: 2–3.
44   'Trade must harness technological change', *Travel Trade Gazette*, 8 May 1996; 'Airlines to Boost Sales on Internet', *Travel Weekly*, 5 June 1996.
45   reference 29: 2–3.
46   Computer Intelligence CITM. The authors are indebted to Mike Snelgrove's MPhil in progress for this reference.
47   reference 15: 5.
48   reference 15: 4.
49   reference 15: 19.
50   reference 15: 3.
51   Fingleton, E. (1996) 'Tokyo Inc. confounds its critics', *The Observer*, 20 October: 22.
52   EIU (1994) 'Outbound Markets: Japan Outbound', EIU *Travel & Tourism Analyst* No. 1, The Economist Intelligence Unit: 42.
53   Ikuo Amano, 'The bright and dark sides of Japanese education', *Royal Society of Arts Journal*, vol. CXL, no. 5425, January 1992, quoted in Chisnall, P.M. (1995) *Consumer Behaviour*, 3rd ed., McGraw Hill, Maidenhead, Berks: 328.
54   reference 51.
55   Said, E. (1978) *Orientalism. Western Conceptions of the Orient*, Penguin, London: 322–4.
56   reference 55: 324–5.
57   National Geographic, 'Endless Beauty . . . Eternal serenity' (1940), NTO and Japanese Government Railways plate in O'Barr, W. (1994) *Culture and the Ad. Exploring Otherness in Advertising*, Westview Press, Oxford: 168.
58   O'Barr, W. (1994) *Culture and the Ad. Exploring Otherness in Advertising*, Westview Press, Oxford: 164.
59   ibid.
60   ibid.
61   'We're all you expect Japan to be', in reference 58: 167.

62   advertisement in reference 58: 169.
63   reference 15: 216.
64   reference 15: 217.
65   ibid.
66   reference 15: 10.
67   reference 15: 218.
68   reference 15: 219.
69   ibid.
70   reference 15: 220–21.
71   reference 15: 227.
72   reference 15: 249.
73   Beeghley, L. (1996) *What Does Your Wife Do? Gender and the Transformation of Family Life*, Westview Press, Oxford: 1.
74   Nelson, C. (1994) *How to Market to Women*, Visible Ink, Detroit: 34.
75   reference 74: 33.
76   reference 73: 135.
77   reference 74: 281.
78   quoted in reference 15: 245.
79   reference 34: 35.
80   reference 73: 4.
81   'America's Vanishing Housewife', *Adweek's Marketing Week*, 24 June 1991, 28–29.
82   Mediamark Research Product Summary Report, Fall 1988, New York: Mediamark Research, Inc., 1991, iii, quoted in Schiffman, L.G. and Kanuk, L.L. (1994) *Consumer Behaviour*, 5th ed., Prentice Hall, Englewood Cliffs NJ: 56.
83   Henley Centre for Leisure Forecasting (1993) 'Generation X: an army of ageing Bart Simpsons or the wave of the future? Today's cohort of 16 to 24s', *Leisure Futures*, 3: 5–97: 94.
84   Hughes, H. (1997) 'Holidays and Homosexual Identity', *Tourism Management*, 18 (1).
85   Mulryan, D. (1995) 'Out of the Closet', *American Demographics*, 17, May, 40–46: 43.
86   Ritchie, K. (1995) *Marketing to Generation X*, Lexington Books, New York and Holcomb, B. and Luongo, M. (1996) 'Gay Tourism in the United States', *The Annals of Tourism Research*, August, 711–13.
87   Ritchie, K. (1995) *Marketing to Generation X*, Lexington Books, New York: 157.
88   reference 85: 42.
89   Holcomb, B. and Luongo, M. (1996) 'Gay Tourism in the United States', *The Annals of Tourism Research*, August, 711–13: 711.
90   reference 85: 42.
91   reference 85: 46.
92   ibid.
93   ibid.
94   ibid.
95   reference 4: 42–5.
96   Dychtwald, K. and Flower, J. (1989) *Age Wave, Los Angeles*, Jeremy P. Tarcher, quoted in Schiffman, L.G. and Kanuk, L.L. (1994) *Consumer Behaviour*, 5th ed., Prentice Hall, Englewood Cliffs NJ: 462.
97   See Henley Centre (1992) 'The Young Consumer', *Leisure Futures*, 3.
98   Jefferson, A. (1992) 'Tourism in Europe', British Tourism Authority/English Tourist Board, *Tourism Intelligence Quarterly*, 14 (1) August, 57–63: 57.
99   Henley Centre for Leisure Forecasting (1992) 'Europe's Ageing Population', Henley Centre, *Leisure Futures*, 3: 6–10.
100 Wolfe, D.B. (1987) 'The Ageless Market', *American Demographics*, July 26–28 and 55–56.
101 Henley Centre for Leisure Forecasting (1992) 'Time Use', Henley Centre, *Leisure Futures*, 3: 30–32.
102 Henley Centre for Leisure Forecasting (1992) 'Demographic Background', Henley Centre, *Leisure Futures*, 3: 16–20, 16.

103   reference 4: 64.
104   See Middleton, V.T.C. (1994) *Marketing in Travel and Tourism*, Butterworth Heinemann, 2nd ed., 39; and Kotler, P., Bowen, J. and Makens J. (1996) *Marketing for Hospitality & Tourism*, Prentice Hall: 189.
105   reference 87: 16–17.
106   reference 87: 165.
107   reference 87: 87.
108   reference 55: 324.
109   reference 55: 325.

6 Power, image and markets

In Chapter 5 we discussed some of the contradictory forces which are shaping the world – global trends which, whilst provoking some power shifts, are in many ways reaffirming the discourses underpinning tourism advertising. Here, we examine in more detail some of these trends and point out that some of the new markets which are emerging as a result have historically been the disenfranchised and the dispossessed in society – women, gays, seniors, and ethnic minorities. Now, however, some of these groups are becoming the new targets of the tourism industry as it constantly searches for new markets. This reflects not only the saturation of the marketplace, but also, on a different level, the fact that these groups are gaining more of a voice and becoming more *visible* – their rising economic power means that marketers are being drawn to these newer segments. On closer examination of the methods used to appeal to these groups, however, it is apparent that they still contain all the old stereotypes which have long underpinned and animated societies' key ideological structures. As we suggested in Chapter 5, whilst the world is changing, the old orders still remain extremely powerful and in its discussion of market segmentation and women, gay and senior consumers, this chapter highlights the inherent (hetero-) sexism, ageism and ethnocentrism of much tourism imagery. Part III is devoted to more detailed discussions of how tourism marketing is highly gendered, but here we examine them within the framework of market segmentation.

Segmentation is a technique based on the highlighting of a number of significant characteristics which distinguish one group of consumers from another. In the process, however, the characteristics which are selected often draw on stereotypical assumptions of those consumers (as with older tourists). Conversely, when marketers *do not recognise difference* they often subsume the needs of some consumers into a generic whole which is white, male and heterosexual (as those of female and black business travellers are submerged into a masculine, white 'norm'). Perhaps the most instructive way to illustrate this is to examine how tourists themselves are portrayed. Representations of tourists draw on an extremely narrow range of stereotypes, images which reveal a great deal about how the image-creators see the world.

John Urry has pointed out that in the material produced by the image creators there are really only three advertising images. These are the 'family' image – couples with school-age children; the 'romantic' image – heterosexual couples – and the 'fun' image – 'same-sex groups each looking for other-sex partners for "fun".'[1] Breathnach *et al.* endorse this observation, pointing out that, in tourism, the underlying assumption is that tourists travel in family groups or as couples, with common aspirations.[2] This leads us to our central contention in this chapter –

that the overwhelming majority of tourist representations revolve around beautiful, white, young, heterosexual couples, particularly in 'exotic locations'. Those in society who do not conform to this model (constructed in the image of the master subject) rarely, if ever, feature as tourists and, if they appear in travel literature at all, it is as part of the tourism product itself – some ethnic groups only ever appear as hosts in far-flung destinations. Given this narrow, restricted view of the tourist, it is unsurprising that we suggest that the tourism image reflects the dominant ideologies and, as such, mediates the world in ways which appeal to white, western, male, heterosexual tourists.

The power of segmentation

The term 'market segmentation' first appeared in the late 1950s and since then, has received considerable attention in the marketing literature.[3] Theodore Levitt once famously proclaimed 'If you ain't segmenting, you ain't marketing.'[4] The technique has been variously defined, although most of the definitions are very similar.[5] Perhaps one of the most succinct is that of Chisnall who defines it as a tool which 'assists marketing management by dividing total market demand into relatively homogeneous sectors that are identified by certain characteristics. Market strategy can then be devised which will be related to the needs of these market segments. There may be changes in styling . . . or in advertising appeals.'[6]

Market segmentation is considered to be the very core of marketing.[7] It recognises that consumers differ in their tastes, needs, lifestyles, motivations and maximises market demand by directing marketing efforts at what are regarded as economically *significant* groups of consumers. The strategy of segmentation enables marketers to avoid direct competition in an increasingly crowded marketplace as it enables them to distinguish their particular product, perhaps on the basis of price, often through styling and promotional appeal. It is important to remember that market segmentation is not itself a marketing strategy, but merely the first phase in a three step strategy. After *segmenting* the market into relatively homogeneous sectors, the marketer then has to identify one or more segments to *target* with a particular product or promotional appeal. The final phase is to *position* the product so that the target market regards it as satisfying its needs better than other offerings. Positioning and repositioning can be accomplished through any aspect of the marketing mix, but particularly through branding, which is our focus in Chapter 7.

Although market segmentation is a key element in marketing theory, many practitioners are dissatisfied with segmentation as a concept and it is often difficult to apply to certain markets. It is important to recognise that segmentation is a creative tool which should not be done as a one-off exercise and needs constant monitoring and re-evaluation. Segmentation will be different for every situation; there is no one right way of segmenting a market and most markets can be segmented in many different ways. Nevertheless segmentation is a very widespread tool and there are high stakes: marketers receive plaudits for getting it right, but incur penalties for getting it wrong.

The discourse of segmentation

Market segmentation is not simply a highly sophisticated marketing technique – seen from a different perspective, it is a process underpinned by power relationships in just the same way as is the entire image creation process. Segmentation implies and enhances difference. Some groups of consumers gain a high profile as a market segment (and are therefore empowered through their consumption), others are ignored or not recognised. Whilst most observers would agree that marketers decide which segments are economically viable, fewer would consider that those decisions are also *cultural* and *ideological*. The recognition of gay people as a market segment is a case in point. Only in the 1990s have they been discussed as a 'market segment' since previously, political and ideological dogma precluded such a description and made widespread targeting of this market untenable. It still remains impossible in many countries and in America, the world's leading consumer society, it remains a high risk strategy for marketers.

Segmentation as a process is therefore clearly inherently ideological. Nichols has said: 'Ideology is how the existing ensemble of social relations represents itself to individuals; it is the image a society gives of itself in order to perpetuate itself.'[8] Challenges to the dominant perspectives of society therefore can pose a fundamental threat to that prevailing order. As a result, ideology manipulates and constructs images and representations 'to persuade us that how things are is how they ought to be. . .'.[9] Thus, if you are a single traveller, you will find a small number of specialist tourism operators which cater for your needs, yet the mainstream operators still insist on charging supplements; hotels and restaurants often direct single people to inferior tables; and the service is generally poorer, even stigmatising.[10] Similarly, whilst the gay consumer has recently emerged as a viable market segment,[11] at the same time, the airline industry barely recognises female business travellers as a segment, suggesting – in direct contrast to the feelings of the businesswomen themselves[12] – that they have no gender-specific needs. Marketing managers regard air travel as a gender-neutral product, but subconsciously what they are doing is subsuming women's needs into some masculinised 'norm'. This, of course, reveals the prevailing ideologies underpinning the actions of marketers – as Weedon comments: 'In patriarchal discourse the nature and social role of women are defined in relation to a norm which is male.'[13]

In such ways, the decisions as to which segments are deemed to be viable are influenced by the perceptions and priorities of the marketers themselves. This emerges clearly when age is used as a criterion for segmentation. Since the 1950s it has been the Baby Boom generation which have dominated marketing in the post-industrial world both because of their numbers and because most senior marketers are themselves drawn from their ranks. Marketers have learned 'that the sheer weight of this birth cohort we call Baby Boomers was often the difference between success and failure for a marketing concept'.[14] The Boomer generation has been the dominant post-war target audience: as 'kids' in the 1950s; as 'teens' in the 1960s; as 'hippies' in the 1970s; as 'yuppies' in the 1980s; and as 'woopies' in the 1990s. As Boomers have aged, so have marketing targets crept towards older age groups. In the early 1980s, the main audience was 18 to 34 year olds, in the mid-1990s it has become the 25 to 54 age group.[15] Other age cohorts have not been so courted and, as we will see, the older age groups in particular have often been neglected. This chapter takes a market segmentation-orientated approach in analysing its case studies but, in looking at these various market segments, we hope to encourage the reader to consider each from a different perspective. Every one reveals something about power relationships and the strength of the prevailing ideologies – from business women, to gay tourists, senior tourists, and black tourists in the USA – they all illustrate the prevalence of the forces of (hetero-) sexism, ageism and ethnocentrism.

The (hetero-) sexist image

The tourism image (like all advertising) is a reflection of youth and beauty, the twin aspirations of western society and consumerism. This dominance of representations of beautiful young people not only reinforces notions of ageism but, as we shall first explore, sexism and heterosexism by highlighting how the male, heterosexual 'norm' structures the segmentation process itself and the images which are its end product. Advertising aimed at the business traveller continues to be constructed to appeal to a male audience; and in the marketing of tourism packages to young people, whilst men are becoming objectified, women are most frequently depicted as sexualised objects. The emergence of the gay market may appear to challenge this heterosexual norm, but the power of heterosexism is such that it still dominates tourism spaces and places.

As we move into the next millennium, there is a substantial growth in the numbers of women business travellers. In the USA, women are starting businesses at twice the rate of men,[16] whilst in Eastern Germany, one of the unforeseen results of the collapse of Communism has been the numbers of women starting new companies. Since the fall of the Berlin Wall over 150 000 businesses have been set up by women, employing a million people and contributing $15 billion to Germany's GDP.[17] In the UK there are 3.5 million women in managerial and professional positions[18] and, as we have seen in Chapter 5, women are highly significant as entrepreneurs in Asia. In the USA, almost 40% of the 35 million-plus business travellers are women[19] – a multi-billion dollar market segment in which women spend well over $10 billion on business travel each year.[20] Recognising the USA as a trendsetter for the developed world, Expotel suggest that by the millennium, women business travellers will account for over one-half of the entire corporate travel market.[21] Much of this worldwide business traffic will, of course, be highly dependent on the airline industry and so it is salutary to explore how airline marketers are responding to the increasing numbers of female business passengers.

Airlines and women business travellers

Women and men business travellers display very similar membership rates of frequent flyer clubs[22] yet airlines have been heavily criticised for failing to reach out to their female customers.[23] In particular, it seems that airlines are, in fact, failing to address women as the equals of men. A British Airways (BA) survey in 1990 revealed that sex discrimination was an issue among almost half of all the women interviewed. Many respondents thought that men were served first and were 'pampered' by stewardesses, whilst they were often treated as partners of men – even those simply seated next to them! Above all, many airlines were perceived to be essentially masculine organisations – from their aeroplanes' colour schemes and interiors to the design and decor of their business lounges.[24]

Five years after that BA survey, another study suggested that the airlines have failed to address these issues – in fact, if anything, women's discontent has grown. The differential service given to women and men was again highly criticised: 'Attitude, attitude, attitude. Stewardesses virtually ignore or are rude to business women travellers.'[25] In addition to service, flight upgrades, advertising and the product itself (especially food, safety, entertainment and hygiene facilities) generated substantial criticism.[26] Interestingly, in view of our contention that marketers read from male 'scripts', despite the overwhelming evidence of women's dissatisfaction with the airline product, airlines (with one or two exceptions) have done little to recognise even the existence of female business travellers. Recent research, in fact, suggests that airlines, in contrast, believe that their business product is gender-neutral and, as such requires no specific targeting or accommodation of women – one marketing manager recently commented: 'We have never considered a difference between men and women business travellers'[27] whilst a research manager said of his company: 'We look at what business people want, not women in particular.'[28]

These attitudes prevail despite research which suggests that a gender-neutral approach is by no means adequate and indeed, often alienating to a group of consumers who will soon constitute *half* the airlines' business. It is important to note here that this notion of gender neutrality is rather misleading. In essence, gender-neutrality is an approach which assumes that women require no services other than those 'normally' provided, but that norm is a essentially a *masculine* standard for measurement. As Millum pointed out as early as the mid-Seventies, stereotypes influence our construction of what is 'typical' and in business travel what is the norm is masculine – women are thus perceived to have no needs which differ from this norm, constructed and dominated by men.[29] It is yet another area in which the standards and norms of society are essentially masculine. Therefore, to be female is to be different (to be Other) – women are more conscious of being a woman than men are of being a man[30] – and, as Carol Nelson forcefully argues: 'The business woman of the 1990s retains a sensitivity parallel to that of a prisoner recently released because late evidence found her innocent.'[31] To illustrate the reason for this sensitivity, we have to look no further than airline advertising (case study 6.1).

Case Study 6.1 Sexist Airline Advertising and the Female Business Traveller

Airlines spend more on advertising than any other sector of the travel industry. Between June 1995 and June 1996 airlines spent £62.4 million on advertising compared to the £18.8 million spent by hotels and £43.2 million by travel agents.[32]

Recent research indicates that women continue to feel that advertising is consistently out of touch with the 1990s woman. Issues such as stereotypical portrayals and sexism continue to dominate the agenda despite the number of articles and studies which should alert marketers to these issues.[33] Old stereotypes, particularly those of submissive, smiling and decorative Asian women remain popular amongst Asian airlines[34] and, amongst Western carriers new stereotypes have emerged, such as the 'business woman with long, slim legs wearing a short-skirted suit and lipstick.'[35]

The stereotypical and sexist nature of these representations are by no means confined to the images used to represent women – they are as much about how men are represented in relation to women. One recent campaign which generated much controversy was that run by BA in 1996.[36] The campaign included a series of images where the heads of male business travellers were superimposed onto the bodies of young children and infants, sometimes in 'Oedipal' situations. The advertisements were designed to appeal to the business traveller by conveying the message that the new business class seats on BA flights were '. . . as embracing as a mothers' arms'.[37] Some women considered these advertisements to be very male-orientated, appealing to the 'little boy' in men, whilst others felt that the BA depiction of men was distasteful, and demeaning to women.[38] One focus group participant commented: 'I am uncomfortable with the image of men as babies – creepy creepy, creepy – this is just one step away from breast feeding.'[39] In the same research project Asian airline advertisements were also criticised for the messages and images they projected. Women considered that they conveyed a message of being 'pampered by Oriental handmaidens' who were not only servile but 'appeal to the sexual instinct in men . . . very distasteful when you consider the level of prostitution in Asia'.[40]

The business people featured in the overwhelming majority of airline advertisements are men, and women were very sensitive to their unrealistic and unrepresentative portrayal in advertisements. One participant commented: 'Why have so many men – I feel slightly insulted.'[41] On the rare occasions when women *were* featured, the messages which were conveyed were not always welcome. For instance, one Air France advertisement featuring a photograph of a beautiful woman and the words: 'The chances of her being seated next to you are so slim that you won't regret the extra space between our seats', provoked universal condemnation amongst female air travellers. Participants commented that it conveys 'all the wrong sentiments'; that 'it could make me feel quite cross'; in 'bad taste'; and that it appealed to 'those deep dark thoughts that you are worried about some man harbouring about travelling in the mile high club and all that sort of thing'.[42] Above all, there was a strong demand for women to be recognised as legitimate business travellers in airline advertising:

> I want to feel recognised as an equal in the workforce and as a customer . . . advertisements don't need to have pictures of women, but they should somehow recognise women have just as serious travel requirements as men . . . certainly less of this underlying sexist rubbish.[43]

As we have seen, by failing to recognise the specific needs of women in either their product or their advertising, airlines are rejecting consumer demands that women are a distinctive segment, requiring different marketing approaches. Far from appealing to women, their advertising is sexist – designed to attract a male audience, and significantly, a heterosexual male audience. This use of (hetero-) sexual imagery is by no means confined to airline advertising and can be seen in many sectors of the tourism industry – in this, tourism is no different from other advertising, as we saw in Chapter 2. Whilst it is seen across tourism advertising, some of the most successful applications of such sexual imagery can be found in campaigns aimed at the younger market, especially young singles and couples. The heterosexual couple is the epitome of the tourist image and the celebration of youth, beauty and sexual encounters lies at the core of the tourism marketers' art. Advertising produced by the all-inclusive couples-only resorts of *Sandals*, *Couples* and *Hedonism II* and by the tour operators *Twenties*, *Priority* and *Club 18–30* are merely some of the most prominent examples of this sexually-oriented imagery (Figure 6.1). Case study 6.2 analyses the marketing imagery used by *Club 18–30*, the UK market leader of young singles holidays, a relatively small but distinctive segment, often characterised by the use of prominent sexual imagery in its promotional literature.

Case Study 6.2   Hetero-sexism Dominates Youth Marketing

In 1995 Club 18–30, having experimented briefly with marketing campaigns which focused on good clean fun, returned to its tried and tested and above all, successful core campaign, of 'sun, fun and sex'. Posters were launched carrying slogans such as 'Discover your erogenous zone', 'Summer of 69' and 'Girls, can we interest you in a package holiday?', with a picture of a man, described by *The Times* as wearing 'a well-padded pair of boxer shorts'.[44] In addition to this high profile poster campaign (which was later extended to cinemas), the company continued the sexual theme in the pages of their brochures. Indeed, sexually-oriented marketing messages dominate the Club 18–30 brochures. The brochures are highly pictorial – there are few photographs of the product – the hotel, location, etc. – which appears simply as a backdrop to fun-loving young tourists. Photographs of attractive, young tourists fill the brochure pages – night-clubbing, lounging by swimming pools, playing in the sea and, above all, enjoying the company of the opposite sex. It is the sheer dominance of these images – many of them taking up a whole page – which creates the brochures' atmosphere of sexuality. In Chapter 9 we explore the sexual and gendered nature of tourism marketing in much more detail, but at this point, it is useful to highlight the heterosexual nature of such imagery.

Significantly, however, the sexual images are not evenly divided between photographs of men and women. Over 60% of the photographs are of women – and two-thirds of these are overtly sexual. Such sexual imagery is not wholly restricted to women and a relatively high number of men are seen in similarly sexual or decorative poses, although in rather smaller proportion, at just over one-third. This development in tourism marketing literature is interesting in view of the increasing use of men as sex objects in other marketing literature (Figure 6.2).[45] Overall, however, whilst operators such as Club 18–30 are featuring men as sexual objects in the tourism advertising aimed at young people, the overwhelming majority of sexual imagery still portrays women.

Through such advertising images tourism is promoted as a (heterosexual) couple's or a family's annual pursuit. Most vacation packages are usually sold on the assumption that there will be (at least) two participants and 'the "honeymoon" images of many resorts reinforce specific types of gender relationships at home' – the advertising images thus mediate society's expectations of what is appropriate

Figure 6.1   Heterosexism Sells. Reproduced by permission of Superclubs

Figure 6.2 The Sexualised Male Image. Reproduced by permission of Flying Colours Holidays Ltd.

male and female behaviour.[46] In this, we see the incorporation into everyday life of a discourse of what is normal and appropriate and what is not – similar to Foucault's discussion of sexuality in the Victorian era.[47] It is not just the state which polices sexual behaviours – we all participate in sanctioning what is seen to be 'acceptable' – and we may use disapproval or even aggression to maintain that norm. One of the clearest ways in which that sanction operates is in the maintenance of the heterosexual nature of places and spaces – a key issue that marketers who would target gay tourists as an emergent segment should consider.

Some tourism marketers are recognising the gay market as a viable market segment, as highlighted in case study 6.3. This recognition demonstrates the economic power of gay consumers and, as their profile is raised, gay events, festivals and spaces are becoming increasingly popular with both gay and straight tourists. In targeting the gay market, however, such is the power of the heterosexual norm that a number of key issues have not even been considered – particularly issues of place and space. There are many homophobic destinations, including Brazil, Columbia, Mexico, Nicaragua, Peru, Iran, Afghanistan and Bavaria,[48] places which do not welcome openly-gay tourists. For example, in Zambia homosexual relations between men of any age are illegal according to Article 155–158 of the Penal Code and the maximum penalty is fourteen years' imprisonment.[49] Even destinations such as popular Caribbean resorts which may, on the surface, seem liberal, may not welcome gay tourists. Richard Fairbrass, lead singer of the UK music band Right Said Fred, recently commented: 'I feel strongly that travel companies should advise on areas not tolerant to certain sections of society', having been subjected to homophobic insults and the threat of arrest whilst on holiday in St Lucia with his partner.[50]

Notions of space and place are of great significance to the gay community primarily because homosexual expressions of identity do not belong in social spaces and public places such as shops, cafés and bars – homosexuals 'are only allowed to be gay in specific spaces and places'.[51] They are marginalised, relegated to gay ghettos and privatised spaces as 'the street . . . is not an asexual place. Rather, it is commonly assumed to be "naturally" or "authentically" heterosexual'.[52] Heterosexuals 'take the street for granted as a "commonsense" heterosexual space precisely because they take for granted their freedom to perform their own identities'.[53] These identities involve public expressions of affection such as holding hands, kissing, using terms of endearment, fleeting touches and meaningful glances.

As a public space which is subject to much tension, the heterosexual street is not immutable, and its heterosexual nature is continually being re-established and challenged. Heterosexuals seek to deny homosexuals legitimacy in the street through official sanction or through disapproval and even aggression. As Myslik has commented, heterosexual men have identified 'Gay men . . . as a group requiring ridicule, policing and/or punishment.'[54] Despite, or because of, such practices, the importance of space has been particularly seized upon by 'queer activists' who have sought to renegotiate it through subversive body language or through more obvious aggressive actions which attempt to contest 'the very production of public space'.[55] Such activities simultaneously challenge the heterosexual norm which defines and dominates the street and empowers those who are currently excluded and disenfranchised.

Part of this challenge to the heterosexual street has been the development of spaces which 'have come to be identified in and outside the gay community as gay spaces'.[56] These are places which enable not only open displays of behaviour and affection but also access to a variety of gay services and facilities including shops, bars, housing, and legal and medical services. Such gay spaces are by no means safe spaces, however – as with public spaces, they have become 'hunting grounds' for those who wish to commits acts of violence against gay men.[57] Despite this, gay spaces do provide homosexuals with a strong sense of safety and they are arenas in which behaviour does not have to be edited to conform to a heterosexual norm. Gay spaces, in essence, provide community and territory as well as a sense of order and power. They are 'sites of cultural resistance with enormous symbolic meaning', providing 'cultural and emotional support for a political movement comprised of an increasingly diverse and geographically scattered community'.[58]

Case Study 6.3 Tourism and the Gay Tourist – Degaying Spaces

Awareness of the gay market is clearly already well established in the wider leisure sector, attracting the attentions not only of the media industries, but also the fashion, food and drinks industries. The gay travel consumer is also a rapidly growing and lucrative, if relatively recent, segment of the tourism industry. It seems that gay couples travel more frequently than their straight counterparts and gays have been described as 'the closest thing to a recession-proof market'.[59] The New York Gay and Lesbian Visitor Center, for instance, estimate that gay couples average 4.5 trips a year compared to a 'straight' average of one trip.[60] Similarly, whilst in the early 1990s most cruise companies experienced a downturn, RSVP, a US gay travel company, reported consecutive annual increases in cruise business.[61]

It is important to point out that any figures on the size of the gay tourism market cannot take into account travel purchases made by gays through mainstream operators or booked directly, yet despite this, its recent growth is nevertheless unmistakable. The Tourism Industry Intelligence suggests that an estimated 5–25 million gay men and lesbians spend more than US$10 billion on travel products each year.[62] The International Gay Travel Association (IGTA) is a global umbrella organisation of over 1500 gay and gay-friendly organisations, 900 of them based in the USA. The IGTA estimates that its members book over a billion dollars in airline tickets alone, with almost US$450 million expenditure in other travel purchases.[63]

To cater for this growing, lucrative segment in the travel market there are a number of gay travel guides, including *Spartacus*, *Best*, *Gai Pied* and *Ferrari for Men*[64] and an increasing number of specialist gay travel companies. These include RSVP in the USA; Man Around, In Touch Holidays and Pride Travel in the UK, and Beach Boy Holidays, the Netherlands' largest gay-only travel company which advertises regularly in the *Gay Krant*, one of Europe's most popular gay newspapers. In addition to these specialist gay companies, there are an increasing number of large-scale gay-friendly companies, such as American Airlines, Quantas and Virgin Atlantic Airways, which are recognising gay consumers by sponsoring events or advertising in gay media.[65] Interestingly, Sandals Resorts, which has ten clubs accepting only heterosexual couples, is now launching a line called Beaches that welcomes singles, families and any couples. The first opened in January 1997 in Negril, Jamaica, the second in April in the Turks and Caicos Islands, and a third will open in Barbados in 1998. 'We are a couple of years behind' in reaching out for a wider market said the company chairman, Gordon Stewart, who has been criticised for years for excluding gay travellers, singles and children.[66] The tourism industry does seem to be slowly recognising and accepting gay tourists. Whilst many hotels are still reluctant to accommodate promoters of lesbian events, as the wealth of the market becomes apparent, that is changing and now annual events such as 'The Dinah Shore Weekend' – a huge lesbian party which runs alongside a women's professional golf event – attract sponsors including American Airlines and Absolut Vodka.[67]

Gay destinations are not confined to the USA: London, Blackpool and Brighton in the UK and Ibiza, Mykonos and Gran Canaria in the Mediterranean are all popular with gay travellers. In the UK the fastest emerging destination is Manchester. The city has a gay and lesbian population of 300 000 which has created a more gay-friendly atmosphere and provided the infrastructure for the Phoenix Mall Project, whose businesses include many types of gay-friendly stores and services, as well as bars and restaurants.[68] This, Europe's first gay shopping mall, opened in early December 1996 in an old textile mill in the city's Gay Village.

The largest and most significant gay event for Manchester, however, is its annual *Mardi Gras*, previously known as the 'Carnival of Fun', 'Tickled Pink' and the 'Absolutely Fabulous Event of the Year'. The event began as a small-scale one-day street market in 1991 and has grown into a four-day festival attracting 60 000–80 000 person visits.[69] The festival currently includes carnival parades, fireworks displays, a funfair, street markets, discos and a candle vigil commemorating those who have died from AIDS. The event organisers are the Village Charity, a group which sees it not only as a fun festival but also as a vehicle to break down barriers, to raise HIV and AIDS awareness and, most importantly, to raise funds for its Aids projects and charities in North West England.[70]

Manchester's success as one of the few UK cities to attract the gay visitor and to capitalise on the market's spending power has, however, become a victim of its own success. The popularity and size of the *Mardi Gras* is threatening the Village's ability to accommodate it, but of more concern for the gay community is the fact that both the Village and the festival are losing their *gay* identities. The Gay Village Guide itself comments that 'this unique and very gay British phenomenon may be degayed' as more and more straight visitors to the city are drawn to its excellent bars, restaurants and cafes.[71] Such a process may, as Hindle, Whittle and Hughes have argued, echo degaying processes elsewhere.[72] Here it may alienate many of the Village's gay visitors, since 'for many gay people it is no longer a safe place', whereas 'a gay bar was a safe place inside for lesbian, gay and other queer people – a place where you finally be yourself – you could drop the mask'.[73]

Concern within the Village about this degaying process is typified by one Village employee who commented that if gay culture 'gets diluted any more than it has already, I wouldn't be surprised if the Village just ups and moves'.[74]

Case study 6.3 highlights why notions of space and place have particular significance for both the homosexual and the heterosexual communities. Public gay space provides an open challenge to the heterosexual nature of the street whilst providing homosexuals with an arena in which heterosexism can be resisted. The emergence of gay festivals can be viewed in similar terms. However, as discussed earlier, the nature and content of public spaces is continually being negotiated and fought over – gay spaces are as much open to challenge as are heterosexual spaces. Both communities are in competition, which can be violent but is also manifested in other, more subtle ways. As the discussion of degaying in Manchester highlighted, gay spaces are undergoing a process of touristification and it would be naive to believe that this process is somehow immune from the forces and power relationships which structure society. Whilst the touristification of gay space may seem to indicate a heterosexual acceptance and even an embracing of those spaces, it could equally be viewed as a more effective means to re-establish heterosexual dominance. As Valentine has argued, 'control over the way space is produced is fundamental to heterosexuals' ability to reproduce their hegemony'.[75]

Gay spaces are centres of empowerment and cultural strength for the homosexual community and the degaying of gay festivals signals both a heterosexual invasion and consumption of this space and a challenge to the hard-won power and control of 'gay' streets. The challenge posed by degaying is as much a threat to gay space, place and public identity as state legislation or civilian disapproval and aggression. Its implications are at least twofold: from the heterosexual perspective it could signal a new development in the maintenance of heterosexual hegemony, and from the homosexual perspective it could represent disempowerment, disenfranchisement and a loss of control over place and space.

The ageist image

In a similar way to the experience of gay consumers, older people have also long been marginalised as a significant market segment. As we outlined in Chapter 5, however, one of the biggest marketing challenges in the late 1990s will be the record numbers of senior citizens in most of the developed countries of the world – the tourism-generating countries. Older people and their needs will become increasingly important to post-industrial societies in ways they have never been before, in any place or time. This mature and informed segment is already impacting on tourism, demanding high standards and value for money. They are today's discerning travellers with the time and financial resources to travel and whilst the propensity to travel amongst the older age groups has traditionally been relatively low, today's seniors are reversing that trend.

In the USA half of all over-65's already take vacations and their vacation expenditure is above average. In Canada the seniors are the fastest growing segment of the tourism market.[76] The European Travel Intelligence Centre predicts that by the year 2000 total travel by Europe's seniors will be 80% above the 1990 level.[77] Their relatively high disposable incomes are the result of two factors: earned income and inheritance. For instance, the 45–59 year old age group have amongst the highest levels of earned income of any group. Moreover, despite the exaggerated importance of inherited income and decreasing mortgage costs, the real value of inheritance has been predicted to rise by 50% during the 1990s and over half of this will go to the 45–59 age group.[78]

However, it is not simply the sheer numbers and disposable income of potential tourists in the older age groups which attracts the interest of tourism marketers – it is also the lifestyles of many of them. It has been said that the 'third age' in particular is as much 'an aspirational category as a new demographic classification, as much a personal affair as a collective circumstance'.[79] The relevance of this senior segment to tourism marketers is, therefore, of crucial importance. Even if its full potential is only partially realised, it implies the existence of a large cohort of older consumers with very different lifestyles and consumption habits from older people in the past. Targeting this market should be of critical importance to tourism professionals since for the first time it has the ability to make choices about consumption habits and, unconstrained by the responsibilities of employment and child-care, this group are increasingly able to enjoy leisure and travel – almost half of the people taking winter holidays in the UK are aged between 45 and 65.[80]

There is considerable evidence that the travel industry is increasingly aware of the lucrative nature of this emerging segment. Case study 6.4 examines the response of the UK travel industry to the seniors market. The UK industry has a long history of targeting the seniors, particularly through Saga – the best-known operator in this sector. The growth in the seniors vacation market has stimulated all of the major UK operators (First Choice, Cosmos, Sunworld etc.) to develop packages specifically designed to attract them. Nevertheless, despite the appearance of these packages, there remains considerable doubt whether marketers really *understand* older consumers and recent research suggests that many marketers and market researchers still ignore older people.[81] It seems that many marketers regard them as only responsive to price inducements or as too old to be persuaded to try new products and/or switch brands. It has also been argued that many marketers take the view that it is young consumers who are the future for their products.[82] At the same time, many older people are rejecting much of the advertising for the products they are likely to buy as the implicit assumption in the style and tone of the messages is that they are not the intended market. 'Lifestyle' advertising is seen as patronising in tone and content and stereotypical seniors in casting and styling – as they are on tourism brochures – are particularly disliked.[83]

Case Study 6.4   UK Tour Operators' Marketing and the Seniors Market

There appears to be some mismatch between the current mainstream marketing messages and the expectations and needs of older tourists. Whilst over a third of the UK population is over 45 years of age, there are very few images of tourists in short- or long-haul tourism brochures which actually represent these age groups. For instance, Middleton identified long-haul destinations as appealing to older, more affluent experienced travellers,[84] yet an examination of these brochures reveals an almost total absence of any tourists over the age of 40. Where older people are portrayed they are passive, non-threatening members of the host community, appearing as 'background' or 'local colour'. There is little evidence of the existence of the affluent, active, culturally-hungry older traveller. Instead, young couples dominate the long-haul and families the short-haul brochures.

It is only in the marketing literature promoting travel products specifically targeted at these age groups that older tourists are portrayed. However, analysis of these suggests that many operators do not seem to know how to represent this segment. There is an overwhelming emphasis on accommodation and product imagery. Few photographs focus on people – where older people are the main focus of the imagery, they are only portrayed undertaking a very narrow range of vacation activities. Leisure pursuits are limited and few images appear of older people participating in outdoor activities such as walking, playing golf, swimming, cycling or playing tennis, even though these activities are often available in the destinations and have relatively high participation rates amongst older people.[85] Instead the brochures emphasise 'traditional' leisure pursuits for seniors including ballroom dancing, bingo and bowls. Quizzes, tea dances and 'sing-alongs' are also heavily featured.

Whilst these are popular activities for some, but not all, segments of the fourth-age segment, it is highly questionable how relevant they are for many third-agers. Given the growing body of research which indicates that seniors undertake a wide range of activities on vacation, it is surprising that there are so many images of empty swimming pools and so few images of seniors enjoying them. Similarly, with evidence of seniors' interest in culture and sightseeing, few images reflect these activities. Women are particularly narrowly represented in the marketing literature. With the exception of keep fit activities and dancing, very few older women are portrayed in active leisure pursuits.

Seniors' responses

There is overwhelming evidence that older people do not think of themselves as old and should not be treated as such. Research consistently suggests that people's perceptions of their ages are more important in determining behaviour than their chronological ages. People may have a number of cognitive or perceived ages. Elderly consumers perceive themselves to be younger than their chronological age on four perceived age dimensions: feel age (how old they feel), look age (how old they look), do age (how involved in activities they are favoured by a specific age group) and interest age (how similar their interests are to a specific age group). Elderly consumers have relatively younger cognitive or ideal ages than their chronological ages.[86] Despite this evidence, qualitative research supports the argument that marketers regard these consumers as uniformly 'old'. Many seniors do not feel that the tourism industry caters for them. Many tend to reject the brochures aimed at them and make their own arrangements. Interestingly many (including a high number of people over 70) do not feel that they are old enough to go on the typical seniors package holidays.[87]

The ethnocentric image

As marketers have made mistakes in their failure to recognise the needs of older consumers (as well as female and gay consumers), the tourism image emerges as not just (hetero-) sexist and ageist, but also ethnocentric. Despite the emergence of relatively significant numbers of affluent, non-white consumers discussed in Chapter 5, looking through the tourism marketing literature, one might be forgiven for concluding that there is still really only one kind of tourist and that that tourist is most definitely white. Despite the multi-racial nature of many tourism generating countries, there are very few non-white faces to be seen as tourists. On the very rare occasions where non-whites do feature, they are almost exclusively black – Asians and Hispanics never feature. Whilst the ethnocentric nature of the tourism image is evident in the dearth of non-white tourists in brochures, on posters and in television commercials, the prevalence and the insidious nature of ethnocentrism can be clearly understood in the context of heritage promotion.

In a discussion of the role of power, place and position in the development of heritage tourism, Hollinshead comments that heritage, legends and myths are not 'innocuous storylines and neutral projections about the past, but . . . collective coercive acts'.[88] Certain truths are sanctioned, others are not, empowering some groups, marginalising others. As we mentioned in Chapter 1 and will return to in Chapter 10, the construction of heritage tourism and its promotion is at some times, a 'pasteurization of the state's public past',[89] at others, a virtual fabrication of history. Thus, Urry has commented that in the UK the heritage industry largely tells a white story, ignoring those aspects of history which may make the majority feel uncomfortable or which may reveal unpleasant aspects of their past. One example he discusses is the Maritime Museum in Liverpool's Albert Dock which includes no interpretation or comment 'on the complex patterns of ethnic sub-ordination which has produced in Liverpool one of the most racist cities in Britain'.[90]

The racialised realities of history are similarly ignored in much of the main-stream marketing material used to promote the Southern States of America. It is marketed with images which are unchanged from those described by Mellinger as current in the early twentieth century. Then the South appeared as a region of 'broad plantations draped in Spanish Moss and magnolias'.[91] Today, in *Mississippi, The South's Warmest Welcome* we are invited into 'The South of magnolia trees and paddle wheel river boats, of cotton plantations, and Civil War battlefields, of white-columned antebellum mansions and live oak trees swathed in Spanish moss. . . .'[92] Tourists are thus presented with a history neatly packaged and transformed. The emphasis is on plantation owners and their southern belles, no mention is made of the fact that the State was built on slavery: 'Mississippi was given its wealth by the cotton planters, river boat tycoons and enterprising merchants who developed the rich lands.'[93] In Mississippi's *Civil War* Guide slavery is briefly mentioned as 'the catalyst issue' but it is made clear that '"Billy Yank" fought to preserve the Union; "Johnny Reb" to ensure states' rights.'[94]

Whilst this sanitised, ethnocentric interpretation of Southern history is promoted in the general literature, a very different view appears in brochures such as *Alabama's Black Heritage* – material produced for America's emerging black tourist market. In many ways, we are witnessing the construction and telling of *two distinct histories*, one which largely ignores the oppressive role of the white majority and one which documents 'the struggles, triumphs, losses, and gains'[95] of the civil rights movement. If we accept that places, peoples and identities are fundamentally shaped by representations of their past, this is a significant manifestation of how power and tourism interact.[96] Heritage tourism products are emerging which are aimed at a black as well as a white tourist gaze, but they tell contrasting stories – different scripts for different segments (case study 6.5).

The appearance of tourism products marketed specifically to a black audience reflects the emergence of African-Americans as the fastest-growing segment of the US travel market, a trend which itself reveals the growing economic power of that particular community.[97] Until recently, however, it was a largely unexplored market which in itself reveals much about the extent of white ideological hegemony in the industry, a dominance reinforced by the travel media who do much to 'provide the framework for perceiving reality'.[98] In the late Seventies the African-American travel market was estimated to be worth just over $7 billion, but by the beginning of the Nineties this figure had grown to $25 billion.[99] Ten million black Americans attend an historical or cultural event each year[100] and the minority business meetings market is worth an estimated $10 billion annually.[101] Moreover, research indicates that African-American convention delegates spend around one and a half times more per delegate per visit than their white counterparts and are much more likely to extend their business visit into a family short vacation.[102] To cater for this lucrative market image creators from Ontario to Philadelphia, Alabama and Louisiana are beginning to promote products specifically aimed at black tourists.

Case Study 6.5 Alabama Embraces its Black Heritage

Alabama is the first state to produce an official guide to its African-American heritage. It invites people to visit a South which is in stark contrast to that of the white plantation owners, of colonnaded mansions and magnolia trees: this is a South of black struggle, enterprise and achievement. *Alabama's Black Heritage* guide contains information on over 300 historic sites, lists key dates in the black struggle for civil rights and offers black heritage tours for visitors who prefer a more structured experience. These include: the Civil Rights Trail; the Martin Luther King Jr Pilgrimage; and the Two Centuries of Black History tour. These initiatives aim to achieve not just a better understanding of black history, but also to promote awareness of the consequences of racism. Richard Arrington Jr, Mayor of Birmingham, Alabama, introduces the Civil Rights District by saying:

> We hope we can try to tell our own story. We want to help ourselves and others understand what happened here, why it happened, and how we overcame the violence through nonviolence and changed the nation.[103]

We are reading a very different script here from that presented in the main marketing literature which largely ignores white oppression. As Odessa Woolfolk, president of the Birmingham Civil Rights Institute Board, comments: '. . . we are saying we no longer hide from our history. We recognize that we were once a city that housed two people, black and white . . . . Now we are a different city, embracing our past and . . . utilizing it as a guidepost for the future.'[104]

Windsor, Ontario has a plethora of historic sites relating to the efforts of African-Americans to achieve freedom from slavery in the nineteenth century. These include the home of Josiah Hensen, a fugitive slave and the man on whom Harriet Beecher Stowe based *Uncle Tom's Cabin*.[105] Windsor has packaged these heritage attractions in an attempt to become a destination for black Americans 'hungry to learn about their past'.[106] In 1991 its Convention Bureau launched the African American Heritage Tour which includes the North American Black Historical Museum, the John Freeman Walls Historic Site, the Elgin Settlement and the Rosa Parks Peace Chapel and in 1997 will launch 'The Road That Led to Freedom' reaching from Ontario to Louisiana.[107] Other cities which are trying to attract this market include Philadelphia, whose Convention and Visitors Bureau in 1994 produced a guide to the city's African-American historical and cultural attractions – over 60 of which 'reflected the history of Black Americans in the "City of Brotherly Love"'.[108]

The Philadelphia initiative, as Tamara Real points out, is a good example of strategies employed to market to a culturally-distinct group. It avoided some of the mistakes which can characterise such initiatives by working in close collaboration with community leaders and travel professionals – of particular importance being the establishment of an ongoing hospitality programme directed by African-Americans prominent in the local travel industry.[109] This development raises important questions which merit further investigation but which can only be posed in this text. Who is developing these new tourism products, which images are being constructed and, above all, whose versions of history are being articulated?

It is being recognised – albeit slowly – that black tourists (like female, gay and older tourists) do have specific needs – they are a market segment in their own right. Additional considerations for those attempting to attract African-American travellers include: attractions of specific interest to African-Americans; service provisions for black travellers (such as comfort and welcome afforded to black travellers and a sensitivity to their needs); and promotional material which reflects cultural diversity.[110] This recognition of the requirements of black travellers is relatively new, however – as Real says – the Windsor Convention Bureau 'luckily discovered its gold mine just as interest in African-American travel opportunities was emerging'.[111]

However fortuitous, it is an example of how the tourism industry can widen both the products and the range of images aimed at tourists. In this instance we see what Berry and Manning-Miller have described as the 'slight increase in the number . . . and . . . kinds of images' of African-Americans appearing in the contemporary media.[112] At this stage we need to ask what happens when the tourist gaze is no longer white, male or heterosexual? To date, as Hollinshead comments: 'the knowledge base of mainstream and dominant heritage interpretations in tourism . . . is anthropocentric . . . androcentric . . . Anglocentric.'[113] Will the rise of previously disenfranchised segments challenge these prevailing ideologies and create new tourism discourses? It is much too soon to comment as we are only seeing the beginnings of the process, but, as we discuss in Chapter 7, we can discern how changing political and cultural circumstances is leading to shifts in the tourism identities of products, peoples and places.

References

1   Urry, J. (1990) *The Tourist Gaze. Leisure and Travel in Contemporary Societies*, Sage, London: 142.
2   Breathnach, P. *et al.* (1994) 'Gender in Irish Tourism Employment', 52–73 in Kinnaird, V. and Hall, D. (eds) *Tourism: a Gender Analysis*, John Wiley and Sons, Chichester.
3   Smith, W.R. (1956) 'Product differentiation and market segmentation as alternative marketing strategies', *Journal of Marketing*, 21, July.
4   Theodore Levitt, quoted by Silvester, S. (1994) Why Pretesting Sucks, speech to the Association of Qualitative Research Practitioners. Background Papers, Market Research Society, Advertising Research Seminar.
5   See, for instance, Schiffman, L.G. and Kanuk, L.L. (1994) *Consumer Behaviour*, Prentice Hall, 5th ed., 47; Loudon, D.L. and Della Bitta, A.J. (1993) *Consumer Behaviour*, McGraw-Hill, 4th ed., 31; and Solomon, M.R. (1994) *Consumer Behaviour*, 2nd ed., Allyn and Bacon: 11.
6   Chisnall, P.M. (1994) *Consumer Behaviour*, McGraw Hill, 3rd ed., 373

7   Sheth, J.N. (1967) 'A review of buyer behaviour', *Management Science*, (13) 12, August.
8   Nichols, B. (1981) *Ideology and the Image*, Bloomington, Indiana University Press: 1.
9   ibid.
10 *Holiday Which* (1992) 'Travelling Solo': 170–71.
11 Pritchard, A. and Morgan, N.J. (1997) 'The Gay Consumer: A Viable Market Segment?', *Journal of Targeting, Measurement and Analysis for Marketing*, 6 (1): 9–20.
12 McGee, R. (1988) 'What do women business travellers really want?', *Successful Marketing*, 37 (9): 55–7: 56.
13 Weedon (1987) 2–3, quoted in Clegg, S.R. (1989) *Frameworks of Power*, Sage, London: 149–50.
14 Ritchie, K. (1995) *Marketing to Generation X*, Lexington Books, New York: 3.
15 reference 14: 19.
16 Zellner, W. *et al.* (1994) 'Women Entrepreneurs', *Business Week*, 3367: 104–10: 104.
17 'Kinder, Kirche, Korporation. . . .', *Holland Herald*, June 1996, KLM.
18 Chetwynd, C. (1995) 'Travails of a lone woman', *The Times*, 3 November: 7.
19 Nelson, C. (1994) *How to Market to Women*, Visible Ink Press, Detroit: 233.
20 reference 12: 55.
21 quoted in Westwood, S. (1997) A Missed Marketing Opportunity? Is the Airline Industry Catering for the Needs of Today's Business Woman?, University of Wales Institute, Cardiff, unpublished dissertation: 24.
22 reference 12: 56.
23 ibid.
24 British Airways (1990), quoted in Westwood, S. (1997), *op cit.*
25 Chambers Travel (1995) The Business Woman Traveller Survey, Chambers Travel, quoted in Westwood, S. (1997), *op cit.*
26 see also Reed Travel Group (1996) Official Airline Guides 1996 Survey – OAG Business Travel Lifestyle Survey: 23 and 25; and Westwood, S. (1997), *op cit.*
27 Marketing Manager Air UK, quoted in Westwood, S. (1997), *op cit*: 32.
28 Research Manager Virgin Atlantic, quoted in Westwood, S. (1997), *op cit*: 32.
29 Millum, T. (1974) *Images of Women: Advertising in Women's Magazines*, Chatto and Windus, London: 58.
30 Simmel in reference 29: 70.
31 Nelson, C. (1994) *How to Market to Women*, Visible Ink Press, Detroit: 234.
32 Mintel Marketing Intelligence (1996) Business Travel Mintel Intelligence Group Ltd, London, October.
33 Marshall, S. (1996) 'Out of date images anger young women', *Marketing*, 30 May: 11; and Marshall, S. (1996) 'Women "fed up" with sexist ads', *Marketing*, 28 November: 12.
34 Kinnaird, V. and Hall, D. (1994) (eds) *Tourism: a Gender Analysis*, John Wiley and Sons, Chichester: 146.
35 Westwood, S. (1997) A Missed Marketing Opportunity? Is the Airline Industry Catering for the Needs of Today's Business Woman?, University of Wales Institute, Cardiff, unpublished dissertation: 59.
36 Matthews (1996) commentary on reaction by Association of Women Business Travellers: 8, quoted in Westwood, S. (1997), *op cit.*
37 Westwood, S. (1997) *op cit*: 60.
38 Westwood, S. (1997) *op cit*: 75.
39 Westwood, S. (1997) *op cit*: 75.
40 Westwood, S. (1997) *op cit*: 78.
41 Westwood, S. (1997) *op cit*: 81.
42 Westwood, S. (1997) *op cit*: 85.
43 Westwood, S. (1997) *op cit*: 90–1.
44 Rogers, L. and Harlow, J. (1995) 'Return of the Sun and Sex Holiday', quoted in Prichard, A. and Morgan, N.J. (1996) 'Sex Still Sells to Generation X: Promotional practice in the youth package holiday market', *Journal of Vacation Marketing*, December 3 (4): 69–80: 75.

45   Moore, S. (1987) 'Target Man', *New Statesman*, January; and Pritchard, A. (1992) Images of Masculinity and Femininity in Magazine Advertising: A Case Study of Playboy and GQ, unpublished University of Wales M.Sc Econ. dissertation.
46   reference 34: 213.
47   Foucault, M. (1978) *The History of Sexuality*, Allen Lane/Penguin Books, Harmondsworth.
48   Amnesty International report detailing persecution of gays across the third world, quoted in *The Observer*, 23 February 1997: 20; and *The Guardian*, 23 August 1995, quoted in Hughes, H. (1997) 'Holidays and Homosexual Identity', *Tourism Management*, 18 (1): 6.
49   *Spartacus* (1996).
50   quoted in *Observer Life* magazine, 23 February 1997: 50.
51   Bristow, J. (1989) 'Being Gay: politics, pleasure and identity', *New Formations*, 9: 61–81: 74.
52   Valentine, G. (1996) '(Re)negotiating the Heterosexual Street', 146–55 in Duncan, N. (ed.) *Bodyspace. Destabilizing geographies of gender and sexuality*, Routledge, London: 146.
53   reference 52: 149.
54   Myslik, W.D. (1996) 'Renegotiating the Social/Sexual Identities of Places', 156–169 in Duncan, N. (ed.) *Bodyspace. Destabilizing geographies of gender and sexuality*, Routledge, London: 160.
55   reference 52: 152–3.
56   reference 54: 157.
57   reference 54: 162.
58   reference 54: 167.
59   Schulz, C. (1994), 'Fill The Valleys Between Your Peak Occupancies', *Hotels*, June: 72.
60   Holcomb, B. and Luongo, M. (1996) 'Gay Tourism in the United States', *Annals of Tourism Research*, August 711–13: 711.
61   ibid.
62   Tourism Industry Intelligence (1994) 'Focus on the Gay Market', *Tourism Industry Intelligence*, 2 (1): 3.
63   reference 60.
64   Hughes, H. (1997) 'Holidays and Homosexual Identity', *Tourism Management*, 18 (1).
65   Mulryan, D. (1995) 'Reaching the gay market', *American Demographics*, 17, May, 46–48: 46; Button, K. (1993) 'The gay consumer', *The Financial Times*, 9 September: 18 and advertisement for the 1996 Sydney Gay and Lesbian Mardi Gras in *Attitude*, February 1996.
66   'Resorts are embracing the all-inclusive trend', *USA Today International*, Monday 11 November 1996: 8A.
67   'The Invasion of the Big Hairy Lesbians', 12 July 1997 Channel 4 TV programme.
68   Channel 4 News Programme, May 1996.
69   Manchester City Council, Arts and Leisure Committee. Equal Opportunities and Anti-Discrimination Sub-Committee, March 1996.
70   ibid.
71   Manchester Gay Village Guide, Healthy Gay Manchester and Manchester City Council, 1996.
72   Hindle, P. (1994) 'Gay Communities and Gay Space in the City', 7–25 in Whittle, S. (ed.) *The Margins of the City: Gay Men's Urban Lives*, Arena, Aldershot; Whittle, S. (1994) 'Cultural Differences: The Collaboration of the Gay Body Within the Cultural State', 27–41 in Whittle, S. (ed.) *The Margins of the City: Gay Men's Urban Lives*, Arena, Aldershot; and Hughes, H. (1997) 'Holidays and Homosexual Identity', *Tourism Management*, 18 (1).
73   Whittle, S. (1994) 'Cultural Differences. The Collaboration of the Gay Body Within the Cultural State', 27–41 in Whittle, S. (ed.) *The Margins of the City: Gay Men's Urban Lives*, Arena, Aldershot: 38.
74   *Independent on Sunday*, 9 June 1996. 5.

75 Valentine, G. (1996) '(Re)negotiating the Heterosexual Street', 146–55 in Duncan, N. (ed.) *Bodyspace. Destabilizing geographies of gender and sexuality*, Routledge, London: 154.

76 Romsa, G. (1992) 'Behaviour Patterns of Elderly German Tourists 1979–89', R20–R37 in the Proceedings of Tourism in Europe the 1992 Conference, Durham, the Centre for Travel and Tourism.

77 'Today's older consumers: an emerging third age of personal fulfilment or a wasted era of frustrated possibilities?', Henley Centre, *Leisure Futures*, 1, 1994: 100.

78 'Time Use', Henley Centre, *Leisure Futures*, 3, 1992: 30–32: 30.

79 reference 77: 7.

80 Elliott, H. (1995) 'Australia Beckons', *The Times*, 13 April.

81 Salmon, B. (1994) Third Agers and Brand Loyalty, unpublished paper by The Research Business.

82 ibid.

83 ibid.

84 Middleton, V.T.C. (1994) *Marketing in Travel and Tourism*, 2nd ed., Butterworth Heinemann, Oxford: 135.

85 Sports Council for Wales (1994) Participation in Sport and Leisure, Sports Update, Sports Council for Wales, Cardiff.

86 Schiffman, L.G. and Kanuk, L.L. (1994) *Consumer Behaviour*, Prentice Hall, 5th ed.: 462–3.

87 Morgan, N.J. and Pritchard, A. (1997) 'Seniors Tourism: A Marketing Challenge for the Next Millennium?, paper presented at the 10th European Leisure and Recreation Association Congress, Dubrovnik.

88 Hollinshead, K. (1996) 'Culture and Capillary Power: Texas and the Quiet Annihilation of the Past', 49–98 in Robinson, M. *et al.* (1996) *Tourism and Culture: Image, Identity and Marketing*, Centre for Travel and Tourism, Sunderland: 50.

89 reference 88: 57.

90 reference 1: 143.

91 Mellinger, W.M. (1994) 'Towards a Critical Analysis of Tourism Representation', *Annals of Tourism Research*, 21 (4): 756–779: 761.

92 Mississippi Department of Economic and Community Development (1997) *Mississippi, The South's Warmest Welcome*, London: 2.

93 ibid.

94 ibid.

95 Alabama Bureau of Tourism and Travel, *Alabama's Black Heritage*, Alabama: 4.

96 reference 88: 50.

97 Richter, L.K. (1995) 'Gender and Race: Neglected Variables in Tourism Research', 71–91 in Butler, R. and Pearce, D. (eds) *Change in Tourism. People, Places, Processes*, Routledge, London: 74.

98 Hall, S. (1981) 'Television as expression of ideology' *Communication Research Trends*, 2 (3): 5–6.

99 reference 97: quoting *Travelling the Globe 1990–91*: 53–56.

100 Real, T. (1996) 'Looking Good: How Cultural Tourism has changed the face of North American Travel Destinations', 171–184 in Robinson, M. *et al.* (ed.) *Tourism and Culture: Image, Identity and Marketing*, Centre for Travel and Tourism, Sunderland: 178.

101 reference 100: 179.

102 ibid.

103 'Living Black History', *Alabama's Black Heritage*, Alabama Bureau of Tourism and Travel, Montgomery, Alabama: 9.

104 ibid.

105 reference 100: 177.

106 reference 100: 171.

107 reference 100: 178.

108 reference 100: 180.

109 ibid.
110 1991 study conducted by the National Coalition of Black Meeting Planners, quoted in reference 100.
111 reference 100: 178.
112 Berry, V.T. and Manning-Miller, C.L. (1996) (eds) 'Introduction' in *Mediated Messages and African-American Culture*, Sage, Thousand Oaks California: xii–xiii.
113 reference 88: 86.

7 Branding, identity and power

Chapter 5 outlined the fragmentation of global identities and their implications for tourism marketing, a fragmentation which, as we suggested in Chapter 6, is beginning to impact on market segmentation, if only on the margins. In this chapter we continue the theme of marketing responses to a changing world, but focus particularly on another key marketing technique – branding. Branding is a familiar term in tourism marketing and, whilst we review its role briefly, our main emphasis is to argue that branding exercises, just like advertising images themselves, can be read at a number of levels: branding says much about power and discourse, and is equally reflective of global power relationships and the dominant ways of seeing the world.

Most discussions of branding have been marketing-orientated, and have therefore been more concerned with the marketing impact of the various strategies than with their sociological implications. They discuss, for example, the relative success of branding the seaside resort of Torbay as *The English Riviera* in the early Eighties[1] or of rebranding the hotel group Trust House Forte as *Forte* in the early Nineties.[2] The key interests of studies such as these are the rationales behind, and impacts of, branding campaigns. Whilst these are clearly crucial questions, such analyses can overlook other, equally significant issues. The brand images, values and propositions used to promote tourism organisations, products and places are grounded in various discourses and reveal how companies and destinations *see* the world and their place in it. As this chapter's first two case studies reveal, something of the politics of branding can be seen in the activities of private sector organisations such as British Airways and P&O Cruises as they reposition to maintain or increase their industry share in a shifting marketplace.

Managing change is not just about companies responding to a shifting external situation – it is also about recognising a changing internal situation. Whilst many branding analyses have examined the former, few have considered the latter, particularly where the tourism product is a destination. The spotlight has never focused on what rebranding – the promotion of a new identity – means for such places and their peoples. This is where analyses based purely on marketing criteria can be one-dimensional as few reveal that places can reposition as much for themselves as for an external audience. Identities are never static or monolithic yet attempts to re-present changed identities are often time consuming and expensive, particularly as they can challenge concepts and ideas which can be deeply rooted in the popular psyche, are often drawn from popular culture and which conform to prevailing ideologies.

The second half of the chapter highlights what such re-creations of destination identities reveal about power and tourism discourses, and we illustrate the discussion by focusing on the emergent destinations of Eastern Europe, on the Balearic Island of Majorca and on Wales in the UK. In Eastern Europe, something of a political and cultural renaissance is in progress as countries previously subordinated to Moscow seek to redefine their national, ethnic and cultural identities. In a similar fashion, Majorca is attempting to shed its former identity, associated with sun and sangria, in an attempt to reclaim its Catalan identity and culture eroded by popular tourism and cultural practices. Finally, Wales could also be described as a country at a crossroads – politically, economically, culturally and socially. Its attempt to redefine its identity, particularly in relation to the overseas tourism market, can be read not merely as an attempt to attract more tourists, but as an attempt to reclaim and reaffirm Wales and Welshness – concepts which, as we shall discuss, have been subject to powerful discourses which have tried to erase the challenge of a separate culture in the predominantly anglicised UK.

Branding, services and power

In tourism marketing, 'brand' is understood to represent an unique combination of product characteristics and added values, both functional and non-functional, which have taken on a relevant meaning which is inextricably linked to that brand, awareness of which might be conscious or intuitive. Brand advantage can be secured through image-building campaigns which highlight the specific benefits of a product, culminating in an overall impression of a superior brand. Huge sums of money are expended annually on such image promotion. Global megabrands like McDonalds, Nike and Coca-Cola have brand symbols which are recognisable in any language or culture. The Coke symbol, for example, is reputed to be worth $35 billion for its recognition value alone. The Shell and McDonald's logos are two of the world's three most recognised symbols, recognised by almost 90% of the global population and exceeded only by the rings symbol of the Olympic Association. This places the recognition value of commercial brands well above religious symbols such as the Christian Cross, which is recognised by about half of the global population.[3]

As recently as 1993 when, on 'Marlboro Friday', the financial markets cut Philip Morris' value by $13 billion in one day, marketing gurus declared 'Brands are dead.' If it could happen to a giant like Marlboro, it could happen to any brand and the media quickly proclaimed the Nineties a 'value decade', arguing that consumers would always shop for the lowest price and buy only on sale.[4] Within two years, however, Marlboro's US market share reached an all-time high of 31% as Philip Morris created 'a Marlboro steamroller' based on the courageous strategy of doubling advertising spend and cutting back on coupons and price-off programmes which 'cheapened the Marlboro image'.[5] It does seem that predictions of the death of brands were premature and today branding remains as powerful a global marketing device as ever. Furthermore, whilst many western marketers were moving away from brand building, their Asian counterparts were energetically building theirs up and the Asian success has been to build brands not around products, but around reputations. The great Asian names imply quality, price and innovation rather than a specific item, they are 'attribute brands' which relate to a set of values. Thus, Mitsubishi is everything from a bank to a car manufacturer to a textiles and an electrical goods manufacturer. In fact, Mitsubishi is not a single company at all but a brand name that belongs to several companies.[6]

The managers of these 'attribute brands' recognise that the image their product has in the consumer's mind, how it is *positioned*, is of more importance to its ultimate success than its actual characteristics. Brand managers try to position their brands so that they are perceived by the consumer to occupy a niche in the marketplace occupied by no other brand. They try to differentiate their product by stressing attributes they claim will match the target markets' needs more closely than other brands and then they try to create a product image consistent with the perceived self-image of the targeted consumer segment. As such, they appeal to consumers' values and self-images and in doing so they are thereby appealing to the powerful discourses which have shaped those self-same values and images. Such is the power of positioning that it has been described as 'the essence of the marketing mix',[7] embodying the concept or essence of the product. It therefore conveys how the product will satisfy a consumer need, and different consumer meanings can be assigned to the same product via different product images. In this way it can be positioned differently to simultaneously appeal to different market segments and it can subsequently be repositioned for the same or a different audience in the later phases of its life cycle. As we outlined in Chapter 2, when consumers make brand choices about tourism services and destinations (as with other products) they are making lifestyle statements since they are trying to buy into an image.[8]

In today's communication-saturated society, it is imperative to create a unique product image in the consumer's mind. Whilst the first priority of brand managers should be to increase the average net value of a brand – or how much consumers like it on average – their second priority should be to increase its distinctiveness. In other words, 'to develop the ability of the brand to "polarise" consumers by differentially developing its appeal to those consumers to whom it is particularly suited'.[9] This also has the effect of reducing the risk of competing head-to-head with other similar products in the market. The result of a successful positioning strategy is a distinctive brand image on which customers rely in making product choices. In developing these brand images, however, brand managers draw on distinctive social and cultural markers to frame their brand identities.

Whatever brands are saying, in today's marketplace, it is becoming more and more critical for brands to be able to 'shout above the crowd'.[10] As recently as the early Eighties, brand managers knew that if they spent enough money on a campaign some of it would work, but in the late 1990s they have to communicate with an increasingly sophisticated audience, whilst both the marketplace and the media have fragmented. Mass markets have been transformed into niche markets, each with their particular needs, wants, desires and resources; consumer choice has exploded; and at the same time, media choices have grown beyond all recognition as new technology continues to push the media frontiers beyond previously established boundaries.

The discourse of branding

The *marketing power* of branding is undoubted, but what has yet to receive attention is what branding reveals about *cultural power*. The discourse of branding can be read in much the same way as any changes in tourism policy should be read. Any maintenance, alteration or redirection of branding strategies should therefore involve an exploration of:

> the socio-political conditions in which the political system operates . . . [in order] to explore the links between the environment, the political system and policy outputs and impacts.[11]

Such an exploration should consider the relationship between tourism marketing and ideology alongside issues of good or bad marketing practices. To date, however, the ideological aspects of branding have received relatively little attention, resulting in an incomplete analysis of a powerful political and cultural phenomenon. The branding of tourism products, in both the public and private sectors, must be analysed in terms of their relationship with the prevailing political, economic, and social systems – such analysis would address Hall's criticism that despite the importance of ideology, 'discussions of the ideological dimensions of tourism have been virtually non-existent'.[12]

Whilst such insights may be easier to find in place marketing, the discourse of branding can also be seen in private sector marketing. British Airways' (BA) 1997 launch of a new identity celebrated the world community and highlighted the airline's claim to be the first truly global carrier. This rebranding can be seen as a response to shifting contemporary power relationships, since the airline regarded its former identity – redolent with concepts of masculinity and colonialism – as inappropriate and disadvantageous in a dynamic and rapidly evolving global community. In contrast, in our second case study, the Oriana, the new flagship of P&O Cruises, is a branding exercise which re-emphasises the company's 'Britishness'. It can be read as a celebration of a certain era and identity which has largely vanished, but from which the organisation and one of its key market segments take comfort. The Oriana may thus represent the last echoes of empire and a desire for a world which has been largely lost. These two case studies represent very different responses to the shifting patterns discussed in Chapter 5, one embracing change, the other continuing to appeal to a notion of historic continuity.

Case Study 7.1   British Airways – Repositioning for a Global Consumer

Over three years – from 1997 to 2000 – British Airways (BA) will introduce a new corporate identity at a cost of £60 million. In June 1997 the new identity was launched simultaneously in 63 countries linked by satellite.[13] The rebranding emerges as a move to embrace globalization and planet Earth and shrug off empire and imperialism. BA, it could be argued, in removing the sober blue and red livery crest – itself an echo of the Union Jack   from its aeroplane tail fins is divesting itself of ethnocentrism and vestiges of imperialism. In rejecting a monolithic corporate identity in favour of a celebration of diversity and humanity, the company is attempting to demonstrate how it differs from its competitors. In future, its new livery will include 50 different 'ethnic' designs drawn from different parts of the globe from Poland to South Africa – a bold move to maintain brand consistency through diversity – portraying BA as 'British but modern; rooted in the UK heritage but at home wherever it travels.'[14]

In many ways, this new identity is merely the most outwardly visible sign of a massive organisational change necessary, so BA have argued, to meet the challenges which the next millennium will bring. A key aspect of this review is BA's decision to offer mono-lingual cabin staff voluntary redundancy and replace these crew with bi- or multi-lingual flight attendants who will be able to deal more effectively with BA's varied customer base. The airline's relationships with airlines in France, Germany, Australia and the US mean that it is handling ever greater numbers of foreign passengers and staff[15] and 60% of its passengers are now generated from outside the UK.[16] The company's change of identity is thus designed to show its customers that it is both 'global and caring' and able to deliver service to passengers of any background.[17] The airline wants to appear as warm and cosmopolitan, not as cold, aloof and chauvinistic – as a company with roots in a modern, not an imperial, Britain.

Whilst this new identity has been deliberately and very carefully chosen by the organisation, not surprisingly such a radical change of style has generated some controversy and criticism – especially in the UK. One very 'traditional' UK newspaper accused the airline of dropping its Britishness, of burning the flag and 'desecrating' what it used to proudly 'fly'.[18] The same newspaper also asked 'If the new, self-hating BA really finds Britishness so outmoded and nationalistic, then why not drop the word "British" altogether?'[19] Interestingly, the furore over BA's latest new look disguises the processes which lie behind its previous revamp in 1984. Then, BA went to San Francisco-based identity consultants, Lander Associates, to develop an identity which appeared 'British in a way that American customers would appreciate rather than authentically British to domestic flyers.' The result of this mid-Eighties re-imaging was the adoption of 'a heritage-themed identity focused on part of the Union flag and fake crest'.[20] Interestingly, this scripted identity was less that of Britain than 'Brit-ish', an identity crafted to appeal to a hugely powerful and profitable US market. In this sense, therefore, the current move to replace the crest with new global 'ethnic' designs, is less the removal of something which is authentic, and more the swapping of one artificially-crafted identity for another.

In embracing cultural expressions from around the globe, BA is presenting itself in a different, and it hopes, more attractive way, especially in the Asian market which regards BA's 'Britishness' as a hindrance.[21] This may well be a reflection that the Asian experience of empire is rather more familiar than that of the American market in the 1984 relaunch. As such, Wally Olins, founder of Wolff Olins (a corporate identity consultancy) commented that 'It may not be in BA's interest to appear to be too British any more.'[22] BA itself commented that: 'In the 1990s, "global and caring" does not mean post-imperialist flag-waving. It has to mean intelligently sensitive relations with customers and communities.'[23] The company also commented that 'Instead of being a British airline with global operations, British Airways has become a world airline whose headquarters happen to be in Britain.'[24] As a prediction with which to close, Adrian Day, Director of Lander Associates, predicted that the airline would, in years rather than decades, drop the word 'British' from its name altogether. He said: 'The company's quest is to become the first global airline. . .' – identities are becoming more flexible and the message is one of diversity – 'It makes sense for where the company is at the moment.'[25]

In contrast to BA's recognition of changing global power and the importance of newer markets in Asia, other companies are more concerned to appeal to existing powerful segments in the old world. Whilst BA looks forward and rejects post-imperialist flag-waving, companies like P&O, in rebranding their new cruise flagship the Oriana, embrace tradition to take them into the future. P&O's invocation of empire is an example of the power of tradition, in this case, one which uses strong colonial markers in a celebration of Britishness. It also represents the powerful pull of a current market possibly at the expense of emerging markets – after all, the ship has been designed in accordance with the brand values of the over-45 UK market. However, in selecting these brand values, it could be argued that future generations of cruisers – young couples, families and international travellers – may not appreciate an experience 'biased towards older, less sophisticated users'.[26] In trying to establish a brand for the Nineties and beyond, it may be that P&O has looked to currently powerful users but at the expense of emerging markets' preferences.

Case Study 7.2   Oriana – The Last Gasp of Empire?

The cruising market has grown rapidly throughout the 1980s and 1990s, particularly in the USA, and is often seen as one of the tourism industry's new frontiers. Whilst total UK passenger numbers leapt from 90 000 in 1986 to over a quarter of a million in 1993,[27] North America dominates the world cruise market, accounting for 60%, against 20% for Europe and 20% for the rest of the world.[28] The most dynamic geographical sub-markets are western and southern Caribbean, the Panama Canal, the Baltic and Black Seas, the Canaries, Antarctica, as well as the fastest growing markets of the Far East and South East Asia.[29] Clearly, the cruise industry is a global one. It is also one which is increasingly attracting younger markets, more family cruisers and more short-break cruisers, trends reflected by the entry of newer players, notably Disney Cruise Lines, into the market.[30]

Interestingly, when P&O was faced with the challenge of identifying key brand values for its proposed replacement to its flagship, the Canberra, it commissioned a study of *current* UK cruisers to discover the brand values associated both with the company and the Canberra. The aim was to establish which brand attributes could and should be transferred to the new ship to design 'the first cruise liner custom built for Britain'.[31] Thus, despite the global trends towards younger, more family-oriented cruisers, the company conducted research exclusively with the core of the UK market – ABC1 couples aged over 45 years. Based on these findings, the Oriana was launched in 1995, at a cost of over £200 million. Aside from the requirements for a variety of things to do, the brand attributes which were most valued by these customers included Britishness (in the form of officers and crew), the English language, and tea, or more specifically, the ability to have 'a good cup of tea' whenever it was desired.[32] The ship was christened by Elizabeth II[33] and the name was chosen for its British credentials. Dingle and Harding comment that it had to be 'British rather than international' and Oriana fitted the bill perfectly, having been the name of a sixteenth-century madrigal which celebrated the triumphs of Queen Elizabeth I, as well as being the name of an earlier P&O cruise ship.[34]

Designed for the British market and based on UK-based market research, the Oriana offers a very different experience from other ships that cater for the North American market. British officers were retained, and the ship's design has a more traditional appearance. It has open decks, a British pub, a smaller, more low-key casino and offers more restrained entertainment in 17 small venues as opposed to the few large ones more common in other cruise ships. In addition, the decor of the public rooms is much more sedate, echoing that of formal English drawing rooms. All the fixtures and furnishings are designed to convey quintessential Englishness, from the carpets, the Wedgwood china and Sheffield silverware to the richly designed library finished with English walnut. Indeed, *Porthole*, the premier US cruise magazine, describes the rooms as looking like 'a transplanted English gentleman's club [where]. . . you almost expect to meet old men in cravats sharing tales of the Raj'.[35]

In this example, we can see certain powerful processes at work, particularly the sway of tradition and existing segments. The Oriana was the newest flagship in a long line of P&O cruise ships but its destiny was inextricably linked with its predecessor, the Canberra, which possessed 'a strong history and a powerful brand personality',[36] associated with its role in the Falklands-Malvinas conflict of the early Eighties. Those qualities most valued by its consumers also echoed certain notions of empire and Englishness – attributes highly valued by the present main UK market for cruising, which is older and upscale. Whilst such values may well appeal to today's third agers, it is questionable whether they will have an enduring appeal for the younger market – the future cruisers. Moreover, whilst the sophistication and formality of a British cruising experience may well appeal to a number of international travellers, ignoring global tastes could alienate others. Thus, *Porthole*'s reviewer of the new ship comments that the Oriana's food is 'decidedly British' and places too much emphasis on red meat and fried foods and not enough on healthy alternatives.[37] Whereas the Oriana was intended to establish itself and P&O as 'the cruising brand for the 1990s and beyond',[38] such a strategy may well be compromised by its overwhelming focus on an existing market segment which is geographically and demographically limited.

Branding, places and power

The marketing of places has become increasingly competitive in recent decades and public sector marketing strategies are becoming ever more sophisticated as the stakes are raised. As Kotler, Haider and Rein comment:

> In our new world economy, every place must compete with other places for economic advantage. Various communities launch drives to attract business firms . . . tourists and conventioneers, sports teams, . . . all of which promise increased employment, income, trade, investment.[39]

Competition for place advantage in tourism extends to restaurants, facilities, sports, cultural amenities, and entertainment – there is a competition over which place has the most four-star hotels, best cuisine, most museums and theatres, and the top-ranked athletic facilities. This process has indeed become global at the end of the twentieth century and not only has the range of marketing tools and activities become more diverse, but the rewards are now enormous. It is estimated that Atlanta, Georgia, in staging the 1996 Summer Olympic Games, secured approximately $3 billion for the city's businesses and citizens.[40]

Discussions of image are gaining increasing importance as tourism expands around the globe, bringing new challenges to destination marketing. One of the outcomes of the increasing number of tourist destinations is increased competition amongst established destination identities.[41] The relative ease of substitutability in tourism products is well established and destinations offering a similar product at a similar price are highly interchangeable.[42] In this ever more competitive market-place, tourist destinations – from resorts to countries – are increasingly adopting branding strategies in an effort to differentiate their identities. In particular, newer, emerging destinations are attempting to carve out a niche and to create images emphasising the uniqueness of their product. In order to rise above the media clutter of the tourism marketing world, more and more destinations are pursuing a highly focused and choreographed communications strategy in which branding plays a critical role. Increasingly, in order to achieve individuality destinations are using images and icons which are specifically associated with themselves both to create and to reinforce their destination image. These images and icons are, however, not merely or exclusively innocent expressions of a country's identity. Instead, they are the culmination of historical, social, economic and political processes. Thus images and icons may be selectively used by national tourist organisations and place marketers to appeal to particular target markets – itself an interaction redolent of the power of the image makers.

Branding places

Some tourism products, like airlines and hotels, do have highly branded identities which can evoke emotional commitment and brand loyalty but can destinations be marketed on the same basis as – for example – Virgin Airlines and Hilton Hotels and Resorts? Arguably they can, as the potential to evoke an emotional attachment is even greater for tourism destinations. Vacations are expensive, involving purchases with high 'badge value'[43] and destinations have very strong and pervasive associations for tourists. In the last decade, tourism marketers (as other marketers)[44] have begun to question, if branding works for consumer products, could it work for a destination? The answer depends largely on how branding is defined. Chernatony and McDonald's definition is typical, describing a successful brand as:

> . . . an identifiable product, service, person or place, augmented in such a way that the buyer or user perceives relevant unique added values which match their needs most closely . . . its success results from being able to sustain these added values in the face of competition.[45]

As definitions such as this suggest, there is a general agreement amongst tourism academics (as well as practitioners)[46] that places can be branded in the same way as products and services. Indeed, de Chernatony and McDonald comment that 'the concept of branding is increasingly being applied to people and places', whilst Kotler argues that the 'concept of a brand name extends to tourist destinations . . . Acapulco, Palm Springs, and the French Riviera have developed strong reputations, consumer perceptions, and expectations'.[47] In similar ways, Virginia builds on 'Birthplace of Presidents', Mississippi on 'The Heart of Dixie', Niagara Falls is

'Romance', Greece is 'The Birthplace of Democracy' and Florence 'The Centre of the Renaissance'. Such positioning appeals transcend specific attractions and are a platform for building a place's image.[48]

Although there is this general agreement that branding does apply to tourism destinations, there is less certainty about how the concept translates into practical marketing activity and there are few empirical studies which investigate the realities of branding destinations. It is more difficult to brand a destination as it is not a single product but a composite product one, consisting of a bundle of different components, including accommodation and catering establishments, tourist attractions, arts, entertainment and cultural venues, and even the natural environment. Packaged goods normally have an obvious core, they can anchor themselves to product performance and attributes, but with destinations the situation is less clear – the atmosphere of a resort, the hotel the tourist stays in, and the friendliness of the local people all contribute to its overall image and affect how the tourist views the experience. This lack of overall product control which the majority of destination marketers experience means that there is a tendency to concentrate on the promotional element of the marketing mix. As such, place branding activities are more accurately described as consistent, focused communications strategies.

The politics of branding places

Clearly, it takes time to establish destination brands and brand building yields incremental and not exponential results – any brand manager seeking to create an identity must have long-term commitment to the brand. However, destination brand managers in the public sector face several key constraints which often undermine attempts at brand building. Firstly, the actual product must correspond with the brand image and with consumer expectations and destinations face difficult challenges as their brand managers are not in control of the product. A diverse range of agencies and companies 'assume responsibility for enhancing and ensuring favourable brand images'.[49] These include: local and national government agencies; environmental groups and agencies; chambers of commerce; and civic groups. In addition to the numbers of players involved, the political heterogeneity of geographical regions often makes it difficult to market them effectively as tourism entities and administrative boundaries rarely coincide with marketable areas. As we saw in Chapter 3, particularly in case study 3.5, the political map of any tourism destination is unlikely to be homogeneous in terms of the political will to construct particular campaigns or, if it is, there are likely to be divisions over its content.

Even where such divisions do not exist, finance is a critically important factor which frequently undermines successful place branding. This funding dimension can be further complicated by the uneven allocation of resources on a political basis and by the interests of the many competing audiences for the branding campaigns. Destination marketers have extremely limited budgets in comparison with the marketers of many consumer goods. For instance, if Levi's spent £1 on advertising for every pair of jeans sold in the UK, their budget would be £8 million for the UK *alone* – approximately four times the *global* marketing budget of the

WTB, our case study in 7.3.[50] Finally, public sector destination marketers are often pressed by their political paymasters to demonstrate instant results, pressure which is inconsistent with the long-term investment required by brand building.

Despite the increasing emphasis on tourism as a vehicle of economic and regional development, 'the politics of tourism is still the poor cousin of both tourism research and political science and policy studies'.[51] Yet, examination of the development, marketing and branding of destinations can be extremely revealing. Peck and Lepie point out that the nature and development of tourism in any destination is the product of a number of complex, interrelated economic and political factors, as well as its particular geographic and recreational features.[52] As an illustration, the development and branding of various resorts in Devon (Southwest England) are not merely successful marketing exercises but also effective visitor management strategies. In most cases, the objective of the policy creators was to maintain a middle and upper class clientele and exclude working class visitors. In pursuit of this goal, the resort of Sidmouth followed policies designed to maintain resort selectivity and:

> . . . a systematic strategy of exclusion emerges from the Council minutes and the advertising literature. Moreover, far from being confined to the earlier decades of the century, such attitudes and policies continued to underpin Council activities in the 'sixties, 'seventies and beyond.[53]

Sidmouth's tourism advertising and development strategy shunned popularity, and appealed instead to a minority of wealthy and older people, 'excluding the masses'.[54] Other Devon resorts, such as Ilfracombe, followed similar strategies throughout the nineteenth century and for the first two-thirds of the twentieth century – arguing that it 'was wise to advertise in better class papers to attract better class people'.[55] Torquay similarly aspired to a select clientele, positioning itself as 'The English Riviera' in order to attract middle and upper class visitors. In Torbay the promotional managers cleverly mixed traditional and modern images to create an impression of a very modern resort capable of providing old-fashioned service and elegance, a sophisticated and successful blend.[56]

Despite the obviously political overtones of such tourism strategies, rarely does anyone question who makes the policy decisions and for whom, or indeed, how these choices are influenced by policies and ideologies and how the decisions are implemented. These decisions which shape tourism policy, the extent and nature of government intervention and the kind of tourism development which is encouraged, are *political acts* which result from *political processes*. Equally, the images used in the promotion of destinations are similarly ideological – springing from the same political processes.[57] Too often such questions are overlooked in the rush to analyse the response of the intended market for such activities and, as Ritchie has argued, the political impacts of tourism need to be examined at both a micro and macro level. The resorts of Devon are a useful example of the politics of *local* government tourism policies. At the macro or *national* level analysis could focus on the relationships between image building and ideological advancement and here the countries of Eastern Europe provide an ideal example.

Between the end of the Second World War and the late Eighties the countries of Central and Eastern Europe formed a particular entity, differentiated from those of Western Europe both politically and economically. Following the political upheavals of the late 1980s, however, the former Eastern Bloc states are variously moving from a one-party to a pluralist democratic system, a change accompanied by a shift from a centralised to a market-orientated economy. The pace and depth of this change varies from one country to another – in Hungary, where tourism is seen as playing an important role in economic transition, the process is going relatively smoothly, whilst in countries such as Romania, the change has been much more complex.[58] In many of these states tourism is seen as an industry which has the ability to revive their entrepreneurial base because of its low threshold of entry, its flexibility and its responsiveness to dynamic forces.[59] As a result, these countries, notably Hungary and Croatia, are investing resources in an effort to encourage their tourism industries. This policy has begun to yield positive results as, for example, Hungarian international tourism arrivals doubled from 10.6 to 22.8 million between 1986 and 1993, whilst the same figure for Romania rose from 1.3 to 5.8 million.[60]

Notwithstanding the importance of its role as 'an economic escape route',[61] it is important to highlight that tourism development is also regarded as highly significant ideologically for these states. As the more comprehensive discussion of the imaging of Eastern Europe in Chapter 10 suggests, such states are concerned to advertise their historical and cultural links with the West. A major feature of the emergence of these 'new' European destinations has been the re-creation and re-presentation of their cultural identities and rebirth and new beginnings is a common theme: 'Croatia is a recently added name on the list of European states, yet it is a well-known destination. If you have ever been to Dubrovnik, Split, . . . or Zagreb, you have known the Croatian wonders by another (Yugoslav) name.' Moreover, Eastern Europe is not only familiar to the West, but it is a place where you can actually experience the meeting of East and West. Vilnius (Lithuania) is 'a cultural meeting point of West and East', as is Estonia, 'a land at the meeting point of the East and the West'.[62] Croatia places even more emphasis on its role as a cultural crossroads:

> Croatian culture is an integral part of Western European culture; indeed it is at the eastern outpost. But Croatia is unique in Europe: four cultures meet here: the West meets the East, and Central Europe meets the Mediterranean South.[63]

These are not just places where West *meets* East, but where the West *confronts* the East. Countries such as Lithuania, Poland and particularly Croatia, are keen to refer to their historical role as defenders of the Christian West against the Islamic East. Tourists are told that Lithuania held back 'the invasion of the West by the Golden Horde' in the fourteenth century and that Poland, under King Jan III Sobieski, defended Vienna 'and the bulwarks of Christian Europe were saved'.[64]

Such strategies are obviously concerned to ameliorate and enhance these countries' images in the West. Less obviously, they are also designed to signify and facilitate their ideological shift from an atheist, socialist and eastern to a Christian, capitalist and western orientation. The script has changed but the process remains the same as there are remarkable parallels with Hall's analysis of tourism in communist Eastern Europe. Hall suggested that the influence of Stalinist economic priorities in Eastern European tourism could be seen in a number of areas, especially in the need to communicate to visitors the superiority of the socialist system.[65] Then, as now, history is being reworked and re-presented in an attempt to construct a new political and social reality. Whilst this new identity draws on a historical age much more ancient than the Communist period, its construction and presentation is as ideological as anything constructed during the Communist era.

In such a fashion, power and ways of seeing the world articulate the tourism image, indeed Papson has suggested that people's perceptions of destinations are:

> created by the marketing arm of government and of private enterprise . . . government and private enterprise not only redefine social reality but also recreate it to fit those definitions.[66]

Whilst there are many variables which influence perceptions of destinations, we can take our discussion of how 'the state translates values, interests and resources into objectives and policies'[67] further by examining the case of the Spanish Balearic Island of Majorca. Here, changes within the political makeup of the state offered opportunities for different perspectives to assert different values and interests and thus effect changes in the identity communicated to potential tourists.

The rebranding of the Island is, at first glance, merely a reflection of a destination seeking to maintain market share as in 1989–90 visitor numbers began to fall, prompting the Balearic Island's regional government to introduce a number of initiatives. A £115 million refurbishment programme funded by regional government and local district councils improved the resorts' environment and infrastructure;[68] development controls were tightened, limiting new hotel developments to four-star or higher; development was completely banned in conservation areas (which covered 30% of the Island); and legislation encouraged older hotels to upgrade. These improvements formed the basis of a promotional campaign orchestrated by the *Fomento del Turismo de Mallorca* (the Majorcan Tourist Board) and the Balearic Islands Tourism Council. The key objectives were firstly 'to draw attention to the . . . improvements', secondly to 'counter the "lager lout resort image" by creating awareness of the island's other attractions' and finally, to attract back the family, the older and the more upscale markets.[69]

The aim was thus to shake off an image of a Majorca 'inextricably linked with a certain kind of tourism; charter flights and crowded beaches and sand and drunken sex'.[70] In addition to the infrastructural improvements, a key vehicle in achieving these objectives was a public relations campaign, linked to the launching of a new corporate logo. The island began to refer to itself as Mallorca, using the spelling of the local language, Mallorquin, to emphasise its cultural identity and some individual resorts rebranded themselves – Magaluf and Palma Nova became Costas de Calvia.[71] To negate its 'lager-lout' image, Mallorca launched a public relations offensive which drew particular attention to its scenery and to Palma and its associations with Chopin, Miro and Robert Graves. The campaign has been extremely successful, as one commentator said in 1997: Mallorca is 'moving upmarket' as film stars and royalty have begun 'flocking there, . .'.[72]

Whilst the marketing objectives were to redress the declining tourist numbers, and to counter negative images of young, drunken tourists causing nuisances in all-night disco-bars, one could question whether such actions also represent a parallel agenda concerned to reclaim Mallorca for the Mallorcans, to retake its identity from the Majorca of the foreign tourists and the Franco era. Such an interpretation is particularly pertinent when the differing political contexts of Majorca and Mallorca are considered. Majorca developed as a tourist resort during the Franco regime when tourists meant money and negative environmental and cultural impacts were of no interest to those dedicated to a downmarket, mass tourism product. The death of Franco, however, saw the return of democracy and more of an emphasis on regionalism as opposed to centralisation. The culmination of these two forces:

> brought a new . . . awareness, a flourishing of the arts and a revival of the Catalan language . . . [as well as] a concern for the environment and culture . . . The new approach to tourism can be directly traced to political change.[73]

This was a political change which in 1983 saw Palma become the capital of the Balearic Islands and which has led to the emergence of a more vibrant society – confident and proud to be Catalan. The Catalan language itself, banned under Franco, has been reinstated and rehabilitated and is now the official language of government as well as the language of the people. Catalan is now everywhere – it is heard on the streets and in the shops and seen on the signs – and is not merely a language, but an 'issue of cultural identity'.[74]

Mallorca's experience is echoed by the repositioning campaign being implemented by the *Ministerio De Comercio Y Turismo* which is rebuilding and reimaging Spain as *España*. As with Majorca, Spain's tourism developed under Franco in an era where controls and impacts – environmental, social or cultural – were irrelevancies. The dictator's death, together with a newly invigorated democracy and a cultural revival, stimulated a similarly proud and confident España, ready to take its place as a full partner in the European Community of nations. It also stimulated the political will to reclaim Spain as a Spanish entity, just as regionalism had enabled Mallorca to reaffirm its identity as Catalan. It was no longer enough for Spain to be merely another sun, sand and sea destination, although this was also obviously being threatened by moves away from mass tourism and the increasing numbers of long-haul competitors for European tourists. In the *España – Passion For Life* campaign Spain is trying to reacquaint the world with an identity which was lost in the development of the Costa tourism. The focus is no longer a Spain of beaches and disco-bars, but the 'Other' Spain, cultural, exotic and Carmanesque, the Spain of flamenco dancers, bull fighters, vibrant cities and beautiful rural villages.[75] Whilst the objective in the campaign was to attract cultural tourists and increase earnings, to neglect the political and cultural context of the campaign is to tell only a part of the story.

The experiences of Majorca and Spain reveal how central politics are to tourism identities and thus to destination branding – the death of Franco signalled a fundamental shift in the direction of Spain's tourism development and marketing by altering the balance of power between central government and the regions. This enabled rather different values and interests to take precedence over others and changes in the political direction of the state was joined by other factors including an increasing concern for the environment, the socio-cultural impacts of tourism and the demands for greater local involvement in tourism. In our final case study, we see the same forces animating the branding of Wales in its overseas tourist markets, especially the USA.

Wales has little in the way of an 'ethnic roots and discovery' market and currently has neither the transport links nor the image strengths to compete for overseas visitors on equal terms with the other countries in the UK. The positive side of this position, however, is that there are few negative perceptions of Wales in the US market segments, for the very reason that they know very little about Wales. This means, that, as a WTB marketing manager recently commented: once the Board has decided what the 'core brand values of Wales should be', it can 'be creative and consistent in the messages' it conveys to the US consumer.[76]

This is not to suggest that the Board has a blank canvas on which to work – the Board cannot create an identity 'Wales' which bears little or no resemblance to what Wales actually represents – it can only select from a range of images which have traditionally been associated with or are representative of Wales and, unsurprisingly, it selects those which most appeal to its target market. However, notions of Welshness reflect complex historical and political relationships – they are by no means value-neutral but are value-laden. Thus, the branding of Wales, like that of Spain, is not just about attempts to attract more tourists, it is also about moves to raise Wales' international visibility and prestige and about the emergence of Wales as a more self-confident nation. To illustrate this argument, we need to examine how powerful discourses have shaped what is Wales and analyse the context which has stimulated Wales' rebranding.

No ethnicity or ethnic identification can be explained without understanding the role of power and culture as 'different modes of domination are implicated in the social construction of ethnic and other identities'.[77] Cultural discourses are of course strongly intertwined with political discourses and the cultural history of Wales has itself long been sharply politicised. As an internal colony,[78] Union with England:

> marked the beginning of a sustained campaign of cultural homogenization by the central state . . . Welsh . . . was banned for administrative and legal purposes . . . . children were punished for speaking Welsh in schools.[79]

This desire for cultural homogenisation was emphasised in a *Times* editorial of 1866 which described the Welsh language as 'the curse of Wales'. It continued to say that:

> Their antiquated and semi-barbarous language, in short, shrouds them in darkness. If Wales and the Welsh are . . . to share the material prosperity and . . . the culture and morality of England, they must forget their isolated language.[80]

Jenkins argues that ultimately one of the defining features of Welshness is the 'sharing of a common ethnic boundary – with and against the English'.[81] The relationship between the 'Welsh' and the 'English' has been defined by powerful discourses which continue to be manifested today, although more punitive control has been replaced by civilian sanction, perhaps no less effective, in the form of social and cultural ridicule. Echoes of *The Times* editorial of 1866 linger on and in many London-oriented cultural arenas Wales and the Welsh are dogged by clichéd and stereotypical derogation. For some, Wales is a primitive backwater where the people speak a curious language; newspaper columnists feel at liberty to describe the Welsh as 'dingy, untalented and sly' and they are vilified without any foundation for having never made 'any significant contribution to any branch of knowledge, culture or entertainment'.[82] In October 1997 an article in *The Sunday Times* went so far as to describe the Welsh as: 'loquacious dissemblers, immoral liars, stunted, bigoted, dark, ugly, pugnacious little trolls'.[83]

As Pitchford notes in her work on ethnic tourism, these stereotypes and stigma have been difficult to destroy:

> attitudes towards the Welsh language and culture range from ignorance and indifference to outright hostility; school children are taught little about Wales, and the media continue to portray the Welsh in derogatory ways.

Despite these efforts to denigrate and ultimately to destroy Wales' distinctive identity, in the latter part of the twentieth century, the country remains culturally distinct in the UK's Celtic fringe and 'the defence and promotion of Welsh culture – symbolised most sharply by the Welsh language – is the dominant item on the nationalist agenda.'[84] Wales, in fact, is linguistically the most 'Celtic' strand in the UK's Celtic fringe,[85] its Welsh cultural identity is strong and 1993 saw the establishment of the Welsh Language Board which is charged with promoting and facilitating the use of Welsh in public and private life.[86] Similarly, its tourism agency is charged with protecting and enhancing the Welsh culture in all its activities – a remit which is exclusive to Wales and not part of any other UK national tourist board's agenda. As its mission statement suggests, the Board seeks to develop and market tourism in ways which will yield the optimum economic and social benefit to the people of Wales. Implicit within this objective is the need 'To sustain and promote the culture of Wales and the Welsh language'[87] and the Board has committed itself not to attracting:

> the largest possible number of tourists at the expense of our heritage, our language, and culture . . . [but to] draw together all kinds of activities, cultural as well as historical, to create a strong image, especially abroad . . . . It is our aim to show the visitor that Wales is a bilingual country.[88]

In the late 1990s Wales is, therefore, seeing a fusion of processes which certainly facilitated (if not prompted) the promotion of a peculiarly Welsh identity, particularly to the overseas market. There are a number of external and internal factors which have combined to facilitate this re-identification of Wales. Perhaps the most obvious of these is the rise of the European Union (EU), independent membership of which would offer Wales an alternative arena in which to air political interest and grievance. The rise of Europe in many ways parallels the decline of Westminster in both reputation and significance in Wales – as Jenkins points out: 'The legitimacy of the present constitutional arrangements for the government of

Wales has been called into question over the last decade.'[89] Almost two decades of Conservative government domination of Parliament did little to enamour Wales with the political *status quo*, particularly as this domination was never reflected in Wales which consistently elected socialist representatives espousing more radical policies and programmes. The dominant political discourse has also been challenged by the experience of Ireland within Europe and many in Wales have recently cast envious eyes over the Irish Sea and asked for a stronger voice for Wales in Europe. Politically there are strong arguments for a more powerful, independent voice for Wales, arguments realised in a recent referendum vote in favour of an assembly which, when it is convened, will be Wales' first independent political institution to be elected for almost 600 years. The extent of political change should not be underestimated as 20 years ago a similar referendum vote on devolved power was rejected by 80% of Welsh voters. In embracing what was once unthinkable, Wales' change of political direction both represents and gives impetus to the promotion of a distinctive Welsh identity.

A further reflection of this re-emergence of a Welsh identity is the status of the Welsh language (as an embodiment of Welsh culture). In the mid Nineties it at last achieved legal parity with English in Wales – despite the campaign to eradicate it. This contemporary celebration of Welsh language and culture is, as the preceding discussion has shown, in direct contrast to their historical treatment. Similarly, in many other areas of Welsh life there is a recognition that tourism can be used to 'promote and protect Welsh culture, to consciously and deliberately craft its messages about Wales that are sent through the medium of tourism'.[90] This is an aim which was facilitated by the granting of overseas marketing powers to the Wales Tourist Board in 1992, some ten years after its Scottish equivalent. This wrested control away from a London-based British Tourist Authority which has been frequently criticised for neglecting the interests of Scotland and Wales in overseas tourism promotion because of its concentration on London. It is interesting to note, for example, that Northern Ireland has found it more profitable to work with Dublin than London on such matters.

This celebration of Welsh culture and identity through tourism promotion can be read as an attempt to reclaim that culture and identity as Welsh. To take pride in Europe's oldest living language is thus to begin to shake off the history and oppression which has bedevilled both it and the Welsh psyche. This celebration is, however, as we pointed out earlier, a celebration which is essentially aimed at the overseas market. This in itself reveals an added dimension to the powerful discourses which have shaped the relationship between Wales and England in the twentieth century. In part, it is these attitudes and stereotypes which could make a tourism campaign similar in style and tone to the overseas one – celebrating Welsh language, arts and culture – very difficult in the domestic market. These negative stereotypes of Wales are obviously not shared by those who visit Wales as studies have repeatedly shown that for many of these the language and culture are significant attractions.[91] However, amongst some of those who have never been to Wales, 'there is evidence to suggest that the idea of an ethnically-distinct, bilingual region within the United Kingdom sometimes arouses hostility'.[92] It is this particular strand in English nationalism which would make the campaign outlined in case study 7.3 highly problematic in both political and marketing terms

Case Study 7.3   Creating 'Wales' the Brand in the US Market

Wales is an emerging destination as far as the US market is concerned. It is currently a destination only for the US traveller who is already familiar with the UK, probably on a third or fourth trip. Yet, of all the major overseas growth markets for Wales, the US is currently the most important single market, both in terms of visitors and expenditure. Just under one quarter of all overseas visitors are American, spending £22.9 million.[93] In addition to its current importance, the US also offers huge growth potential for Welsh tourism. It has a total population of almost 249 million, of which fewer than 10% currently take overseas vacations.

Those US citizens who have the highest propensity to travel to Wales tend to be college educated, in professional or managerial occupations, aged 35 or over, of household incomes earning in excess of US$50 000 per year and travelling in couples.[94] They are attracted to the UK for a number of reasons, particularly its history, heritage, culture and environment and because the UK and the USA share a common heritage and language (see Table 7.1). In addition, the countries of the UK are perceived in North America as congenial and safe destinations associated with images of quaint and charming countries.[95]

Table 7.1   SWOT Analysis of Wales in the US Market.

Strengths	Weaknesses	Opportunities	Threats
• friendly people	• no image or identity	• activity oriented	• increased other market competition
• history/heritage	• product weaknesses	• emerging markets (independents, seniors)	• smaller and declining US holiday entitlement
• outdoor activities	• no direct transport links	• distinctive	
• shared and own languages	• distance from US	• Welsh language and culture	• not sufficiently exotic or adventurous
• quality products	• seasonality	• inexpensive	
• green/unspoilt environment & scenery	• weather	• continuing weakness of £ against $	
	• inadequate marketing budget		

Source: adapted from Wales Tourist Board Marketing Plan 1994/5.

Wales' branding strategy

Wales' ultimate marketing objective in the US is to increase tourism volume and value. Given the budgetary constraints facing the WTB, the vacation brochure is the key marketing tool for targeting potential visitors, although Wales relies heavily on travel agency initiatives, trade shows and joint press activity.[96] It also runs media and public relations campaigns, and familiarisation trips for influential journalists. In all of these promotional activities, however, the key objective is to raise Wales' profile in the US, specifically, to develop a clear and cohesive branding for Wales.[97]

The key focus of the Wales Tourist Board's current marketing strategy is therefore to create a brand for Wales and in this there are a number of associations and values on which it can capitalise. Today Wales has thriving design, craft and film

Table 7.2 Brand Icons in Wales' USA Brochure.

Images	% of Welsh icon images
national costume/dress	65
Welsh language	14
national flag	12
culturally specific activities	4
famous Welsh personalities	3
Welsh emblems/symbols	2
Base figure	*156*

Note: figures to nearest per cent.

and animation industries. It also has a distinctive language and living cultural heritage, and it is on these latter associations that the tourist board is founding its branding. It is attempting to construct an image of a Celtic, Welsh-speaking and, therefore, unique destination within the UK and a key element of this strategy is the use of brand icons in its marketing imagery.[98]

Analysis of Wales' promotional literature aimed at the US market clearly illustrates the range and the depth of this branding exercise. In the vacation brochures aimed at the US traveller the WTB is using branding symbols to communicate the distinguishing characteristics of the Welsh vacation product. Content analysis reveals that such branding symbols account for a third of all the images seen in the brochures. Thus the branding strategy emphasises Celtic heritage, language, myths and legends and Welsh emblems, such as the daffodil, the leek, the Welsh dragon, and the Welsh flag (Table 7.2). Also heavily featured are images of Wales' vocal and musical tradition, which research indicates sets Wales apart from competitor destinations. The second most commonly occurring images, accounting for just under 30%, are 'heritage' images – principally castles – itself a secondary brand signature for Wales.[99] The extent of the branding exercise emerges not just from the frequency of the use of brand signatures, but also from their prominence. Images of the Welsh flag and the Welsh language are central to each brochure page layout. The use of the Welsh language is perhaps the most significant brand signature in the attempt to craft an unique identity as it differentiates Wales from other UK destinations. As the brochure text proclaims: 'We are a nation which is distinctive, with its own Celtic language and culture, which is as proud of its past as its present and future.'[100]

This strategy – promoting Wales as a distinct, individual country in the UK – is a clear attempt to woo the 'play-it-safers' in the US market, those who want to feel comfortable abroad, with a similar culture and language but also with a hint of the exotic. Thus, when the WTB launched its first advertising campaign in partnership with American Airlines in 1995 the Welsh language featured prominently in a campaign emphasising that Wales has its own language, culture and history. Discussing this role of the language, the WTB's Communications Director commented that the US visitor enjoys visiting another country but does not like to cope with a foreign language and 'to avoid this . . . the ad copy says we speak English fluently as well'.[101]

Given the rise of a global culture where there is so much information and so many competing brands, products and destinations, the existence of a brand signature will be critical. In fact, it may be that as consumers are confronted by an increasingly fast-moving, sound-bite, snapshot world, such shorthand images of products and places will become more prevalent. In the case of destinations, developing their own brand signatures may be the only weapon for emerging destinations to compete with the existing destination megabrands – just as branding has become a useful shorthand device for consumer products. As we have tried to highlight in this chapter, however, it is important to recognise not just the marketing context of branding activities, but also their wider cultural, political, social and economic context.

The images chosen by companies like BA and P&O and by places such as Wales and Majorca are the culmination of historical, social, economic and political processes. Images and icons are used selectively by national tourist organisations and place marketers to appeal to particular target markets – itself an interaction echoing the image-makers' power – but the images which they use are highly political. They are also often highly stereotypical and clichéd and this reliance on shorthand images is likely to increase as the sound-bite media becomes more dominant. In this scenario, the power of stereotyping is central to the articulation of the tourism image, as is the power of the camera – the essential conduit for the image. It is these two aspects of the image which Chapter 8 will now explore.

References

1 See Morgan, N.J. (1991) Perceptions, Politics and Patterns of Tourism: The Development of the Seaside Resorts of Devon in the Twentieth Century, unpublished PhD thesis, University of Exeter, Chapter 7.
2 Repositioning Forte, *Insights*, English Tourist Board.
3 International Olympic Committee survey of 10 000 adults worldwide, asking them to match symbols to organisations, *The Observer*, 3 December 1995.
4 Hallberg, G. (1995) *All Consumers Are Not Created Equal. The differential marketing strategy for brand loyalty and profits*, John Wiley and Sons, Chichester: 2.
5 Sellers, P. (1995) 'A Brand New Day in Marlboro County', *Fortune*, 12 June: 16.
6 'Brand New World', interview with Richard Branson in *The World in 1997*, *The Economist* Publications (1996), London: 124.
7 Schiffman, L.G. and Kanuk, L.L. (1994) *Consumer Behaviour*, Prentice Hall, New Jersey: 187.
8 Brassington, F. and Pettitt, S. (1997) *Principles of Marketing*, Pitman, London: 123.
9 Marchant, L.J., Hutchinson, P.J. and Prescott, P. (1990) 'A practical model of consumer choice', *Journal of Market Research Society*, 32: 1.
10 Alan McCulloch, Saachti & Saachti Vision, interview on EBN Future File, 14 February 1997.
11 Jenkins, W.I. (1978) *Policy analysis: a political and organizational perspective*, St. Martin's Press, New York: 26–7.
12 Hall, C.M. (1994) *Tourism and Politics: policy, power and place*, John Wiley and Sons, Chichester: 11.
13 Elliott, H. (1997) 'BA takes ethnic route in £60 million bid to stay in front around the world', *The Times*, 11 June: 5.
14 Smith, A. and Skapinker, M. (1997) 'Flights of Imagination', *Financial Times*, 11 June: 27.

15 Rowe, M. (1997) 'Hullo John, got a new motif?', *The Independent on Sunday*, 15 June:
    8.
16 *The Times* editorial 11 June 1997.
17 reference 14.
18 *Daily Telegraph* editorial 11 June 1997.
19 ibid.
20 'By their tailfins shall we know them?', *Independent on Sunday*, 15 June 1997.
21 reference 15.
22 ibid.
23 quoted in Marston, P. (1997) 'BA stops flying the flag in £60 million facelift', *Daily
    Telegraph*, 11 June: 12.
24 ibid.
25 ibid.
26 Dingle, D. and Harding, G. (1995) 'From Canberra to Oriana: A £200 million
    investment in the identification and management of brand values', *Journal of Vacation
    Marketing*, 1 (2): 195–201: 199.
27 reference 26: 196.
28 Charlier, J.J. (1996) 'New Geographical Trends in Cruise Shipping', 51–60 in Roehl,
    W.S. (ed.) *Proceedings of the Second Environments for Tourism Conference*, Las Vegas:
    William F. Harrah College of Hotel Administration, University of Nevada, Las Vegas:
    51.
29 reference 28: 59.
30 Miller, A.R. (1996) 'Toward the Year 2000: Trends in the Cruise Industry', 178–182 in
    Roehl, W.S. (ed.) *Proceedings of the Second Environments for Tourism Conference*, Las
    Vegas: William F. Harrah College of Hotel Administration, University of Nevada, Las
    Vegas: 178.
31 reference 26: 196.
32 reference 26: 198.
33 Petrie, G. (1997) 'P&O's Oriana: British Traditions Sail On', *Porthole. A View of the
    Sea and Beyond*, July/August 40–43: 40.
34 reference 26: 200.
35 reference 33: 41.
36 reference 26: 197.
37 reference 33: 43.
38 reference 26: 196.
39 Kotler, P. *et al.* (1993) *Marketing Places. Attracting Investment, Industry and Tourism to
    Cities, States and Nations*, The Free Press, New York: 10.
40 reference 39: 21.
41 Travis, A.S. (1994) 'Tourism Destination Area Development (from theory to practice)',
    29–40 in Witt, S. and Moutinho, L. (eds), *Tourism Marketing and Management
    Handbook*, Prentice Hall, London.
42 Goodall, B. *et al.* (1988) 'Market Opportunity Sets for tourism', Geographical Papers
    100: Tourism Series, 1, University of Reading, Department of Geography; and Medlik,
    S. and Middleton, V.T.C. (1973) 'The Tourist Product and its Marketing Implications',
    28–46, *International Tourism Quarterly*, 9.
43 Wagner, W. (1997) 'Modernization and Prestige: Tourism as a Motor of Social
    Change', paper presented to the 10th ELRA Congress, Leisure, Culture and Tourism in
    Europe, Dubrovnik, September.
44 Levy, M. (1996) 'Current accounts and baked beans: Translating FMCG marketing
    principles to the financial sector', *Journal of Brand Management*, 4 (2): 95–99.
45 de Chernatony, L. and McDonald, M.H.B. (1992) *Creating Powerful Brands: the
    strategic route to success in consumer, industrial and service markets*, Butterworth
    Heinemann, Oxford: 18.
46 Vial, C. (1997) 'Success Stories of Tourism Campaigns', paper presented at the First
    International Tourism and Leisure Advertising Festival, Dubrovnik September.

47   reference 45 and Kotler, P., Bowen, J. and Makens, J. (1996) *Marketing for Hospitality & Tourism*, Prentice Hall, New Jersey: 285.

48   Kotler, P. *et al.* (1993) *Marketing Places. Attracting Investment, Industry and Tourism to Cities, States and Nations*, The Free Press, New York: 213–4.

49   Kotler, P., Bowen, J. and Makens, J. (1996) *Marketing for Hospitality & Tourism*, Prentice Hall, New Jersey: 285.

50   'Branded', BBC2 television programme screened 1 March 1997.

51   reference 12: 1.

52   Peck, J.G. and Lepie, A.S. (1989) 'Tourism and development in three North Carolina coastal towns', 203–222 in Smith, V. (ed.) *Hosts and guests: the anthropology of tourism*, 2nd ed., University of Pennsylvania Press, Philadelphia: 216.

53   Morgan, N.J. (1991) Perceptions, Politics and Patterns of Tourism: The Development of the Seaside Resorts of Devon in the Twentieth Century, unpublished PhD thesis, University of Exeter: 208.

54   Pimlott, J.A.R. (1947) *The Englishman's Holiday. A Social History*, Faber & Faber, London: 209.

55   reference 53: 225.

56   Morgan, N.J. (1997) 'Seaside Resort Strategies: The Case of Inter-War Torquay', 84–100 in Fisher, S. (ed.) *Recreation and the Sea*, University of Exeter Press, Exeter.

57   reference 12: 7.

58   Fletcher, J. and Cooper, C.P. (1996) 'Tourism Strategy Planning. Szolnok County, Hungary', *Annals of Tourism Research*, 23 (1): 181–200: 182.

59   reference 58: 183.

60   reference 58: 184.

61   reference 12: 29.

62   Lithuanian Tourist Board, *Welcome to Lithuania*, 1996:6; and Estonian Tourist Board, *Eesti, Estonia*, 1994: 2.

63   Croatian National Tourism Office, *Croatia*, 1996.

64   Lithuanian Tourist Board, *Welcome to Lithuania*, 1996: 4 and Polish Tourist Information Centre, *Poland Invites*, Warsaw, 1997.

65   Hall, D.R. (1984) 'Foreign tourism under socialism: the Albanian "Stalinist" model', *Annals of Tourism Research*, 11 (4): 539–55: 542.

66   Papson, S. (1981) 'Spuriousness and tourism: politics of two Canadian provincial governments', *Annals of Tourism Research*, 8 (2): 220–235: 225.

67   Davis *et al.* (1993) Public policy in Australia, 2nd ed., Allen & Unwin, St Leonards: 19.

68   Morgan, M. (1991) 'Majorca: Dressing Up to Survive', *Tourism Management*, 12 (1) March; and Morgan, M. (1996) *Marketing for leisure and tourism*, Prentice Hall, Hemel Hempstead: 255–6.

69   ibid.

70   Kelly, T. (1997) 'You Say Majorca, I Say Mallorca', *Independent on Sunday*: 3.

71   reference 68.

72   reference 70.

73   ibid.

74   ibid.

75   *Ministreio De Comercio Y Turismo*, Secretaria General De Turismo (1994), Espana.

76   Snelling, A. (1997) 'Letter From America', *The Leisure Monitor*, 1 (3): 3.

77   Jenkins, R. (1997) *Rethinking Ethnicity. Arguments and Explorations*, Sage, London: 73.

78   Davies, C.A. (1987) *Welsh Nationalism in the Twentieth Century*, Praeger, New York.

79   Pitchford, S.R. (1994) 'Ethnic Tourism and Nationalism in Wales', *Annals of Tourism Research*, 35–50.

80   *The Times* editorial 8 September 1866, Times CD ROM.

81   reference 77: 32.

82   Wilson, A.N. (1996) 'Never Say Dai', *The Evening Standard*, March, 5: 4.

83   quoted in the *Western Mail*, 9 October 1997: 10.

84   reference 77: 126.

85   reference 77: 148.

86 Welsh Language Board, (1996) Annual Report, Welsh Language Board, 28 June 1996.
87 Wales Tourist Board (1994) *Tourism 2000. A Strategy for Wales*, Wales Tourist Board, Cardiff.
88 Wales Tourist Board (1991) 'Selling Wales – No Thanks', 4–7, translation of Chairman's Lecture at Bro Delyn National Eisteddfod (transcript), Cardiff, Wales Tourist Board.
89 reference 77: 34.
90 reference 79: 44.
91 Light (1992) 'Bilingual Heritage Interpretation in Wales', *Scottish Geographical Magazine*, 108: 3; Wales Tourist Board, All Wales Visitor Survey 1996; ECTARC (1988) Study of the Social, Cultural and Linguistic Impact of Tourism on Wales, Wales Tourist Board.
92 reference 79: 40. See also Wanhill, S. (1992) *Tourism 2000: A Perspective for Wales*, Wales Tourist Board, Cardiff.
93 Wales Tourist Board (1994) Marketing Plan, 1994/5, Cardiff.
94 Pritchard, A. and Morgan, N.J. (1996) 'Selling the Celtic Arc to the USA: a comparative analysis of the destination brochure images used in the marketing of Ireland, Scotland and Wales', *Journal of Vacation Marketing*, 2 (4), September, 346–65.
95 British Tourist Authority (1992) *USA Market Guide*, British Tourist Authority, London; and Louis Harris & Associates, 'The American Travel Consumer – A Profile', *Travel & Leisure Magazine Survey*, 1989, quoted in the WTB Overseas Marketing Plan, 1994–95.
96 WTB (1995) *A Review of the Wise Wales Initiative in the USA*, WTB, Cardiff.
97 reference 87.
98 Pritchard, A. and Morgan, N.J. (1996) 'Marketing Emerging and Established Destinations: a case study of Ireland, Scotland and Wales in the US Market', in Roehl, W.S. (ed.) *Proceedings of the Second Environments for Tourism Conference*, Las Vegas, Nevada: 202–11.
99 reference 98.
100 WTB (1995) *Wales. The Country That Makes Britain Great*, WTB, Cardiff: 1.
101 *Western Mail* (1995) 'Selling Wales with Castles and Coracles', 3 May.

Part Three:
Changing Worlds, Changing Images?

8 The image, politics and power

Power relations are as much about the politics of everyday life as they are about the grand issues of politics and sovereign power[1] and in Parts I and II we tried to show how these power relations impact on tourism processes. In this chapter, we return to the discussions of Chapters 1 and 2 to analyse the discourse of imagery, but focus in much more detail on power in relation to tourism promotion. In particular, the chapter discusses some of the structures behind image creation and examines the role the photographic image plays in constructing identities and creating stereotypes.

This discussion is set against a backdrop in which the roles and rationales for tourism are increasingly being questioned. It is no longer viewed as the global panacea, the answer to every nation's economic problems, that it was in the 1960s and 1970s. Instead, there is as much concern over the costs of the industry as its benefits to local economies and questions have been raised as to whether the money invested in attracting tourists would be better spent elsewhere.[2] This is particularly true in a global system in which the economic and political forces which underpin the affluence of the First World are largely maintained by the underdevelopment of the Third World. Tourism is an activity in which some participate whilst others do not. Much of the tourism infrastructure is supported by, and indeed, reliant upon armies of poorly paid workers servicing the needs of relatively affluent tourists. Questions have also been raised about an industry which draws heavily on the derogatory, often racialised, stereotyping of indigenous peoples,[3] an issue which is particularly pertinent to our interests here. Tourism is therefore an arena in which we can legitimately observe the operation of power and examine its impacts. That the tourism industry has hitherto been dismissed by conventional political commentators as less important than, say, the arms or oil industries reveals, as Enloe says, more about 'the ideological construction of "seriousness" than about the politics of tourism'.[4]

Power: expanding the boundaries of tourism

To provide a framework for the study of tourism and, more specifically, tourism imagery, it is essential to locate the industry and tourism representation in the wider social, economic and political systems which shape our world. These systems embody power relations which, as Foucault argued, concern 'our bodies, our lives, our day-to-day existence . . . . Between every point of a social body . . . there exists relations of power'.[5] Recognising this, we need to re-examine notions of power, culture and history if we are to fully understand tourism processes. In doing this, tourism can usefully learn from the debates which have animated leisure studies for some time. As a significant leisure experience, tourism should be included in such debates in any case since an understanding of leisure and the kinds of constraints and influences which frame leisure choices can only lead to a more insightful analysis of tourism.

Leisure has been described by John Wilson as 'part of the struggle for the control of space and time in which social groups are continually engaged', a struggle in which dominant groups seek 'to legitimate, through statute and administrative fiat, . . . appropriate use of space and time, and the subordinate groups resist this control through individual rebellion and collective action'.[6] Such commentators have stripped leisure of its seeming neutrality and freedom from constraining forces, turning it into a highly politicised field. Leisure has increasingly become regarded as:

> less a matter of individual choice than a concomitant of social position, less a means by which society is unified through a leisure-consuming democracy than divided by material and cultural inequality.[7]

Wilson and Chris Rojek have both pointed out that the word leisure derives from the Latin word *licere*, meaning to be lawful or allowed.[8] However, license has a double meaning: it can imply liberty or official sanction. As Wilson notes, this duality 'indicates the complex of associations the word "leisure" has for us, suggesting both freedom and constraint. Regulation and control – in short, politics – is thus an inherent part of the meaning of leisure to us'.[9] Etymological evidence thus implies that leisure is not free time but activity subject to constraints and therefore to power relations. Thus, 'the concept of "free time"', Rojek argues, 'has no intrinsic meaning. Rather, its meaning always depends on the social context in which it occurs.'[10] The same is true of tourism whose *meaning* is historically – and culturally – specific, conveying different meanings to different people at different times. It can only be understood in the context of its relation to a specific historical and cultural situation. Tourism, like leisure, is concerned with power relations at all levels within societies and although those relations are subject to constant renegotiation, inequality dictates the nature of the bargain. As Nancy Duncan writes: 'personal relationships are also power relationships . . . everyone is implicated in the production and reproduction of power relations . . . . Although places may be more or less overtly politized, there are no politically neutral spaces.'[11]

The perception of tourist spaces as neutral and tourism activities as 'free time', allowing maximum discretion over the disposal of non-work time, therefore emerges as something of an illusion. Marxist and neo-Marxist scholars have redefined our understanding of the leisure experience by focusing on its social and economic context, as have feminists by highlighting the impact of gender and sexuality. Similarly, Foucault's emphasis on the 'micropolitics of power' now enables us to see power at work in many diverse sites 'far removed from the materiality of the state and its ideology'.[12] As a result of the emergence of these perspectives, no new theoretical work on leisure or tourism should now overlook the constraints placed upon their operation by socio-economic class, gender, race, age, sexuality or abilism. Similarly, none of these factors should be viewed in isolation as they intersect at different points, combining to generate particular relations of power, privilege and disadvantage. In essence, therefore, *tourism manifests power* and it mirrors and reinforces the distribution of social and cultural power in individual societies and in the global community, power which springs from an assemblage of interconnected sources. Clarke and Critcher have said that in the first world's so-called 'leisure democracy, a substantial minority remain disenfranchised'.[13] This observation is even more relevant when the focus shifts to other worlds and the 'minority' becomes the majority.

The international tourism system

As the most significant global industry, tourism has been the subject of much debate and controversy. Regardless of their political or ideological perspective, however, many of the world's governments and countries attach great importance to an industry which has been variously seen as a route to economic diversification; as a generator of much-needed foreign currency; and as a means to stimulate fast-track hi-tech service skills or infrastructural improvements. Tourism is also regarded as a means of raising the international profile and even prestige of nations, regions and cities.[14] Despite the fact that many of these hopes and aspirations have proved to have been ill-founded, tourism continues to be viewed as a means to bring equilibrium to an unequal and unstable international system.[15] However, far from accelerating global parity or convergence, Crick has argued that tourism actually enhances neo-colonial relationships between the world's rich and poor countries. Whereas once the latter exported primary products to fuel their colonisers' economies, now the colonisers export tourists with high levels of disposable income who vacation in the Third World because it is relatively cheap. Others, such as Holvik and Heiberg have similarly commented on how international tourism is frequently characterised by colonialism and by the political economy of North–South relations.[16] Leisure imperialism has thus replaced economic colonialism. In such a context it is easy to understand why Hawaiians refer to the islands' large hotels owned by American and Japanese corporations as 'the new plantations'. Here, Caucasian men are the hotel managers, Hawaiian men and women are the entertainers and Filipino women are the chambermaids.[17]

It does seem an inescapable conclusion that the global tourism industry is still characterised by neo-colonial employment patterns where certain ethnic groups and women tend to be concentrated in the poorest or least desirable positions, undermining any suggestions of equality or meritocracy. The top personnel in tourism operations and facilities outside Europe and North America are often First Worlders[18] and the industry itself is largely controlled by governments, banks, multinationals and international tourism bodies which are 'primarily white or Asian and almost certainly male enclaves of influence'.[19] The tourism industry is, of course, characterised by an increasing participation of women and non-white ethnic groups, both as employees and tourists. Equally clear, however, is that the gendered and racial relationships which characterise the global community channel their participation in particular directions, in many ways constraining their opportunities. As Richter points out: 'In much of the world, tourism is something that non-whites participate in only as employees, if at all.'[20] The tourist is, therefore, largely portrayed as white. As we saw in Chapter 6, although 'more racially and gender diverse tourism is emerging . . . largely stimulated by rising economic power amongst women and particular ethnic groups, such as African-Americans',[21] the forms of that development are still articulated by a male, white script. Understandably, advocates of various forms of 'alternative', 'just' or 'fair' tourism, from which the local people will benefit while a situation of intercultural understanding develops, suggest that this is a long way from the reality of the Third World.[22] This is hardly surprising in a global economy characterised by historical and contemporary relations of domination and subordination – dimensions of power which any analysis of tourism must consider.

Tourism processes reinforce the way in which the powerful nations perceive, and relate to, the rest of the world[23] and the tourism image provides a superb window onto those relationships. As Crick says: 'The imagery of international tourism is not . . . about socioeconomic reality at all. It is about myths and fantasies, and . . . it can harm a country's development efforts precisely because its own image making creates a false picture of the Third World.'[24] What is the impact, for instance, of the construction of certain countries as 'timeless' and 'primitive', as inferior to their western, technological counterparts? Thus, Vietnam is described by western tour operators as 'still a country out of time . . . a real travel experience [which] . . . should be visited now before western influence takes too strong a hold'.[25] Likewise, 'Zimbabwe and Botswana are largely unaffected by the march of time'[26] and the whole of Eastern Europe is described by one operator as 'wrapped up in a time warp and delivered . . . courtesy of us'.[27] These descriptions both mirror and reinforce pervasive Western perceptions which may well hold significant implications for such countries' economic development.

The application of such descriptions to countries, and even whole regions, is by no means restricted to tourism or to less economically developed countries. The international global economy provides an excellent example of how ideology can ignore and distort a 'reality' which contrasts with established Western mores and beliefs. Japan's continued economic strength still baffles many Western economic experts, 'in particular, writers for *The Economist* magazine, whose free market views are holy writ for many opinion formers and policy makers in the United States and across Europe'.[28] These writers persist in predicting economic decline and failure regardless of the relative success of the Japanese economy. Whilst common elsewhere, the description of other cultures as inferior to the West is, however, a particular feature of tourism promotion and travel writing. For example, in a *Condé Nast Traveler* article on Malaysia, the writer comments that: 'the economic miracle . . . has transformed this onetime backwater Islamic nation into the fastest growing country in South East Asia', clearly implying the superiority of western-style capitalism and linking the Muslim faith with primitive economics.[29]

International tourism in its contemporary form, 'linked as it is with transnational corporations, ruling elites and political hegemonies',[30] is not simply about power relationships between societies, but also within them. Tourism processes parallel the pre-existing socio economic processes which animate a society they do not exist outside of them.[31] Within countries, power is manifested in various ways, for example, in the relationship between the government and local groups and cultures. In this situation, the government is at one and the same time the planner and marketer of the identities, products and practices displayed to tourists.[32] The continued success of the international tourism system is vitally dependent on the involvement of national and local élites. The global economic system is characterised by relations of advantage and disadvantage but within the disadvantaged societies, there are economic and political élites which attempt to 'associate' themselves 'with the values, imagery etc. of the superior group'.[33]

It would, of course, be naive to suggest that the West could somehow simply impose its perspective on a particular country or culture – as we outlined in Chapter 1, the dominance of the prevailing ideology creates *consensual* marketing. There are many manifestations of power within any one society or context and we have to look at the interplay between foreign, national and local governments, finance and elites. Elites in any given society are constantly engaged in relationships with those in other societies. These relationships promote and reinforce ways of seeing which, as we will examine in Chapters 9 and 10, serve to confirm and promulgate racist and (hetero-)sexist stereotypes and relations of domination and subordination. Our discussion in this chapter has so far focused on the international dimensions of power. It is time to shift the emphasis somewhat, whilst retaining a global perspective, to the relations of power which characterise everyday life. Tourism 'involves processes which are constructed out of complex and varied social realities and relations are often hierarchical and unequal'.[34] It is to two of those relations – gender and race – that we are now going to turn.

Gender, race and power

Gender and race have received significant attention in other social science disciplines, including leisure studies.[35] In tourism, however, these variables have, until recently, been largely ignored or marginalised, despite the fact that tourism is a field profoundly influenced by perceptions of image and identity.[36] This has begun to change with research gaining momentum, as we saw in Chapter 1, through the work of authors such as Enloe and Richter.[37] Gender and race are two of the key determinants of power relations and their interplay creates new dimensions to inequalities – 'Space and race, when combined, have different implications for women and men, even of the same social class.'[38] The wielding of power in and through the tourism industry can be investigated through the experiences of different races and genders. Their touristic representations portray and reinforce existing power structures and reflect a masculine and 'Western desire for an exotic "other"'.[39] Thus, the relationship between the West and the Other is expressed through racialised and gendered exchanges. In this sense, when a western brochure advises tourists to Asia that: 'When you see a girl in a bar . . . dancing suggestively with a live snake, then instead of thinking of her as a harlot, picture instead a little girl trying to shock an adult out of pure bedevilment',[40] we see not just the exertion of male power over female bodies, but also the ability of the West to portray Orientals as childlike and relatively powerless.

Power thus operates through the variables of race, ethnicity, class, age and abilism, all of which are filtered through gendered views of the world and acceptable gendered behaviours. There is a growing recognition that in order to understand how tourism mediates existing power relationships, we need to expand the scope of a subject which has largely overlooked 'the role of sexual ideology in maintaining and reproducing these systems and structures'.[41] To push back the boundaries further in tourism and to expand its relevance there must be a move to situate tourism more centrally within the 'long phallic tradition of desire for those with less power and privilege'.[42] This is even more critical given that notions of masculinity and femininity are vital to the maintenance of the tourism industry – 'The very structure of international tourism *needs* patriarchy to survive.'[43]

Gender roles and relationships are grounded in society and refer to social classifications into 'masculine' and 'feminine'.[44] These distinctions are sites of struggle since, as Foucault wrote: 'For the state to function in the way that it does, there must be between male and female . . . quite specific relations of domination which have their own configurations and relative autonomy.'[45] In this sense, 'most women's and men's actions are "gendered", that is, they give men advantages over women'.[46] Gender differences have declined in the developed world a great deal, but they remain highly significant, and, whilst differences vary from one country to another, in all cases women remain dependent on men.[47] Despite this, however, all too often 'no allowance is made for gender differences in social research' due to 'a gender bias which subsumes female behaviour into that of the dominant male pattern'.[48] This oversight is all the more surprising in tourism as the desire to travel has traditionally been characterised in masculine terms and 'infused with masculine ideas about adventure, pleasure and the exotic'.[49] Masculinity has defined travel whilst, in contrast, femininity has frequently been defined in opposition to notions of travel and independent experience and has revolved around notions of domesticity. In this way, the gendered nature of the tourism industry is linked to specific western notions of masculinities and femininities since, together with imperialism, these were instrumental in the formation and development of the global tourism industry.

Historical evidence of the interplay between gender and imperialism can be found in the nineteenth century World Fairs discussed in Chapter 1. In many ways, these exhibitions were forerunners of mass tourism since they enabled people to 'visit' other cultures and nations by proxy. The similarity also exists in the way in which the World Fairs and the contemporary tourism industry both characterise countries and peoples in oppositional terms – civilised and savage, developed and primitive, 'us' and 'them'. World Fairs represented other peoples and cultures in cliched terms 'at opposite ends of the modernity scale',[50] in which the imperial nations represented the zenith of development and the colonised its nadir. The mission of imperialism and the role of the World Fairs was not only racial, however, but gendered. Men colonised, women stayed at home. The only way the latter could view the exotic, which was experienced directly by their adventurous sons and husbands, was at the Worlds Fairs.

Just as gender and race collided historically in the World Fairs, so they do today in tourism. The industry has yet to fully recognise the female audience – the advertising images are designed to appeal to men[51] and remarkably few efforts have been made to create destinations and attractions targeted at women.[52] Moreover, it is an industry which is overwhelmingly subject to the complex relationship which exists between the West and the so-called 'Other', the non-white, non-westerners.[53] MacCannell has argued that mass tourism is in fact a powerful shaper of ethnic identity which produces 'new and more highly deterministic ethnic forms than those produced during the colonial phase'.[54] This is because 'Westerners continue to write the true story of the existence of other peoples.'[55] Thus, images of the Third World, or ethnic minority groups within societies tend to reflect a western, white, male, colonial perspective of the 'Other'. Such representations defend white racial advantage by marginalising and excluding non-whites and demeaning female bodies.

Ways of seeing the tourism image creators

The construction of the tourism image and the direction of its gaze is one discourse amongst many and it draws on other gazes and other discourses, one of which is colonialism. Karen Anderson has demonstrated how racism 'has long structured socio-structural relations' in settler nations and has 'been woven into a range of power differentiated regimes . . . into the present'.[56] In this context, it will come as no surprise to find that the images portrayed by the travel media assume a particular kind of tourist – white, western, male and heterosexual.[57] This is the model of the typical tourist largely because those behind the camera, the image creators themselves, are predominately male, white and western and where they are not from this group, they read from a script which privileges its view. 'Moreover, those ideologies can be so powerful that they may blind consumers to other interpretations',[58] as well as the people who themselves work in the industry.

There are two immediately noticeable features about the key agents of image creation – the advertising agencies, market research bureaux and marketing consultants. The first is the location of the offices of the leading companies at the heart of metropolitan life.[59] Seven of the top ten global advertising agencies are US-based[60] – as we mentioned in Chapter 3, it is typical that the creative agency for the ITT Sheraton group is based in Boston, Massachusetts and The Leading Hotels of the World group has its headquarters on Third Avenue in Manhattan. The second key feature is the lack of any scholarly work on the make-up of advertising and marketing practitioners as occupational groups.[61] Nixon, in his discussion of advertising, comments that 'the kinds of gender, "racial" and ethnic identities or scripts that are sanctioned within these creative industries' needs further investigation. Such filters produce particular ways of seeing the tourism world, the tourist and the visited in advertising imagery, ways of seeing which have independent political significance.[62] We cannot comment in detail here about the organisational practices of agencies or on the composition of their staff. We can, however, examine the output of the agencies and the marketers to discern their 'scripts'. As we shall see, it clearly provides a white, male, heterosexual norm against which others are compared.

Much has been made about the rise of women, particularly in the fields of advertising, marketing and tourism. Yet despite the emergence of female executives, it is obvious that equality does not exist. It may be that in the USA women currently account for almost one-third of marketing managers, but the flip side of that figure is that 70% of these professionals are male.[63] As Nelson comments in her book, *How to Market to Women*, 'I've been in the advertising business most of my professional life, and I haven't concluded that most media buyers are women.'[64] In addition, the history and organisational cultures of advertising agencies are male dominated and Nixon points out how 'particular masculine scripts were privileged within the culture of advertising'.[65] The tourism image, like all advertising images, is created, filtered and mediated through cultural and ideological structures. Sceptics of this perspective may do well to bear in mind that despite the growing economic power of blacks in the USA, only two African-American advertising agencies have travel accounts.[66] Similarly, as we saw in Chapter 6, those tourism products which are aimed at African-Americans, particularly Black heritage trails, have actually been constructed by white marketers for black consumption.

Whilst it is true that the powerful in contemporary tourism, as creators and consumers of the image, share a particular profile, to portray the powerful as monolithically Western or male or white is far too simplistic. This is to 'erase' the 'refinements to the dominator perspective' and to create a 'falsely tidy dichotomy of relations between *a* racialized "us" versus *a* racialized "them", when in reality the social processes constituting social relations were [and are] complex and differentiated'.[67] Instead, the reality is one where colonialism and imperialism, key precursors of tourism discourses, relied on the '. . . leadership – less of whites *per se* than – of a specific "master subject" who was white, adult, male, heterosexual and bourgeois'.[68] Today this master subject continues to construct the media, powerful players in the creation of the images and identities which characterise the tourism industry, although this dominance is not deliberately orchestrated, for instance, 'Masculinism is not understood as a conscious conspiracy' but rather 'a complex series of . . . discursive positions, relations and practices'.[69] Instead:

> Discourses intersect, so that certain identities are constituted as more powerful and more valuable than others; thus, in the dominant culture of the West now, a white bourgeois heterosexual man is valued over a black working class lesbian woman.[70]

It is difficult to underestimate the potential influence of this master subject-dominated media in the construction of the tourist's world view. Silver, writing on the marketing of Third World destinations, argues that the images and information disseminated by the travel industry are critically important influences on First-Worlder perceptions.[71] Whilst they draw on cultural markers, advertisements and travel brochures are themselves vital sources of information for the potential tourist.[72] Mellinger argues that the media act as:

> powerful tour guides that can produce ideas, identities, and role models for tourists, and define their situations, set their agendas, and establish the boundaries of their gaze.[73]

In such cases, tourists' knowledge and understanding, for example, of Third World peoples and places '. . . seem to derive most immediately and explicitly from images marketed in travel magazines, advertisements and brochures'.[74] Yet whilst the travel literature becomes the framework through which the tourist filters experience and perception, the image creator:

> remains firmly lodged in the cultural values and orientations of his own society. He deals in the ethnicity of others, packaging and marketing it to members of his own culture . . . [he is a] 'broker in ethnicity'.[75]

In the process of marketing images of 'exotic' places and peoples, travel brochures draw upon 'a small set of indigenous markers . . . through which the tourist filters his perceptions' and which create a marketable ethnic stereotype.[76] Whilst these image creators may use genuine ethnic markers and cultural symbols in their marketing literature, their perceptions are channelled through particular lenses which themselves have established ways of seeing other people and cultures. They are thus mediated at a number of levels which further complicate and distort 'reality', whatever that may be. As O'Barr comments:

> Many advertisements for travel photography deal with foreign peoples and cultures, offering blueprints for their readers to use, in constricting their own touristic experiences and about representing otherness.[77]

He goes on to argue that photographs represent 'the social patterns and cultural values that govern our lives'. Through these images we can see 'how representations of other peoples' lives reflect, shape and even construct our perceptions of them'.[78] As we shall now examine, photography is a powerful shaper of the tourism image.

The power of the camera

Photographic representations are selective not just in terms of what is portrayed, but also in which images are photographed and the meanings and values which are conveyed by them. Importantly, such representations can also define the parameters within which the representations of peoples and places are constructed. The ambiguous nature of the photograph may convey many potential meanings. However, of these potential meanings, one meaning tends to be privileged above others. This preferred meaning may well be supported or indicated by the text which accompanies the photographic image. As such it is essential to look not just at the image but also the text in order to establish these preferred meanings.[79] It is the visual representations which are particularly important, however, because of the peculiar attributes associated with the camera, attributes which are themselves highly questionable and contested. The power of the photographic image lies in its ability to seemingly objectively represent reality, yet the active processes which lie behind the image – how photographers select, construct and frame their subjects – normally remain obscured (case study 8.1).

Case Study 8.1   A Play on Fantasy Reveals the Power of the Image Creators

The July 1997 front cover of *Condé Nast Traveler*, one of the most popular travel magazines in the USA, depicts a beautiful young woman standing on a tropical beach 'dressed' as a mermaid – a creature of myths and fantasies. The notion of fantasy is echoed in the magazine's editorial which recognises and understands that when we visit an island paradise we cast off not only our normal form but also 'normal' standards of behaviour and indulge in those dreams we associate with paradise islands. The editorial, in describing the cover, says it is:

> A PLAY ON FANTASY – the transforming notion that once we set foot on an island we shed our normal form and become . . . part of the paradise we associate with islands.

We can look at this photograph in a number of ways, just as we did with our examples in Chapter 2. On a superficial level, it is merely a photograph of a beautiful woman on an island beach. Once we look below the surface, however, it reveals the interplay of various discourses of power. The photograph was constructed by a white, male photographer, in consultation with the magazine's editorial staff. The choice of model, her appearance and pose are all designed to depict a certain image. What we are seeing here is a reflection of the heterosexual male gaze – woman is objectified and photographed. As a mermaid, she is blonde, unclothed and beautiful, evoking a myriad of myths and fantasies drawn from western legends. Mermaids are siren-seducers, erotic but perfidious and deadly. Whilst she protects her modesty with folded arms, her face is uplifted, her eyes closed and her lips pouted, tempting a (male) kiss.

The photograph not only reflects gendered power relations, but also reveals the everyday realities of power which structure the West's encounters with the rest. This photo shoot took place, not on Moorea, as the reader might infer from the editorial, but in Langkawi, Malaysia. Langkawi is a staunchly Muslim island and the photographer, in his contributor's notes, recognises the paradoxical relationship between the subject of the photograph and the country which forms its backdrop. He says: 'It is a Muslim country, so I felt strange shooting a topless woman on the beach.'

Rarely does such background information feed into our knowledge of the image creation process, yet in this instance it reveals much about the power relationships which characterise all international transactions. The powerful take the pictures they want, even when this contradicts local customs and religious beliefs. In Muslim countries women's hair is covered, but here we have not only hair but naked breasts. In many ways the photograph provides a microcosm of the power relationships which underpin the international tourism industry and the creation of the tourism image.

It is the camera's apparent objectivity which gives it a representational legitimacy. In the sense that the camera appears to:

> deal with the images of real people . . . the photograph seems closer to lived experience than words ever can be. This tends to privilege the photographic image over the written word for many viewers, and therefore underpins its claim to documentary objectivity.[80]

The photograph is so powerful precisely because of this notion 'that the images produced are not the product of a human brain but of an impersonal camera eye'.[81] Photographs therefore offer particular perceptions of a society and can create new ways of regarding people and places as Hamilton demonstrated in his study of photo-journalism in post-war France. This was 'a photography of the cultural' – a collection of images which 'created a system of representations of what made France French in a particular era'.[82] In this fashion, the visual representation:

> offers a certain vision of the people and events that it documents, a construction which rests on how they were represented by the choices of both photographers and the press.[83]

Unlike text, which is by default constructed with a certain point or perspective in mind, photographs appear to be reflections rather than constructions of reality and have 'special value as evidence or proof'.[84] The camera seems to reflect not distort, objectify not subjectify. As such, photographs can persuade where the written word would be disregarded or even dismissed as mere window dressing. Photography has become 'a principal medium for our understanding of the world', a two-dimensional medium which we trust and to which we attach special significance.[85]

The photograph is not a mere replication of fact, however, but 'a mode of representation deeply coloured by ambiguities, and generally representative of the paradigm in which it has been constructed'.[86] The photograph is a subjective interpretation since it is 'mediated through the perspective of the person making it . . . it is . . . a mixture of emotion and information'[87] and, in the case of tourism, a marketing brief or agenda. Reality is thus interpreted by the marketer, the photographer and the viewer. In tourism, photographs (and text) familiarise and interpret the unfamiliar, yet they are neither factual records nor innocent of value. Photographs thus tend to legitimate certain interpretations at the expense of others. They are designed to communicate a particular view of a particular people or place at a particular point in time and they are intended to elicit a particular response from the potential tourist. The interpretative framework is also defined in promotional literature by the desire to sell vacations to potential tourists. The 'reality' which emerges therefore revolves around the construction of images in which people and places are assigned particular roles in order to enhance the tourism product and increase the chances of sale to an already culturally dominant clientele. Images are thus designed to appeal to a clientele which is currently largely western and white (and male) and are thus constructed within that particular paradigm.

Tourist postcards and photographs

Postcards and tourists' collections of photographic images of tourism destinations and peoples represent particular interpretations of these places at a particular point in time in the same way as promotional literature. Postcards are an important, if somewhat neglected, part of the tourism image discourse. Enloe has commented that 'selecting postcards is one of those seemingly innocent acts that has become fraught with ideological risks' as we search for the 'picturesque' rather than the 'reality' of peoples' lives.[88] As Edwards has commented, the 'Exoticism' they depict 'is not merely the . . . regurgitation of stereotypes on the one hand or, on the other, insignificant ephemera. Rather . . . this exoticism both influences and is influenced by the central motivating structures in the touristic process itself. . .'.[89]

As we briefly discussed in Chapter 3, photographs and photography have a particularly significant place in the process of tourism representation, both through 'public' and 'private' images.[90] Indeed, it has been said that 'the camera and tourism are two of the uniquely modern ways of defining reality',[91] and thereby of defining relations between countries and peoples. The cameras that the tourists themselves purchase are sold as a 'mechanism to bring home, preserve and display photographic souvenirs'.[92] In many ways, their own cameras frame the tourists' gaze. From Monument Valley to the Pyramids and the Parthenon, tourists around the world are advised by their tour guides of the perfect spot to capture 'a Kodak moment'. Certainly such photographs, preserved in albums, have 'become substitutes for memory and constitute both the structure and context of travel recollections'.[93]

Whilst Kodak may be on the lips of every tour guide, all the main photographic companies are closely associated with tourism promotion. A full page advertorial by Canon invites readers of *Condé Nast Traveler* to: 'Get the Big Picture in Texas.' Here there is 'A Whole World of Images . . . For photographers of every ability . . . [Texas] offers more than 300,000 square miles of photo opportunities.'[94] Teaching the tourist to use the camera to capture photographic moments is an ongoing process. Texas offers the tourist 'a host of images you'll want to capture, bring home and treasure for a lifetime', whilst the reader is clearly told that Canon offers you 'Tips for Taking Great Shots in Texas'.[95] In a different issue of the same magazine, a seven page joint Kodak-Jamaica Tourist Board advertorial, 'Picture Jamaica', informs readers that 'a trip to Jamaica will take you beyond your wildest imagination. . . and Kodak will help you capture it all'.[96] In such ways, travel photography advertisements have promoted this idea of collecting photographic souvenirs and 'helped standardize cultural expectations about travel photographs'.[97]

In this process of capturing the perfect shot, however, there is a very clearly defined power relationship between the photographers and the photographed, where the former are powerful and the latter are like actors, 'dancing to directions'.[98] In fact, such are the power inequalities in this process of travel photography that O'Barr has described 'advertisements for travel photography as a continuous discourse'. He argues that the differences between the visitors and the visited are invariably emphasised over the similarities and that this repetition of difference itself contributes to the construction of otherness amongst foreign peoples and amongst ethnic minorities in the tourists' own countries. 'Advertisements that depict foreigners, . . . depict ideologies about relationships between us and them'[99] as travel photographs seek to tell a story not of a 'common humanity but of fundamental economic, political and cultural differences'.[100] Us and Them are often in contrast, the former being associated with wealth and leisure, and the latter with poverty and labour. Above all, the visited peoples in foreign places are almost always depicted as having to work for their living, whilst the visitors have the freedom of leisure.[101] These ideas are not only reflected in the tourists' and marketers' photographs but also in the how to do it books on photography. These describe what O'Barr terms 'photographic colonialism' as they construct the people who live in other parts of the world as the raw materials for our photographs, whose images we 'appropriate'.[102] In such ways, 'the inequality of relationships runs throughout the discourse of advertising depicting the experience of tourism. . . . [and] The camera serves to boost it.'[103]

The power of stereotyping in representation

The body is perhaps the ultimate site of the operation of knowledge and power through a photographic lens. Men and women, black and white have been 'seen' differently and described in different terms throughout history. Their bodies have been inscribed with particular meanings and thus constrained or empowered in particular ways. Rational masculinity contrasts with irrational femininity, the abstract thus confronts the passionate body, the superior the inferior.[104] In fact, there are remarkable similarities between how women and blacks have been scripted and defined by an empowered white masculine tradition.[105] From this we can see that how people are portrayed and described has implications not only for how they are seen and how they may act, but also how they perceive themselves. As Said concludes, 'cultural domination is maintained . . . as much by consent as by direct and crude economic pressure'.[106] When examining the representation of difference we need to look at variables such as sexuality, gender, race and ethnicity. We also need to recognise that representations are not exclusive to one particular arena or industry. Tourism is but one 'site of representation'[107] in which difference is portrayed. There are many sites of representation and, as we shall see, the images used are repeated across sites.

The role of stereotyping

Stereotyping is a technique which we make use of to classify people and places according to particular traits and roles. It reduces people to those traits, exaggerating and simplifying them, producing caricatures which are resistant to change.[108] Stereotyping:

> sets up a symbolic frontier between the 'normal' and the 'deviant' . . . the 'acceptable' and the 'unacceptable', what 'belongs' and what does not or is 'Other', between 'insiders' and 'outsiders', Us and Them.[109]

Stereotyping is all about power, the power of one to label or define another and thus to represent peoples and places in particular ways. Dominant groups and perspectives thus:

> attempt to fashion the whole of society according to their own world view, value system, sensibility and ideology . . . they make it appear . . . as 'natural' and 'inevitable' . . . in so far as they succeed, they establish their hegemony.[110]

Stereotypes abound in the tourism image, for example, in the portrayal of men and women. As we look closer, we can see that, as in all advertising,[111] depictions of their relationships are seldom egalitarian. Men drive rental cars, women ride as passengers; men select from menus, women praise the choices; men swim and water-ski, women lounge seductively by poolsides; men invite women out and they accept and dress to conform to male expectations. The contradictory representations that strike us as unusual – of a man looking after children whilst a woman goes scuba-diving – merely confirm the usual messages. Clichés operate in the same way and it is not enough to dismiss either them or stereotypes as evidence of lazy thinking. Rather we need to enquire, why it is that certain words or phrases are used so frequently by certain people at certain times – by tourism marketers – what is it about such words which makes them so popular? The answer, in the words of Fiske, is that 'Clichés are the commonsense, everyday articulations of the dominant ideology.'[112]

This ability of powerful groups to manage and manipulate cultural as well as economic power has resulted in the production of a 'radicalised knowledge of the Other . . . [which is] deeply implicated in the operations of power (imperialism)'.[113] This is a racialised knowledge of the Other highlighted – not just in the Orient by Said, but by McClintock in Africa,[114] by Fredrikson in the pro-slave states of the USA,[115] and by Mellinger in his historical analysis of postcards of African-Americans from the Southern States (1893–1917).[116] In all of these studies, the images which are portrayed are selective and make no attempt to communicate the rich diversity of other peoples' cultures. This racialised knowledge, in which the West has labelled and defined Others, could largely be described as the product of three ages. The age of slavery, of empire and more latterly, in the post-war period, the age of migration from the 'Third World' into the West.[117] In many ways, however, contemporary representations are more insidious and ultimately more dangerous in the sense that whilst colonialism has been rejected economically and politically, it continues to construct cultural perspectives of peoples and places, but in a way which is covert.

The significance of such imagery is far wider than the impact of seeing a photograph in a brochure. Representations reinforce cultural stereotypes. Peoples are not represented as they would represent themselves but as the West sees them.[118] This in turn influences how peoples are perceived and how they perceive themselves. Particular identities are consumed and reinforced at the expense of others. The identities which are portrayed have a wider significance, just as Perry and Bussey comment on the impact of stereotypical gender portrayals on children's behaviour,[119] so Wood argues that there is evidence to suggest that:

> state definitions of tourist attractions, embodied in tourism planning, marketing and development, affect local perceptions of national identity and cultural heritage.[120]

Therefore, as we saw in Chapter 7, what states choose to celebrate in tourism are political acts which communicate certain aspects of societies and particular identities. It would be naive to imagine, however, that this was somehow the end of the matter. This selection process conveys messages both to those who are visitors and to those who are visited, influencing how tourists see those they visit and ultimately how the visited see themselves. This 'racial grammar of representation' is well documented in the twentieth century[121] and echoes are clearly heard in contemporary tourism marketing. MacCannell has argued that certain ethnic identities are maintained and promoted over others in order to entertain the tourist[122] and, as we shall see in Chapter 10, non-whites rarely feature in tourism advertisements. Thus, the 'Other' continues to be described in the terms highlighted by Spivak:

> People of colour are seen but do not see, are represented but do not represent, and are photographed but do not photograph. . . . This racist regime of representation preserved and defended the racial privilege of European Americans.[123]

Hall has commented that 'The marking of "difference" is thus the basis of that symbolic order we call culture.'[124] People who differ from the majority (Them as opposed to Us) have traditionally tended to be represented in binary terms, such as good or bad, civilised or primitive; and ugly or attractive.[125] This racialised knowledge of the Other frequently makes use of binary representations which label and define the world in terms of us and them, superiority and inferiority, intellect and instinct. Peoples and places are assigned key characteristics which conform to this two-dimensional or oppositional world view (Table 8.1).[126]

These binary representations between the primitive, sexual and violent blacks and the civilised, cerebral and restrained whites are, according to Segal, 'internationalised by Black people themselves' because of the essentially white-dominated culture in which they live.[127] Wrapped up in these stereotypes are certain notions of black sexuality – black men as 'studs' and black women 'whores'. In this gaze, we can see how black sexuality has been constructed as masculine, animalistic, elemental and unrestrained; and Oriental sexuality as feminine, sophisticated and decadent. This reminds us that, despite the binary depiction of others, it is important to note Anderson's comment that 'relationships between dominant and minoritized groups are crossed not only by discursive fields but also by multiple

Table 8.1 The Difference Between 'Them' and 'Us'.

Black	White
savage	civilised
instinctual	intellectual
natural	cultured
simple	complex
primitive	advanced
emotional	scientific
feeling	learning
custom	knowledge
ritual	reason
barbaric	developed

positionings that are not reducible to the binary division of 'us' and 'them'.'[128] In this sense, racism, for example, often draws on gender as a form of oppression, an intersection of power relations which needs to be understood to fully appreciate the 'wider discursive network' which structures racism, sexism and homophobia.

Historically, the African man or woman has been characterised at best as a noble, innocent and simple savage, and at worst, as beastly, even evil, rather than human, the division reflecting the divergent views of the anti- and pro-slavery groups and the missionary forces.[129] Africa was 'a kingdom of darkness', or 'a dark continent' from which its people had to be rescued by 'the Englishman. . . [a] superior being, obliged reluctantly but inevitably to bring "civilisation" to the inferior races of the world'.[130] These others were seen as inferior – because of a supposed proximity to the ape, humanity's ancestor – yet compellingly sensual and expressive, in stark contrast to white Victorian repression and restraint.[131]

In this polarised gaze, we can see how the West 'set Africa up as a foil to Europe',[132] just as it constructed the Orient. In the same way as Said argued that the Western conceptions of the Orient continue to structure how the West sees the East, Segal comments that 'The image of Africa as dark and malevolent, primitive and unchanging is with us still . . . increasingly the idea grew that Africa was not simply unchanged, but unchangeable.'[133] Whilst this may seem a highly historical view, we would do well to note that the legacy of colonialism continues to dominate western thinking on those who are not Western. As Jablow and Hammond concluded in their study of four centuries of British writing about Africa: 'The liquidation of empire by no means bankrupted the traditional messages. On the contrary, the new situation has been as much a stimulus for proliferation of the tradition as had been the growth of empire.'[134]

This 'racial grammar of representation' is well documented, not only in the colonialism of the nineteenth century but also in the twentieth century history of the cinema.[135] To echo our discussions of Chapters 3 and 4, it is not just specifically tourism-related photographs which influence how we construct others, for popular culture, in visual terms art, the performing arts, the cinema and television, all contribute to constructing our world view. All spheres of culture draw on the same stock of knowledge and thus privilege the same stereotypes and ways of seeing. For example, Denzin, drawing on the work of Foucault, has analysed Hollywood's manipulations of class, race and gender, arguing that the cinematic gaze must be understood as part of the machinery of power which regulates social behaviour.[136] Amongst others, notably de Lauretis, Denzin contends that:

> the cinematic apparatus operated as a technology of gender (and race) which reproduced the structure of patriarchy (and racism) by implementing a concept of looking and spectatorship which often made women (and non-whites) the objects of the male (white) gaze. . . .[137]

Here, again, we see the ways in which race and gender overlay each other. Not only is the cinematic gaze white, it is also male. Thus, despite the recent changes in the role of women, this view of the gaze remains accurate, as 'Hollywood's contemporary female . . . gaze is still defined by the masculine eye, even as recent texts expose the limits of the male look and give women the power to gaze on themselves and the male figure.'[138] Thus, although films such as *Broadcast News*, *Blue Velvet*, *Black Widow* and *Fatal Attraction* 'made women active, aggressive voyeurs . . . in the end, each woman . . . found her body coded in patriarchal terms, she remained the object of the male's look. . . .'[139] The cinematic gaze is similarly racially structured and, for example, a number of Oriental stereotypes emerge, including: the beautiful Oriental woman (the exotic China doll); the sinister Oriental man (the drug kingpin); and the ageing, wise Oriental (the revered priest).[140] Hollywood, as other sites of cultural production, has thus been an agent in the creation of racial and gendered stereotypes, representations which the tourism image draws on and reinforces. In fact, tourism imagery continues to construct and recreate stereotypes, it certainly does not break them down.

This racial grammar of representation can be clearly seen in contemporary tourism. The Other continues to be described in terms which are childish, simple, dependent, mischievous, primitive, and fixed in a paternalistic relationship with the first world.[141] The racial grammar is also particularly relevant in terms of gender, of 'women of colour' and how they are seen or represented in the tourism literature. It is also significant to point out that this racialised knowledge or stereotyping is also about fantasy as much as perceived reality, as Hall has said, about 'what is not being said, but is being fantasised, what is implied but cannot be shown'.[142] Images of black men and women appear to be tied up with a white obsession of black sexuality, revealing deep-seated white fantasy views and fears of black men as 'supermen, better endowed than whites and sexually insatiable'.[143] This fantasy dimension revolves around perceived beliefs about the highly sexual nature of 'Them' – a nature which is at one and the same time dangerous but compelling. Difference is thus 'powerful, strangely attractive, precisely because it is forbidden, taboo, threatening to cultural order'.[144] As Marchetti has pointed out in her work on ethnicity and the cinematic image, ethnicity is never neutered and images of race, ethnicity and sexuality are always interweaved. She argues that racial hierarchies are maintained 'through fantasies which reinforce those differences through references to gender. Thus fantasies of threatening Asian men, emasculated eunuchs, alluring Asian "dragon ladies", and submissive female slaves all work together to rationalize white, male domination.'[145] This linkage is apparent in contemporary tourism imagery, and just as Denzin describes the portrayal of the Asian film detectives Charlie Chan, Mr Moto and Mr Wong during 1929–49 as 'feminised Asian men, even eunuchs',[146] never sexually threatening to the white majority, so we will argue, the same portrayals of Asian males appear in tourism images – either as the young Buddhist monk or the aged, wise, even stoic, Oriental.

Just as African-Americans and Asians have been constructed in clichéd roles and identities by the vehicles of popular culture, so too have images of native Americans. There are a number of stereotypical images which prevail. These range from negative images of 'the bloodthirsty savage' and 'the whisky Indian' to more positive images of 'the Noble Savage', a romantic, noble, natural and spiritual representation and 'the stoic Indian', accepting and uncomplaining. These are celluloid images, in that 'Hollywood has given people the image of the stoic Indian who feels no pain or bears it with dignity.'[147] These cinematic stereotypes are grounded in a historical relationship, the present day culmination of which sees the 'white man' presenting 'himself to the Indians in . . . another role, the tourist'.[148] By drawing on these stereotypes, tourists 'dehumanize the Indian, patronisingly turn[ing] him into something "cute" and see[ing] him as a fit object for consumption'.[149] This echoes our earlier discussion of the role of the tourist camera, since here:

> The tourist is so preoccupied with *photographing* Indian culture that he fails to *see* the totem pole – but it does not matter to him anyway because back home his photograph will appear to be the real thing.[150]

In such ways, the tourist constructs indigenous peoples. When they see other cultures through the tourist lens they often see what they choose to, not always what is actually there.[151]

It would be foolish to suggest from this discussion that the process of representation is one way. Every visit by a tourist provokes some kind of interaction with those who are visited. These interactions produce similar but alternative clichéd identities for consumption. Not only are the less powerful groups engaged in a struggle with more dominant groups, they also represent or stereotype the tourists themselves. As Evans-Pritchard observes in an analysis of how tourists and Native Americans interact:

> Pueblo and Navajo silversmiths in New Mexico express and manipulate stereotypical images of tourists and Indians in making and selling their work.[152]

Similarly, Laxson reminds us that the Indians see the tourists in certain ways:

> Thus, the Indians, too, see the tourist as 'other', an anonymous person who passes through, only to be replaced by another anonymous person. This sense of 'otherness' . . . originates in part from the stereotypes each group has of the Other.[153]

Stereotyping is not one way and the Indians regard the tourists as ignorant, greedy, pushy and acquisitive. In this way, 'Indian stories about tourists help shape actual interactions as well as being shaped by them.'[154] Such devices help to mediate relationships with the tourist just as similar devices are used by the tourism industry to mediate the tourists' relationship with local people. In this sense, stereotypes do not merely discriminate but they can also defend:

> For a minority, for 'fourth-worlders', ethnic labelling can be devastating: majority stereotypes of minorities generally oppresses. Minority stereotypes of majorities often seems to empower.[155]

Resistance and change

In the course of this chapter's discussion of power, two particular issues which have yet to feature significantly are change and resistance. Whilst we cannot ignore a reality in which some achieve more power than others, opportunities for change and resistance or their possibilities are central to Foucault's analysis of the operation of power and knowledge. Points of resistance develop, and power relationships may shift or destabilise, thereby fracturing specific dominant discourses. Power is by no means monolithic and it is not merely exercised from above, but within societies. When examining the wider power structures which inform and underpin tourism marketing, it would be a mistake to see the structures and relationships within tourism as static or immutable. There has, and probably always will be, conflict and change within and between cultures. Tourism is merely one more way through which people's cultures and relationships change, through contact and through the incomes generated by the industry. The outcomes are not necessarily negative. Thus, in Bali, for example, the centrality of Balinese culture to the tourism experience has enabled the Balinese to successfully resist Indonesianisation of their educational institutions.[156]

It would also be a mistake to see the imaging process as being somehow linear or one way. As we saw in Chapters 3 and 4, tourists themselves are not passive recipients of marketed images, although, without the tools to assess the accuracy of images, tourists will by necessity have their views shaped by the images promoted in popular culture and in tourist literature and advertisements. It should not be forgotten that tourists themselves are products of particular socio-economic and cultural systems and so share with those responsible for tourism marketing common values and perspectives. It would also be misleading to portray the objects of the tourist gaze, for instance, ethnic minorities and indigenous peoples, as helpless in the face of the power of the representators. They may well attempt to subvert and resist marketed images, however, their ability to do so is severely constrained because the powerful tourist organisations often control the terms and the boundaries of the encounter.[157] As we argued in Chapter 1, what is produced, therefore, is a consensual as opposed to a conspiratorial framework for seeing, albeit one grounded in an unequal, multi-dimensional relationship of domination and subordination.

Discussions on power and powerful groups in society may sometimes suggest, either deliberately or inadvertently, that the opportunities for change and resistance are highly circumscribed because of the sheer dominance of the master subject. We can see some fracturing of power and the development of new alliances to challenge dominant discourses in tourism. The sex tourism industry is one such case in point. The upheaval in the Philippines' political system caused by the removal of Ferdinand Marcos as president presented an opportunity to challenge the domination of the islands by sex tourism. Women activists pressed for change and indeed action was taken. Yet, the punitive consequences were largely inflicted on the relatively powerless. 'In the name of cleaning up the city [Manilan] . . . police arrested hundreds of women. [However,] Virtually no pimps, businessmen or male clients were jailed.'[158] As Clegg has argued in his *Frameworks of Power*, whilst 'there is no reason to expect that representations will remain contextually and historically stable', it is equally apparent that power will be exercised to attempt to maintain the representations or to manage the change. In such ways '. . . knowledge that is used to structure and fix representations in historical forms is the accomplishment of power'.[159]

In Chapters 9 and 10, we expand on this argument and consider tourism identities crafted by marketers which affirm gendered relations; reflect and distort historical colonial relations; and reinforce current economic realities. This chapter has argued that it is highly misleading and disingenuous to see the travel media as being mere value-free representors of some objective reality. Instead they represent a particular reality. After all, they are in the business of selling dreams, of promoting destinations and products, not the business of accurately portraying places and peoples, although it is not in their long-term interest to portray false or misleading images (though this can and does happen). Instead tourism imagery is an arena where power and ideology are manifested. Tourism images can be examined as sites of struggle where particular ideologies triumph at the expense of others, successful ideologies structure how tourists see the world and its inhabitants. The failure to critically analyse such representations contributes to the view that such representations are normal and natural as opposed to being constructed and value laden and thus reflective of particular viewpoints in society. Tourism imagery is part of a discursive formation in which some represent and others are represented. The process of representation is informed by the dominant socio-economic and historical context and similarly contributes to the reinforcement of this context. By considering the marketing of destinations in the Americas, the Orient, Africa and in Europe, the next two chapters will ask just whose myths, whose histories, whose identities and whose heritages are being constructed and presented by tourism agencies and marketers and consumed by tourists? Although these chapters consider gender and race in turn, it is vital that the reader recognise that such a divide is artificial purely to facilitate discussion, and that there is, in reality, a close relationship between the representation of race and gender in the tourism image.

References

1   Clegg, S.R. (1989) *Frameworks of Power*, Sage, London: 149.
2   Crick, M. (1989) Representations of international tourism in the social sciences: sun, sex, sights and servility, *Annual Review of Anthropology*, 18: 307–44: 316–18.
3   See Harrett-Bond, B.E. and Harrett-Bond, D.L. (1979) 'Tourism in the Gambia', *Review of African Political Economy*, 14: 78–90; and Machlis, G.E. and Burch, W.R. (1983) 'Relations Between Strangers: cycles of structure and meaning in tourist systems', *Sociological Review*, 31: 666–92.
4   Enloe, C. (1989) *Bananas, Beaches and Bases. Making Feminist Sense of International Politics*, Pandora, London: 40.
5   Foucault, M. (1980) 'The history of sexuality', *Power/Knowledge: Selected Interviews and Other Writings 1972–1977*, Gordon, C. (ed.), Random House, New York: 187.
6   Wilson, J. (1988) *Politics and Leisure*, Unwin Hyman, London: 12.
7   Rojek, C. (1985) *Leisure and Capitalist Theory*, Tavistock, New York: 146–7.
8   reference 6: 11 and reference 7: 16.
9   reference 6: 11 and reference 7. 13.
10 reference 7: 13.
11 Duncan, N. (1996) 'Sexuality in Public and Private Spaces', 127–45 in Duncan, N. (ed.) *Bodyspace: destabilizing geographies of gender and sexuality*, Routledge, London: 135.

See also Eisenschitz, A. (1988) paper presented at the Leisure Studies Association Third International Conference, Brighton: 1.

12 reference 1: 182–3.

13 Clarke, J. and Critcher, C. (1985) *The Devil Makes Work: Leisure in Capitalist Britain*, University of Illinois Press, Urbana: 174.

14 reference 4: 40. See also Kotler, P. *et al.* (1993) *Marketing Places. Attracting Investment, Industry and Tourism to Cities, States and Nations*, The Free Press, NY.

15 reference 4: 40.

16 Holvik, T. and Heiberg, T. (1980) 'Centre-periphery tourism and self reliance', *International Social Science Journal*, 32 (1), 69–98; Britton, S. (1982) 'The political economy of tourism in the Third World', *Annals of Tourism Research*, 9, 331–338; Nash, D. (1989) 'Tourism as a form of imperialism', in Smith, V. 'Hosts and Guests: an Anthropology of Tourism'; and Selwyn, T. (1992) 'Tourism, Society and development', *Community Development Journal*, 27 (4): 353–60.

17 reference 4: 34.

18 Silver, I. (1993) 'Marketing Authenticity in Third World Countries', *Annals of Tourism Research*, 20: 302–18; and Britton, R. (1979) 'The Image of Third World Tourism in Marketing', *Annals of Tourism Research*, 6: 318–29: 322.

19 Richter, L.K. (1995) 'Gender and Race: Neglected Variables in Tourism Research', 71–91 in Butler, R. and Pearce, D. (eds) *Change in Tourism. People, Places, Processes*, Routledge, London: 85.

20 reference 19: 74.

21 reference 19: 83.

22 reference 2: 319.

23 Hiller, H.L. (1979) 'Tourism: Development or Dependence?', 51–61 in Millett, R. and Will, W.M. (eds) *The Restless Caribbean*: 51, quoted in reference 2: 321.

24 reference 2: 329. See also Britton, R.A. (1979) 'The Image of the Third World in Tourism Marketing', *Annals of Tourism Research*, 6: 318–28.

25 Airwaves America Latina brochure: 45.

26 reference 25: 74.

27 Intra Travel, New Europe 1997 brochure: 2.

28 Fingleton, E. (1996) 'Tokyo Inc. confounds its critics', the *Observer*, 20 October: 22.

29 Torregrosa, L.P. (1997) 'Malaysia to the Max', *Condé Nast Traveler*: 72.

30 O'Grady, R. (1980) (ed.) *Third World Tourism*, Singapore, Christian Conference Asia: 3, quoted in reference 2: 320.

31 Young, R.C. (1977) 'The Structural Context of the Caribbean Tourist Industry. A Comparative Study', *Economic Development and Cultural Change*, 25: 657–71.

32 Wood, R.E. (1984) 'Ethnic Tourism, The State & Cultural Change in South-East Asia', *Annals of Tourism Research*, 11: 353–74.

33 MacCannell, D. (1984) 'Reconstructed Ethnicity, Tourism and Cultural Identity in Third World Communities', *Annals of Tourism Research*, 11: 375–91: 383.

34 Kinnaird, V. and Hall, D. (1994) (eds) *Tourism: a Gender Analysis*, John Wiley and Sons, Chichester: 6.

35 reference 7.

36 reference 19: 71.

37 references 4 and 19.

38 reference 4.

39 Cohen, C. (1995) 'Marketing Paradise, Making Nation?', *Annals of Tourism Research*, 22: 404–21: 418.

40 Selwyn, T. (1992) 'Peter Pan in South-East Asia. Views from the brochures', 117–37 in Hitchcock, M. *et al.* (eds) *Tourism in South-East Asia*, Routledge, London, quoting Redwings Go Places 1989/90 brochure: 123.

41 reference 39: 418.

42 Gallop (1988) 169, cited in reference 39: 418.

43 reference 4: 41.

44 Oakley, A. (1982) *Sex, Gender and Society*, Maurice Temple Smith, London: 16.

45 Foucault, M. (1980) 'The history of sexuality', 183–93 in *Power/Knowledge*, Harvester, Brighton; Gordon, C. (ed.) *Selected Interviews and Other Writings 1972–1977*, Harvester Wheatsheaf, London: 188.

46 Beeghley, L. (1996) *What Does Your Wife Do? Gender and the Transformation of Family Life*, Westview Press, Oxford: 4. See also Acker, J. (1990) 'Hierarchies, Jobs, Bodies: A Theory of Gendered Organizations', *Gender & Society*, 4: 139–58.

47 Beeghley, L. (1996) *What Does Your Wife Do? Gender and the Transformation of Family Life*, Westview Press, Oxford: 129.

48 Breathnach, P. *et al.* (1994) 'Gender in Irish Tourism Employment', 52–73 in reference 34.

49 reference 4: 20.

50 reference 4: 26.

51 Swain, M. (1995) 'Gender in Tourism', *Annals of Tourism Research*, 22: 247–66: 249.

52 reference 19: 74.

53 reference 18.

54 reference 33: 377.

55 ibid.

56 Anderson, K. (1996) 'Engendering Race Research: Unsettling the Self-Other dichotomy', 197–211 in Duncan, N. (ed.) *Bodyspace: destabilizing geographies of gender and sexuality*, Routledge, London: 198.

57 reference 19: 81.

58 Mellinger, W.M. (1994) 'Towards A Critical Analysis of Tourism Representations', *Annals of Tourism Research*, 21 (4): 756–779: 775.

59 Nixon, S. (1997) 'Circulating Culture', 179–234 in Du Gay, P. (ed.) *The Production of Culture/Cultures of Production*, Sage, London: 215.

60 Walker, C. (1996) 'Can TV save the planet?', *American Demographics*, 18 May: 42–7: 43.

61 reference 59: 211.

62 ibid.

63 reference 47: 133.

64 Nelson, C. (1994) *How to Market to Women*, Visible Ink, Detroit: 42.

65 reference 59: 217.

66 reference 19: 80.

67 reference 56: 198.

68 reference 56: 198. See also Rose, G. (1993) *Feminism and Geography: The Limits of Geographical Knowledge*, Polity Press, Cambridge.

69 Rose, G. (1993) *Feminism and Geography. The Limits of Geographical Knowledge*, Polity Press, Cambridge: 10.

70 reference 69: 6.

71 reference 18.

72 Adams, E.M. (1984) 'Come to Tana Toraja. "Land of the Heavenly Kings". Travel Agents as Brokers in Ethnicity', *Annals of Tourism Research*, 11: 469–484.

73 reference 58: 776.

74 reference 18: 303.

75 reference 72: 472.

76 ibid.

77 O'Barr, W. (1994) *Culture and the Ad. Exploring Otherness in the World of Advertising*, Westview, Boulder, Colorado: 17.

78 reference 77: 44.

79 Barthes, R. (1977) 'Rhetoric of the Image', in *Image, Music-Text*, Hill & Wang, New York.

80 Hamilton, P. 'Representing the Social: France and Frenchness in Post-War Humanist Photography', 75–150 in Hall, S. (ed) (1997) *Representation: cultural representations and signifying practices*, Sage and the Open University, London: 87.

81 reference 80: 86.

82 reference 80. 77.

83   reference 80: 76.

84   Newhall, quoted in reference 80: 82.

85   Fulton, M. (ed.) (1988) *Eyes of Time: photojournalism in America*, Little Brown & Co., Boston: 106, quoted in reference 80: 84.

86   reference 80: 87.

87   reference 80: 83.

88   reference 4: 19.

89   Edwards, E. (1996) 'Postcards: Greetings from Another World', 197–222 in Selwyn, T. (ed.) *The Tourism Image. Myths and Myth Making in Tourism*, John Wiley and Sons, Chichester: 197.

90   Berger (1980) as quoted in Botterill, T.D and Crompton, J.L. (1996) 'Two Case Studies. Exploring the Nature of the Tourist's Experience', *Journal of Leisure Research*, 28 (1): 57–82.

91   Horne, D. (1984) *The Great Museum. The Representation of History*, Punto Press, London: 21.

92   reference 77: 18.

93   reference 77: 26.

94   advertisement run in *Condé Nast Traveler*, July 1997: 57.

95   reference 94: 59.

96   advertisement run in *Condé Nast Traveler*, August 1997, 41–48: 41.

97   reference 77: 21.

98   ibid.

99   reference 77: 12

100   reference 77: 36.

101   reference 77: 26–29.

102   reference 77: 41.

103   reference 77: 29.

104   reference 69: 9.

105   reference 69: 81.

106   Said, E. (1978) *Orientalism. Western Conceptions of the Orient*, Penguin, Harmondsworth: 324.

107   Hall, S. (1997) 'The Spectacle of the "Other"', 223–90 in Hall, S. (ed.) *Representation. Cultural Representation and Signifying Practice*, Sage and the Open University, London: 232.

108   Dyer, R. (1977) *Gays and Film*, British Film Institute, London in reference 107: 257.

109   reference 107: 258.

110   Dyer, R. (1977) *Gays and Film*, British Film Institute, London in reference 107: 259.

111   reference 77: 4.

112   Fiske, J. (1989) *Understanding Popular Culture*, Routledge, London: 118.

113   Said, E. (1978) *Orientalism. Western Conceptions of the Orient*, Penguin, Harmondsworth: 260.

114   McClintock, A. (1995) *Imperial Leather*, Routledge, London.

115   Fredrikson, G. (1987) *The Black Image in the White Mind*, Wesleyan University Press, Hanover, NJ.

116   reference 58.

117   reference 107: 239.

118   references 18 and 39.

119   Perry, D.G. and Bussey, K. (1979) 'The Social Learning Theory of Sex Differences. Imitation is alive and well', *Journal of Personality and Social Psychology*, 37: 1699–1712.

120   reference 32: 366.

121   Hall, S. (ed.) (1997) *Representation: cultural representations and signifying practices*, Sage and the Open University, London: 251.

122   reference 33: 385–6.

123   Spivak, G.C. (1988) 'Can subaltern speak?', in Nelson, C. and Grossberg, L. (eds) *Marxism and the Interpretation of Culture*, University of Illinois Press, Chicago.

124   reference 107: 236.

125   reference 107.

126   see reference 107: 243.

127   Segal, L. (1990) *Slow Motion. Changing Masculinities, Changing Men*, Virago, London: 179.

128   reference 56: 199.

129   reference 127: 170–1.

130   ibid.

131   see also Kovel, J. (1988) *White Racism: A Psychohistory*, Free Association Books, London.

132   Achebe, C., quoted in reference 127: 173.

133   reference 127: 174.

134   Jablow, A. and Hammond, D. (1970) *The Africa That Never Was: Four Centuries of British Writing About Africa*, Twayne Press, New York: 108.

135   reference 107: 251.

136   Denzin, N.K. (1995) *The Cinematic Society. The Voyeur's Gaze*, Sage, London.

137   reference 136. See also de Lauretis, T. (1987) *Technologies of Gender*, Bloomington, Indiana University.

138   reference 136: 139.

139   ibid.

140   reference 136: 59.

141   reference 39.

142   reference 107: 263.

143   ibid.

144   reference 107: 237.

145   Marchetti, G. (1991), 'Ethnicity, the Cinema, and Cultural Studies', 277–309 in Friedman, L.D. (ed.) *Unspeakable Images: Ethnicity and the American Cinema*, University of Illinois Press, Urbana: 289.

146   reference 136: 93.

147   Laxson (1991) 'Tourism and Native Americans', *Annals of Tourism Research*, (18): 365–391: 372.

148   Evans-Pritchard, D. (1989) 'How "They" See "Us"', *Annals of Tourism Research*, (16): 89–105: 90.

149   reference 148: 93.

150   reference 148: 94.

151   reference 148: 95.

152   reference 148: 89.

153   reference 147: 373.

154   reference 148: 98.

155   reference 148: 102.

156   reference 32: 370.

157   reference 18 and reference 58: 775.

158   reference 4: 39.

159   reference 1: 151–2.

9 The gendered and sexualised image

In this chapter we focus on two of the dimensions of power discussed in Chapter 8 – gender and sexuality. We begin by reviewing extant work on gender and tourism, the majority of which has been concerned with female employment patterns and with the complexities of host and guest relationships, particularly sex tourism. There is a notable lack of image-based research on gender and tourism and this forms a central theme of our discussion. We examine the role and use of gender stereotypes in tourism promotional literature and travel writing and introduce a scale for measuring sexism in tourism imagery. The chapter concludes with a discussion of the way in which tourism landscapes are constructed by marketers and travel writers as gendered and racialised, highlighting the close relationship between the language of (hetero-)sexuality and the language of tourism promotion. The discussion reveals how Foucault's web of power engenders tourism, dictating interactions at all levels – from everyday contacts between women and men to the broader relationships between men, women, the media and the state.

The construction of gender

The promotion of gender-related views of the world are ongoing, pervasive processes. Butler has commented that gender is constituted by 'regulated pattern or repetition' of appropriate behaviours[1] and, in a similar vein, Joanne Sharpe has written that gendered identities appear to be 'natural . . . through the repeated performance of gender norms'.[2] Indeed, 'there is mounting evidence that they are packages of expectations that have been created through specific decisions by specific people',[3] and that conventional notions of masculinity and femininity are not innate or inalienable but are learnt, created and constructed. There are many forces and agents which help to construct our expectations of suitable gender behaviours. The mass media is one of the many cultural phenomena which contribute to the construction of gender in the shape of masculine and feminine ideologies. As we have already discussed, media images reflect the prevailing cultural values of a society, drawing upon current images and stereotypes and by this selection, they not only reflect but also help to shape and reinforce such values.[4] Marketers and advertisers select and utilise particular images and aspects of society and ignore or discard others. This selection process reflects and reinforces particular preferred meanings in society which are chosen from the existing collective body of cultural knowledge. This selection has important implications for the representation of men and women in society through its creation and maintenance of stereotypical perceptions and behaviour – particularly as girls and boys tend to imitate what is constructed as appropriate female and male behaviour.[5]

A considerable amount of attention has focused on media representations of women. The most notable early commentators include Millum[6] and Goffman[7] and there are now studies which examine representations across a range of media – from magazine and television advertising[8] to the cinema.[9] Rather fewer studies have examined representations of men[10] and analyses which simultaneously examine the roles and representations of men and women are very uncommon.[11] There is a variety of explanations for this imbalance, including the growth in feminist-related research, the women's movement and the subsequent attention to the roles and relationships confining women in media representations and in reality. Much of this work has demonstrated that the range of images presented within the media have tended to be very narrow, particularly with regard to women. Indeed, the developments in the reality of women's lives in the West seem to be largely irrelevant to the ways in which the media have continued to depict women.[12]

This picture has been modified recently as certain authors, particularly Moore,[13] have argued that there has been a shift towards a more egalitarian media portrayal of men and women, although this view itself is not without its challengers.[14] The marginal shift which does seem to have occurred is most obviously seen in the relationships between men and women in advertising imagery, in the emergence of man as a consumer and in the increasing commodification of the male body.[15] As a result of societal change, contradictory representations of manhood and woman-hood have come to exist and often appear in the same visual image. Perhaps the greatest change can be seen in male representations where advertising traditionally defined men by their family role. For example, in the July 1951 issue of *Time* magazine over 80% of the men depicted in advertisements had obvious family ties; in the same magazine issue in 1986, the figure had fallen to 12.5%.[16] Moreover, where men are shown with others, it is now usually as a young heterosexual couple where the marital context is left vague. Instead of the family, the peer group is emerging as the dominant referent group in advertisements, where it operates as a symbol of a wider social belonging. There is also a significant trend within adver-tising to show people – both men and women – on their own. This individualisa-tion of the represented is in part a response to the individualisation of society and in part a device by which advertisers encourage the viewer or reader to project themselves into the advertisement.[17]

Gender and tourism

Scott and Godley posed the question, 'Are leisure worlds generally segmented along the lines of gender identification?'[18] Although a seemingly obvious question, it is one which has been largely overlooked in the tourism marketing literature. As tourism itself is a phenomenon constructed from gendered societies it follows that tourism processes are gendered in their construction, presentation and consumption. The form of this gendering is configured in different and diverse ways which are both temporally and spatially specific.[19] Despite the gendered nature of travel, until relatively recently gender roles and relationships have been largely ignored in tourism research, unlike in leisure studies where a substantial body of work has developed.[20] Two collections of work appeared in the mid Nineties – Kinnaird and Hall's *Tourism: a Gender Analysis* and a special issue of the *Annals of Tourism Research*[21] – both of which attempted to redress the balance and recognised that 'gender is an unevenly represented but expanding focus in tourism studies'.[22] Although many commentators have argued that human societies are characterised by a division of labour by sex,[23] we have seen that gender is 'a system of cultural identities and social relationships between females and males'.[24] In this sense, economic structures such as tourism have 'grown out of gendered societies which inform all aspects of tourism development and activity and all these processes embody gender relations'.[25]

The failure to fully incorporate gender into examinations of the tourism industry, and the processes which inform it, leads to an analysis which is at best partial and at worst superficial and naive. This is because 'notions about femininity and masculinity create and sustain global inequalities and oppressions . . . patriarchal ideas and practices link all of these sectors to each other'.[26] Gender relations therefore simultaneously reflect and reinforce notions of reality in society – gendered realities which, as Swain remarks, shape 'tourism marketing, guests' motivations and hosts' actions'.[27] Wearing and Wearing similarly point out that:

> Gendered tourists, gendered hosts, gendered tourism marketing and gendered tourism objects each reveal power differences between women and men which privilege male views and which have significant impacts on tourism image and promotion.[28]

In so far as tourism research has addressed the issue of gender, it is possible to discern two particular concerns which have captured the imagination of researchers. The first major research strand has focused on the economic relationships which characterise the practical involvement of women in the tourism industry.[29] This involvement takes place not on a level playing field but within societies founded on unequal relationships. Whilst some research has shown that involvement in tourism may bring benefits to individuals or even groups of women within specific communities,[30] tourism has not provided a fundamental challenge to unequal gender relations. More often, it has confirmed and reinforced gendered roles and relationships since the tourism industry is founded on notions of masculinity and femininity. Women largely service the tourism industry as their labour is cheap, particularly when they are employed in jobs which are paid versions of what has traditionally been constructed as 'women's work'. In essence, the tourism industry is founded on an army of poorly paid women who cook, clean, wash and service the needs of incoming tourists. In addition, women's involvement in the industry is not restricted to these practical, domestic tasks, but also encompasses servicing the sexual and emotional needs of tourists.

This brings us to the second major strand of gender research in tourism – studies which have examined the various relationships developed as a result of host and guest contact in tourism destinations. Interest has ranged from the romantic and sexual relations between women guests and male hosts,[31] to the impact of tourists on hosts' traditional social and cultural behaviour patterns.[32] Significant attention has also been devoted to the emergence of sex tourism and the gender relationships which characterise this activity, several studies focusing on the relationship between the sexual 'entertainment' provided by host females on the one side and male guests on the other.[33] Sex is one of the oldest motivators for tourism and the sex tourism industry is one of the logical outcomes of a gendered tourism industry and a gendered international system. It is an industry whose development has been founded on three factors according to Enloe. The first is a poverty-stricken population which encourages women to participate, either voluntarily or forcibly, in the sex industry. The second is male tourists who have been socialised into seeing women in certain countries, for instance in Thailand, as somehow more willing and available. The triumvirate is completed by political and economic institutions and businesses who are prepared to nurture a trade which:

> encourages men . . . to travel to . . . countries specifically to purchase the sexual services of local women. The countries that have been developed . . . [for] sex tourists include those which have served as 'rest and recreation' sites for the American military: Thailand, South Korea, the Philippines.[34]

Sex tourism, and the gendered and economic power relations which characterise it, is of course neither an exclusively female nor an exclusively adult industry. Rogers, for instance, in an examination of the relationships between tourism and child prostitution, suggests that 90% of child prostitutes in Sri Lanka and 60% in the Philippines, are male.[35] It is interesting to note that some Western governments have recently considered the possibility of prosecuting those who travel for child-sex tourism. This was a response stimulated in part by pressure group activity, but largely prompted by western media interest, provoking a public outcry which may not have been unrelated to a number of high-profile child-sex scandals in the West. This vignette reveals two dimensions of global power discourses. Firstly, 'problems', once recognised in the West, seem to assume more world importance; secondly, when the victims of sex tourism are also male, the condemnation of the industry is much more vociferous – a response much different from that generated when the victimised body is female.

The sex trade does not, however, cater exclusively for men and recently there has been an emergence of male host and female guest relationships which, as described by Pruitt and Lafont:

> create an opportunity for women to traffic in men. This situation illuminates the links between economic status and dominance in gender relations and contradicts conventional notions of male hegemony.[36]

The emergence of women as economic powers in the West has led to the development, as yet small-scale, of this so-called 'romance tourism'. Interestingly, however, such relationships are described as romantic rather than sexual, largely because with romance tourism, it is argued that women travel in search of relationships rather than a simple sexual exchange. Neither partner 'considers their interaction to be prostitution, even while others may label it so'.[37] This in itself provides an interesting commentary on gender and power relationships in tourism and society, since the implication is that when women seek sexual encounters they cannot be described in terms which place their male partners in a relatively powerless position.

Just as women are beginning to create a demand for a sex tourism of their own, attention has also been paid in the tourism literature to the impact of organised gender-specific behaviour which can exert pressure on the policymakers of destinations which have hitherto had flourishing sex tourism industries. Leheny, in particular, has focused on the emergence of a greater women's rights movement in Japan and its implications for other countries' sex tourism industries.[38] This social movement in Japan has impacted on the market for Japanese sex tourism in Thailand as Japanese women increasingly avoid sex destinations – a situation which Thai policymakers can ill afford to ignore if they are not to lose a highly lucrative market.[39]

What emerges from this brief review of the extant work on gender and tourism is the lack of image-based research. Abbot Cone has looked at how the construction of Mayan women's self-images changed as a result of the employment and social opportunities offered by tourism in Chiapas, Mexico, but this is a relatively isolated example.[40] The failure to look at gendered tourism marketing, at the representations and presentations of gender, gender relations and sexuality is an omission which has not, however, gone unrecognised in the tourism literature. Kinnaird and Hall noted that tourism brochure representations of men tend to be associated with action, power and ownership, whilst representations of women tend to be associated with passivity, availability and being owned.[41] They also commented that tourism promotion and the myths and fantasies pedalled by tourism marketers are dependent upon shared conceptions of gender, sexuality and gender relations and that women are often used in the promotion of the exoticised nature of destinations:

> Sexual imagery, when used to depict the desirability of places in such a way, says a great deal about the gendered nature of the marketing agents and their fantasies . . . the sexual myths and fantasies extolled in the tourism promotion lead to the construction of these ideas in the hearts and minds of tourists.[42]

In summarising the, then current, state of research, Kinnaird and Hall called for an analysis of gendered tourism marketing, focusing on sexuality and gender relations. Despite this comment, little of the extensive research elsewhere on gender imagery has yet to permeate the tourism literature.[43] As we shall see, the gendered nature of tourism imagery is not merely created by the marketing literature, but is the result of shared cultural values and beliefs regarding gender roles and relationships which are reinforced by their continued use and re-use in popular culture.

Gender in tourism imagery

As we indicated earlier, research into gendered representations has a long tradition in other subjects, notably media studies and sociology. Of particular interest is

Goffman's work on magazine covers,[44] a phenomenon which has many parallels with the tourism brochure. He suggested that magazine covers act as a gender advertisement projecting desirable female attributes such as youth, beauty, sexuality or the possession of a man and, by implication, desirable male states, such as social or economic power and sexuality. Female stereotypes of sweetly submissive, aggressively vibrant and sensual women are endorsed, as are male stereotypes of the caring man, the macho man and the high-powered male executive.[45] Tourism brochures and advertisements can be seen to operate in much the same way. As all advertising media, they make use of desired gendered attributes in the hope of communicating more effectively with their intended target markets. These socially-defined attributes carry messages which have implications for male and female roles, for instance, through their idealisation of certain roles and relationships. As such, tourism advertisements, just like magazines, carry reinforcements of masculinity and femininity. Thus, Disney Cruiselines' advertisements invite the male reader to 'Promise Her The Moon And Stars. [whilst] We'll Provide The Magic'. Here, although it is a vacation in which *a couple* can 'Discover Uncharted Magic', the audience and facilitator is *a man*, whose choice his partner will endorse – 'she'll think *you* hung the moon'.[46]

Such advertisements beg the question, just for whom are the tourism professionals catering? Cohen points out that:

> the representations in tourism brochures and the promotional videos are largely self conscious constructions . . . they are presumably created to be representative enough of what is being marketed to ensure consumer satisfaction upon purchase, while sufficiently idealised to attract and perhaps even to construct a particular tourist gaze.[47]

This gaze clearly emerges as male and heterosexual – the signs, symbols, myths and fantasies are invariably male-orientated[48] and exclusively heterosexual. Women and sexual imagery are used to portray the 'exotic' nature of a destination, the airline which takes you there – the Singapore Girl – and, in some cases, as in Thailand, the main reason for the visit.[49] Selwyn has written of brochures which describe the Thai people as 'the most sensual and overtly sexual on earth', speak of Malaysia as 'Dazzling Even After Dark . . . [with] Endless Possibilities' and which say of Pattaya 'If you can suck it, use it, eat it, taste it, abuse it, or see it then it is available in this resort'.[50]

Clearly, the marketing of tourism-related activities has the potential to reinforce stereotypical roles for women and men. These may manifest themselves in terms of sexual or decorative roles, the sexual division of labour or, more culturally specific, the portrayal of Asian women as passive traditionalists, uninfluenced by western feminism. Although it is simplistic to see the appeal of sex as catering purely for the West, ignoring the appeal of that market to Japan,[51] it does seem that promotional images via media such as tourist brochures and satellite travel shows are vehicles for disseminating the ideologies of the West. Thus, Selwyn has argued that:

> Tourist brochures help to construct the myths and fantasies that are characteristic of certain key ideological features of Western culture which include representations

of men and women which associate action, power and ownership with the former and passivity and being owned with the latter.[52]

As we have seen in Part I, these brochures are carefully constructed objects, produced by governmental tourist organisations, tourism operators and advertising agencies who draw on the wider cultural sphere. Most of their images 'depend on femininity, masculinity and heterosexuality to make their appeals and achieve their goals'.[53] The representations of gender and heterosexuality have led to women being represented as exotic but more than this, as an exoticism which is there to be experienced. The more exotic, in other words, the less western the women, the more western male tourists are encouraged by marketers to 'shed civilization's constraints' and leave behind 'standards of behaviour imposed by respectable women back home'.[54]

The language of sexuality is closely allied to the language of tourism promotion: destinations are sexualised, as are tourists and locals. Indeed, Sharp has commented that 'tourism . . . depends upon sensual mythologies of exotic places'.[55] Thus *Destination Jamaica*, produced by the island's Hotel and Tourist Association, describes it as 'the Caribbean's answer to the fabled "Garden of Eden". . . There's a certain magic – or romantic allure that brings people back again and again.'[56] Vacations are often marketed as hedonistic experiences, where sex is often part of the trip, whether within the framework of a romantic getaway for two or the chance of a romantic encounter with a fellow tourist or local. Thus sex is often used to sell tourism products, whether visually or literally. Even the activities tourists enjoy whilst on vacation are heavily sexualised. Shopping, often seen as a feminine activity, is clearly an erotic experience in Jamaica: 'Pretend you're a goddess sprinkling your bronzed body with sensuous imported perfumes – the essence of the gods. . . . Pamper your passion'.[57]

Indeed, a trip to the Caribbean, just as to the Orient, is marketed as a highly sensual experience. In an analysis of Caribbean tourism, Henshall-Mansen has argued that 'The regional "tourist gaze" includes clear sexual imagery with women portrayed as both the strong mother and the quintessential exotic temptress to be experienced by man, the adventurer'.[58] Caribbean women are portrayed in tourism literature as 'sexual objects and publicity props; the tourist industry presents them as sexual mulattos with endless free time to enjoy the beaches and, of course, the (male) visitors'.[59] This gendered relationship implied in the imagery is interesting given Pruitt and Lafont's analysis of romance tourism in Jamaica[60] and Meisch's analysis of changing tourist relations in Otavalo, Ecuador,[61] both of which suggest that women are also travelling for sexual excitement – a fact which has yet to be reflected in tourist promotional literature. Instead the preferred image in the tourism-generating countries continues to be one of: 'scantily clad young women in exotic surroundings appealing to the fantasies of middle-aged businessmen who are feeling threatened by the improvement of women in the North'.[62]

Even where women are portrayed in situations which may be termed as active and work-oriented they are still presented as passive and attractive adornments to the tourism product. For instance, in airline advertisements, the stewardesses appear in uniform and at work but are mostly depicted smiling passively, as if part of the plane.[63] The significance of these advertisements is not confined to the gendered representation of the air stewardess, for in Asian countries such as Singapore and Thailand, it also represents 'the feminine essence of that nation. For that distinctive femininity is a major attraction in the eyes of the flight attendants' employer and her government'.[64] Such advertisements are not always received positively, however, and Polynesian Airlines had to withdraw an advertisement depicting scantily clad women because of complaints that Samoan women do not dress like that in public but are much more dignified.[65]

Measuring gendered representations

The preceding sections have argued that there is a need to examine gender representations in tourism marketing. This, however, is not sufficient since research methods have to be developed to analyse the style and content of such representations, as they have been in media and consumer studies.[66] These methods could then be used in a time-series analysis to establish the degree of continuity or change in gendered representations. We propose here a technique which adapts a textual analysis technique developed by Butler-Paisley and Paisley-Butler known as the consciousness scale.[67] Originally developed to evaluate magazine advertising imagery, the scale is based on an ordinal, as opposed to a nominal, classification which facilitates the measurement and comparison of media representations. Images can thus be placed in relation to each other, as opposed to being merely enumerated as sexist or non-sexist. The scale operates as a continuum describing points ranging from sexist to non-sexist portrayals of roles and relationships. There are four levels.

- Level one images are classified as those which depict women and men in very limited, essentially sexual and decorative roles.
- Level two images are traditional images which show women and men within a heavily circumscribed activity or sphere. Here women are seen engaging in 'traditional' female pursuits, such as caring for children, shopping or grooming themselves, or as passive spectators of active men. Men, in contrast, appear in 'traditional' male roles, such as participating in sport or as figures of authority which could include them choosing dinner or ordering drinks for a female partner.
- Level three images portray men and women in 'non-traditional' roles. For instance, women are seen actively participating in sports and men appear caring for children.
- Level four images are those which represent women and men as equal individuals (Table 9.1).

Our use of the scale incorporates a number of refinements to the original Butler-Paisley and Paisley-Butler methodology. The most obvious involves the weighting of images according to size, a methodology used by Dilley in his analysis of tourism brochure imagery.[68] It cannot be denied that an image occupying a double page in a brochure or an advertisement is far more eyecatching and influential in the reader's mind than a smaller image which may be less than an eighth of a page in size. To allow for this, in the following case study each image was assigned to

Table 9.1   A Scale for Measuring Sexism in Tourism Representations.

	Level IV Women and Men as individuals	

Level III Women in non-traditional role (sport, authority, etc.)	**Level III** Men in non-traditional role (child-care, submissive)
Level II Women in traditional role (passive or in beauty or child-care activities)	**Level II** Men in traditional role (sport, authority)
Level I Women as a one-dimensional sexual object or decoration	**Level I** Men as a one-dimensional sexual object or decoration

Source: adapted from Butler-Paisley, M. and Paisley-Butler, W.J. (1974) Sexism in the Media: Frameworks for Research, paper presented to the annual meeting of the Association for Education and Journalism, San Diego. Reproduced by permission.

one of six size categories, ranging from A3 to significantly smaller than a quarter page, with values of six, five, four, three, two and one used to weight the overall significance of the images. Case study 9.1 examines the nature of gendered tourism representations in two major market divisions in tourism – the short and the long haul markets.

Case Study 9.1   Gendered Tourism Marketing Representations

A total weighted image base of 12 832 images was analysed, applying the consciousness scale to representations of male and female tourists in fourteen separate brochures used to promote overseas holidays to potential holidaymakers in the United Kingdom. The brochures promoted a range of tourism products and targeted a variety of markets, including singles, couples and seniors. As such they were a representative sample of brochures, and provide valuable case study material for an analysis of gender images.

The most significant finding in the short haul market was the overwhelming dominance of female images, with women constituting 60% of all the images of tourists. Furthermore, this dominance of women was concentrated in certain imagery types, for instance 64% of all level I images were female (Table 9.2). It is also interesting how the level I images were used for both men and women, since 78% of these images were presented not merely as attractive people, but set against the backdrop of the tourism product. In other words, these were images of people which 'decorated' some aspect of the product, whether hotel bedrooms, swimming pools, or the destination itself. In contrast, only 22% of these level I images in the short haul brochures were images where the main focus of the photograph were the people themselves. The overwhelming majority of the male level III images were photographs of men in child-care situations, whereas most of the female level III were the result of women shown undertaking sports and active pursuits.

In the long haul travel brochures there were far fewer images of people – just over 700 compared with over 3000 in the short haul brochures (Table 9.3). The

Table 9.2 Gender Images in Short Haul Brochures.

Level	Women %	Men %	Totals %
level I	64	36	100
level II	46	54	100
level III	52	48	100
level IV	66	34	100
Base figure	2004	1346	3350

Table 9.3 Gender Images in Long Haul Brochures.

Level	Women %	Men %	Totals %
level I	62	38	100
level II	10	90	100
level III	93	7	100
level IV	53	47	100
Base figure	393	329	722

typical photograph was of an empty beach or deserted countryside, landscapes awaiting the arrival of the tourist. Where men and women did appear, they were represented in more equal numbers, with women forming 54% of all the images of people. This more equal match of numbers largely reflects the fact that most people were depicted as heterosexual couples. Whilst this type of brochure differed significantly from the short haul market on this figure, the dominance of women at level I, the decorative and sexually attractive level, was remarkably similar, accounting for 62% of this classification.

The key significant difference between the long and short haul visitor imagery was at levels II and III, a reflection of the different target markets of the two types of brochure. The short haul brochures are aimed at potential family holidaymakers with children, whereas the long haul brochures are often aimed at couples. Thus the low numbers of level II female images in the latter was the result of few family-oriented photographs, and most of the female level II images were of women caring for children. In contrast, the high number of level III female images was because there were a high number of photographs of women participating in traditional 'male' sports and activities, particularly watersports. This emphasis on activities and the lack of family images also explains the high number of male level II images and the low number of level III images, since children hardly feature as tourists in the long haul brochures, and most male level III images in the short haul brochures were of men looking after children.

In both types of brochures the kinds of activities men and women were portrayed doing were extremely stereotypical. Men hold menus and drive cars; women are featured in passive or 'domestic' roles, at kitchen sinks in self-catering apartments or looking after children. Women do drink and enjoy sports activities, but usually only in the company of men, rarely alone or with other women. The dominant female image is that of a sexually attractive, 'decorative' woman. Although in brochures aimed at younger markets, such as Club 18–30 and 'twenties brochures, men also appear as sex objects, their frequency does not match that of the objectified, sexualised woman who seems to spend most of her vacation posing seductively by swimming pools, draped across hotel beds or dining with her (male) partner.

The results of the above case study are similar to others conducted in the Seventies and early Eighties, one of which found that 75% of female images in magazine advertisements were either of levels I or II.[69] Of note in all such analyses is the sheer consistency of these images – research continues to demonstrate that, despite the passage of time and changes in women and men's roles, representations have changed little. The one exception is that male representations are undergoing a subtle change, particularly in the use of male decorative representations in some promotional situations, for instance in the new male lifestyle magazines[70] and here in the tourism literature aimed at a younger audience.[71] It still remains the case, however, that women are overwhelmingly portrayed either in domestic roles or as sex objects, whilst men tend to appear in authority roles or as active, dynamic figures.

The implications of such findings may at first appear trivial. The issue is not that tourism images featuring women deferring to men, or as competent wives and mothers, or even as sexually attractive people are inherently sexist. However, when female images are *overwhelmingly* restricted to these representations, they serve not only to distort reality, but also, by maintaining sexist stereotypes, to constrain female identities. It is not the mere existence of images featuring women in particular prescribed and subordinate roles which is significant, but rather the numbers in which such images occur throughout all media. Such images play a vital role in creating and maintaining everyday perceptions of accepted roles for the sexes – if the majority of images are limiting or even degrading they contribute significantly towards legitimising such images.

Gendered tourism landscapes

In the same way that gendered tourism marketing extols particular myths and fantasies of a sensualised and sexualised tourism experience, the language of tourism promotion also constructs 'a sensual (rather than, say, an intellectual) link between tourists and the landscape of the tour. . .'.[72] Indeed, Kinnaird and Hall have argued that tourism landscapes, just like tourism activities, are gendered:

> . . . different landscapes take on a gendered perception . . . the rough rugged natural environment of wild national parks, Arctic tundra or high mountains are there to be 'conquered', usually by men. Similarly, family-orientated entertainment or 'shopping' as a leisure pursuit are often marketed toward women in their role as carers of the family.[73]

Despite Kinnaird and Hall's assertion, they recognised that the concept of gendered landscapes required substantially more research in order to explore their role within tourism. This is a phenomenon which we explore in some detail below, beginning with a discussion of historical gendered landscapes, before moving to analyse contemporary tourism landscapes.

Sociologists, geographers, historians and students of international politics have recognised for some time that space has a gender identity and, as we saw in

Chapter 6, Duncan[74] and Valentine[75] have argued that public space is masculine and heterosexually dominated. Sparke, in a discussion of geography fieldwork and gender, has described how the discipline feminised space as the object of the masculine gaze, 'cast as a seductive but wild place that must be observed, penetrated and mastered by the geographer'.[76] Similarly, Rose has noted that geography portrays landscapes in feminine and beauteous terms – a significant observation given that landscape is 'a form of representation and not an empirical object'.[77] Representations of landscapes are grounded in the gendered power relationships which characterise societies: 'Woman becomes Nature and Nature Woman . . . both can thus be burdened with men's meaning and invite interpretation by masculinist discourse'.[78] This feminisation of nature and landscape was accompanied by, indeed was dependent on, the existence of its binary opposite, 'the masculine gaze'. This is a gaze which is active in contrast to a passive landscape waiting to be explored. Similarly, it is a gaze which is technological, scientific and rational as opposed to feminised nature which is irrational, wild and seductive.[79] Despite these charms of the latter, the masculine gaze ultimately triumphs in the geographers' mastery of the feminine landscape. As Sparke suggests, the construction of landscapes, particularly faraway landscapes, as feminine reveals a reality in which 'masculinity, militarism, imperialism and science all come explicitly together in a fantasy of fieldwork in foreign lands'.[80]

This same gendering process can be discerned in history and international politics. Arguably the international political system is riven with examples of feminised landscapes under threat of invasion and needing defence by their masculine populaces. Within this nation-state masculinity, militarism and imperialism combine to actively repel a foreign (male) penetration of the passive, vulnerable, feminized landscape. As Sharp has pointed out, it is not surprising that symbolic representations of nation-states have often been women – Britannia, Marianne and Mother Russia come immediately to mind. 'In the national imaginary, women are mothers of the nation or vulnerable citizens to be protected . . . male citizens . . . act to save or protect the female nation'.[81]

Given the tendency to engender landscapes in these ways, the concept of gendered and sexualised tourism landscapes is an extension of this view of space, a view which can be found throughout the history of travel, as evidenced by Karen Dubinsky's *The Imaginary Geography of Niagara Falls in the Nineteenth Century*.[82] She argues that Niagara Falls is and always has been 'gazed upon as a specifically female icon'.[83] The engendering process does not end there, however, as by:

> incorporating female imagery into their descriptions of Niagara, many writers also projected onto the landscape suitably gendered physical attitudes and emotional responses.[84]

It is not surprising, then, that sexual imagery abounds in descriptions of the Falls. Its spray was 'a kiss', the sound of running water 'a moan', whilst the water 'writhes', 'gyrates', and 'caresses the shore'. Above all, 'Niagara . . . is "seductively restless", and "tries to win your heart with her beauty".'[85] Such sexual imagery in turn leads to the construction of sexualised responses to Niagara Falls they become not merely a natural phenomena, but a woman, a mistress, a lover, and an enchantress who allures, captivates and enslaves man. This is not, therefore, a female landscape which was alone, but was viewed and consumed by the male. This positioning of the waterfall as female and the viewer as male is traced by Dubinsky as enhancing the spectatorial pleasure of 'doing' Niagara. Pratt has pointed out that imagery reveals more about the observer than the observed,[86] and here we see the (male) observer's social and cultural priorities – objectifying and possessing the (feminine) waterfall.

This gendering of landscapes is by no means unique to Niagara, and in fact, 'The gendering of nature has been a staple feature of western culture.'[87] Stott, in a discussion of the novels of the Victorian author Rider Haggard, describes how the colonialists' horror of Africa – nature at its wildest and most threatening – was embodied in the tyrannical figure of 'She Who Must Be Obeyed.'[88] In a similar vein, Kolodny's discussions of the USA in the eighteenth and nineteenth centuries reveal that the unknown land was initially gendered as a bountiful mother, an image which 'gave way to a more sexualized, "seductive virgin" motif . . . a field for exercising sexual mastery' once the continent had become less dangerous through exploration.[89] Thus, in both Niagara and the USA, 'the discourse of masculine domination clearly stands out'.[90]

It is, however, merely one example of how nature and science have been consistently gendered. Wernick discusses how in the 1950s man was often positioned as technological, as the driver behind the consumer revolution, whilst nature was feminised as passive, subordinate and without threat. Occasionally landscapes could acquire a 'siren-like power', but for the most part feminised nature was either a bountiful source of raw materials or a picturesque backdrop for the world of plenty created by technological man.[91] This, as we have seen, is a phenomenon which has a long history and has characterised and dominated western culture. As we will now discuss, it continues to be played out today as the masculine, advanced West and North, turns its gaze to consume tourism delights in the 'natural' 'feminine' landscapes of the south and east, overlaying a racial dimension to the landscapes. Today's gendered tourism landscapes offer feminine seduction and masculine adventure – attractions which seem to be constructed to appeal to a certain type of tourist – the white, male heterosexual.

Female landscapes offer seduction

Feminine landscapes abound in tourism imagery, particularly in the less powerful nations which provide First World tourists with more exotic tourism products. The Caribbean is one such destination which is heavily imbued with feminine, sexualised imagery. Cohen, in one of the very few tourism studies of gendered landscapes, focused on the British Virgin Islands (BVI). In her analysis of the themes and images used to market the BVI she found that the campaigns link the allure of the Islands to 'the allure of virginity and sexual possession . . . sell[ing] the islands as a tourism destination by appealing to sexual desire'.[92] Tourists are invited to 'discover nature's little secrets' while marketing focuses on the Islands as 'Virgin holiday territory'. Within the BVI, therefore, the association of travel with the masculine search for adventure and discovery of the exotic and pleasurable is juxtaposed with the passive, virginal and feminine landscape awaiting masculine exploration.

> Naturalized within relations of sexual difference as female and eroticized through references to the allure of virginity, the British Virgin Islands is rendered a site where to 'discover nature's little secrets' is to achieve the transcendence of the knowing male subject . . .[93]

Similar themes and images can be found in the promotional material of many other destinations, associations which naturalise gendered power relations and thus legitimise sexual inequalities. For instance, Fiji offers a sensual feminine landscape which invites the tourist to discover 'waterfalls tumbling through virgin forests. . . the scent of wild, exotic blooms. . . Dreams and fantasies? – Fiji realities'.[94] Similarly potential tourists are told the Seychelles offer 'seas that were made for pleasure',[95] and that Tahiti is 'often called "The Island of Love"'.[96] Indeed, 'The Islands of Tahiti . . . have allured, inspired and enamoured a wide range of visitors . . . [as] These are islands of beauty, of love and of passion'.[97] These are sentiments which echo geographical encounters with Tahiti, as Rose notes: 'Tahitian women represent the enticing and inviting land to be explored, mapped, penetrated and known.'[98]

Case Study 9.2   Constructing a Female Landscape – 'Jamaica, Me Love you'

The language and atmosphere of seduction is never far away when the destination is Jamaica. Terms laden with innuendo are used liberally to describe the Jamaican tourism product – a product which is at one and the same time 'tempting' and 'innocent', 'sinful', 'sensuous', 'seductive', 'teasing' and 'hypnotic'. Tourists are invited to participate in this heady sexual cocktail at Runaway Bay, 'a place where you can let your imagination run wild. A place that defines the word "vacation".'[99] Not only is Runaway Bay a place where your imagination can run wild and, by implication, be satisfied whatever the dreams may be, it is also a place where 'there's something sensuous in the undulating seas that massage the sand, in the way the winds tease the palm trees and the hypnotic rhythm of the peoples' patois.'[100]

   Here, the people of Jamaica are linked to the sexual imagery of the landscape and there is no doubt that the landscape is female – and no less clear that the camera and the tourist gaze is male. The linking of a desirable female landscape with the female inhabitants of the island continues:

> Rugged cliffs give way to pure white beaches, making a luscious mixture of seduc- tiveness and innocence. The sun is so warm it's almost sinful. As it melts into the tranquil Caribbean sea, tempting sunsets appear as girls with cinnamon-coloured skin walk the beach wearing bikinis the size of butterflies. This is your Eden. Welcome to Negril.[101]

It is here, in Negril, that the sensuous nature of Jamaica is most explicitly com- municated. This is a destination of:

> Soft Sensuous Beaches, Rugged Cliffs and Tempting Sunsets [which] Create a Luscious Mixture of Seductiveness and Innocence. Welcome to The Ultimate Getaway. The Capital of Casual.[102]

The ambiguous phrase, 'Capital of Casual' has an interesting connotation, given the clear sexual references. The rugged, masculine cliffs both submit to and seduce the pure, white innocent feminine beaches. Appeals to the masculine tourist are abundant, with sinful suggestions beneath the tempting sunsets – maybe, we seem to be invited to think, with the barely clad, tempting girls with exotic skin. This is a white, male Garden of Eden, crammed with sensuous delights ready for consumption – a place where everything is available, even 'nude cruises'.[103]

Promotional brochures are not the only place to find such sexualised tourism landscapes. Travel features similarly make use of sexualised fantasies to describe both destinations and their inhabitants. In a *Condé Nast Traveler* article on Moorea, an island in the South Pacific, a description of a gendered landscape is neatly interweaved with one of its sexualised and feminised inhabitants.[104] Readers are first introduced to Moorea's inhabitants by a full page photograph of young Moorean girls in short sarongs, their traditional dress, and wearing flowers in their hair and around their necks. One of the girls has her face turned towards the camera, smiling. Despite her youth, the accompanying text suggests that she is representative of all the women of the island who use 'antique traditions to tempt tourists'. If this is only a suggestion, this is confirmed over the page where bold print declares that Moorea's main attraction: '. . . IS THE WOMEN. . . . IT IS THIS LONG HAIR, THIS VELVET TYPE OF SKIN, THIS FRAGRANCE'.[105] This description is heavily laden with sexuality, but in case the reader misses the point, the author hints at his sexual arousal, having to wipe 'the beads of sweat' from his forehead.[106] Not only are its women highly desirable, but Moorea is represented as a beautiful, voluptuous young woman – 'Like the pretty girl next door, Moorea is Tahiti's enticing neighbor.'[107] Moorea and its women are there to be encountered by the male writer and his audience. As the article closes we are left with a clear image of this destination and its inhabitants, as we are told of a girl 'dressed in a red and white wrap-around pareu, sitting all by herself . . . the perfect image of paradise was locked in my head forever'.[108] This is a paradise for the male eye – an attractive young woman sitting alone, by implication awaiting the arrival of the male tourist or mourning his departure.

These descriptions are typical of gendered representations of feminised landscapes. They are landscapes which are feminine and attractive, but also powerless and vulnerable – epitomised by the images of young girls who decorate the pages of the travelogues and brochures. Such imagery is not restricted to Caribbean or Pacific 'paradise' style destinations it also abounds in descriptions of an exotic and erotic East. Promotional material for Vietnam exudes sexual overtones, inviting the potential tourist with 'Vietnam awaits you'. She not only awaits, but 'Vietnam is now as alluring as ever.'[109] Similar sensual invitations seduce the tourist considering India.

> India awaits you . . . The timeless mystery and beauty of India has been waiting for you for 5000 years. She is an indescribable and unforgettable land and only by visiting the country can the truth be experienced. . . . Everything you desire can be found in India. . . every whim will be gratified.[110]

So accept the invitation:

> if you have ever dreamt of a warm land of space and light . . . where the glittering sea
> always beckons you, . . . where the succulent juice from a bite of ripe pineapple or
> papaya drips on your hot skin as you luxuriate lazily on the white sand.[111]

Such offers are particularly appealing if you want to be 'freed from standards of
behaviour imposed by respectable women back home' to indulge in the imagined
pleasures of the exotic 'other'.[112]

Male landscapes offer adventure

Whilst some tourism researchers have begun to discuss sexualised and feminised
landscapes, we would argue that gendered landscapes are by no means exclusively
feminine. Whereas it has been suggested that the unexplored North American
landscape was portrayed as a woman awaiting male discovery,[113] in the language
of contemporary tourism, we see under-explored destinations described as masculine, awaiting exploration by men. In contrast to the passive, seductive feminine
landscapes described above, male landscapes are active, wild, untamed and often
harsh and even penetrative. In Chile 'smouldering volcanoes *tower* over *stark* lava
fields' and '*mighty* turquoise glaciers' are adrift 'in *a wilderness untamed* by man'.[114]
Similarly, 'Papua New Guinea is the Land of Adventure, from its *mighty* rivers
and deep valleys, to its volcanic islands, *imposing* mountains and remote undis-
covered corners.'[115]

What is significant is that these wild landscapes have no place for female
exploration. The images and themes used to promote Canada's Yukon are
grounded in a masculine country, with a masculine past, waiting to be relived by
today's male adventure tourist: 'The Yukon is one of the world's great adventure-
travel destinations. . . . [A] Union of incredible geography, wildlife, history,
mystery and challenge.'[116] Its description echoes themes of coming of age and rites
of passage and hints at a life with which we (men) have lost touch but secretly
yearn to recover:

> in a time when travellers look more and more for an 'experience', the Yukon has
> come of age. Here's a land which will fill you with the rhythms of a place that we all
> remember as our undeniable ancestry.[117]

Tourists are invited to revisit their childhood fantasies and 'relive the bygone era of
the gold rush and retrace a route marked with abandoned shovels, boots and
picks'.[118] The Yukon, a land resplendent in masculine icons and a testament to
man's endeavour and quest for adventure offers 'A special man to nature' as
opposed to a male to female romance since 'nothing compares to the romance of
dog mushing'.[119]

These themes of adventure, excitement and exploration are found elsewhere,
from Australia to Africa and South America. Papua New Guinea is '. . . the "last
unknown" . . . untouched by western influence. . .'. [Clearly] 'If you have the heart

of a pioneer and the spirit of adventure, a holiday in Papua New Guinea can offer you the experience of a lifetime.'[120] Likewise in Southern Africa '. . . something of the sense of excitement and discovery that lured the explorers and settlers of old still awaits today's visitor'.[121] Finally, 'At Latin America's most southern extremity . . . there is some of the wildest and most astonishing scenery on earth. In this . . . wilderness of giant glaciers and mountains . . . there is little evidence that man has ever arrived.'[122]

There is romance and seduction in both male and female landscapes, yet we would suggest that both are constructed to appeal to Haraway's master subject and that more often than not the language of tourism promotion addresses men not women. The feminine landscape seductively invites the man to come and discover her treasures and (hetero-)sexual allure structures her description. In contrast, masculinised landscapes like the Yukon offer an environment in which man can rediscover himself and reacquaint himself with the real, natural world. It offers the romance of man with man's best friend, a return to the natural elemental world and a reliving of (a masculinised) history.

Here, we would draw a parallel between the construction of these gendered landscapes and Edensor and Kothari's work on the masculinisation of the heritage of Stirling in Scotland.[123] They have described the ways in which:

> heritage production, interpretation and consumption are gendered . . . these processes articulate masculinised notions of place and identity, and male dominated versions of the past which privilege white, male, heterosexual experience and activity.[124]

Their discussion highlights the 'persistent masculinised themes that run throughout the heritage industry, such as militarism and the glorification of "Great Men"'.[125] Similarly, the Yukon offers a history from which women are absent, a history which is then grafted onto a contemporary tourism landscape exclusively aimed at men. What role do female tourists play in the feminised, sexualised landscapes which offer an opportunity to explore exotic, sexual fantasies? The gendering of landscapes in this way raises serious questions about how marketers and image creators use and construct images and who they perceive as their intended audience. It has been argued by Pearce that women are the primary decision-makers in the choice of American family vacations,[126] yet the evidence would seem to suggest that women as consumers are peripheralised in a world dominated by male heterosexual marketing fantasies which celebrate men 'militarized in their manliness' and women as 'welcoming and available in their femininity'.[127]

Although our discussion has centred largely on the *gendering* of landscapes, it is important to recognise that the complexity of power relationships also promotes the *racialisation* of space. These power relationships and representations cross at many points and in many ways. As Sharp comments, 'National identity . . . is constructed in particular times and places through relations of power already existent in society.'[128] A fuller discussion of racial representations in tourism appears in the next chapter, but the following case study indicates the way in which gender and race collide in landscape portrayal. This particular study is drawn from the work of Anderson who has examined how British Columbia's identity came to be crafted in the nineteenth century as white and female in response to the perceived threat posed by Chinese immigration. It reveals how the:

> making of 'Canada' in its symbolic dimension entailed representational practices that were deeply saturated with race and gender concepts . . . out of which a dominant imagined geography of nation grew.[129]

Case Study 9.3   Constructing a White and Feminised Landscape for British Columbia

The late nineteenth century witnessed attempts by government officials in Canada and British Columbia to construct an identity for the country embodied in the shape of a white woman. They sought to create:

> a racialized and gendered aesthetic that interconnected the spaces of nation and body. 'Canada' appears scripted in official texts as a pure space . . . the iconic body of white woman was grafted onto the space of nation (and province).[130]

The use of a white woman as the iconic embodiment of Canada was designed to symbolically convey the 'passive' and 'pure' qualities of the landscape which were perceived to be threatened by Chinese immigrants:

> Like other symbolic figurations of nation such as Miss Britannia and Lady Liberty . . . Miss BC [British Columbia] is made to emblematically stand as an essence under peril of violation.[131]

Miss BC was not only passive and pure, she was defenceless, requiring protection by her masculinised officialdom. The discourse of Canadian nation building therefore was one which:

> created and appropriated . . . notions of 'British Columbia' and . . . of 'Canada', drawing on specific codes of race, femininity and masculinity, within Canadian culture.[132]

Just as Canada and British Columbia were constructed as both racialised and gendered landscapes, so too was the embodiment of the threat to Canada's white, feminine landscape – Vancouver's Chinatown. This was similarly constructed on racial and gendered lines, condemned because of its 'presumed proclivities for opium, gambling, sexual exploitation and over-crowding' encapsulated in notions of 'vice, mystery, danger and disease'.[133] In 1919 the Women and Girls Protection Act outlawed white women's employment on Oriental restaurant premises and in the interwar years Vancouver's Chief Constable closed down numerous premises for employing white women on the grounds that they would be 'induced . . . to prostitute themselves with Chinese'.[134] Chinatown was constructed as an alien landscape populated by those who would corrupt the white, feminine landscape which was British Columbia – one regional government resolution described them as:

> alien in sentiment and habit [with] . . . a system of secret societies which encourages crime . . . to the demoralization of the native races. . . This House urgently requests that some restrictive legislation be passed to prevent our Province from becoming completely overrun by Chinese.[135]

Representations of the Chinese were somewhat schizophrenic, at times characterised in feminine, docile terms, at others, as sexual predators. The imagined corruption of the British Columbia landscape was encapsulated in the supposed sexual threat that Chinese men posed to white women. These sexually lustful and 'energetic pursuers of white women'[136] directly challenged the hegemony of white men. 'Thus Chinatown, like that mythical region of western imagining called the Orient, was recurrently white Vancouver's Other.'[137] Such representations of the Chinese were by no means restricted to popular newspapers but also informed British Columbia's political apparatus. Thus, in 1878 an Official Select Committee Report on the Chinese said that:

> A large majority of the men are in a state of semi-bondage, while all the women are prostitutes . . . A state of marriage is unknown amongst them; hence the influence exerted upon society by such wholesale vice cannot be otherwise than highly pernicious.[138]

The portrayal of Miss (white) British Columbia is in direct contrast to how Miss Black Africa was portrayed in the same period of history. Whereas the former was there to be protected in all her innocence, the latter was there to be explored, penetrated and conquered. As Segal comments in her discussion of nineteenth-century white novelists' portrayals of Africa:

> Just as Africa itself is persistently depicted as 'female' (passive and inviting, wild, dangerous and deadly), so the language of the colonial narrative is one of sexual conquest. Like Africa itself, however, Black women are but the backdrop for the white man's testing of himself.[139]

We will explore the implications of such racial representations in Chapter 10.

Understanding the gendered complexities of tourism, and the power relations they involve, is vital. If we fail to do so, then we 'fail to recognise the reinforcement and construction of new power relations that are emerging out of the tourism process'. Kinnaird and Hall continue, as tourism constitutes one of the largest sectors in global trade, 'it is essential that we reformulate our focus to identify associated societal change and what it means for men and women'.[140] Whilst the image creators may be beginning to portray women in more active, less 'traditional' roles, the shift is marginal and the emphasis continues to be on their attractiveness and sexual appeal. Whereas ten years ago, tourism marketers routinely posed a bikini-clad young woman by swimming pools, now they are just as likely to photograph an athletic, bikini-clad young woman posing on water skis. In brochures targeted at a younger audience, the woman is likely to be accompanied by an equally attractive, swim-suited young man. Clearly, gendered relationships still structure tourism, image and identity – Haraway's 'master subject' is alive and well in contemporary tourism imagery creation.

References

1   Butler, J. (1990) *Gender Trouble: Feminism and the Subversion of Identity*, Routledge, New York: 145.

2   Sharp, J.P. (1996) 'Gendering Nationhood', 97–108 in Duncan, N. (ed.) *Bodyspace: destabilizing geographies of gender and sexuality*, Routledge, London: 98.

3   Enloe, C. (1989) *Bananas, Beaches & Bases. Making Feminist Sense of International Politics*, Pandora, London: 3.

4   Sengupta (1995) 'The Influence of Culture on Portrayals of Women in Television Commercials: A Comparison Between the US and Japan', *International Journal of Advertising*, 14: 314–33.

5   Perry, D.G. and Bussey, K. (1979) 'The Social Learning Theory of Sex Differences. Imitation is alive and well', *Journal of Personality and Social Psychology*, (37): 1699–1712.

6   Millum, T. (1975) *Images of Women: Advertising and Women's Magazines*, Chatto and Windus, London.

7   Goffman, E. (1979) *Gender Advertisements*, Macmillan.

8   Courteney, A.E. and Lockeretz S.W. (1971) 'A Woman's Place: An Analysis of the Roles Portrayed by Women in Magazine Advertisements', *Journal of Market Research*, 8 Feb: 92–5; Wagner, L.C. and Banos, J.B. (1973) 'A Woman's Place: A Follow Up Analysis of the Roles Portrayed by Women in Magazine Advertisements', *Journal of Market Research*, 10 May: 213–4; Sexton, D.E. and Haberman, P. (1974) 'Women in Magazine Advertisements', *Journal of Advertising Research*, 14 (4), August: 41–6; Venkatesan, M. and Losco, J. (1975) 'Women in Magazine Ads: 1959–71', *Journal of Advertising Research*, 15 (5) Oct: 49–51; Poe, A. (1976) 'Active Women in Advertisements', *Journal of Communication*, 26 (4), Autumn: 185–92; Culley, J.D. and Bennett, R. (1976) 'Selling Women, Selling Blacks', *Journal of Communication*, Autumn: 160–72; Lundstrom, W.J. and Scimpaglia, D. (1979) 'Sex Role Portrayals in Advertising', *Journal of Marketing*, 41, July: 72–8; and Ferguson, M. (1980) 'The Woman's Magazine Cover Photograph', *Sociological Review Monograph*, 29 Oct: 219–38.

9   de Lauretis, T. (1987) *Technologies of Gender*, Indiana University, Bloomington.

10 Wolheter, M. and Lammers, H.B. (1980) 'An Analysis of Male Roles in Print Advertisements Over a 20 Year Span: 1958–78', 760–1 in Olsen, J. (ed.) *Advances in Consumer Research*, Ann Arbor, Michigan; Skelly, G.V. and Lundstrom, W.J. (1981) 'Male Sex Roles in Magazine Advertising, 1959–79', in *Journal of Communication*, Autumn: 52–6.

11 McArthur, L.Z. and Resko, B.G. (1975) 'The Portrayal of Men and Women in American Television Commercials', *Journal of Social Psychology*, 97, Dec: 209–20; Manstead, A.S.R. and McCulloch, C. (1981) 'Sex Role Stereotyping in British Television Advertising', *British Journal of Social Psychology*, 20 (3), September: 171–80; and Pritchard, A. (1993) Images of Masculinity and Femininity in Magazine Advertising: A Case Study of Playboy and GQ, unpublished University of Wales M.Sc Econ. dissertation.

12 Jacobson, M.F. and Mazur, L.A. (1995) *Marketing Madness. A Consumer's Survival Guide*, Westview Press, Oxford.

13 Moore, S. (1987) 'Target Man', *New Statesman*, Jan.

14 Matthews, V. (1987) 'Merely Male in Admen's Markets', *Guardian*, Monday 30 November.

15 Pritchard, A. (1993) Images of Masculinity and Femininity in Magazine Advertising: A Case Study of Playboy and GQ, unpublished University of Wales M.Sc Econ. dissertation.

16 Wernick, A. (1991) *Promotional Culture. Advertising, ideology and symbolic culture*, Sage, London: 52.

17 reference 16: 52–3.

18 Scott and Godley (1992) quoted in Kinnaird and Hall (eds) (1994) *Tourism: a Gender Analysis*, John Wiley and Sons, Chichester.

19 Kinnaird, V. and Hall, D. (eds) (1994) *Tourism: a Gender Analysis*, John Wiley and Sons, Chichester: 2.

20 See Rojek, C. (1985) *Capitalism and Leisure Theory*, Tavistock Publications, London.

21 reference 19 and *Annals of Tourism Research*, 22 (2) 1995.
22 Swain, M. (1995) 'Gender in Tourism', *Annals of Tourism Research*, 22 (2): 247–266, 256.
23 Murdock, G.P. (1937) 'Comparative Data on the Division of Labour by Sex', *Social Forces*, 15 (4): 551–53.
24 reference 22: 247.
25 Rao, N. (1995) 'Commoditisation and Commercialisation of Women in Tourism: Symbols of Victimhood', *Contours*, 7 (1), March: 30.
26 reference 3: 18.
27 reference 22: 249.
28 Wearing, B. and Wearing, S. (1996) 'Refocussing the tourist experience: the "flaneur" and the "choraster"', *Leisure Studies*, 15 (4): 229–244: 231–2.
29 Abbott Cone, C. (1995) 'Crafting Selves. The Lives of Two Mayan Women', *Annals of Tourism Research*, 22 (2): 314–327; Wilkinson, P. and Pratiwi, W. (1995) 'Gender and Tourism in an Indonesian Village', *Annals of Tourism Research*, 22 (2): 283–299; Garaa-Ramon, M.D. *et al.* (1995) 'Farm Tourism, Gender and the Environment in Spain', *Annals of Tourism Research*, 22 (2): 267–282; Creighton, M.R. (1995) 'Japanese Craft and Tourism. Liberating the Crane Wife', *Annals of Tourism Research*, 22 (2): 463–478; Scott, J. (1995) 'Sexual and National Boundaries in Tourism', *Annals of Tourism Research*, 22 (2): 385–403.
30 Creighton, M.R. (1995) 'Japanese Craft and Tourism. Liberating the Crane Wife', *Annals of Tourism Research*, 22 (2): 463–478; Scott, J. (1995), op. cit.
31 Meisch, L. (1995) 'Gringas and Otavalenos. Changing Tourist Relations', *Annals of Tourism Research*, 22 (2): 441–462; Pruitt, D. and Lafont, S. (1995) 'For Love and Money Romance. Tourism in Jamaica', *Annals of Tourism Research*, 22 (2): 422–440.
32 Moore, R.S. (1995) 'Gender and Alcohol Use in a Greek Tourist Town', *Annals of Tourism Research*, 22 (2): 300–315.
33 Senftleben, W. (1986) 'Hot Spring Resorts and Sexual Entertainment. Observations from Northern Taiwan – A Study in Social Geography', *The Philippine Geographical Journal*, 30, January–June: 21–41; Hall, C.M. (1994) 'Gender and Economic Interests in Tourism Prostitution: the nature, development and implications of sex tourism in South-East Asia', 143–164 in reference 19.
34 reference 3: 36.
35 Rogers, J.R. (1989) 'Clear Links: tourism and child prostitution', *Contours*, 4 (2): 20–22.
36 Pruitt, D. and Lafont, S. (1995) 'For Love and Money Romance. Tourism in Jamaica', *Annals of Tourism Research*, 22 (2): 422–440, 422.
37 reference 36: 423.
38 Leheny, D. (1995) 'A Political Economy of Asian Sex Tourism', *Annals of Tourism Research*, 22 (2): 367–384.
39 ibid.
40 Abbott Cone, C. (1995) 'Crafting Selves. The Lives of Two Mayan Women', *Annals of Tourism Research*, 22 (2): 314–327.
41 cited in reference 22: 249.
42 reference 19: 214.
43 reference 19: 251
44 Goffman, E. (1959 and 1979) *The Presentation of Self in Everyday Life*, Doubleday, NY.
45 ibid.
46 Advertisement in the *Condé Nast Traveler*, July 1997: 11.
47 Cohen, C. (1995) 'Marketing Paradise, Making Nation', *Annals of Tourism Research*, 22: 404–21: 411. See also Urry, J. (1990) *The Tourist Gaze. Leisure and Travel in Contemporary Societies*, Sage, London: 66–67.
48 reference 3.
49 Antrobus, P. (1990) quoted in reference 19: 14.
50 Selwyn, T. (1992) 'Peter Pan in South-East Asia. Views from the brochures', 117–37, in

Hitchcock, M. *et al.* (eds) *Tourism in South-East Asia*, Routledge, London: 123, quoting Redwing's Go Places 1989/90 brochure and 136, quoting Malaysia Incentive produced by the Tourist Development Corporation of Malaysia.

51   Senftleben, W. (1986) 'Hot Spring Resorts and Sexual Entertainment. Observations from Northern Taiwan – A Study in Social Geography', *The Philippine Geographical Journal*, 30, January–June: 21–41.

52   Selwyn, T. (1992) 'Tourism, Society and Development', *Community Development Journal*, 27 (4): 353–60: 355.

53   reference 3: 32.

54   reference 3: 28.

55   reference 2: 106.

56   The Jamaica Hotel and Tourist Association Official Guide, *Destination Jamaica*, 1996: 24.

57   reference 56: 62.

58   Henshall-Mansen, J. Tourism, gender and development in the Caribbean, 107–120 in reference 19: 107.

59   Dogenais, H. (1993) 'Women in Guadeloupe: the paradoxes of reality', 83–108 in Mansen, J.H. (ed.) *Women and Change in the Caribbean: a pan Caribbean perspective*, London, James Currey, Indiana University Press, Bloomington.

60   reference 36.

61   Meisch, L. (1995) 'Gringas and Otavalenos. Changing Tourist Relations', *Annals of Tourism Research*, 22 (2): 441–462.

62   reference 58: 117.

63   Sexton, D.E. and Haberman, P. (1974) 'Women in Magazine Advertisements', *Journal of Advertising Research*, 14 (4), August: 41–6.

64   reference 3: 33.

65   Fairbairn-Dunlop, P. (1994) 'Gender, Culture and Tourism Development in Western Samoa', 121–141 in reference 19.

66   Two examples of this kind of work in media studies include: Englis, B.G. *et al.* (1994) 'Beauty Before the Eyes of Beholders: The Cultural Encoding of Beauty Types in Magazine Advertising and Music Television', *Journal of Advertising*, 23 (2) June: 49–63; and Sengupta, S. (1995) 'The Influence of Culture on Portrayal of Women in Television Commercials: A Comparison Between the United States and Japan', *International Journal of Advertising*, 14: 314–333.

67   Butler-Paisley, M. and Paisley-Butler, W.J. (1974) Sexism in the Media: Frameworks for Research, a paper presented to the annual meeting of the Association for Education and Journalism, San Diego, August.

68   Dilley, R.S. (1986) 'Tourist Brochures and Tourist Images', *The Canadian Geographer*, 30 (1): 59–65.

69   Pingree, S. *et al.* (1976) 'A Scale for Sexism', *Journal of Communication*, Autumn; 193–200.

70   reference 15.

71   See also Pritchard, A. and Morgan, N.J. (1996) 'Sex Still Sells to Generation X', *Journal of Vacation Marketing*, 69–80.

72   Selwyn, T. (1992) 'Peter Pan in South-East Asia. Views from the brochures', 117–37 in Hitchcock, M. *et al. Tourism in South-East Asia*, Routledge, London: 131.

73   reference 19: 214.

74   Duncan, N. (1996) 'Sexuality in public and private spaces', 127–45 in Duncan, N. (ed.) *Bodyspace: destabilizing geographies of gender and sexuality*, Routledge, London.

75   Valentine, G. (1993) 'Hetero(sexing) space: lesbian perceptions and experiences of everyday spaces', *Society and Space*, 11: 395–413.

76   Sparke, M. (1996) 'Displacing the Field in Fieldwork', 212–33 in Duncan, N. (ed.) *Bodyspace: destabilizing geographies of gender and sexuality*, Routledge, London: 212.

77   Rose, G. (1993) *Feminism and Geography. The Limits of Geographical Knowledge*, Polity Press, Cambridge: 89.

78   reference 77: 94.

79   See reference 16: 55–7.
80   reference 76: 215.
81   reference 2: 99.
82   Dubinsky, K. (1994) '"The Pleasure is Exquisite but Violent": The Imaginary Geography of Niagara Falls in the Nineteenth Century', *Journal of Canadian Studies*, 29 (2): 64–88: 64.
83   reference 82: 74.
84   ibid.
85   reference 82: 75.
86   Pratt (1992) in reference 82: 78.
87   reference 82: 80.
88   quoted in Rose, G. (1993) *Feminism and Geography. The Limits of Geographical Knowledge*, Polity Press, Cambridge: 106.
89   quoted in reference 82: 80.
90   reference 82: 80.
91   reference 16: 55–7.
92   Cohen, C.B. (1995) 'Marketing Paradise, Making Nation', *Annals of Tourism Research*, 22 (2): 404–421, 405.
93   reference 92: 410.
94   Fiji Visitors Bureau (1995), *Fiji Islands Travel Guide*, 22.
95   Seychelles Tourist Office (1995), Seychelles.
96   Tahite Tourisme (1996) *The Islands of Tahiti Travel Planner to Islands Beyond the Ordinary*: 37.
97   reference 96: 3.
98   Rose, G. (1993) *Feminism and Geography. The Limits of Geographical Knowledge*, Polity Press, Cambridge: 94.
99   Jamaican Tourist Board (1995) *Jamaica Me Love You*: 124.
100 reference 99.
101 reference 99: 144.
102 reference 99: 173.
103 reference 99: 157.
104 Payne, B. (1997) 'Beauty Beyond Measure', *Condé Nast Traveler*, July: 83–91.
105 reference 104: 84.
106 reference 104: 91.
107 ibid.
108 ibid.
109 Vietnam Travel Agency (1995) *Vietnam Awaits You*, 1.
110 Government of India Tourist Office (1995) *Indiahhh. Only 9 hours away*, 1.
111 reference 110: 6.
112 reference 3: 28.
113 quoted in reference 82: 80.
114 Cox and Kings (1997) Latin America brochure: 14, italics added.
115 Papua New Guinea. Land of Adventure and Excitement. Air Niugine Paradise Tours 1996 brochure: 62, italics added.
116 Alaska Travel Guide (1994) Canada's Yukon, 20.
117 ibid.
118 reference 116: 21.
119 reference 116: 22.
120 reference 115: 4.
121 Sunset Travel Holidays 1997 brochure: 99.
122 Cox and Kings Latin America brochure: 12.
123 Edensor, T. and Kothari, V. 'The Masculinisation of Stirling's Heritage', in reference 19.
124 Edensor, T. and Kothari, V. 'The Masculinisation of Stirling's Heritage', in reference 19: 166.
125 reference 124: 183

126 Pearce, D. (1989) *Tourist Development*, Longman, London: 12.
127 reference 3: 32.
128 reference 2: 103.
129 Anderson, K. (1996) 'Engendering Race Research', 197–211 in Duncan, N. (ed.) *Bodyspace: destabilizing geographies of gender and sexuality*, Routledge, London. See also Bhabba, H. (1990) 'The other question: difference, discrimination and the discourse of colonialism', 71–88 in Ferguson, R. *et al.* (eds) *Out There: Marginalisation and Contemporary Cultures*, New Museum of Contemporary Art and Massachusetts Institute of Technology, New York.
130 Anderson, K. (1996) 'Engendering Race Research', 197–211 in Duncan, N. (ed.) *Bodyspace: destabilizing geographies of gender and sexuality*, Routledge, London: 202.
131 ibid.
132 reference 130. See also Schaffer, K. (1995) 'The Elisa Fraser story and constructions of gender, race and class in Australian culture', *Hecate*, 17 (1): 136–49.
133 reference 130: 204.
134 Anderson, K. (1991) *Vancouver's Chinatown. Racial Discourse in Canada 1875–1980*, McGill-Queen's University Press, Montreal: 160, quoting Chief Constable W.W. Foster.
135 Anderson, K. (1991) *Vancouver's Chinatown. Racial Discourse in Canada 1875–1980*, McGill-Queen's University Press, Montreal: 51.
136 reference 130: 204.
137 reference 130: 200.
138 reference 135: 49.
139 Segal, L. (1990), *Slow Motion. Changing masculinities, changing men*, Virago, London: 172–3.
140 reference 19: 27.

10   Images of 'them' and 'us'

This chapter will explore the configuration of power, ethnicity and the tourism image. As we shall see, a range of definitions of ethnicity exist in the sociological literature, yet in tourism a very narrow view has been adopted, a view which itself reflects the power/knowledge relationship which we take as our theme in this book. That which is ethnic (which is 'Other') is frequently associated with that which is exotic. Ethnicity and exoticism imply difference and so our focus here is on how difference is mediated for the tourist. We explore the tourism literature's use of a number of mediation strategies, including echoing the importance of colonial relationships and portraying hotels as oases of western luxury, from which the tourist can explore other (less developed) worlds.

Tourism is much more than hotels and destinations, however, it is also about people and we shall explore how the peoples of these destinations are themselves mediated in ways which confirm the power of Haraway's 'master subject'. This confirmation of power is not simply the affirmation of First World power over the Third World. Much attention has focused on tourism processes in certain 'exotic' destinations, including the Caribbean and Asia, but less research has focused on how tourism impacts on the ethnic peripheries and less powerful worlds in Europe. These groups are being imaged and represented in ways similar to portrayals of so-called 'exotic' locales. This is significant in terms of our discussion of ethnicity and how tourism defines tourists as 'us' and the Others, the non-whites, the visited, as 'them', a definition which entails notions of power over ways of talking about and representing subjects and peoples.

Constructing ethnicity

The construction of ethnicity, a phenomenon critical to the production of traditionally defined 'ethnic' tourism opportunities, relies on a particular way of seeing the world. Ethnicity is a disputed concept – as Max Weber said, ethnicity, like its close relative, the nation, cannot easily be defined precisely for sociological purposes.[1] Perhaps the best discussion of the concept is that of Hughes, who argues that:

> An ethnic group is not one because of the degree of measurable or observable difference from other groups; it is an ethnic group, on the contrary, because the people in it and the people out of it know that it is one. . . . If it is easy to resign from the group, it is not truly an ethnic group.[2]

Identity is thus concerned with the 'outs' as well as the 'ins', and as a result, a minority group, which is of course a relative concept, cannot be studied in isolation from the majority. Yet in tourism, work has concentrated on the minorities – itself an illustration that ethnicity is related to the power of some to define it as such, or to exclude others. Some groups are defined as ethnic and therefore as minorities excluded from power, whilst the West is viewed by the tourism image creators, and by those tourism academics who have studied them, as some composite non-ethnic and therefore, more powerful majority. Jenkins' comment in *Rethinking Ethnicity* could equally be applied to its study in tourism:

> the construction of ethnicity is typically – or even only – an attribute of the Other. Ethnicity thus becomes something which characterises other people rather than ourselves. We need, however, to remind ourselves all the time that each of us participates in an ethnicity – perhaps more than one – just like them, just like the Other, just like the minorities.[3]

There is a distinct reluctance for white Anglo-Saxon Protestants (WASPs) to perceive themselves as an ethnic group. Similarly, definitions of ethnicity offered by the tourism literature have tended to use the term ethnic to refer to all those groups in society which do not share a Judeo-Christian heritage and a Western cultural perspective.[4] This ethnocentric definition adopts a Western cultural standard against which ethnicity is measured and which construes any discussion of race, ethnicity or 'others' to mean non-whites. In this chapter we will take issue with this narrow discussion and examine how races, ethnic groups and cultures across the world are represented in the tourism image.

Traditionally-defined 'ethnic' tourism is based on an asymmetrical relationship between relatively affluent First Worlders and relatively poor 'Other Worlders'. It is a relationship based on superiority and marginalisation.[5] Images are created by the First World of 'other worlds' for First World consumption. This is not just a device adopted by contemporary tourism marketers but rather is the culmination of a historical tradition which continues to structure perceptions today. As we saw in Mellinger's work, 'Postcard photographs of African Americans were markers of . . . tourists' quests for a primitive, natural and unalienated world. They reveal an imperial nostalgia in which white tourists appropriated black bodies to satisfy their own lurid fantasies.'[6] Such identities created almost 100 years ago still impact on the perceptions and beliefs of those who create and consume images today. Contemporary images and identities are therefore grounded in and reinforce an historical context which confirms the superiority of certain sections of the global community over others.

Tour operators invite tourists to 'See the world through our eyes' (Figure 10.1).[7] They are also exhorted to see the world through the eyes of familiar First Worlders since destinations are often described by the words of famous individuals. Brochures present us with Colonel T.E. Lawrence's diary account of his 'awestruck first impression of Wadi Rum in Jordan', and invite us to walk 'In the Footsteps of Lawrence' before we 'take lunch at Azraq, the oasis in the Wadi Sirhan which [he] . . . chose as his strategic base'.[8] We are told of Jamaica that 'Columbus Described This Lush Tropical Playground As . . . "The Fairest Land

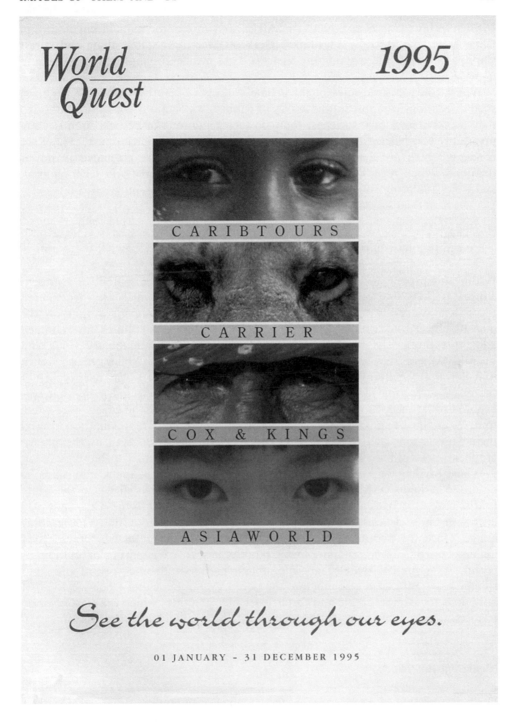

Figure 10.1 Mediating the 'Other'. Reproduced by permission of Bales Worldwide.
Note: The *World Quest* brochure is no longer available.

My Eyes Have Ever Seen"', whilst in Africa we can see 'the magnificent setting of Cape Town, described by Sir Francis Drake as "the most stately thing and fairest Cape. . ."'[9] and 'the magnificent Victoria Falls which [Livingstone] . . . was to name after the Queen. . .'.[10]

Whilst tourism academics might debate concepts of authenticity and tradition such discussions can obscure the reality of cultures which are never static. Although they are contemporary societies, touristic representations of certain countries are invariably constructed around concepts of 'tradition' and 'timelessness'. These are concepts which are by no means innocent of value but are grounded in power relations, which regard some cultures as progressive, dynamic and technological, and others as primitive, immutable and natural. Silver has pointed out that:

> While Europeans invented indigenous tradition in order to ideologically justify colonial rule, tour operators do so to compete in a market whose customers want to experience a taste of cultures they perceive as timeless and unchanging.[11]

Within this process, marketers do not necessarily artificially construct or represent ethnic 'markers' but rather elaborate on existing markers which are then filtered through a particular view.[12] This view from behind the camera is that of 'the master subject' which provides the norm against which other cultures are examined and represented. The perspective is therefore oppositional and binary – 'us' and 'them', – where 'they' are culturally inscribed with otherness. Mellinger has shown that it was the cultural exoticism of African-Americans which was part of, if not the chief, attraction for tourists, but it was an attraction grounded in what was believed to be the local population and culture.[13] In this case the gazers were white tourists at the beginning of this century and the postcard representations reveal their expectations and their fantasies of Southern blacks, as well as the photographers' perceptions of the type of images the tourists wanted to buy.[14]

Whilst Mellinger's was a historical study, the interaction of the relationships he discussed remains current. Today we can investigate the ways in which the white tourist gaze objectifies and represents others in order to discern the wider interplay of power in societies. Chapter 8 demonstrated the power of the photographic image. Once the photograph is taken and the identity represented, 'ethnic' lives undergo a transformation into living representations of a particular culture or group. As representatives of an interpreted, pseudo-authentic way of life, that change has significance reaching into the political, economic and ideological.[15] Not only does the camera create and foster particular identities which are consumed by tourists, it also contributes to the shaping of the way of life of those it images.

Mediating the 'exotic'

Dann has examined how travel writers 'manage' unfamiliar situations for their readers.[16] One of the most popular techniques is to establish expatriate connections between the potential destination and visitor and this is particularly common in tour operators' brochures and advertisements. In the Caribbean marketing literature aimed at a UK audience, for example the tourist is told that '. . .

Barbados is an ideal introduction to the Caribbean. . . . It's known as Little England for its old colonial customs, which range from unobtrusive courtesy and colonnaded houses to afternoon tea and cricket whites.'[17] In this way Barbados is mediated via a link with the UK, regardless of the fact that this romanticised view of old England is itself a perception far removed from the reality. In the same vein, tourists are told that 'Argentina is not only a land of immense space and exotic traditions. It's also one country in South America with which the European visitor will feel a strange affinity, for here the population is essentially of Spanish, Italian and other European descent and strong British connections provide a fascination of their own.'[18]

A second technique which tourism marketers and writers use to mediate the unfamiliar is to denigrate the local population and culture. In their examination of language and tourism, Cohen and Cooper noted how tourists tended to talk down to indigenous peoples and the latter reciprocally tended to talk up to the foreigners.[19] However, as Dann points out, their discussion failed to examine the language of the tourism industry itself – where the industry addresses tourists and vice versa.[20] These conversations are just as revealing, as would be examinations of tourists' conversations with each other. Thus, when the marketers describe hotels, they are often portrayed as familiar base camps for tourists, enabling journeys to be taken from within privileged cocoons of luxury. Thus, the Hotel Grande Bretagne in Athens is 'A privileged point of reference for a journey through Greek culture, without sacrificing the class and comfort of The [Sheraton] Luxury Collection.'[21]

If tourists are told that they do not have to compromise on facilities, the language of tourism also warns them to adjust to other non-Western and (by implication) less developed cultures which invariably display characteristics which clash with western ideas or notions of appropriate behaviour. 'In Papua New Guinea your patience may be tested to the extreme with unexpected delays or primitive facilities . . . part of the country's . . . charm.'[22] In Mexico 'Punctuality and a sense of urgency are not generally part of life . . . although any delay is invariably accompanied by a wide smile.'[23] Similarly, in India, the tourist should be aware that:

> . . . the slow pace of life and the top heavy bureaucracy for which India is famous, [means] . . . a measure of patience and a sense of humour will help [them] . . . to enjoy what will unquestionably be a fascinating and rewarding experience.[24]

The analysis in this chapter makes some comment on the significance of such language and imagery. Tourism marketing images of the remote or unfamiliar are best drawn from travel brochures and advertisements[25] and we will suggest that they reveal more about how the West constructs the world than about how the world really exists. Images of the remote and unfamiliar are inherently contradictory, however, precisely because whilst retaining their exoticism, these places and peoples need to be accessible to tourists. This accessibility has to be not merely physical but cultural, as the cultural unfamiliarity of peoples has to be mediated for the potential tourist, a process which makes use of a number of techniques, the first of which is to highlight bridges with the First World.

'A Little European, a Lot of Caribbean' [26]

As the above quote from the Sint Maarten advertisement in Chapter 2 exemplifies, tourism images and text routinely juxtapose the exotic with the familiar. Since people's capacity for the exotic varies, a number of techniques are utilised to accentuate the familiar whilst retaining a controlled spirit of adventure. As Cohen has argued, international hotel chains such as Hilton attempt to bridge the gap between the tourist and local by offering a mix of local life and reassuring American-style facilities which operate as oases or outposts of Americana in a foreign land:

> After seeing the jewels and Topkapi, the fabled Blue Mosque and bazaars, it's awfully nice to come home to the Istanbul Hilton. [27]

It is in the marketing of destinations, however, where we can particularly observe how the language of tourism mediates the exotic via the familiar. This is a familiarity which often juxtaposes exoticism with well known European geography. In the late 1990s, on a *Thomas Cook* holiday British tourists can enjoy 'an Oriental Journey beyond the wildest dreams of Marco Polo', where they can visit: Bangkok ('the Venice of the East'); Hong Kong ('where Britain meets China'); and Macau ('the oldest European settlement in Asia'). [28] Alternatively, they can visit Delhi (the 'Paris of India'). [29] Even closer to home culturally: 'South Africa is, in many ways, more European than African', a destination where 'visitors will find a measure of sophistication and a good standard of accommodation, food, shopping and entertainment'. [30]

This mediation device is used to appeal to tourists throughout the developed world, not just in Europe. Thus, the US Virgin Islands appeal to the American visitor with the strapline 'They're Your Islands', there for US visitors to explore, safe in the knowledge that:

> As an American territory, the US Virgin Islands offers United States citizens significant advantages over other Caribbean vacation getaways. Even if you are an international traveler, you will find the American system of laws and customs under which the US Virgin Islands operates to be convenient and trouble-free. [31]

'Journey into the depths of the jungle . . . stroll through timeless colonial streets' [32]

Colonial relationships between the old world and the new are, like the above description of Mexico, one of the most common mediating techniques. Examples of such bridging devices are not restricted to what might be termed the early years of the search for mass exoticism. People can now pick up brochures and buy vacations to all parts of the world, frequently at all levels of comfort, yet although the exotic is more obtainable, tourism imagery retains its colonial familiarity, as in India:

> Shimla, set in the foothills of the Himalayas, was the summer capital of the British Raj. . . . The Cecil, in Shimla, where the cream of society convened, has been lovingly

restored to its original splendour . . . retain[ing] its original charm while discreetly
providing levels of service, facilities and amenities to meet the needs of the more
sophisticated leisure traveller. . . .[33]

Here (in an announcement of a major new development opening in 1997) a hotel
group establishes colonial connections through references to the British Raj, and
historical and contemporary exclusivity is linked by the fact that whilst the cream
of (colonial) society once met at The Cecil, the hotel now provides the reassuring
levels of service and facilities which the modern traveller requires. Interestingly,
there are no references to the indigenous society or heritage and the bridge with
Empire is completed by the accompanying photograph which is more reminiscent
of some English idyll than an independent India.

Destinations, even more than tourism products like hotels, are mediated via
these familiar, colonial markers. For the British tourist to Antigua 'One of the
most popular sights is the English Harbour and the restored Nelson's Dockyard –
headquarters of his Caribbean fleet.'[34] Similarly, 'Bermuda is a relaxing destination
with a distinctive atmosphere reflecting the traditions of over 400 years as a British
colony . . . [offering a] secure "villagey" feel.'[35] Elsewhere in the Caribbean: 'A
heady cocktail of colony and calypso, Barbados serves up a unique blend of
imperial tradition and Caribbean spirit. And Tradewinds offers you so many ways
to savour it. . . .'[36] Often, echoing our discussions in Part I, these colonial markers
are fused with others from popular culture to orientate the would-be traveller. In
this way, one brochure describes Calcutta as: '. . . the headquarters of the East
India Company and . . . capital of the British Empire in India. . . . second only to
London'. It also tells us that 'Mother Theresa has lived and worked in Calcutta for
decades and it was popularised by the book and film "City of Joy".'[37]

Colonial links are by no means restricted to the former imperial powers of
Europe. US readers of an advertorial in *Condé Nast Traveler* are told that the
Philippines' '. . . history of Spanish and American colonialism combine' to make
the country uniquely interesting.[38] Perhaps even more explicit is an advertisement
for Puerto Rico in the same magazine.[39] A young white couple dressed in
swimming costumes are pictured beneath a cascade, amidst the splendour of
'America's rain forest'. The reader is invited to 'Discover the Continent of Puerto
Rico. Right here in the U.S.A.' Here we have an advertisement which appropriates
a country and its attractions for the States but which obscures its 'Commonwealth'
status. After all, Puerto Rico's foreign, defence and immigration policies are
decided by a Washington legislature at which Puerto Rico only enjoys non-voting
representation.

A 'home away from home for the discerning traveller'[40]

The third major device used to mediate the unfamiliar reassures tourists that whilst
on vacation they will enjoy all the amenities of home – as in the above description
of the Ritz-Carlton in Sydney. In the same way American travellers are informed
that whilst the Hyatt Regency Kauai will take them 'back in time, recapturing the

pristine Hawaii of years gone by', they can still rely on 'a state-of-the-art health spa. And 18 holes of breathtaking championship golf'.[41]

Whilst this device is as common in the First World as in less developed worlds, Silver has pointed out that:

> Many brochures for luxury hotels in the Caribbean [include] images of natives in the background (often as menial labourers). . . . Such images seem to convey to the mass tourist that natives only matter insofar that they fulfil a Western desire to experience authenticity.[42]

Such images serve to confirm the exploitative relationships which characterise global realities. Often the hotel is a familiar marker of the West in the midst of a fascinating but intimidating and overwhelming 'Other'. Clearly, the tourist is asked to see the hotel as an outpost of Western comfort, even civilisation, a halfway house from which to explore.

> The secrets of the east and the comfort of Forte Meridian hotels make the perfect combination for a fascinating holiday. . . . At the very heart of the city, Le Meridien Singapore provides a relaxed oasis of comfort and calm. French elegance and Asian flair are complemented by impeccable service, superb cuisine and outstanding facilities.[43]

Many hotels, particularly in the Middle and Far East, are presented as 'refuges', 'oases' and 'havens' in the midst of the frantic hustle and bustle of the unfamiliar. In Damascus, Le Meridien Hotel is 'an oasis of calm';[44] in Sao Paulo, the Sheraton Mofarrej can be found 'in the midst of the bustle and excitement, . . . a place of elegance, comfort and distinctive service';[45] the Cairo Forte Grand Pyramids provides 'a perfect refuge from the bustle of the city';[46] and the Forte Grand Abu Dhabi, 'whilst at the hub of the city . . . remains a haven of luxury where beautifully appointed rooms and first class service combine to satisfy even the most discerning traveller'.[47]

The growth of all-inclusive resorts and purpose-built constructions take this concept of 'refuge' even further and add another dimension to the significance and power of representation. Dann and Potter describe a hotel in Barbados which has:

> constructed a mock-up village in its grounds . . . thereby making it unnecessary for its guests to leave the enclave and visit the living environment outside the gates. . . . Representation has [therefore] supplanted reality.[48]

Alternative realities, identities and opportunities for interaction are thus severely constrained whilst the created image – of life, culture and history – assumes even greater importance as a framework within which to construct and interpret reality. Opportunities for Wearing and Wearing's chorasters to interact with indigenous peoples are obviously severely circumscribed in these settings. Resorts (such as ClubMed) with their self-contained facilities represent 'the antithesis of cultural tourism'[49] even though they make use of local culture in their appeal to tourists, offering demonstrations and cultural dances for tourist consumption.

In this vein, one must also question the currently popular (re)construction of cultural productions where whole villages are built at a location convenient to centres of tourism. Wood, in a discussion of one such facility, a Korean Folk village, describes how:

> the tourist is presented with juxtaposition rather than relations, static essence rather than history and change. The smiling inhabitants of these villages apparently never wore rags, even the poorest workers in the most despised crafts are decked out in beautiful special occasion dress.[50]

Such facilities thus operate in a similar fashion to native entertainment shows. To satisfy the need for a touristic experience of the local culture, the historical reality is obscured and an 'imagined reality' is created based on a romanticised interpretation of the past. The end result is:

> the international homogenization of the culture of tourists and the artificial preservation of local ethnic groups and attractions so that they can be consumed as tourist experiences.[51]

Constructing identities

Tourism marketing is concerned with more than tourism products and attractions. It is also about the representation of whole societies or particular communities within those societies. In this context language is as vital as visual imagery in constructing identities. Cohen, in his analysis of the representations of Thai hill tribes, argues that the language of tourism imagery is one of rhetoric.[52] The exotic is described as 'authentic', 'original' and 'real' and indigenous peoples are characterised as strangers who are presented as primitive, simple, colourful, exotic, spectacular, remote and unspoilt. The overwhelming thrust of the tourism promotional literature is to portray indigenous peoples as members of primitive, static, somehow timeless and unchanging societies. These societies lack context because of the failure to reference the economic and social forces which have shaped those societies. Such societies are somehow magically taken out of time to exist in a 'reality vacuum' far removed from the relationships and realities which characterise the rest of the world, regarded as almost ahistorical curios immune to economic and social inequalities. The reality of exploitative global relations can thus be conveniently suspended as the visitor gazes upon the visited. As we shall see later, this situation is by no means unique to the portrayal of non-European destinations. We begin our discussions, however, with an examination of representations of Latin America.

Ways of seeing Latin America

In Latin America we can find clear markers which link the old and new world, the familiar and the exotic. We read that Buenos Aires is 'The Paris of the Americas'[53] and that we can 'stroll through timeless colonial streets lined with elegant Spanish mansions and white washed churches' in Mexico.[54] These links can be seen clearly, for instance, in the marketing of Cuba. We are told that 'Christopher Columbus . . . considered the island "a paradise". . . since then Cuba has come under the sway of the Spanish, the English, the French and the Americans.' This colonial past lingers on in 'Old Havana . . . steeped in the atmosphere of Spanish colonial times.'[55] If colonial markers are too historical, as we saw in Chapter 4, tourist packages such as 'Hemingway's Cuba' also offer the opportunity to explore a more recent and thus more familiar, yet still highly romanticised island positioned in the past.[56]

Although we see our familiar markers, it is the local people who really take centre stage in Central and South America. Caribbean-style resorts in destinations such as Cancun in Mexico heavily feature tourists, but once the tourist gaze moves beyond the beach, we are introduced to an older, traditional, 'ethnic' Latin America and echoes of the timeless native resound in such representations. Typically, and more significantly, it is women who portray this face of Latin America and the tourist is presented with images of a very traditional way of life such as colourful market scenes, where women sell crafts and textiles, and cradle children in brightly-coloured ponchos. The potential tourist may also catch very fleeting glimpses of gauchos who occasionally ride across the pages of the tourism brochure. Whilst there is some brief reference to 'modern' Latin America, there is no doubt that the central appeal is an ancient past – 'Mexico City looks to the future . . . [but] visitors gaze at its Mayan past.'[57] In Peru 'legends have evolved from the mysterious remains of ancient civilisations and [despite] the struggles of New World conquerors . . . the spirit . . . remains mysteriously Inca. . . .'.[58] The very packages which the tourist operators sell echo the developed world's fascination for the continent's past; tourists are invited to experience the 'Land of the Maya',[59] to see 'The Lost World of the Incas'[60] and listen to the 'Echoes of the Incas' in Peru.[61]

Whilst the people of South America are overwhelmingly depicted as female (Figure 10.2), the second most significant image of its tourism product, the continent's spectacular scenery is, as we saw in Chapter 9, male. This echoes the masculine construction of travel, as an adventure to discover and conquer inhospitable male landscapes. 'Chile is a . . . wilderness untamed by man', whilst elsewhere we can 'head south by car, through the lush green landscapes and superb mountain scenery of the "Avenue of Volcanoes", passing the snowy peaks of Illinza and Cotopaxi . . . through exhilarating and unspoilt high-altitude scenery. . . .'[62]

Ways of seeing the Caribbean

The key theme which characterises the promotional literature's portrayal of the Caribbean is that of a 'playground' but, in contrast to Latin America, this is a tourist playground from which the local people are virtually absent. Analysis of images of the Caribbean reveals an island paradise dominated by expensive chartered yachts, wealthy playboys and voluptuous girls. Jamaica is marketed as a 'Playground of the Rich and Famous', and jet-set tourists are invited to join, at least for two weeks.

Figure 10.2 The 'Other' is Female, Child-like and Timeless. Reproduced by permission of Cox and Kings.

> With so many of the rich and famous choosing to work and play in Jamaica's technicolor splendor, how can you not have a wonderful and memorable vacation on this picture-perfect island?[63]

The playground theme does not end here. The island is itself one giant playground – 'The Caribbean's Amusement Park'[64] – to rival Disneyland. It is '. . . the Magic Kingdom of the Caribbean' where tourists are invited to 'Hop on a magic carpet and take a look at this king-size amusement park.'[65]

Whereas tourists have long been invited to visit this island playground of James Bond, in today's Jamaica tourists are told: 'Instead of James Bond, it's you.'[66] This paradise, populated by celebrities and royalty, is, however, one where exclusivity is based not just on affluence but on race. Tourists are invited to enjoy a playground which, according to the advertisements, is populated by a clientele consisting almost entirely of white, young, beautiful couples. Jamaica is not unique in this, as Dann and Potter comment of an advertisement for Barbados: 'The young couple might as well have stayed at home in an all Caucasian setting bereft of Bajans.'[67] One might well ask where exactly are the *local people* in the Caribbean? To the image creators, it is irrelevant that, for instance, in Barbados, over 90% of the population are black. Indigenous African-Caribbeans hardly feature at all in this white Garden of Eden of beaches, swimming pools and luxury hotels and, when they do appear, they are only there to service the white holidaymakers, whether as waiters, masseurs, beauty therapists or bar staff.

Examination of touristic images of the Caribbean not only highlights the theme of play and the absence of local people, but also the reconstruction of Caribbean identity in the image of another as:

> Caribbean locales [are] fabricated into a pastiche of Polynesian architecture, exotic voodoo and Creole cuisine, which becomes more real than reality.[68]

Similarly, Caribbean peoples are being recreated in an Oriental image. Bajans are described in terms, often, as we shall see later, reserved in the tourism marketing literature for the Far East and the South Pacific. They are: '"serene", "gracious" and make you feel at home in paradise'.[69] Destinations therefore appear to be 'identically unique', grounded in some sort of universal, marketed and recon-structed Polynesian mythic image.[70] The question must be asked: Why Polynesian as opposed to Caribbean? Perhaps the answer is that Polynesia poses a less problematic identity for image creators than that of the Caribbean which was built on slavery and black African Caribbean identities, just like Africa, the other destination from which indigenous peoples are absent.

The few representations of Caribbean peoples which appear in the tourism literature severely limit local identities and acceptable spheres of action. They also combine to rewrite Caribbean history – built on plantations, slavery and brutality – to facilitate western consumption of the Caribbean. In this scenario, local peoples are 'spectacles' which tourists can consume on a nightly basis:

> Dancers wearing spectacular costumes twirl across the stage to the rhythm of Caribbean sounds. Talented singers entertain. . . . Limbo dancers challenge the flames as they slide across the floor. Fire dancers jump to the front, lighting up the night.[71]

As spectacles, representations of people echo representations of nature. The rhythms of the Caribbean seem like the rhythms of the night, frenzied dances and fire rituals take the people much closer to nature, in contrast to their technological, rational and therefore supposedly superior western audience. Constructed images thus distort the reality of people's lives, heritage and culture and in so doing transform and reconstruct historical relationships. As Dann and Potter write: 'The plantation, once the scene of iniquitous black slavery, has now been transformed into a carnival of entertainment.'[72] Plantation life has been rehabilitated and glamorised, denying the existence of the oppressed majority. *Destination Jamaica 1996* proclaims that 'The English turned the island into one vast sugar plantation. Sugar became "king". Everyone prospered.' – even those condemned to slavery?[73] In this sense, tourists consume and gaze upon a Jamaican history bearing more resemblance to a fairytale or a swashbuckling Hollywood movie script – Jamaica has been Disneyfied:

> From pirates to sugar barons, the island's history is a tapestry of colorful characters and events. Jamaica's history is a turbulent story of sugar and slaves, Spaniards against Englishmen, fragrant tropical evenings, howling hurricanes, crushing earthquakes, pirate and naval heroes.[74]

Just as Caribbean history has been recreated and remade to entertain the white, male, western tourist, so too have power relationships been reproduced. Arguably, slavery has to all intents and purposes been replaced by or exchanged for another form of exploitation which enslaves and recreates identity and history. Reality is eschewed in favour of a represented myth which conveniently ignores issues of poverty, low wages and illiteracy. Caucasian superiority is once again reaffirmed, only this time instead of by slave chains, power is characterised by sequinned costumes.

In arguing this, we are not trying to deny the abilities of local people to negotiate, resist or even locally exploit the terms of the tourism exchange. Nor does this analysis deny that Caucasian power is to some extent mediated through indigenous élites who are themselves exploiters participating in the re-creation of identity and reality. We cannot, however, escape or ignore the inescapable: that such images and relationships re-create and reinforce existing inequalities. White men (and women) have exchanged their 'mission to educate' with one to be entertained. The tourist is confirmed in his or her economic, cultural and historical superiority. As MacCannell points out:

> tourism has helped in getting beyond the phase of ethnic relations where minorities are kept in place with light salaries, heavy prison terms and redneck cruelty. But one may have come full circle . . . one is only doing with admiration what he earlier did with dogs and guns.[75]

Repression and exploitation thus remain, although perhaps in more obscure forms than in the past. The findings of this analysis of Caribbean imagery which reveals the under-representation of black people is confirmed when the focus switches to the other major black destination – Africa.

Ways of seeing Africa

Here, the same processes of marketer mediation can be seen in operation. Thus, the *South African Airways Holidays 1996/97* brochure offers, as one of its special interest tours, 'Young Winston', a tour which at the same time mediates the African experience and reaffirms the old colonial links. Here, working with Churchill's granddaughter, South African Airways Holidays 'has created a unique tour celebrating the exploits of young Winston's life as a war correspondent during the Boer War in 1899'.[76] In Africa, as elsewhere, the old world links are strongly evident in the text and imagery of tourism: 'In 1855 explorer David Livingstone stumbled upon the magnificent Victoria Falls which he was to name after the Queen. . . .'[77] Here, as in Central and South America, we can clearly recognise the same ways of constructing the exotic and the same techniques of tourist mediation.

Perhaps the most significant feature of the African imagery, however, is that in the literature produced by tour operators and in travel writing, Africa is a destination populated almost exclusively by wild animals. Not only are there very few tourists but there are virtually no inhabitants. Tourists are sold images of the continent as an unexplored land. This is in stark contrast to Latin America, and, as we shall see below, to the Middle and Far East, where there are many more images of local people. In fact, African destinations are the least likely to be marketed by operators on the basis of the attractions of the local people, and this includes destinations in the developed world. The few black faces which are seen in brochures promoting sub-Saharan Africa are usually presented as a local 'spectacle', wearing tribal dress or in occupations servicing the (white) tourists. The *South African Airways Holidays 1996/97* brochure is typical of those marketing the continent. Thirty-five per cent of its imagery is devoted to empty landscapes; 30% to both wild animals and tourist facilities, such as hotels, and only 5% to images of the indigenous black population.[78] The contrast with the Orient could not be more striking.

Ways of seeing the Orient

In their search to examine and understand the 'exotic' Other, tourism researchers have been particularly interested in Oriental identities.[79] In addition, it could also be argued that attempts to understand how the Orient has been constructed have also underpinned the development of the 'emergent' conflict perspective in tourism theory discussed in Chapter 1. One of the most influential authors in this debate must surely be Said, although his ideas have taken some time to filter through to the tourism literature. In *Orientalism* he explored the ways in which Occidentals have attempted to come to terms with the Orient.[80] This is an Orient which he describes as one of 'the deepest, most recurring images of the Other' for the Occident.[81]

The Occidental construction of the Orient is grounded in Western dominance and authority over the Orient which has in turn managed and produced a particular Oriental identity ultimately grounded in colonialism. Images of the Orient thus reveal the dominant global power relations – political, economic, intellectual, cultural and moral.[82] Orientals were long unable to construct their own identities and even now image creators read from an Occidental script. In this way, those who dominated thus retain power over those who were, and are, dominated – those who represent, and thus create, identities have power over those who are represented and recreated in the image of a particular world view.

Tourism, like all other representations of the Oriental and the Occidental, are oppositional. The latter has been instrumental in developing a discourse in which the Oriental is portrayed as 'irrational, depraved, childlike and different', whilst the Occidental is seen as 'rational, virtuous, mature and normal'.[83] The world is thus divided between us and them, between the familiar and the strange, between the powerful and articulate and the defeated and mute.[84] Images of the Orient revolve around the 'passive, sensual, feminine, even silent and supine East'.[85] By comparison, the West is represented in terms of the authoritative 'spectator, judge and jury'.[86] The oppositional characters of the East and the West are reflected in tourism imagery and an advertisement for the Ritz-Carlton Resorts in the *Condé Nast Traveler* is typical. In a scene which invites the tourist to place him/herself in the photograph – a view of palm trees set against a night sky, with two full glasses and a champagne bucket in the foreground – the advertisement copy claims *'while passion and civility may reside in opposite corners of the soul, here we encourage them to dance.'* Clearly, we are invited to see that exotic Eastern passions and Western civility can come together in 'evenings when an alabaster moon lures the civility of the day into the night'.[87]

In popular culture, in literature and film, images of this Oriental discourse revolve around daydreams of 'harems, princesses, princes, slaves, veils, dancing girls and boys. . .'.[88] These fantasies represent a constructed opportunity in which Westerners (largely men) can escape from western morality. As we saw in Chapter 4, such daydreams are not merely the preserve of the individual but are 'socially organised . . . through television, advertising, literature, cinema, photography and so on'.[89]

These images continue to structure the contemporary tourism image. This Orient described by Said, the Orient of harems, sultans and legends, can still be visited today:

> On the eastern part of the Arabian peninsula, the Sultanate of Oman is the legendary home of the Queen of Sheba and said to be the inspiration of such explorers as Marco Polo and Sinbad the Sailor.[90]

At Marrakech, 'Few visitors will resist the appeal of . . . its singers, sorcerers, herbalists, acrobats, preachers and snake-charmers.'[91] Images and daydreams of the East are thus more about Western fantasies than Eastern realities. Even where the modern Orient cannot be repressed, it is tempered by an Occidental view of the East (Figure 10.3 and case study 10.1). Thus, it is acknowledged that Singapore 'is now a thriving modern community with a dynamic cosmopolitan life'. Yet, we are told, it was 'Once the haunt of tigers, crocodiles and pirates', and even now 'the mysterious East is ever-present, whether in the lush vegetation sweeping down to the harbour or in the thronged bazaars of Chinatown'.[92]

Case Study 10.1   Seeing Singapore, Seeing Raffles

Kathy Taylor, former athlete and current holiday show presenter, is our guide for a journey around Singapore in the BBC's *Holiday Programme*. The first thing we learn about Singapore is that 'a mere 200 years ago it was a barren pirates' island full of opium dens and British colonials.' Whilst it has since been transformed into one of the world's most modern city states, some 'colonial relics live on', most obviously in the shape of the Raffles Hotel, which as we shall see, represents and symbolises the transformation of Singapore.

We are invited to visit the hotel named after 'the man who founded Singapore' – Sir Stamford Raffles. We are also told that the links between the UK and Singapore, as symbolised by Raffles, are not merely colonial, they are also literary. Indeed, 'in its heyday this grand hotel of the Orient inspired the writings of Rudyard Kipling, Somerset Maugham and Noel Coward who were regular guests.' Apparently 'they even shot a tiger hiding under the billiard table' one evening.

If the literary icons failed to establish the link between the viewer and Raffles, we need not worry for, as we are told, 'Tenko fans will recall in the 'eighties, . . . [Raffles] was used for filming the hit BBC wartime drama.' A link which paves the way for our introduction to modern Singapore, transporting us from the colonial to present-day city. In a scene from Tenko, a character proclaims 'Raffles never changes', to which Kathy replies that indeed it has, largely due to a £60 million pound refurbishment. Whilst you can still enjoy its famous Tiffin curries and Singapore Slings, the hotel has 'lost some of its original colonial feel to more designer aspirations'.

Singapore's colonial heritage has largely been lost to modern-day symbols of consumption which include Gucci, Versace, Vuitton, Chanel and Burberrys. These expensive labels represent what Singapore has become for Western tourists: a 'shoppers' paradise'. Although, in keeping with its designer image, we are warned that it is 'not as inexpensive as it used to be'. Just when we are in danger of being seduced by the trappings of such conspicuous consumption, Kathy tells us that 'there are more interesting things to see than American-style shopping malls' and that, even in this most western of Oriental cities, we do not have to look far to find the exotic Orient. In many ways, within Singapore we can take a tour of the Magic Kingdom of Asia, a somehow timeless and unchanging oasis of difference, but we can see it from the comfort of our western-style hotel room (Figure 10.3).

Next, the viewer is advised that 'Chinatown is a must and little has changed over the generations, from the old Buddhist temples to the traders and their Chinese takeaways.' Chinese food may be a familiar symbol to those who may be wary of this exotic Singapore, but it is only one 'world' in this Magic Kingdom. We can also sample a selection of 'Middle Eastern delights, including silks, perfumes and carpets' in the Arab quarter. Snake charmers, magic carpets and harems seem only an imaginative breath away in this most ancient culture which also provided 'some of the original settlers in Singapore'. Yet, in Singapore we can experience not only China and Arabia but also that other Oriental giant: India. 'Little India' provides us with 'a microcosm of India and 'this is the sort of thing [Kathy] . . . travelled thirteen hours across the world for – no Armani, Gucci or Versace here!' Singapore is truly a box of delights where the tourist can experience other 'Disney-type attractions', including a tropical rainforest in downtown Singapore where 'it always (perhaps comfortingly) rains at twelve o'clock'.

This vision of a colonial, consumerist and exotic Singapore offers one more icon for the potential visitor, a marker which is both representative of its international and yet exotic nature. We are told that 'eating out is one of the high points in Singapore – practically every taste is catered for with great cuisine from all around the world.' This cuisine might also cure ailments in the traditional Chinese fashion;

Figure 10.3 Seeing Singapore, Seeing Asia. Reproduced by permission of the Singapore Tourism Board.

if you're into healthy eating, you have to give the Imperial Herbal Restaurant a go: they add lots of interesting ingredients to your meal to help certain ailments.

These ingredients include black ants, dried lizards, seahorses and scorpions, together with ox and deer sweetbreads. The Doctor 'can tell the strength of all the various organs in your body by first feeling [your] . . . wrists'. In Kathy's case, he gives her 'a bit of everything'. In doing so, the veracity of the medicinal properties are questioned, if only implicitly and, as if to question it further, Kathy heads for a Western alternative to these 'concoctions' by going for a late night swim in the hotel pool. Our trip to Singapore is almost at an end but before we leave, Kathy gives us 'a couple of pieces of vital advice'. Singapore's laws have received quite a lot of publicity in the West recently and we are reminded that possession of chewing gum carries a £500 fine and failure to flush a lavatory a £250 fine.

The content and tone of this case study is by no means unique and in many ways is typical of Western travelogues and travel shows. Whilst their aim is to entertain, it is also to inform and as such, they are vital players in the tourism image business. Just as advertisements for camera equipment in the Fifties instructed Americans how to see other peoples, so these programmes instruct and advise today's tourists. Moreover, the processes by which the shows are constructed are also similar to the taking of photographs discussed in Chapter 3. Similar questions pertain. Which images did its producers deem worthy of inclusion, which were excluded; which images ended up on the floor of the editing suite and which featured in the finished film? These are questions as relevant to this tourism media as to others. Referent systems, including colonialism, exoticism and the familiar markers, and audio and visual cues combine to form a highly selective and choreographed collection of images. These elements are by no means randomly chosen but are carefully crafted and highly stage managed.

Source: BBC1 The Holiday Programme, May 1997.

Said's construction of the Orient is clearly reflected in contemporary tourism literature, as we saw in our discussion of gendered and racialised landscapes. Tour operators market Oriental destinations as the most heavily populated destination. There are far more photographs of indigenous people featured in the pages of the tour operators' brochures devoted to India, the Far and the Middle East than in those on Latin America and substantially much more than in those promoting the black destinations of the Caribbean or Africa. Not only do the local people form a major part of the tourism 'product', but they also feature in particular ways. The scenes represented portray 'traditional' as opposed to technological ways of life – markets, rural landscapes, agricultural life and religious worship. Male Buddhist monks and female Balinese dancers (often young) are the key icons of eastern destinations (Figure 10.4).

Whilst there emerges a common way of seeing the Orient, there are clear differences between specific regions. The Middle East is largely populated by men, usually in a service capacity or as 'local colour', often astride camels or trading in souks. Images of Indians and Sri Lankans are also dominated by tradition – traditional dress and activities abound – we see snake charmers, tea pickers, fishermen and elephant handlers, usually in rural landscapes. There are no references to the modern, economic powerhouses which constitute today's Asia. As we move further East, into Hong Kong, Vietnam, Thailand and Indonesia, markets and agricultural scenes continue to predominate but images of the local population

Figure 10.4 The Face of the Far East. Reproduced by permission of British Airways Holidays.

become more clearly *the focus* of the tourist gaze. Particularly important are images of the Thai hill tribes, Buddhist monks and Balinese dancers. Thus when people are seen in advertisements and brochure images of Hong Kong, aside from one or two city scenes, they are depicted in very traditional pursuits. They take part in dragon boat races, worship in temples, and shop in floating markets. The urban inhabitants of modern Hong Kong, the world's fifth most important financial centre[93] and one of the commercial capitals of the Far East, are totally absent.

Case Study 10.2   Thailand – in the Caribbean?

Just as we suggested above that Caribbean identities are being recrafted as Polynesian and Creole, so other destinations are being remade in constructed 'realities'. In the case of Thailand it is the Caribbean which forms the tourism image creators' template. Wood has pointed out that South East Asian countries appear to be moving away from emphasising cultural attractions to selling beaches to the mass tourist. This has long-term implications, however, as 'the choice of which parts of a country's cultural heritage to develop for tourism constitutes a statement about national identity, which is conveyed to both tourists and locals.'[94]

In promoting beach vacations, advertising strategies tend to focus on sun, sea, sand and sex. The location itself is not particularly relevant and in fact a plethora of culturally and historically diverse societies are becoming grouped in what Matthews has termed the 'pleasure periphery'.[95] Concerns of play are paramount in this periphery which has been transformed into a playground for the economically advantaged First World. As with the Caribbean, destinations are therefore becoming 'identically unique'.[96]

This can be clearly seen in an advertisement for Thailand run on CNN in November 1996. It communicated a Thailand which to all intents and purposes could be anywhere, but appears to be an additional Caribbean island. Tourists are invited to come to Thailand for sun and fun. This is a Thailand of not one but 'hundreds of islands'. It is a Thailand of empty, white beaches, of clear blue seas, of golf and of exotic food and drink. There is nothing peculiarly Thai in the advertisement imagery, apart perhaps from the three boys who are its key participants. Smiling, happy, mischievous and playful, the boys invite the viewer to come and play in Thailand.[97] The use of children is itself significant in constructions of the Orient, as already discussed. Symbols and descriptions of Thailand are totally absent from this creation and would seem to confirm the trend amongst tourism image creators to create interchangeable destinations for tourist consumption – destinations which are based on play and pastiche rather than reality.

Perhaps the most significant feature of the touristic construction of the Orient is its childlike portrayal. More than in any other continent, where children very rarely feature, there are many images of smiling young children in tourism promotional literature and in travel articles devoted to the East (case study 10.2). They are often seen in traditional dress, and particularly in the case of young boys, as Buddhist monks. Adult and child images in the Orient are interchangeable – even the adults have a childlike quality, a feature previously highlighted by Selwyn.[98] This relationship between adult and child is clearly one of power and Oriental adults are presented as childlike and innocent in a relationship where parental power is exercised by the (Western) consumer. Such representations are by no means innocent of meaning or value, and represent the balance of power between the West and the rest and between races (case study 10.3). As Mellinger has discussed, in historical representations black children had a rascally and mischievous quality which signified an underlying belief in American society that blacks themselves were merely grown up children who should be treated as such.[99]

Case Study 10.3 Tourism Marketing Representations of 'Others'

Qualitative examinations of touristic representations of different parts of the world reveal a particular discourse of image in what the tourism literature has termed 'ethnic' destinations. The true extent of this discourse can be most usefully discerned, however, by measuring the nature and the extent of such representations in a methodology which combines qualitative analyses with a quantitative approach. Just as in Chapter 9 where a scale was presented to measure sexism in tourism representations, so here we present a scale for measuring ways of seeing the Other in the tourism image. Five levels of representation are suggested in this scale. The first level is the Other as decorative and welcoming. Here images of indigenous peoples have no context and are simply seen as attractive individuals. This level is similar to level I in the sexism scale and, indeed, there are often sexual overtones when hosts appear in level I images, particularly when they are female. The second level is where local peoples are purely the 'canvas' on which the tourism marketers paint a more detailed picture. Here indigenous peoples appear as 'local colour', merely to provide a backdrop to set the scene – in an exotic marketplace or as tea-pickers in the distance.

Level III in the scale presents people as a tourist attraction in themselves, maybe as an elephant herder or performing in a native dance or at a festival. Arguably, in these three levels other peoples are seen as part of the destination itself. In the last two levels this changes. In level IV local people are less part of the product but are still depicted in ways which emphasise the power of the tourist. They appear as employees or in some serving capacity. This category is dominated by waiters and waitresses, kitchen staff and chefs. The final category, level V, is where the locals are seen as the equals of the tourists, maybe in conversation or having a drink or meal with them. The following case study analysed a total of 752 images of host populations in four long haul UK tourism brochures. Interestingly short haul brochures portrayed virtually no local people, an interesting comment on how tourism marketers 'use' indigenous peoples – in more 'exotic' locales.

The Others: 'local colour', 'spectacle' or 'waiters'

Adult male images are those of 'local colour' or the 'backdrop' to the scene (half of all adult male images); 'attractions' (a quarter) and 'servants' (just under a quarter). It is interesting that 75% of all servants are male, and just under a fifth of all images of the Other are as servants. Perhaps the most interesting statistic is that in only 1% of images is the Other depicted as the equal of the tourist. These images came from a handful of photographs where the local inhabitants appeared as wedding guests.

The welcome of the Other is 'childlike' and 'female'

Whilst just under a fifth of all images are of children, childlike images predominate in the category of decorative/welcoming imagery, since 88% of these images are of children. Moreover, of the decorative images two-thirds are female (both women

Table 10.1   Images of Adults in Long Haul Brochures.

level	description	female %	male %	total %
I	decorative	4	0	2
II	canvas	56	51	53
III	attractions	26	25	26
IV	servants	12	23	19
V	equals	1	1	1
totals		100	100	100
Base figures		*225*	*382*	*607*

Source: Thomas Cook Holidays; Worldwide Faraway Collection 1995; Kuoni Worldwide Holidays 1995; BA Holidays Worldwide 1995.

Table 10.2   Images of Children in Long Haul Brochures.

level	description	female %	male %	total %
I	decorative	61	38	50
II	canvas	31	62	49
III	attractions	8	0	1
IV	servants	0	0	0
V	equals	0	0	0
totals		100	100	100
Base figures		*64*	*81*	*145*

Source: Thomas Cook Holidays; Worldwide Faraway Collection 1995; Kuoni Worldwide Holidays 1995; BA Holidays Worldwide 1995.

and girls) – it is particularly interesting that there are no adult male welcoming images, possibly because adult males may be seen as threatening to the 'master subject's' sexuality. The most dominant image for children, however, is decorative (exactly a half) and local colour (almost a half of all children).

The Other is unseen in black destinations

Whilst the levels at which local peoples are presented is remarkably similar across 'exotic destinations', the numbers in which people occur are strikingly different. The Orient and Latin America are seen as highly populated regions, where the exoticism and the traditions of the local peoples are integral to the tourism experience. In the brochure pages promoting these destinations, photographs of local people appear, on average, every one and a half pages. In stark contrast, in black destinations the local people rarely figure and, if they do it is largely in a service capacity (level IV) or as an attraction (level III). Africa is seemingly devoid of human inhabitants, populated instead by wild animals, whilst the Caribbean appears as an almost exclusive white, heterosexual playground. Images of local people appear in these countries, on average, only once every seven pages.

Ways of seeing Eastern Europe

As we pointed out at the beginning of this chapter, the way in which tourism has used the term 'ethnic' has previously excluded from the discussion those groups who are within the Judeo-Christian tradition, despite the fact that every group on earth is an ethnic group of some description. Yet, despite this academic view of ethnicity, it seems as though the tourism marketing literature is actively 'exoticising' peripheral groups in European destinations, using techniques similar to those used to mediate the 'exotic' elsewhere. In particular, the national tourist boards of many of emergent Eastern European destinations clearly use these devices. The history of these countries is different from those described above, as are their historical relationships with the powerful within the First World, however, attempts to position the unfamiliar alongside the familiar again emerge as common marketing devices. Bucharest (Romania) is 'little Paris', where 'there is even an Arc Triumph'; in Estonia you can find 'the Venice of the Baltics' at Haapsalu and even 'the Athens on the River' at Tartu.[100]

As we saw in the discussion on Eastern Europe in Chapter 7, the tourism marketers, particularly the tour operators and the national tourist boards of these countries, are constructing these destinations as 'new' countries with old traditions. Historical, religious and ethnic imagery is important to this image building process, imagery which has implications for how the people of these places are seen. It is paradoxical that they are politically new countries, yet the vast majority of their imagery anchors these destinations very firmly in the past. Nowhere is this more apparent than in how their peoples are represented. In most of these countries, traditional representations of the people are heavily featured in brochures, in stark contrast to those selling Western European countries (Table 10.3). The people are seen in gaily-coloured peasant dress, welcoming potential tourists with wide smiles. In many ways, they parallel how people are used in representations of the Far East, where the smiling Thai woman is a key icon of eastern hospitality. Tourists are told that 'Music and traditional dress are part and parcel of Romanian life', whilst 'Lithuania's Folklore and Ethnic Culture' offers the tourist a variety of 'Ethnic Holidays'.[101] These destinations juxtapose their rebirth with their innate timelessness: 'A lot of store is set in Estonia in the country's past, be it the graves of the forefathers or grandmothers' handicraft skills.'[102]

Similarly the emphasis on the rural idyll, the pastoral myth, rather than the urbanised modern, contributes to the view of such societies as somehow timeless and unchanging. Images of hay-laden carts, girls in traditional dresses, narrow

Table 10.3 Traditional and Modern Representations of Eastern Europeans.

Destination	'Traditional' Dress %	'Modern' Dress %
Croatia	73	27
Estonia	33	67
Hungary	53	47
Lithuania	67	33
Poland	52	48
Romania	78	22
Slovenija	45	55
totals	61	39
Weighted base figure	*64*	*41*

Source: national tourist board brochures, 1996–97.

cobblestone streets, red-tiled roofs, imposing castles and a Christianity, somehow older and closer to paganism, fill the brochure pages.

> Here, it is as if time itself has stood still; . . . the locals fashion clay pottery, and the typical . . . castles and churches with countless frescos created by the brushes of recognised local masters are, in spite of centuries of Christianity, still charged with a spirit of ancient pagan times; times which the Prekmurians, with their irrepressible love of life, relive over and over again in their picturesque folk customs.[103]

The language and style used is very similar to those which frequently describe other, more obviously exotic (non-western) cultures and peoples. Here, we have a construction of the exotic within the 'new' Europe – and, interestingly, one which is not just constructed by external marketers from tour operators but also by the countries' own national tourist boards.

The use of traditional representations of people by national tourist boards can be seen clearly in Table 10.3. The images of indigenous peoples were analysed according to their style of dress in the national tourist board brochures of seven Eastern European countries. The frequency of traditional appearance was analysed and the images weighed by size, so full page photographs were given higher weightings. It is clear that, with the exception of Estonia, and to a lesser extent, Slovenija, over half of the images of the host population in each destination are presented in 'traditional' dress. It is also interesting that when these images do appear, they are often isolated images – not as a group of people at festivals (although those too are common), but often as individual photographs where the welcome and appearance of the people is clearly part of the destination product. The following case study provides an example of how one destination is attempting to craft a particular identity which is grounded in notions of the past, and of traditions which live on today. It is also a destination which can draw interesting parallels with its counterparts in Western Europe.

Case Study 10.4 'Romania. Come as a Tourist, Leave as a Friend.'

Many of the devices used to mediate Eastern Europe can be seen in operation in the brochure of the Romanian Ministry of Tourism.[104] The idea of a country reborn, yet firmly rooted in a past of strong, rural tradition, is presented timelessly to the tourist gaze, a gaze which is also directed by western markers. The Romanian brochure offers the tourist a new Romania – a Romania which has been 'reborn as a free nation'. It is a country which is welcoming to tourists and which offers a 'wonderfully varied heritage of traditional culture, scenic splendours and leisure opportunities'. A photograph of a smiling girl in traditional dress informs the tourist that 'A new and confident future beckons.' Tourists are also informed that the 'very name "Romania" reminds us that ancient Rome exercised a decisive influence on this country'.[105]

Romania is a land where the tourist can experience 'living cultural traditions' and 'watch folk festivals in Transylvania that are genuine expressions of local culture, not merely staged for visitors'. This is a land not of 'throwaway souvenirs' but of genuine local crafts. Here the rural is important. Music, traditional dress, colourful local festivals are all vital parts of Romanian life where 'The shepherd is honoured as guardian of an ancestral rural heritage' and where tourists can experience 'Living traditions in Maramures villages'.[106] These are described as a heritage which has been fought for and which:

Today you can visit and admire their unique lifestyle in peace, and one hopes with respect. Few other parts of Europe have preserved so distinctive a rural culture. . . . On Sunday afternoons both women and men often parade and dance as they have done for centuries . . . though costumes vary from village to village.[107]

Tourists are also invited to explore the Danube Delta, a place offering 'Tranquillity in a time-warp' and villages which 'seem untouched by time'. Romania is not just about rural folk life, however, it is also about an urbanscape reminiscent of Paris and 'Mediterranean style holidays' enjoyed by tourists 'on perfect beaches'. It is also a Romania of Transylvania, the land of the legendary Dracula. To top it all, the Ministry of Tourism is keen to assure the tourist that the destination is backed up by 'modern facilities and gratifying prices'.[108]

Ways of seeing Western Europe

In stark contrast to other continents and to Eastern Europe, the language of tourism promotion rarely portrays the old world of Europe as exotic. It is hardly ever seen from a hotel which is described as a 'refuge' or 'haven' (except in Latin countries like Spain and Greece). Above all, even in these southern European destinations, the indigenous people are not significant to the tourism product. The brochures produced by the tourist boards of countries such as Greece, Spain, Turkey, Italy, Germany, Finland, and Norway do not feature the indigenous population in anywhere near the same numbers or in the same way as do those of Latin American or Asian destinations. In northern, western and southern Europe the people are rarely seen in traditional dress, although some destinations do feature their folklore, culture and traditions – for instance, we are told that 'Italy is virtually a little continent itself, rich in disparate traditions.'[109] Such references are extremely uncommon, however, and whilst they occasionally appear in the national tourist board brochures, keen to perhaps promote the 'culture' of their country, such references are almost totally absent in the promotional literature of tour operators, which never feature the indigenous population (except perhaps as waiters).

Although there is no general pattern of seeing Western Europeans as 'Others', there are some interesting exceptions, usually on the geographical peripheries of Europe. In the context of our earlier discussions of ethnicity and its definition, it is interesting to return here to Foucault's linking of knowledge and power. The power to define geographically, and often politically and economically, peripheral and relatively powerless groups as 'ethnic' relates to how the discourse of representation is defined. In the national tourist board brochures of Finland, Lappes appear in native dress, as a 'colourful' attraction in 'The last civilized wilderness in Europe'. Tourists are informed that 'The Saame, or Lappes, are the original population, whose unique cultural heritage still thrives. . .'.[110]

On the far west of Europe, we have already seen in Chapter 7 how Wales is being recrafted. Similarly, in Ireland, we also have a construction of a somewhat 'exotic' destination. One of its major marketing strengths has been described as 'the friendliness of the people, [and] a strong folk and cultural tradition. . .'.[111] Another key selling point of Ireland is that its orientation to time is seen as nonlinear and anarchic, echoing notions of a society somehow out of time and pre-modern. Despite the fact that the language of economics has labelled the Republic a European 'Tiger', the language of tourism continues to suggest that it holds '. . . the promise of escape from pressures of modernity to a pre-industrial society where leisure is paramount and the work ethic a foreign notion'.[112] We are told as tourists that: 'You can relax, reflect, and settle into residents' time. Like you, the Irish don't approve of rushing . . . . You'll appreciate the words of the wise old proverb: "there is as much to see in a blade of grass as in the whole meadow."'[113]

The case of Ireland illustrates the longevity of ways of seeing peoples and places. The reality of a rapidly-expanding economy, driven by high-tech developments and increasingly centred around a now quite cosmopolitan Dublin, is eschewed in favour of pre-modern imagery. The touristic representations of Ireland celebrate icons drawn from its rural and agricultural past, and its people appear as genial farmers and almost peasant-like young girls. These are not necessarily the images which *Borde Failte* has chosen to promote Ireland,[114] however, they dominate the tourist discourse of Ireland, particularly in key markets such as the USA and, as we argued in Chapter 4, many of these representations are drawn from popular cultural resources.

In many ways, this final example leads us to the heart of our discussion of tourism representations. Such images are not selected at random, rather they are the culmination of various discourses which, in some cases, have developed over a considerable period of time. When we examine the representations of peoples and places in tourism, we can see how discourses of imperialism, colonialism, racism, gender and heterosexism have combined to structure the dominant ways of seeing. Many commentators would argue that today's expanding media horizons will offer people increased opportunities to represent themselves, and thus to challenge dominant ideologies. We have never suggested in this book that such discourses are monolithic, indeed, in some cases we have shown how groups can actively subvert powerful discourses. However, in our final chapter we will now go on to argue that the increasing fragmentation of the media is, in many ways, less likely to shatter stereotypical ways of seeing and is more likely to cement their power.

References

1   Jenkins, R. (1997) *Rethinking Ethnicity. Arguments and Explorations*, Sage, London, paraphrasing Weber: 10.
2   Hughes, C.E. (1994) *On Work, Race and the Sociological Imagination*, ed. L.A. Coser, University of Chicago Press, Chicago: 91.
3   reference 1: 14.
4   MacCannell, D. (1984) 'Reconstructed Ethnicity. Tourism and Cultural Identity in Third World Communities', *Annals of Tourism Research*, 11: 375–91.
5   Mellinger, W.M. (1994) 'Towards a Critical Analysis of Tourism Representations', *Annals of Tourism Research*, 21 (4): 756–79
6   reference 5: 773.
7   World Quest 1995 brochure cover.
8   Bales Worldwide 1997: 64.

9   The Jamaica Hotel and Tourist Association Official Guide, *Destination Jamaica*, 1996:
    23; and reference 8: 79.
10 Airwaves Africa brochure: 8.
11 Silver, I. (1993) 'Marketing Authenticity in Third World Countries', *Annals of Tourism
    Research*, 20: 302–18: 304.
12 Adams, K.M. (1984) 'Come to Tana Toraja "Land of Heavenly Kings". Travel Agents
    as Brokers in Ethnicity', *Annals of Tourism Research*, 11: 469–85.
13 reference 5: 757.
14 reference 5: 759.
15 reference 4: 388; and Dann, G. and Potter, R. (1994) 'Tourism and postmodernity in a
    Caribbean setting', *Cahiers du Tourisme*, Serie C no. 185.
16 Dann, G. (1992) 'Travelogs and the management of unfamiliarity', *Journal of Travel
    Research*, 30 (4): 59–63.
17 Trade Winds 1995: 96.
18 The World of Abercrombie and Kent, 1995: 74.
19 Cohen, E. and Cooper, R. (1986) 'Language and Tourism', *Annals of Tourism Research*,
    13: 533–63.
20 Dann, G. (1996) *The Language of Tourism. A Sociolinguistic Perspective*, CAB
    International, Wallingford, Oxford: 16
21 The Weekend Collection, The Luxury Collection, ITT Sheraton.
22 Papua New Guinea. Land of Adventure and Excitement. Air Niugine Paradise Tours
    1996 brochure: 6.
23 Kuoni Worldwide, 1996–7: 256.
24 Airwaves Worldwide Holidays, 1997: 52.
25 Cohen, E. (1983) 'Hill tribe tourism', 307–325 in McKinion, J. and Bhruk Sasri, W.
    (eds) *Highlanders of Thailand*, Oxford University Press, Kuala Lumpur: 308.
26 Strapline for Sint Maartens in the Caribbean, 1996 brochure.
27 Cohen, E. (1972) 'Towards a sociology of international tourism', *Social Research*, 39:
    64–182: 171.
28 Thomas Cook Faraway Collection Brochure 1995: 14 and 56.
29 reference 24: 68.
30 British Airways Holidays Worldwide, 1995: 133.
31 US Virgin Islands, 1996: 3.
32 Description of Mexico from World Quest 1995: 70.
33 The Oberoi Group new developments flyer, World Travel Market, London, November
    1996.
34 reference 30: 151.
35 reference 30: 194.
36 Tradewinds Worldwide Holiday and Barbados joint advertisement in the *Mail on
    Sunday You Magazine*, 15 June 1997: 75.
37 Mysteries of the East 1997: 2.
38 'The Best of the Islands. The Philippines' (1997), 125–8 in *Condé Nast Traveler*, July:
    125.
39 'Discover the Continent of Puerto Rico' (1997), advertisement in *Condé Nast Traveler*,
    July: 49.
40 The Ritz-Carlton in Sydney in *The Leading Hotels of the World 1995 Directory*: 103.
41 Advertisement in the *Condé Nast Traveler*, July 1997: 40.
42 reference 11: 306.
43 Forte Gold Card News (58) May/June 1996: 13.
44 Le Meridien and Forte Grand Exclusive Hotels of the World Directory 1995: 55.
45 The Luxury Collection ITT Sheraton Directory: 13.
46 Forte Gold Card News (59) July/August 1996: 12.
47 Forte Hotels & Resorts Worldwide 1996: 53.
48 Dann, G. and Potter, R. (1994) 'Tourism and postmodernity in a Caribbean setting',
    Cahiers du Tourisme, Serie C no. 185: 26.

49 Wood, R.E. (1984) 'Ethnic Tourism, the State and Cultural Change in Southeast Asia', *Annals of Tourism Research*, 11: 353–74: 360.
50 reference 49: 367.
51 reference 4: 387.
52 Cohen E. (1989) '"Primitive and Remote" – Hill tribe trekking in Thailand', *Annals of Tourism Research*, 16: 301–61: 40–51 .
53 Cox and Kings 1997 Latin America: 12.
54 reference 53: 18.
55 reference 8: 60.
56 Airwaves Worldwide Holidays 1997: 70.
57 reference 24: 159.
58 reference 53: 6.
59 reference 53: 18.
60 reference 24: 159;
61 reference 19: 75.
62 reference 19: 78.
63 The Jamaica Hotel and Tourist Association Official Guide, *Destination Jamaica*, 1996: 27.
64 reference 63: 29.
65 reference 63: 30.
66 reference 63: 139.
67 Dann, G. and Potter, R. (1994) 'Tourism and postmodernity in a Caribbean setting', *Cahiers du Tourisme*, Serie C no. 185: 22.
68 reference 67: 20.
69 reference 67: 22.
70 reference 12: 307.
71 reference 63: 139.
72 reference 67: 23.
73 reference 63: 25.
74 reference 63: 24.
75 reference 4: 389.
76 South African Airways Holidays 1996/97: 20.
77 The Cape to Victoria Falls, Journeys through southern Africa, Airwaves, 1997.
78 reference 76.
79 Selwyn, T. (1992) 'Peter Pan in South East Asia. Views from the brochures', 117–37 in Hitchcock, M. *et al.* (eds) *Tourism in South East Asia*, Routledge, London.
80 Said, E. (1978) *Orientalism. Western Conceptions of the Orient*, Penguin, Harmondsworth.
81 reference 80: 1.
82 reference 80: 12.
83 reference 80: 40.
84 reference 80: 43 and 57.
85 reference 80: 138.
86 reference 80: 109.
87 advertisement placed in the *Condé Nast Traveler*, July 1997: 52.
88 reference 80: 109.
89 Urry, J. (1990) *The Tourist Gaze. Leisure and Travel in Contemporary Societies*, Sage, London: 83.
90 reference 30: 117.
91 reference 19: 48.
92 reference 24: 56.
93 Peters, G. (1996) *Beyond the Next Wave. Imagining the Next Generation of Customers*, Pitmans, London: 53.
94 Wood, R.E. (1984) 'Ethnic Tourism, the State and Cultural Change in Southeast Asia', *Annals of Tourism Research*, 11: 353–74. 365.

95   Matthews, H.G. (1978) *International Tourism. A Political and Social Analysis*, Schenkman, Cambridge MA: 81–83.
96   reference 12: 307.
97   Thailand advertisement run on CNN in November 1996.
98   reference 79.
99   reference 5.
100 Romania, Ministry of Tourism, Romania, 1997; and Estonian Tourist Board, Eesti, Estonia, 1994: 8.
101 Romania, Ministry of Tourism, Romania, 1997.
102 Estonian Tourist Board, Eesti, Estonia, 1994: 4.
103 Ministry of Economic Affairs, Slovenija. The green piece of Europe, 1996.
104 'Romania. Come as a tourist, leave as a friend.' Ministry of Tourism, Romania 1997.
105 ibid.
106 ibid.
107 ibid.
108 ibid.
109 Italian State Tourist Office, Italia, Travels in Wonderland, 1991.
110 Finnish Tourist Board, Finland, Summer 1996, Helsinki: 75.
111 O'Cinneide, M., Walsh, J. (1991) 'Tourism and regional development in Ireland', *Geographical Viewpoint*, 19: 47–68, quoted in Breathnach, P. *et al.* (1993) (eds) 'Gender in Irish Tourism Employment', 52–73 in Kinnaird, V. and Hall, D. (eds) *Tourism: a Gender Analysis*, John Wiley and Sons, Chichester: 55. See also O'Connor, B. (1993) 'Myths and Mirrors: Tourist Images and National Identity', in O'Connor, B. and Cronin, M. (eds) *Tourism in Ireland: A Critical Analysis*, Cork University Press, Cork: 78.
112 O'Connor, B. (1993) 'Myths and Mirrors: Tourist Images and National Identity', in O'Connor, B. and Cronin, M. (eds) *Tourism in Ireland: A Critical Analysis*, Cork University Press, Cork: 70.
113 Borde Failte (1995) *Ireland. The Ancient Birthplace of Good Times*, 16.
114 Pritchard, A. and Morgan, N.J. (1996) 'Selling the Celtic Arc to the USA. A Comparative Analysis of the Destination Brochure Images Used to Market Ireland, Scotland and Wales', *Journal of Vacation Marketing*, 346–65.

11 Changing ways of seeing the image

We have seen throughout this book how the tourism image is becoming increasingly fused with other imagery – with literature, art, music and, above all, with the moving visual images of film and even computer-based multi-media. In all spheres of life the media 'have become the arbiters of everyday manners' and we have all become dependent on media-generated information and on 'entertainment capitalism'.[1] Yet, as we have demonstrated in our use of the circuit of culture, the images and representations which appear in this media (and advertising) are by no means neutral or mere reflections of reality – they are drawn from a stock of cultural knowledge which is itself highly ideological and selective. Similarly, the images which appear in tourism advertising are drawn from much wider discourses – as O'Barr comments: 'Contemporary advertising does not constitute a single global discourse but rather a set of discourses that operates within the boundaries of nations and languages.'[2] Tourism advertising (as all other) is instrumental in constructing systems of meaning and assists in defining and describing and even limiting its audience. In tourism's case it presents and represents others for a particular audience's consumption:

> . . . peoples . . . [and] cultures have been freely appropriated by twentieth-century . . . advertising in its promotion of goods and services in the marketplace – a marketplace that also includes ideologies in its offerings.[3]

This book has argued that such an analysis of tourism imagery is by no means peripheral, but is in fact central to any consideration of global power structures and to a fuller understanding of tourism processes. Tourism images are pervasive images which represent peoples, countries, cultures and genders, having important implications for the ways in which we *see* global identities. As we have seen, the outcome of this representation process can be either marginalisation or empowerment. Tourism, like all spheres of society, is underpinned by an axis of power which revolves around the variables of gender, race, class, heterosexism, ageism and ableism. These can configure as points of empowerment or oppression, experiences of which are socially constructed, reflecting the 'diverse locations within power dimensions'.[4] Tourism has only recently begun to recognise the significance of the first three variables, and has yet to consider that of the latter three in any fundamental sense.

One of the debts we owe Foucault is his insistence that 'power relations cannot be adequately explained by class relations, that power is discursive and is to be understood in the specific contexts of its exercise, not in generalized social structures.'[5] This book has focused on the power dimensions which structure touristic representations, images which simultaneously reflect and reinforce particular relationships within the wider global context. Within this imagery discourse, dominant groups have the authority and the ability to represent, whilst weaker, less powerful groups are the represented. The ability of the dominant groups to represent also carries the power to determine what is normal, what is acceptable, what is worthy – what is truth and reality. In time preferred truths become the currency of everyday knowledge, 'truth' and interpretation.[6] Tourism imagery is therefore one of those sites of struggle where particular ideologies triumph at the expense of others – these successful ideologies structure the ways in which tourists see the world and its inhabitants.

For too long, tourism imagery has remained divorced from discussions of power which have been articulated elsewhere. The cultural power of tourism and the discourse of tourism imagery demands more attention, revealing as it does, micro and macro relations of power. Similarly, just as these cultural issues deserve examination, so too do historical perspectives, as these have shaped contemporary realities but rarely figure in analyses of tourism imagery. Indeed, we have seen that tourism imagery lacks any historical context, and in fact is more concerned to distort historical, social and economic relations in marketing destinations. Contemporary tourism images are actively reshaping how we see the past as well as the present. Indeed, it could be argued that many marketers are engaged in presenting us with a touristic vision of the future based on a careful and selective orchestration of the past. The distortion is particularly acute when destinations have a colonial past. Whilst colonialism may have been rejected historically and politically, it continues to exert cultural power in terms of how peoples and places are constructed. This cultural power is insidious and covert and often distorts history, perpetuating a particular view of the past which bears little resemblance to reality. This view is often an ethnocentric and androcentric pastiche of history, events and peoples.

This misrepresentation of historical relationships is just one facet of a much more complex, multi-dimensional power reality in which powerful white worlds dominate and define black worlds; in which male dominates female; and a dynamic First World contrasts itself with a static, timeless and unchanging Third World. This is not power confined to international politics and global players – this is the power and politics of everyday life. The same discourses – the powerful, male, white, heterosexual axis – construct history, heritage and tourism through the representation of others. As we saw in her study of Vancouver's Chinatown, Anderson argues that it 'was not just the object of biased depiction and "prejudice" . . . but . . . of a particular cultural politics of discursive production that enabled one (European) set of truths to acquire the status of truth and normalcy'.[7] There are layers of oppression – when countries are less powerful, they are constructed as female and non-white, and thereby their subordination is confirmed. The language of tourism is racialised, sexualised and gendered. Urry talks of 'the belief amongst people from affluent countries that women of colour are more available and submissive',[8] and as we saw in Chapter 9, the language of tourism overlays nations and countries with this racialised and gendered view.

The gendered nature of the representations is accentuated by the absence of images of adult males in certain countries. This is particularly noticeable in black destinations – above all in Africa and the Caribbean. Black identities and histories are being ignored or only partially told – as we have seen, in the US Southern States it is only publications and guides produced *specifically for black consumption* which confront the realities of white oppression. In the mainstream marketing guides there is a tendency to remake black identities – in the Caribbean, these have been recrafted into some generic Polynesian image. On an international scale, this reflects what Urry identified as the selective touristification of certain ethnic groups when he commented 'certain ethnic groups have come to be constructed as part of the "attraction" of some places. This is most common in the case of Asian rather than Afro-Caribbean groups.'[9] Asian countries and peoples are feminised and made childlike, indeed, in the Orient, as in Latin America, young girls are the key focus of the image-creators' cameras. Why are peoples and places engendered in such ways? We would suggest that it is a way of mediating the Other by constructing what is *different* (and therefore threatening) as feminine and childlike – existing micro and macro power structures are affirmed in our world of difference (Figure 11.1).

This racialised and gendered construction of certain cultures and peoples is not confined to the developing world. As we have seen in this book, the cultural power of the tourism image also has the ability to define, construct and even restrict other identities. The gazer looks upon and constructs those who are visited as unchanging – in this way, the America envisions Europe as 'medieval', as Europe envisions Asia as 'colonial'. On the geographical and power peripheries of Europe, we find 'unchanging', and 'pre-modern' destinations in Ireland and Eastern Europe. Here, countries are being defined as somehow ancient and timeless, a tendency which has important implications for how those countries are seen on the global stage. In an age where image dominates and where tourism images have become influential snapshots, the implications for peoples and places which are constructed or construct themselves in such ways are felt far beyond the tourism sphere.

This view of tourism destinations as timeless and immutable to the forces of change is related to the so-called search for authenticity and the sacred. In our industrialised, urbanised, fragmented world some of us search for the sacred, to compensate for our own alienated existence. This search for the sacred is itself an outcome of nineteenth-century (white, male, heterosexual) anthropology – a social science constructed around binary concepts: savage and civilised; primitive and developed; them and us. In tourism we can see the same opposition between the 'noble savage', the 'happy peasant', the tribal dancer and the technologically sophisticated, camera-toting, 'civilised' tourist. What the West once documented with pseudo-science, now it documents with 'a Kodak moment'. Unfortunately, in their search for 'authentic' cultures, anthropology and tourism often both deny the reality of external and indigenous change. In essence, there can be no one *authentic* touristic experience – there are simply many different experiences.

These issues are not merely the provenance of tourism researchers and academics. They are in fact directly relevant to the work of tourism marketers and image creators. Accepting the tourist as an interactor rather than merely a gazer may, as Wearing and Wearing have argued, open up new marketing avenues and

Figure 11.1 Engendering the 'Other'. Reproduced by permission of Kuoni Travel Ltd.

eventually new tourism markets. Indeed, we would argue that the ways in which Alabama is marketing its black heritage and Wales is promoting itself are all about participatory, inclusive tourism. Visitors are invited to physically engage with peoples and places, to learn and understand their history (interpreted by *those people*, not constructed by marketers) and to converse with the visited on equal terms. Tourism is not simply a focus of oppression but empowerment. In Bali we saw that, because of the popularity of the Balinese culture as a tourist attraction, the Island has been able to resist Indonesianisation of its society.[10] In Alabama and Wales, however, the tourism activities can really be described as *emancipatory marketing* – instead of being marketing by and for an anthrocentric, androcentric and Anglocentric gaze, the destinations are breaking the hold of stereotyping. In doing so this emancipates the visited and visitor, liberating themselves and freeing the tourist from sterile, passive consumption.

It may indeed be that we are on the verge of a new image order, and if we are, it is likely to be facilitated by developments in new technology. Certainly, the image and information revolution, spearheaded by the Internet, is only just beginning. Originally started in the late Seventies by the Pentagon as a way of diffusing information sources as an insurance against a nuclear war, the Internet has expanded into a world-wide network in which consumers can do an ever-increasing number of things: send messages anywhere in the world; download whole books, music or images, moving or still; or access whole libraries and art galleries around the world. Moreover, as computers become cheaper and more powerful, and telephone lines made of hair-thin optical fibres, each with the capacity to handle 200 000 video channels simultaneously, are installed across the national and international highways, the potential for information will be almost unlimited.[11] The Internet will one day become *the* principal medium for communications and images – audio, visual entertainment, travel, ticket booking, home shopping, remote learning and conversation.

One of the key issues surrounding this reconfiguration of the image is whether the Internet will become a deregulated and unlicensed medium or whether dominant groups will maintain control through censorship and commercial weight. If it is absorbed into the existing media superstructure with the big commercial players investing in the most sophisticated web sites, reinforced and advertised in other media, it will become merely another conduit for existing ways of seeing. If it does become less controlled, however, it will have implications for the tourism image (as other images) and we may see an equalisation of ways of seeing the world as the media becomes more egalitarian. If previously marginalised groups have opportunities to project *their* view of the world, the dominance of currently powerful ideologies may be threatened.

Some visionaries talk of electronically facilitated universal and affordable access for all; a golden age in which the biggest gap between rich and poor – the information gap – would be eliminated. It has yet to happen, in fact, we would suggest that the emergence of this electronic media-dominated world has led to:

a reinforcement of the stereotypes by which the . . . [Other] is viewed. Television, the films and all the media's resources have forced information into more and more standardised moulds.[12]

The fast moving images of today demand more not less stereotyping. Ulmer, Denzin and others have pointed out that developed societies, particularly America, have '. . . become dependent upon visual and video modes of communication and entertainment, on . . . representations. . . . These representations . . . furnish knowledge about, but not an understanding of, the other.'[13] The image will continue to define our lives, but how will the image be constructed? Denzin sees a positive future, as 'The feminine, gay and ethnic gaze . . . hears and sees things that escape the white masculine eye' and that when 'the feminine (and ethnic) gaze appropriates the masculine tools of looking', 'different versions of truth (and reality) are produced' and the 'norms . . . are challenged'.[14] Whether his vision of the feminine and ethnic eye displacing the sexualising, male gaze to create alternative, more personal and insightful ways of knowing others materialises remains to be seen. Where these gazes are allowed to develop, they are changing ways of seeing, as our view of emancipatory marketing suggests. Whether the influence of these alternative gazes extends beyond the power peripheries remains open to question.

References

1   Denzin, N.K. (1995) *The Cinematic Society. The Voyeur's Gaze*, Sage, London: 210.
2   O'Barr, W. (1994) *Culture and the Ad. Exploring Otherness in Advertising*, Westview, Boulder, Colorado: 157.
3   reference 2: 158.
4   Chouinard and Grant (1996) 'On being not even close to the project', 170–93 in Duncan, N. (ed.) *Bodyspace. Destabilising geographies of sexuality*, Routledge, London: 185.
5   Fiske, J. (1989) *Understanding Popular Culture*, Routledge, London: 179.
6   Hollinshead, K. (1996) 'Culture and Capillary Power: Texas and the Quiet Annihilation of the Past', 49–98 in Robinson, M. *et al.* (1996) *Tourism and Culture: Image, Identity and Marketing*, Centre for Travel and Tourism, Sunderland: 51.
7   Anderson, K. (1996) 'Engendering Race Research: Unsettling the self-Other dichotomy', 197–211 in Duncan, N. (ed.) *Bodyspace: destabilizing geographies of gender and sexuality*, Routledge, London: 200.
8   Urry, J. (1990) *The Tourist Gaze. Leisure and Travel in Contemporary Societies*, Sage, London: 63.
9   reference 8: 143.
10 Wood, R.E. (1984) 'Ethnic tourism, the state and cultural change in South East Asia', *Annals of Tourism Research*, 11: 353–74.
11 'Brain Storms', *The Guardian*, 5 November 1996: 2–3.
12 Said, E. (1978) *Orientalism. Western Conceptions of the Orient*, Penguin, Harmondsworth: 26.
13 reference 1: 211.
14 reference 1: 217.

Bibliography

Abbott Cone, C. (1995) 'Crafting Selves. The Lives of Two Mayan Women', *Annals of Tourism Research*, 22 (2): 314–327.

Acker, J. (1990) 'Hierarchies, Jobs, Bodies: A Theory of Gendered Organizations', *Gender & Society*, 4: 139–158.

Adams, E.M. (1984) 'Come to Tana Toraja. "Land of the Heavenly Kings". Travel Agents as Brokers in Ethnicity', *Annals of Tourism Research*, 11: 469–484.

Airwaves Africa brochure.

Airwaves Worldwide Holidays brochure

Airwaves America Latina 1996/97 brochure.

Aitchison, C. (1997) book review of Apostolopoulos, Y. *et al.* (eds) (1996) *The Sociology of Tourism: Theoretical and empirical investigations, Leisure Studies*, Routledge: (16) 53–54.

Ajzen, I. and Fishbein, M. (1980) *Understanding Attitudes and Predicting Social Behaviour*, Prentice Hall, Englewood Cliffs, NJ.

Alabama Bureau of Tourism and Travel, *Alabama's Black Heritage*, Alabama.

Alaska Travel Guide (1994) Canada's Yukon.

Anderson, K. (1991) *Vancouver's Chinatown: Racial Discourse in Canada, 1875–1980*, McGill-Queens University Press, Montreal.

Anderson, K. (1996) 'Engendering Race Research: Unsettling the self-Other dichotomy', 197–211 in Duncan, N. (ed.) *Bodyspace: destabilizing geographies of gender and sexuality*, Routledge, London.

Argyle, H. (1975) *Bodily Communication*, Methuen, London.

Ashworth, G.J. (1991) Products, Places and Promotion: Destination Images in the Analysis of the Tourism Industry, 121–142 in Sinclair, M.T. and Stabler, M.J. (eds) *The Tourism Industry: An International Analysis*, CAB Int., Redwood Press, Melksham.

Ashworth, G.J. and Voogd, H. (1990) *Selling the City*, Belhaven Press, London.

Bales Worldwide brochure 1997.

Barthes, R. (1967) *The Elements of Semiology*, Cape, London.

Barthes, R. (1972) *Mythologies*, Cape, London.

Barthes, R. (1977) 'The Rhetoric of the Image', in Barthes, R., *Image, Music, Text*, Hill & Wang, New York: 32–51.

Beeghley, L. (1996) *What Does Your Wife Do? Gender and the Transformation of Family Life*, Westview Press, Oxford.

Bennett, T. (1986) 'Introduction: Popular Culture and "the turn to Gramsci"', vii–xi in Bennett, T., Mercer, C. and Woollacott, J., *Popular Culture and Social Relations*, Open University, Milton Keynes.

Berger, J. (1980) *About Looking*, Pantheon Books, New York.

Berger, J. (1983) *Ways of Seeing*, British Broadcasting Corporation & Penguin, London and Harmondsworth.

Berlowitz, A. (1994) *Creative Development Research*, Market Research Society, Advertising Research.

Berlowitz, A. (1994) *Stimulus Material*, Market Research Society, Advertising Research.

Berry, V.T. and Manning-Miller, C.L. (1996) 'Introduction', in Berry, V.T. and Manning-Miller, C.L. (eds) *Mediated Messages and African-American Culture*, Sage, Thousand Oaks California: xii–xiii.

Bhabba, H. (1990) 'The other question: difference, discrimination and the discourse of colonialism', 71–88 in Ferguson, R. *et al.* (eds) *Out There. Marginalisation and Contemporary Cultures*, New Museum of Contemporary Art and Massachusetts Institute of Technology, New York.

Blackston, M. (1993) 'Advertising Works – and CRA can count the ways', *Research Plus*, November, p.14.

Borde Failte (1995) *Ireland. The Ancient Birthplace of Good Times.*

Botterill, T.D. and Crompton, J.L. (1987) 'Personal Constructions of Holiday Snapshots', *Annals of Tourism Research*, 14 (1): 152–156.

Botterill, T.D. and Crompton, J.L. (1996) 'Two Case Studies Exploring the Nature of the Tourist's Experience', *Journal of Leisure Research*, 28 (1): 57–82.

Bovee, C.L. *et al.* (1995) *Advertising Excellence*, international edition, McGraw-Hill, New York.

Bradshaw, Y.W. and Wallace, M. (1996) *Global Inequalities*, Pine Forge Press, Thousand Oaks, California.

Brassington, F. and Pettitt, S. (1997) *Principles of Marketing*, Pitman, London.

Breathnach, P. *et al.* (1993) 'Gender in Irish tourism employment', 53–67 in O'Connor, B. and Cronin, M. (eds) *Tourism in Ireland: A Critical Analysis*, Cork University Press.

Breathnach, P. *et al.* (1994) 'Gender in Irish Tourism Employment', 52–73 in Kinnaird, V. and Hall, D. (eds) *Tourism: a Gender Analysis*, John Wiley and Sons, Chichester.

Bristow, J. (1989) 'Being Gay: politics, pleasure and identity', *New Formations*, 9: 61–81.

British Airways Holidays Worldwide, 1995.

Britton, R. (1979) 'The image of Third World tourism in marketing', *Annals of Tourism Research*, 6: 318–329.

Britton, S. (1982) 'The political economy of tourism in the Third World', *Annals of Tourism Research*, 9: 331–338.

Brunner, E. (1994) 'Abraham Lincoln as authentic reproduction: a critique of postmodernism', *American Anthropologist*, 96 (2): 397–415.

Butler-Paisley, M. and Paisley-Butler, W.J. (1974) 'Sexism in the Media: Frameworks for Research', a paper presented to the annual meeting of the Association for Education and Journalism, San Diego, August.

Butler, J. (1990) *Gender Trouble: Feminism and the Subversion of Identity*, Routledge, New York.

Butler, R. and Pearce, D. (eds) (1995) *Change in Tourism. People, Places, Processes*, Routledge, London.

Button, K. (1993), 'The gay consumer', *The Financial Times*, 9 September: 18.

Carney, T.F. (1972) *Content Analysis: A Technique for Systematic Inference from Communications*, University of Manitoba Press, Winnipeg.

Chambers, I. (1986) *Popular Culture: the Metropolitan Experience*, Methuen, London.

Charlier, J.J. (1996) 'New Geographical Trends in Cruise Shipping', 51–60 in Roehl, W.S. (ed.) *Proceedings of the Second Environments for Tourism Conference*, William F. Harrah College of Hotel Administration, University of Nevada, Las Vegas.

Chetwynd, C. (1995) 'Travails of a lone woman', *The Times*, 3 November: 7.

de Chernatony, L. and McDonald, M.H.B. (1992) *Creating Powerful Brands: the strategic route to success in consumer, industrial and service markets*, Butterworth Heinemann, Oxford.

Chisnall, P.M. (1994) *Consumer Behaviour*, 3rd ed., McGraw-Hill, New York.

Chon, K.S. (1990) 'The Role of Destination Image in Tourism: A Review and Discussion', *Tourist Review*, 45 (2): 2–9.

Chouinard and Grant (1996) 'On being not even close to the project', 170–193 in Duncan, N. (ed.) *Bodyspace. Destabilising geographies of sexuality*, Routledge, London.

Clarke, J. and Critcher, C. (1985) *The Devil Makes Work*, MacMillan, London.

Clegg, S.R. (1989) *Frameworks of Power*, Sage, London.

Cohen, C.B. (1995) 'Marketing Paradise, Making Nation', *Annals of Tourism Research*, 22 (2): 404–421.

Cohen, E. (1972) 'Towards a Sociology of International Tourism', *Social Research*, 39: 164–182.

Cohen, E. (1979) 'Rethinking the sociology of tourism', *Annals of Tourism Research*, 6: 18–35.

Cohen, E. (1979) 'A phenomenology of tourist experiences', *Sociology*, 13: 179–201.

Cohen, E. (1983) 'Hill tribe tourism', 307–325 in McKinion, J. and Bhruk Sasri, W. (eds) *Highlanders of Thailand*, Oxford University Press, Kuala Lumpur.

Cohen, E. and Cooper, R. (1986) 'Language and Tourism', *Annals of Tourism Research*, 13: 533–563.

Cohen, E. (1989) '"Primitive and remote" – Hill tribe trekking in Thailand', *Annals of Tourism Research*, (16): 30–61.

Cohen, E. (1987) review of Yeshayahu, N. (1985) *The Bible of the Image: The History of Photography in the Holy Land, 1839–1899*, University of Pennsylvania Press, Philadelphia, *Annals of Tourism Research* 14 (1) 157–162.

Coltman, M.M. (1989) *Tourism Marketing*, Van Nostrand Reinhold, New York.

Cook, G. (1992) *The Discourse of Advertisements*, Routledge, London.

Cooper, C. *et al.* (1993) *Tourism Principles & Practice*, Pitman Publishing, London.

Condé Nast Traveler, July and August 1997.

Courteney, A.E. and Lockeretz, S.W. (1971) 'A Woman's Place: An Analysis of the Roles Portrayed by Women in Magazine Advertisements', *Journal of Market Research*, 8 Feb: 92–95.

Cox and Kings 1997 Latin America brochure.

Creighton, M.R. (1995) 'Japanese Craft and Tourism. Liberating the Crane Wife', *Annals of Tourism Research*, 22 (2): 463–478.

Crick, M. (1989) 'Representations of international tourism in the social sciences: sun, sex, sights, savings and servility', *Annual Review of Anthropology*, 18: 307–344.

Croatian National Tourism Office, *Croatia*, 1996.

Crompton, J.L. (1979) 'An Assessment of the Image of Mexico as a Vacation Destination and the Influence of Geographical Location upon that Image', *Journal of Travel Research*, 18, Fall: 18–23.

Cronin, B. (1993) 'Myths and Mirrors: Tourist Images and National Identity', 68–85 in O'Connor, B. and Cronin, M., *Tourism in Ireland: a Critical Analysis*, Cork University Press.

Culler, J. (1976) *Saussure*, Fontana, London.

Culler, J. (1981) 'Semiotics of Tourism', *American Journal of Semiotics*, 1: 127–140.

Culley, J.D. and Bennett, R. (1976) 'Selling Women, Selling Blacks', *Journal of Communication*, Autumn, 160–172.

Dann, G. (1988) 'Images of Cyprus projected by tour operators', *Problems of Tourism*, XI (3): 43–70.

Dann, G. (1992) 'Travelogs and the management of unfamiliarity', *Journal of Travel Research*, 30 (4): 59–63.

Dann, G. & Potter, R. (1994) 'Tourism and Postmodernity in a Caribbean setting', *Cahiers du Tourisme*, serie C, 185.

Dann, G.M.S. (1995) 'A sociolinguistic approach towards changing tourist imagery', 114–136 in Butler, R. and Pearce, D. (eds) *Change in Tourism. People, Places, Processes*, Routledge, London.

Dann, G. (1996) *The Language of Tourism: A Sociolinguistic Perspective*, CAB International, Oxford.

Dann, G.M.S. (1996) 'The People of Tourist Brochures', 61–82 in Selwyn, T. (ed.) *The Tourist Image. Myths and Myth Making in Tourism*, John Wiley and Sons, Chichester.

Davies, C.A. (1987) *Welsh Nationalism in the Twentieth Century*, Praeger, New York.

Davis *et al.* (1993) *Public policy in Australia*, 2nd ed., Allen & Unwin, St Leonards.

de Lauretis, T. (1987) *Technologies of Gender*, Bloomington, Indiana University.

Denzin, N.K. (1995) *The Cinematic Society. The Voyeur's Gaze*, Sage, London.

Dichter, E. (1985) 'What's in an image?', *Journal of Consumer Marketing*, 2 (1): 75–81.

Dilley, R.S. (1986) 'Tourist Brochures and Tourist Images', *The Canadian Geographer*, 30 (1): 59–65.

Dogenais, H. (1993) 'Women in Guadeloupe: the paradoxes of reality', 83–108 in Mansen, J.H. (ed.) *Women and Change in the Caribbean: a pan Caribbean perspective*, James Currey, London, Indiana University Press, Bloomington, Indiana.

Dubinsky, K. (1994) '"The Pleasure is Exquisite but Violent": The Imaginary Geography of Niagara Falls in the Nineteenth Century', *Journal of Canadian Studies*, 29 (2): 64–88.

Duncan, N. (ed.) (1996) *Bodyspace. Destabilizing geographies of gender and sexuality*, Routledge, London.

Duncan, N. (1996) 'Sexuality in Public and Private Spaces', 127–145 in Duncan, N. (ed.) *Bodyspace: destabilizing geographies of gender and sexuality*, Routledge, London.

Dyer, R. (1986) *Heavenly Bodies: Film Stars and Society*, St Martens, New York.

Echtner, C.M. and Brent Ritchie, J.R. (1991) 'The Meaning and Measurement of Tourism Destination Image', *Journal of Tourism Studies*, 2 (2), December.

(The) *Economist* (1996) 'The World in 1997', The Economist Publications, London.

(The) Economist Intelligence Unit (1994) 'Outbound Markets: Japan Outbound', *Travel & Tourism Analyst*, 1, The Economist Intelligence Unit.

ECTARC (1988) *Study of the Social, Cultural and Linguistic Impact of Tourism on Wales*, Wales Tourist Board, Cardiff.

Edensor, T. and Kothari, V. 'The Masculinisation of Stirling's Heritage', in Kinnaird, V. and Hall, D. (eds) (1994) *Tourism: a Gender Analysis*, John Wiley and Sons, Chichester.

Edwards, E. (1996) 'Postcards: Greetings from Another World', 197–222 in Selwyn, T. (ed.) *The Tourism Image. Myths and Myth Making in Tourism*, John Wiley and Sons, Chichester.

Eisenschitz, A. (1988) paper presented at the Leisure Studies Association Third International Conference, Brighton.

Elliott, H. (1997) 'BA takes ethnic route in £60 million bid to stay in front around the world', *The Times*, 11 June: 5.

Embacher, J. and Buttle, F. (1989) 'A Repertory Grid Analysis of Austria's Image as a Summer Vacation Destination', *Journal of Travel Research*, 28 (1): 3–7.

Englis, B.G. *et al.* (1994) 'Beauty Before the Eyes of Beholders: The Cultural Encoding of Beauty Types in Magazine Advertising and Music Television', *Journal of Advertising*, 23 (2), June: 49–63.

Enloe, C. (1989) *Bananas, Beaches and Bases. Making Feminist Sense of International Politics*, Pandora, London.

Estonian Tourist Board (1994) *Eesti, Estonia*.

Evans-Pritchard, D. (1989) 'How "They" See "Us"', *Annals of Tourism Research*, (16): 89–105.

Ewen, S. (1976) *Captains of Consciousness. Advertising and the Social Roots of the Consumer Culture*, McGraw Hill, New York.

Fairbairn-Dunlop, P. (1994) 'Gender, Culture and Tourism Development in Western Samoa', 121–141 in Kinnaird, V. and Hall, D. (eds) *Tourism: a Gender Analysis*, John Wiley and Sons, Chichester.

Featherstone, M. (1991) *Consumer Culture and Postmodernism*, Sage, London.

Featherstone, M. (ed.) (1988) *Postmodernism: Theory, Culture and Society*, Sage, London.

Ferguson, M. (1980) 'The Woman's Magazine Cover Photograph', *Sociological Review Monograph*, 29 Oct: 219–238.

Fiji Visitors Bureau (1995) *Fiji Islands Travel Guide*.

Fingleton, E. (1996) 'Tokyo Inc confounds its critics', *The Observer*, 20 October 1996: 22.

Finnish Tourist Board, Finland. Summer 1996, Helsinki.

Fiske, J. (1992) *Reading the Popular*, Routledge, London.

Fiske, J. (1994) *Understanding Popular Culture*, Routledge, London.

Fletcher, J. and Cooper, C.P. (1996) 'Tourism Strategy Planning. Szolnok County, Hungary', *Annals of Tourism Research*, 23 (1): 181–200.

Forte Grand Exclusive Hotels of the World Directory 1995.

Forte Gold Card News (58) May/June 1996.

Forte Gold Card News (59) July/August 1996: 12.

Forte Hotels & Resorts Worldwide 1996.

Fowles, J. (1996) *Advertising and Popular Culture*, Sage, London.

Foucault, M. (1978) *The History of Sexuality*, Harmondsworth, Penguin.

Foucault, M. (1977) *Discipline and Punishment*, Tavistock, London.

Foucault, M. (1980) *Power/Knowledge*, Harvester, Brighton.

Foucault, M. (1980) *Power/Knowledge: Selected Interviews and Other Writings 1972–1977*, ed. Gordon, C., Random House, New York.

Fredrikson, G. (1987) *The Black Image in the White Mind*, Wesleyan University Press, Hanover, NJ.

Garaa-Ramon, M.D. *et al.* (1995) 'Farm Tourism, Gender and the Environment in Spain', *Annals of Tourism Research*, 22 (2): 267–282.

Gartner, W. (1993) 'Image Formation Process', *Journal of Travel and Tourism Marketing*, 2 (2/3): 191–215.

Gardiner, S. (1994) *Qualitative Pretesting*, Market Research Society, Advertising Research.

Gilbert, D.C. (1991) 'An examination of the consumer behaviours process related to tourism', 78–105 in Cooper, C.P. (ed.) *Progress in Tourism, Recreation and Hospitality*, vol. III, Belhaven Press, London.

Gitelson, R.J. and Crompton, J.L. (1983) 'The Planning Horizons and Sources of Information used by Pleasure Vacationers', 2–7, *Journal of Travel Research*, 21 (3).

Goffman, E. (1959 and 1979) *The Presentation of Self in Everyday Life*, Doubleday, NY.

Goffman, E. (1979) *Gender Advertisements*, Macmillan, London.

Gold, J.R. (1994) 'Locating the message: place promotion as image communication', 19–37 in Gold, J.R. and Ward, S.V. *Place Promotion. The Use of Publicity to Sell Towns and Regions*, John Wiley and Sons, Chichester.

Goodall, B. *et al.* (1988) 'Market Opportunity Sets for tourism', Geographical Papers 100: Tourism Series, 1, University of Reading, Department of Geography.

Goodrich, J.N. (1978) 'The relationship between preferences for and perceptions of vacation destinations: application of a choice model', *Journal of Travel Research*, Fall, 8–13.

Government of India Tourist Office (1995) *Indiahhh. Only 9 hours away.*

Gow (1992) 'Making Sense of Music Videos: Research during the inaugural decade', *Journal of American Culture*, 15 (3): 35–43.

Graburn, N. (1989) 'Tourism, the sacred journey', 21–36 in Smith, V. (ed.) *Hosts and Guests. The Anthropology of Tourism*, 2nd ed., University of Pennsylvania Press, Philadephia.

Graburn, N. (1995) 'The past in the present Japan: nostalgia and neo-traditionalism in contemporary Japanese domestic tourism', 47–70 in Butler, R. and Pearce, D. (eds) *Change in Tourism. People, Places, Processes*, Routledge, London.

Gray, C. and Herbert, M. (1983) Choosing a Country for a Holiday, Seminar on The Importance of Research in the Tourism Industry, Helsinki, ESOMAR.

Grossman, L.M. (1992) 'After Demographic Shift, Atlanta Mall Restyles Itself as Black Shopping Center', *The Wall Street Journal*, 26 February.

Gunn, C. (1988) *Vacationscapes: Designing Tourist Regions*, Van Nostrand, New York.

Gyte, D.M. (1987) 'Tourist cognition of destination: an exploration of techniques of measurement and representation of images of Tunisia', Trent Working Papers in Geography, Trent Polytechnic, Nottingham.

Hack, S. (1997) 'Rock a La Mode', *Condé Nast Traveler*, July, 94–103.

Hadfield, T. (1994) *Strategic Development*, Market Research Society, Advertising Research.

Hall, C.M. (1994) *Tourism and Politics: policy, power and place*, John Wiley and Sons, Chichester.

Hall, C.M. (1994) 'Gender and Economic Interests in Tourism Prostitution: the nature, development and implications of sex tourism in South-East Asia', 143–164 in Kinnaird, V. and Hall, D. (eds) *Tourism: a Gender Analysis*, John Wiley and Sons, Chichester.

Hall, D.R. (1984) 'Foreign tourism under socialism: the Albanian 'Stalinist' model', *Annals of Tourism Research*, 11 (4): 539–555.

Hall, S. (1980) 'Encoding/decoding', 128–138 in Hall, S. (ed.) *Culture, Media, Language*, Hutchinson, London.

Hall, S. (1981) 'Television as expression of ideology', *Communication Research Trends*, 2 (3): 5–6.

Hall, S. (ed.)(1997) *Representation: cultural representations and signifying practices*, Sage and the Open University, London.

Hall, S. (1997) 'The Work of Representation', 13–74 in Hall, S. (ed.) *Representation: cultural representations and signifying practices*, Sage and the Open University, London.

Hall, S. (1997) 'The Spectacle of the "Other"', 223–290 in Hall, S. (ed.) *Representation. Cultural Representation and Signifying Practice*, Sage and the Open University, London.

Hallberg, G. (1995) *All Consumers Are Not Created Equal. The differential marketing strategy for brand loyalty and profits*, John Wiley and Sons, Chichester.

Hamilton, P. (1997) 'Representing the Social: France and Frenchness in Post-War Humanist Photography', 75–150 in Hall, S. (ed.) *Representation: cultural representations and signifying practices*, Sage and the Open University, London.

Hargreaves, J. (1986) *Sport, Power and Culture*, Polity Press, Cambridge.

Harrett-Bond, B.E. and Harrett-Bond, D.L. (1979) 'Tourism in the Gambia', *Review of African Political Economy*, 14: 78–90.

Hawaii Visitors Bureau (1997) *The Islands of Aloha*, The Official Travel Guide of the Hawaii Visitors Bureau.

Henderson, K. (1994) 'Perspectives on Analysing Gender, Women and Leisure', *Journal of Leisure Research*, 26: 119–137.

Henley Centre (1992) 'Europe's Ageing Population', Henley Centre, *Leisure Futures*, 3: 6–10.

Henley Centre for Leisure Forecasting (1992) 'Time Use', Henley Centre, *Leisure Futures*, 3: 30–32.

Henley Centre for Leisure Forecasting (1992) 'Demographic Background', Henley Centre, *Leisure Futures*, 3: 16–20.

Henley Centre for Leisure Forecasting (1993) 'Generation X: an army of ageing Bart Simpsons or the wave of the future? Today's cohort of 16 to 24s', *Leisure Futures*, 3: 5–97.

Henley Centre (1994) 'Todays older consumers: an emerging third age of personal fulfilment or a waster era of frustrated possibilities?', Henley Centre *Leisure Futures*.

Henshall-Mansen, J. (1994) 'Tourism, gender and development in the Caribbean', 107–120 in Kinnaird, V. and Hall, D. (eds) *Tourism: a Gender Analysis*, John Wiley and Sons, Chichester.

Hindle, P. (1994) 'Gay Communities and Gay Space in the City', 7–25 in Whittle, S. (ed.) *The Margins of the City: Gay Men's Urban Lives*, Arena, Aldershot.

Hitchcock, M. *et al.* (eds) (1992) *Tourism in South-East Asia*, Routledge, London.

Hodgson, P. (1983) 'Research into the Complex Nature of the Holiday Choice Process', Seminar on The Importance of Research in the Tourism Industry, Helsinki, ESOMAR.

Holcomb, B. and Luongo, M. (1996) 'Gay Tourism in the United States', *Annals of Tourism Research*, August: 711–713.

Holvik, T. and Heiberg, T. (1980) 'Centre-periphery tourism and self reliance', *International Social Science Journal*, 32 (1): 69–98.

Hollinshead, K. (1992) 'White gaze, "red" people – shadow visions: the disidentification of "Indians" in cultural tourism', *Leisure Studies*, 11: 43–64.

Hollinshead, K. (1996) 'Culture and Capillary Power: Texas and the Quiet Annihilation of the Past', 49–98 in Robinson, M. *et al.* (1996) *Tourism and Culture: Image, Identity and Marketing*, Centre for Travel and Tourism, Sunderland.

Holloway, J.C. and Robinson, C. (1995) *Marketing for Tourism*, 3rd ed., Longman, Harlow.

Horne, D. (1984) *The Great Museum. The Representation of History*, Punto Press, London.

Horner, S. and Swarbrooke, J. (1996) *Marketing Tourism, Hospitality and Leisure in Europe*, Thomson Business Press, London.

Hughes, C.F. (1994) *On Work, Race and the Sociological Imagination*, ed. Coser, L.A., University of Chicago Press, Chicago.

Hughes, H. (1997) 'Holidays and Homosexual Identity', *Tourism Management*, 18 (1).

Hughes, G. (1992) 'Tourism and the geographical imagination', *Leisure Studies*, 11: 31–42.

Hunt, J.D. (1975) 'Image as a factor in Tourism Development', *Journal of Travel Research*, 13 (3): 1–7.

Independent on Sunday Business Supplement (1996) 'Irish exploit liquid assets', 1 December: 7.

The Independent on Sunday (1996) 'A word about the home office', 1 December: 80–81.

Intra Travel, New Europe 1997 brochure.

Italian State Tourist Office (1991) *Italia. Travels in Wonderland*.

Jablow, A. and Hammond, D. (1970) *The Africa That Never Was: Four Centuries of British Writing About Africa*, Twayne Press, New York.

Jacobson, M.F. and Mazur, L.A. (1995) *Marketing Madness. A Consumer's Survival Guide*, Westview Press, Oxford.

Jamaica Tourist Board (1995) *Jamaica Me Love You.*

(The) Jamaica Hotel and Tourist Association Official Guide (1996) *Destination Jamaica*.

Jefferson, A. (1992) 'Tourism in Europe', British Tourism Authority/English Tourist Board, *Tourism Intelligence Quarterly*, 14 (1), August: 57–63.

Jenkins, R. (1997) *Rethinking Ethnicity. Arguments and Explorations*, Sage, London.

Jenkins, W.I. (1978) *Policy analysis: a political and organizational perspective*, St. Martin's Press, New York.

Kelly, J. (1994) 'The symbolic interaction metaphor and leisure: critical challenges', *Leisure Studies*, 13: 81–96.

Kelly, T. (1997) 'You Say Majorca, I Say Mallorca', *Independent on Sunday*: 3.

Kent, P.J. (1990) 'People, Places and Priorities: Opportunity Sets and Consumers' Holiday Choice', in Ashworth, G. and Goodall, B. (eds) *Marketing Tourism Places*, Routledge, London: 42–62.

Kinnaird, V. and Hall, D.R. (eds) (1994) *Tourism: a Gender Analysis*, John Wiley and Sons, Chichester.

Kinnaird, V. and Hall, D.R. (1996) 'Understanding tourism processes: a gender-aware framework', *Annals of Tourism Research*, 17: 95–102.

KLM (1996) *Holland Herald*, June.

KLM (1996) 'Kinder, Kirche, Korporation. . . .', *Holland Herald*, June.

Kovel, J. (1988) *White Racism: A Psychohistory*, Free Association Books, London.

Kres, G. and Van Leeuwen, T. (1990) *Reading Images*, Deakin University Press, Geelang, Australia.

Kotler, P. *et al.* (1996) *Principles of Marketing*, Prentice Hall, European edition.

Kotler, P. *et al.* (1996) *Marketing for Hospitality & Tourism*, Prentice Hall, New Jersey.

Kotler, P. *et al.* (1994) *Marketing Places. Attracting Investment, Industry and Tourism to Cities, States, and Nations*, The Free Press, New York.

Kuoni Worldwide, 1996–7.

Lanfant, M.F. (1995) 'International Tourism, Internationalization and the Challenge to Identity', 24–43 in Lanfant, M.F., Allcock, J.B. and Bruner, E.M. (eds) *International Tourism: Identity and Change*, Sage, London.

Lasch, C. (1978) *The Culture of Narcissm: American Life in an Age of Diminishing Expectations*, W.W. Norton, New York.

Lash (1990) *The Sociology of Postmodernism*, Routledge, London.

Laxson, J. (1991) 'How "We" See "Them": Tourism and Native Americans', *Annals of Tourism Research*, (18): 365–391.

Lazer, W. (1997) *Handbook of Demographics for Marketing and Advertising: New Trends in the US Marketplace*, Lexington, New York.

Leheny, D. (1995) 'A Political Economy of Asian Sex Tourism', *Annals of Tourism Research*, 22 (2): 367–384.

Lett, J. (1983) 'Ludic and liminoid aspects of charter yacht tourism in the Caribbean', *Annals of Tourism Research*, 10: 35–56.

Levy, M. (1996) 'Current accounts and baked beans: Translating FMCG marketing principles to the financial sector', *Journal of Brand Management*, 4 (2): 95–99.

Lidchi, H. (1997) 'The Poetics and the Politics of Exhibiting Other Cultures', 151–222 in Hall, S. (ed.) *Representation: cultural representations and signifying practices*, Sage and the Open University, London.

Light (1992) 'Bilingual Heritage Interpretation in Wales', *Scottish Geographical Magazine*, 108/3.

Lithuanian Tourist Board (1996) *Welcome to Lithuania*.

Loudon, D.L. and Della Bitta, A.J. (1993) *Consumer Behaviour*, 4th ed., McGraw-Hill, New York.

Lull, J. (1992) 'Popular music and communication: An Introduction', 1–32 in Lull, J. (ed.) *Popular Music and Communication*, Sage, Newbury Park, California.

Lundstrom, W.J. and Scimpaglia, D. (1979) 'Sex Role Portrayals in Advertising', *Journal of Marketing*, 41, July: 72–78.

MacCannell, D. (1973) 'Staged Authenticity', *American Journal of Sociology*, 79 (3): 589–603.

MacCannell, D. (1984) 'Reconstructed Ethnicity, Tourism & Cultural Identity in Third World Communities', *Annals of Tourism Research*, 11: 375–391.

MacCannell, D. (1989) 'Introduction to special issue on the semiotics of tourism', *Annals of Tourism Research*, 18.

Machlis, G.E. and Burch, W.R. (1983) 'Relations Between Strangers: cycles of structure and meaning in tourist systems', *Sociological Review*, 31: 666–692.

Manchester Gay Village Guide (1996), Healthy Gay Manchester and Manchester City Council.

Manchester City Council, Arts and Leisure Committee. Equal Opportunities and Anti-Discrimination Sub-Committee, March 1996.

Manstead, A.S.R. and McCulloch, C. (1981) 'Sex Role Stereotyping in British Television Advertising', *British Journal of Social Psychology*, 20 (3), September: 171–180.

Marchand, R. (1985) *Advertising the American Way: Making Way for Modernity 1920–1940*, University of California Press, Berkeley.

Marchant, L.J., Hutchinson, P.J. and Prescott, P. (1990) 'A practical model of consumer choice', *Journal of Market Research Society*, 32: 1.

Marchetti, G. (1991) 'Ethnicity, the Cinema, and Cultural Studies', 277–309 in Friedman, L.D. (ed.) *Unspeakable Images: Ethnicity and the American Cinema*, University of Illinois Press, Urbana.

Marshall, S. (1996) 'Women "fed up" with sexist ads', *Marketing*, 28 November: 12.

Marshall, S. (1996) 'Out of date images anger young women', *Marketing*, 30 May: 11.

Marston, P. (1997) 'BA stops flying the flag in £60 million facelift', *Daily Telegraph*, 11 June: 12.

Matthews, H.G. (1978) *International Tourism. A Political and Social Analysis*, Schenkman, Cambridge MA.

Matthews, V. (1987) 'Merely Male in Admen's Markets', *Guardian*, Monday 30 November.

Mayo, E.J. and Jarvis, L.P. (1981) *The Psychology of Leisure Travel: Effective Marketing and Selling of Travel Services*, CBI, Boston.

McArthur, L.Z. and Resko, B.G. (1975) 'The Portrayal of Men and Women in American Television Commercials', *Journal of Social Psychology*, 97, Dec: 209–220.

McClintock, A. (1995) *Imperial Leather*, Routledge, London.

McCracken, G. (1986) 'Culture and Consumption: A theoretical account of the structure and movement of the cultural meaning of consumer goods', *Journal of Consumer Research*, 13: 71–81.

Medlik, S. and Middleton, V.T.C. (1973) 'The Tourist Product and its Marketing Implications', 28–46 in *International Tourism Quarterly*, 9.

Ministry of Economic Affairs, Slovenija (1996) *Slovenija. The green piece of Europe*.

McGee, R. (1988) 'What do women business travellers really want?', *Successful Marketing*, 37 (9): 55–57: 56.

McLellan, R.W. and Dodd Foushee, K. (1983) 'Negative Images of the United States as Expressed by Tour Operators from Other Countries', *Journal of Travel Research*, 22 (1): 2–5.

McLuhan, M. (1964) *Understanding Media: the extensions of man*, McGraw Hill, New York.

McQuail, D. (1987) *Mass Communication Theory*, Sage, London.

Meisch, L. (1995) 'Gringas and Otavalenos. Changing Tourist Relations', *Annals of Tourism Research*, 22 (2): 441–462.

Mellinger, W.M. (1994) 'Towards A Critical Analysis of Tourism Representations', *Annals of Tourism Research*, 21 (4): 756–779.

Mercer, C. (1986) 'Complicit Pleasure', 50–68 in Bennett, T., Mercer, C. and Woollacott, J., *Popular Culture and Social Relations*, Open University, Milton Keynes.

Middleton, V.T.C. (1994) *Marketing in Travel and Tourism*, 2nd ed., Butterworth Heinemann, Oxford.

Miller, A.R. (1996) 'Toward the Year 2000: Trends in the Cruise Industry', 178–182 in Roehl, W.S. (ed.) *Proceedings of the Second Environments for Tourism Conference*, Las Vegas: William F Harrah College of Hotel Administration, University of Nevada, Las Vegas.

Millum, T. (1974) *Images of Women: Advertising in Women's Magazines*, Chatto and Windus, London.

Mintel International Group Ltd (1995) 'Targeting the Rich and Poor', *Executive Summary*, 17 July, Mintel International Group Ltd.

Mintel Marketing Intelligence (1996) *Business Travel*, Mintel Intelligence Group Ltd, London, October.

Mississippi Department of Economic and Community Development (1997) *Mississippi, The South's Warmest Welcome*, London.

Moore, R.S. (1995) 'Gender and Alcohol Use in a Greek Tourist Town', *Annals of Tourism Research*, 22 (2): 300–315.

Moore, S. (1987) 'Target Man', *New Statesman*, January.

Morgan, M. (1991) 'Majorca: Dressing Up to Survive', *Tourism Management*, 12 (1): March.

Morgan, M. (1996) *Marketing for Leisure and Tourism*, Prentice Hall, Hemel Hempstead.

Morgan, N.J. (1991) Perceptions, Patterns and Policies of Tourism: the development of the Devon seaside resorts during the twentieth century with special reference to Torquay and Ilfracombe, unpublished Exeter University PhD thesis.

Morgan, N.J. and Pritchard, A. (1997) 'Seniors Tourism: A Marketing Challenge for the Next Millennium?', paper presented at the 10th European Leisure and Recreation Association Congress, Dubrovnik.

Morgan, N.J. (1997) 'Seaside Resort Strategies: The Case of Inter-War Torquay', 84–100 in Fisher, S. (ed.) *Recreation and the Sea*, University of Exeter Press, Exeter.

Moss, S. (1994) *The Planning and Role of Research*, Market Research Society, Advertising Research.

Mulryan, D. (1995), 'Out of the Closet', *American Demographics*, 17, May: 40–46.

Mulryan, D. (1995) 'Reaching the gay market', *American Demographics*, 17, May: 46–48.

Murdock, G.P. (1937) 'Comparative Data on the Division of Labour by Sex', *Social Forces*, 15 (4): 551–553.

Myslik, W.D. (1996) 'Renegotiating the Social/Sexual Identities of Places', 156–169 in Duncan, N. (ed.) *Bodyspace. Destabilizing geographies of gender and sexuality*, Routledge, London.

Naisbitt, J. (1997) *Megratrends Asia. The Eight Asian Megratrends That Are Changing The World*, Nicholas Brealey Publishing, London.

Nash, D. (1989) 'Tourism as a form of imperialism', in Smith, V. (ed.) *Hosts and Guests: The Anthropology of Tourism*, University of Pennsylvania Press, Philadelphia.

Nelson, C. (1994) *How to Market to Women*, Visible Ink Press, Detroit.

Nelson, C. and Grossberg, L. (eds) *Marxism and the Interpretation of Culture*, University of Illinois Press, Chicago.

Nichols, B. (1981) *Ideology and the Image*, Indiana University Press, Bloomington.

Nixon, S. (1997) 'Circulating Culture', 179–234 in Du Gay, P. (ed.) *The Production of Culture/Cultures of Production*, Sage, London.

Nolan, D.S. (1976) 'Tourists' use and evaluation of travel information sources', *Journal of Travel Research*, 14, Winter: 6–8.

Oakley, A. (1982) *Sex, Gender and Society*, Maurice Temple Smith, London.

O'Barr, W. (1994) *Culture and the Ad. Exploring Otherness in Advertising*, Westview Press, Boulder, Colorado.

O'Cinneide, M. and Walsh, J. (1991) 'Tourism and regional development in Ireland', *Geographical Viewpoint*, (19): 47–68.

O'Connor, B. and Cronin, M. (eds) (1993) *Tourism in Ireland: A Critical Analysis*, Cork University Press, Cork.

O'Connor, B. (1993) 'Myths and Mirrors: Tourist Images and National Identity', in O'Connor, B. and Cronin, M. (eds) *Tourism in Ireland: A Critical Analysis*, Cork University Press, Cork.

Papson, S. (1981) 'Spuriousness and tourism: politics of two Canadian provincial governments', *Annals of Tourism Research*, 8 (2): 220–235.

Papua New Guinea. Land of Adventure and Excitement. Air Niugine Paradise Tours 1996 brochure.

Parker, S. (1981) 'Change, flexibility, spontaneity, and self-determination in leisure', *Social Forces*, 60 (2): 323–331.

Pateman, C. (1988) *The Sexual Contract*, Polity Press, Cambridge.

Payne, B. (1997) 'Beauty Beyond Measure', *Condé Nast Traveler*, July: 83–91.

Pearce, D. (1989) *Tourist Development*, Longman, London.

Pearce, P.L. (1988) *The Ulysses Factor*, Springer-Verlag, New York.

Pearce, P.L. (1982) 'Perceived changes in holiday destinations', *Annals of Tourism Research*, 9: 145–164.

Peck, J.G. and Lepie, A.S. (1989) 'Tourism and development in three North Carolina coastal towns', 203–222 in Smith, V. (ed.) *Hosts and Guests: The Anthropology of Tourism*, 2nd ed., University of Pennsylvania Press, Philadelphia.

Perry, D.G. and Bussey, K. (1979) 'The Social Learning Theory of Sex Differences. Imitation is alive and well', *Journal of Personality and Social Psychology*, 37: 1699–1712.

Petrie, G. (1997) 'P&O's Oriana: British Traditions Sail On', in *Porthole. A View of the Sea and Beyond*, July/August, Panoff Publishing, 40–43.

Peters, G. (1996) *The New Wave. Imagining the next generation of customers*, Pitman, London.

Pimlott, J.A.R. (1947) *The Englishman's Holiday. A Social History*, Faber & Faber, London.

Pingree, S. *et al.* (1976) 'A Scale for Sexism', *Journal of Communication*, Autumn: 193–200.

Pitchford, S.R. (1994) 'Ethnic Tourism and Nationalism in Wales', *Annals of Tourism Research*, 35–50.

Poe, A. (1976) 'Active Women in Advertisements', *Journal of Communication*, 26 (4), Autumn: 185–192.

Polish Tourist Information Centre (1997) *Poland Invites*, Warsaw.

Pritchard, A. (1992) Images of Masculinity and Femininity in Magazine Advertising: A Case Study of Playboy and GQ, unpublished University of Wales MSc. dissertation.

Pritchard, A. and Morgan, N.J. (1995) 'Evaluating Vacation Destination Brochure Images: the case of local authorities in Wales', *Journal of Vacation Marketing*, 2 (1), December: 23–38.

Pritchard, A. and Morgan, N.J. (1996) 'Selling the Celtic Arc to the USA: A Comparative Analysis of the Destination Brochure Images Used in the Marketing of Ireland, Scotland and Wales', *Journal of Vacation Marketing*, 2 (4): 346–365.

Pritchard, A. and Morgan, N.J. (1996) 'Marketing Emerging and Established Destinations: a case study of Ireland, Scotland and Wales in the US Market', in Roehl, W.S. (ed.) *Proceedings of the Second Environments for Tourism Conference*, Las Vegas, Nevada: 202–211.

Pritchard, A. and Morgan, N.J. (1996) 'Sex Still Sells to Generation X', *Journal of Vacation Marketing*, 3 (4), December: 69–80.

Pritchard, A. and Morgan, N.J. (1997) 'Marketing Practice and Opportunity in the Tour

Operators' Senior Travel Market: Beyond Bowling and Ballroom Dancing', *Journal of Vacation Marketing*, 3 (2), March: 153–163.

Pritchard, A. and Morgan, N.J. (1997) 'The Gay Consumer: A Viable Market Segment?', *Journal of Targeting, Measurement and Analysis for Marketing*, 6 (1): 9–20.

Prue, T. (1994) *Tracking and Effectiveness*, Market Research Society, Advertising Research.

Pruitt, D. and Lafont, S. (1995) 'For Love and Money Romance. Tourism in Jamaica', *Annals of Tourism Research*, 22 (2): 422–440.

Rao, N. (1995) 'Commoditisation and Commercialisation of Women in Tourism: Symbols of Victimhood', *Contours*, 7 (1), March: 30.

Real, T. (1996) 'Looking Good: How Cultural Tourism has Changed the Face of North American Travel Destinations', 171–184 in Robinson, M. *et al.* (eds) *Tourism and Culture. Image, Identity and Marketing*, The Centre for Travel and Tourism, Sunderland.

Relph, E. (1983) *Place and Placelessness*, Pion, London.

Research International, Background Papers, Market Research Society, Advertising Research Seminar, The Research International Approach to Advertising Evaluation Research.

Richter L.K. (1995) 'Gender and Race: Neglected Variables in Tourism Research', 71–91 in Butler, R. and Pearce, D. (eds) *Change in Tourism. People, Places, Processes*, Routledge, London.

Riley, R.W. and Van Doren, S. (1992) 'Movies as tourism promotion', *Tourism Management*, September: 257–274.

Ritchie, K. (1995) *Marketing to Generation X*, Lexington Books, New York.

Roberts, K. (1997) 'Same activities, different meanings: British youth cultures in the 1990s', 1–16 in *Leisure Studies*, (1): 16.

Robins, K. (1996) *Into the Image. Culture and politics in the field of vision*, Routledge, London.

Rogers, J.R. (1989) 'Clear Links: tourism and child prostitution', *Contours*, 4 (2): 20–22.

Rojek, C. (1985) *Capitalism and Leisure Theory*, Tavistock Publications, London.

Rojek, C. (1995) *Decentring Leisure. Rethinking Leisure Theory*, Sage, London.

Romanian Ministry of Tourism (1997) 'Romania. Come as a tourist, leave as a friend.'

Romanian Ministry of Tourism (1997) *Romania*.

Romantic Romania. Fascinating Tours operated by Romantic Travel, Romania.

Rose, G. (1993) *Feminism and Geography. The Limits of Geographical Knowledge*, Polity Press, Cambridge.

Rosenow, J. and Pulsipher, G. (eds) (1979) *Tourism – the Good, the Bad and the Ugly*, Media Production Marketing, Lincoln, Nebraska.

Rowe, M. (1997) 'Hullo John, got a new motif?', *The Independent on Sunday*, 15 June.

Said, E. (1991) *Orientalism. Western Conceptions of the Orient*, Penguin, Harmondsworth.

Salmon, B. (1994) Third Agers and Brand Loyalty, unpublished paper by The Research Business.

Sampson, P. (1982) 'Consumer classification – the state of the art', *European Research*, 10 (4), October.

Sexton, D.E. and Haberman, P. (1974) 'Women in Magazine Advertisements', *Journal of Advertising Research*, 14 (4), August: 41–46.

Seychelles Tourist Office (1995), Seychelles.

Schaffer, K. (1995) 'The Elisa Fraser story and constructions of gender, race and class in Australian culture', *Hecate*, 17 (1): 136–149.

Scott-Malden, D. (1991) Recent Developments in Advertising Theory: A Review of the Work of Davies, Riley-Smith, MacClay and Millward Brown, unpublished.

Schmoll, G.A. (1977) *Tourism Promotion*, Tourism International Press, London.

Schiffman, L.G. and Kanuk, L.L. (1994) *Consumer Behaviour*, 5th ed., Prentice Hall, Englewood Cliffs, NJ.

Schulz, C. (1994) 'Fill The Valleys Between Your Peak Occupancies', *Hotels*, June: 72.

Scott, J. (1995) 'Sexual and National Boundaries in Tourism', *Annals of Tourism Research*, 22 (2): 385–403.

Seaton, T.V. (1989) 'Promotional Strategies in Tourism', 335–339 in Witt, S.F. and

Moutinho, L. (eds) *Tourism Marketing and Management Handbook*, Prentice Hall, Hemel Hempstead.

Segal, L. (1990) *Slow Motion. Changing Masculinities, Changing Men*, Virago, London.

Selby, M. (1995) Tourism and Urban Regeneration: The Role of Place Image, MSc thesis, Department of Management Studies, University of Surrey.

Selby, M. and Morgan, N.J. (1996) 'Reconstruing place image: A case study of its role in destination market research', *Tourism Management*, 17 (4): 287–294.

Sellers, P. (1995) 'A Brand New Day in Marlboro Country', *Fortune*, 12 June: 16.

Selwyn, T. (1992) 'Tourism, Society and Development', *Community Development Journal*, 27 (4): 353–260.

Selwyn, T. (1993) 'Peter Pan in South-East Asia: a view from the brochures', 117–137 in Hitchcock, M. *et al.* (eds) *Tourism in South-East Asia*, Routledge, London.

Selwyn, T. (ed.) (1996) *The Tourist Image. Myths and Myth Making in Tourism*, John Wiley and Sons, Chichester.

Senftleben, W. (1986) 'Hot Spring Resorts and Sexual Entertainment. Observations from Northern Taiwan – A Study in Social Geography', *The Philippine Geographical Journal*, 30 January–June: 21–41.

Sengupta (1995) 'The Influence of Culture on Portrayals of Women in Television Commercials: A Comparison Between the US and Japan', *International Journal of Advertising*, 14: 314–333.

Seymour-Ure, C. (1974) *The Political Impact of the Mass Media*, Constable, London.

Sharp, J.P. (1996) 'Gendering Nationhood', 97–108 in Duncan, N. (ed.) *Bodyspace: destabilizing geographies of gender and sexuality*, Routledge, London.

Shaw, S. (1996) 'A bull market for prisons', The World in 1997, *The Economist*.

Sheth, J.N. (1967) 'A review of buyer behaviour', *Management Science*, (13) 12, August.

Shields, R. (1990) *Places on the Margin*, Routledge, London.

Shimp, T. (1993) *Promotion Management and Marketing Communications*, 3rd ed., Dryden Press, Fort Worth.

Shipton, M. (1997) 'A new era – a brand new Wales', *Wales on Sunday*, 4 May: 20–21.

Silver, I. (1993) 'Marketing Authenticity in Third World Countries', *Annals of Tourism Research*, 20: 302–318.

Silvester, S. (1994) *Is Research Killing Advertising?* Background Papers, Market Research Society, Advertising Research.

Silvester, S. (1994) Why Pretesting Sucks, speech to the Association of Qualitative Research Practitioners.

Skelly, G.V. and Lundstrom, W.J. (1981) 'Male Sex Roles in Magazine Advertising, 1959–79', in *Journal of Communication*, Autumn: 52–56.

Slovenija Ministry of Economic Affairs (1996) *Slovenija. The green piece of Europe.*

Smith, A. and Skapinker, M. (1997) 'Flights of Imagination', *Financial Times*, 11 June: 27.

Smith, P. (1996) 'Africa turns Asian', The World in 1997, *The Economist*, 89–90.

Smith, V. (ed.) (1989) *Hosts and Guests: The Anthropology of Tourism*, 2nd ed., University of Pennsylvania Press, Philadephia.

Smith, W.R. (1956) 'Product differentiation and market segmentation as alternative marketing strategies', *Journal of Marketing*, 21, July.

Snelling, A. (1997) 'Letter From America', *The Leisure Monitor*, 1 (3): 3.

Solomon, M.R. (1994) *Consumer Behaviour*, 2nd ed., Allyn and Bacon, Boston.

Sparke, M. (1996) 'Displacing the Field in Fieldwork', 212–233 in Duncan, N. (ed.) *Bodyspace: destabilizing geographies of gender and sexuality*, Routledge, London.

Sports Council for Wales (1994) Participation in Sport and Leisure, Sports Update, Sports Council for Wales, Cardiff.

Staveley, N. (1994) 'Is it right . . . Will it work?', *Admap*, May: 33–36.

Sunset Travel Holidays 1997 brochure.

Swain, M. (1995) 'Gender in Tourism', *Annals of Tourism Research*, 22: 247–266.

Taft, R. (1959) 'Ethnic stereotypes, attitudes and familiarity: Australia', *Journal of Social Psychology*, 49: 177–186.

Tahite Tourisme (1996) *The Islands of Tahiti Travel Planner to Islands Beyond the Ordinary.*

The Leading Hotels of the World 1995 Directory.

'The Best of the Islands. The Philippines' (1997), 125–128 in *Condé Nast Traveler*, July.

The Times editorial 8 September 1866, Times CD ROM.

The Times (1997) 'Whitby takes fright at the spectre of a Dracula invasion', 14 June: 12.

The Weekend Collection, The Luxury Collection, ITT Sheraton.

The World of Abercrombie and Kent.

Thomas Cook Faraway Collection Brochure 1995.

Trade Winds 1995.

Travel Trade Gazette (1996) 'Trade must harness technological change', 8 May.

Travel Trade Gazette (1996) 'Agents will be bypassed by BT's self-booking kiosks', 5 June: 4.

Travel Weekly (1996) 'Airlines to Boost Sales on Internet', 5 June.

Travis, A.S. (1994) 'Tourism Destination Area Development (from theory to practice)', 29–40 in Witt, S. and Moutinho, L. (eds) *Tourism Marketing and Management Handbook*, Prentice Hall, London.

Theobald, W. (ed.) (1994) *Global Tourism. The next decade*, Butterworth Heinemann, Oxford.

Torregrosa, L.L. (1997) 'Malaysia to the Max', *Condé Nast Traveler*, July: 70–81.

Tourism Industry Intelligence (1994) 'Focus on the Gay Market', *Tourism Industry Intelligence*, 2 (1): 3.

Thurot, J. and Thurot, G. (1983) 'The ideology of class and tourism. Confronting the discourse of advertising', *Annals of Tourism Research*, 10: 173–189.

Turner, L. & Ash, J. (1975) *The Golden Hordes. International Tourism and the Pleasure Periphery*, Constable, London.

Um, S. and Crompton, J.L. (1990) 'Attitude determinants in tourism destination choice', *Annals of Tourism Research*, 17 (3): 432–448.

Urry, J. (1990) *The Tourist Gaze. Leisure and Travel in Contemporary Societies*, Sage, London.

Urry, J. (1991) 'Tourism, Travel and the Modern Subject', *Vrijetijden Samenleving*, 9 (3/4): 87–98.

Urry, J. (1991) 'The sociology of tourism', 48–57 in Cooper, C., *Progress in Tourism, Recreation and Hospitality Management*, vol. III, Belhaven Press, London.

US Virgin Islands, 1996.

USA Today International edition (1996) 'Resorts are embracing the all-inclusive trend', Monday 11 November: 8A.

Uzzell, D. (1984) 'An Alternative Structuralist Approach to the Psychology of Tourism Marketing', *Annals of Tourism*, 11 (1): 79–100.

Venkatesan, M. and Losco, J. (1975) 'Women in Magazine Ads: 1959–71', *Journal of Advertising Research*, 15 (5), Oct: 49–51.

Valentine, G. (1993) 'Hetero(sexing) space: lesbian perceptions and experiences of everyday spaces', *Society and Space*, 11: 395–413.

Valentine, G. (1996) '(Re)negotiating the Heterosexual Street', 146–155 in Duncan, N. (ed.) *Bodyspace. Destabilizing geographies of gender and sexuality*, Routledge, London.

Vial, C. (1997) 'Success Stories of Tourism Campaigns', paper presented at the First International Tourism and Leisure Advertising Festival, Dubrovnik, September.

Vietnam Travel Agency (1995) *Vietnam Awaits You.*

Wagner, L.C. and Banos, J.B. (1973) 'A Woman's Place: A Follow Up Analysis of the Roles Portrayed by Women in Magazine Advertisements', *Journal of Market Research*, 10 May: 213–214.

Wagner, W. (1997) 'Modernization and Prestige: Tourism as a Motor of Social Change', paper presented to the 10th ELRA Congress, Leisure, Culture and Tourism in Europe, Dubrovnik, September.

Wales Information Society Project (1997) Wales Information Society, Cardiff.

Wales Tourist Board (1991) 'Selling Wales – No Thanks', 4–7 Translation of Chairman's Lecture at Bro Delyn National Eisteddfod (transcript), Cardiff, Wales Tourist Board.

Wales Tourist Board (1994) *Tourism 2000. A Strategy for Wales*, Wales Tourist Board, Cardiff.

Wales Tourist Board (1994) Marketing Plan, 1994/5, Cardiff.

Wales Tourist Board (1994) Marketing Areas Study, Wales Tourist Board, Cardiff.

Wales Tourist Board (1994) Promotional Literature – Towards a More Rational Approach. A Wales Tourist Board Consultation Paper, Wales Tourist Board, Cardiff.

Wales Tourist Board (1995) A Review of the Wise Wales Initiative in the USA, Wales Tourist Board Cardiff.

Wales Tourist Board (1995) Wales. The Country That Makes Britain Great.

Wales Tourist Board (1997) The 1996 All Wales Visitor Survey, Wales Tourist Board, Cardiff.

Walker, C. (1996) 'Can TV save the planet?', *American Demographics*, 18 May: 42–47.

Wanhill, S. (1992) *Tourism 2000: A Perspective for Wales*, Wales Tourist Board, Cardiff.

Ward, S.V. and Gold, J.R. (eds) (1994) *Place Promotion. The Use of Publicity and Marketing to Sell Towns and Regions*, John Wiley and Sons, Chichester.

Ward, S.V. and Gold, J.R. (1994) 'Introduction', 1–17 in Ward, S.V. and Gold, J.R. (eds) *Place Promotion. The Use of Publicity and Marketing to Sell Towns and Regions*, John Wiley and Sons, Chichester.

Wearing, B. and Wearing, S., (1996) 'Refocussing the tourist experience: the "flaneur" and the "choraster"', *Leisure Studies*, 15 (4): 229–244.

Wearne, N. and Morrison, A. (1996) *Hospitality Marketing*, Butterworth Heinemann, Oxford.

Welsh Language Board (1996) Annual Report, Welsh Language Board, 28 June 1996.

Wernick, A. (1991) *Promotional Culture. Advertising, ideology and symbolic expression*, Sage, London.

Western Mail (1995) 'Selling Wales with Castles and Coracles', 3 May.

Western Mail (1997) 'Move to avert fresh row over name of visitor brochure', 5 June.

Westwood, S. (1997) A Missed Marketing Opportunity? Is the Airline Industry Catering for the Needs of Today's Business Woman?, University of Wales Institute, Cardiff, unpublished dissertation.

Wicks, B.E. and Schutt, M.A. (1991) 'Examining the role of tourism promotion through the use of brochures', *Tourism Management*, December: 301–312.

Wilkinson, P. and Pratiwi, W. (1995) 'Gender and Tourism in an Indonesian Village', *Annals of Tourism Research*, 22 (2): 283–299.

Wilson, A.N. (1996) 'Never Say Dai', *The Evening Standard*, March 5: 4.

Wilson, J. (1988) *Politics and Leisure*, Unwin Hyman, London.

Williams, R. (1985) 'Culture', 15–22 in McLellan, D. (ed.) *Marx: the first 100 years*, Oxford University Press, Oxford.

Williamson, J. (1983) *Decoding Advertisements. Ideology and Meaning in Advertising*, Marion Boyars, London.

Whittle, S. (1994) 'Cultural Differences: The Collaboration of the Gay Body Within the Cultural State', 27–41 in Whittle, S. (ed.) *The Margins of the City: Gay Men's Urban Lives*, Arena, Aldershot.

Wolheter, M. and Lammers, H.B. (1980) 'An Analysis of Male Roles in Print Advertisements Over a 20 Year Span: 1958–78', 760–761 in Olsen, J. (ed.) *Advances in Consumer Research*, Ann Arbor, Michigan.

Wolfe, D.B. (1987) 'The Ageless Market,' *American Demographics*, July: 26–28 and 55–56.

Wood, R.E. (1984) 'Ethnic Tourism, The State & Cultural Change in South-East Asia', *Annals of Tourism Research*, 11: 353–374

Woodside, A.G. and Lysonski, S. (1990) 'A general model of traveller destination choice', *Annals of Tourism Research*, 17: 432–448.

World Quest 1995 brochure.

Yeshayahu, N. (1985) *The Bible of the Image: The History of Photography in the Holy Land, 1839–1899*, University of Pennsylvania Press, Philadelphia.

Yural Davies, N. (1991) 'The citizenship debate: women, the state and ethnic processes', *Feminist Review*, 39: 56–88.

Young, R.C. (1977) 'The Structural Context of the Caribbean Tourist Industry. A Comparative Study', *Economic Development and Cultural Change*, 25: 657–671.

Zellner, W. *et al.* (1994) 'Women Entrepreneurs', *Business Week*, 3367: 104–110.

Index